AND HOUSING FOR ALL
The Fight to End Homelessness in America

MARIA FOSCARINIS

Prometheus Books

Essex, Connecticut

 Prometheus Books

An imprint of The Globe Pequot Publishing Group, Inc.
64 South Main Street
Essex, CT 06426
www.globepequot.com

Distributed by NATIONAL BOOK NETWORK

British Library Cataloguing in Publication Information Available

Library of Congress Cataloging-in-Publication Data Available

ISBN 9781633889767 (cloth : alk. paper) | ISBN 9781633889774 (epub)

♾™ The paper used in this publication meets the minimum requirements of American National Standard for Information Sciences—Permanence of Paper for Printed Library Materials, ANSI/ NISO Z39.48-1992

For Nathan
And to the memory of Nicolas, Rosa, and Nikos

CONTENTS

INTRODUCTION

The Price of Homelessness

Dullanni stood in front of his tent in the woods near San Diego, explaining how he'd gotten to this point—and how hard it was to get out.

By then it had been years since everything had fallen apart. Dullanni had lost his partner, his job, and his house. Staying with his younger brother hadn't worked. Eventually, he got a tent and set up camp in the woods with a few others in similar straits.

Finding a job wasn't hard. Keeping it was the problem. He figured he'd been arrested and jailed at least twenty times for living outside. Every incident related to being homeless; otherwise, Dullanni wouldn't have a record at all. Usually, he'd be in jail a few days, then he'd be released. By the time he got out, he'd have lost whatever job he'd landed.

Dullanni saw how the system worked: "The time pays for the fines." Giving up three days of his life at a stretch was the price he had to pay for being homeless.[1]

In Denver, homelessness had cost Danny his right leg below the knee and all five toes on his left foot. He'd been living under a tarp in 2023 during the bitterly cold winter when he felt frostbite setting in. Shelters—if they even had space—operated with a 5 p.m. curfew, and he had a job stocking shelves that didn't get out until midnight. Constant "sweeps" by police enforcing the city's camping ban had made it hard to hold on to his cold-weather gear. Danny's visits to urgent care hadn't helped, and eventually, amputation had been the only option.[2]

In Kentucky, state lawmakers were determined to exact an even higher price for homelessness than lost limbs. In April 2024, the state legislature overrode Governor Beshear's veto to enact a new law that makes "unlawful camping" on both private and public property a crime.

The law allows property owners to shoot an unhoused trespasser—fatally. The "Safer Kentucky Act" makes explicit the state's assessment that a homeless person's life has less value than private property.[3]

Standing under the trees that shaded his tent from the California sun, Dullanni made three wishes: to get into permanent housing himself, that others would not harbor such negative views of people experiencing homelessness, and that all unhoused people would have homes. A bit ruefully, he wondered whether his last wish was too "cheeseball."

To my mind, Dullanni's wish isn't overly idealistic at all. While it may be hard to imagine now, large-scale, visible homelessness hasn't always been prevalent in the United States. It exploded across the country in the early 1980s, triggered by the government's deliberate policy choices and the private interests often driving them. These policies were—and are—supported by public narratives that stigmatize those most directly hurt by them. There is nothing inevitable about homelessness in America. We can make and demand different choices.

* * *

Coming into office in 1981 claiming that government was the problem, not the solution, then-president Reagan promoted deep cuts to social programs. Until then, homelessness had been largely limited to the skid rows of urban centers, affecting primarily single men. Some had been patients of mental institutions, discharged without support in the 1960s, then displaced again when developers destroyed their inexpensive lodgings to build luxury housing in the 1970s.

Reagan's massive cuts shredded the social safety net, decimating affordable housing and other support for low-income people, affecting a much more diverse group of people and geographical areas. Seemingly suddenly, families with children as well as younger working men and women were losing their homes. They were not only in cities but also in suburbs and rural areas. At the same time, the president popularized the idea that the individuals most affected by the crisis were entirely to blame for their situation.

As homelessness rapidly became a national emergency, Reagan insisted that no one was really living in the streets other than those who were "homeless by choice." It's a fiction that still finds resonance today, including in otherwise liberal cities, as Dullanni would note decades later. Yet despite the enduring popularity of this demonstrably false narrative, homelessness is almost never a choice—and ending homelessness is not a fanciful wish. But doing so will require fundamentally different policy choices and perspectives.

In the early 1980s, activists in communities across the country mobilized to offer relief, opening shelters and soup kitchens and pressing their local governments for support. In New York City, advocates and legal aid lawyers brought litigation that led to a landmark legal settlement, establishing a right to shelter in the city. While still in effect, it's been targeted for elimination by successive mayors, most recently Eric Adams.

The suit helped spur advocacy in other communities, and as homelessness increased around the country, local activists came together to form the National Coalition for the Homeless (NCH), led by a New York City–based group. By the mid-1980s, homelessness was undeniably a rapidly escalating national problem, and a federal response was urgently needed, yet Reagan and his allies insisted homelessness didn't merit a federal response. A campaign would have to be organized to press the Reagan administration and Congress.

At the time, I was a young lawyer at a Wall Street law firm, litigating cases on behalf of large corporate clients. Two years earlier, I had volunteered for a pro bono case representing homeless families in Nassau County, an otherwise affluent New York City suburb. Part of the precipitous new growth of homelessness, the families were being denied emergency shelter, and legal aid lawyers had filed a class-action suit against the county and the state. Joining them was the New York City–based advocacy group that had successfully brought the right-to-shelter litigation. Over the coming two years, I spent untold hours visiting dozens of families, writing briefs, and arguing in court. Eventually, we won a favorable settlement of our case. And in the process, I had also found my calling. When NCH approached me about leaving my law firm to organize a national campaign in Washington, D.C., I signed up.

* * *

In less than two years, our campaign beat the high odds against us. Mobilizing an improbable, bipartisan team of strange bedfellows, our campaign won an early and unlikely victory: We secured passage of the first major federal legislation to address homelessness. Reluctantly signed into law by Reagan, the landmark law—the McKinney-Vento Act—put homelessness on the map as a national policy issue, shifting the paradigm that defined it as an issue for charities or local governments.

Since that time, the law has expanded, helping millions of people and funding aid programs around the country. But the McKinney-Vento Act was passed as an urgent, initial response, focused mainly on emergency shelter—a Band-Aid at best, not a solution. It was never meant to be the sole response to homelessness. Key members of Congress recognized the law's limitations even as they passed it, cautioning that it was only "a first step towards reversing the record increase in homelessness" and that more comprehensive measures were needed.[4]

Our campaign continued, growing along the way, but despite multiple important victories that followed, those comprehensive measures have yet to come. Emergency systems have become permanent, and shelter providers increasingly beholden to government funding. Once fierce advocates, their voices are often silenced. As a result, homelessness hasn't just persisted, it's proliferated, becoming a seemingly permanent feature of American life.

In 1989, I left NCH to form a new organization, now known as the National Homelessness Law Center (NHLC or the "Law Center"), with a mission to use the power of the law to end and prevent homelessness in the United States. The Law Center would focus not just on the symptoms of homelessness but also on its underlying causes. Those causes have not only remained unaddressed, but they've also deepened and strengthened.

For one thing, federal aid for low-income housing never recovered from the Reagan cuts of the early 1980s. Today, just one in four of those impoverished enough to be eligible for federal low-income housing programs actually receives help. Public housing, once a cornerstone of the New Deal, has been starved of funding, demonized in political and public discourse, and prevented by law from expanding. Income assistance programs, long inadequate, were eliminated—and their recipients smeared as lazy, fraudulent "welfare queens."

In the private market, housing prices skyrocketed while wages stagnated, driving for the highest profit without regard for the people living there. Housing was increasingly treated as a commodity for investment, not a place to live. Even public property—beyond public housing—was being sold for profit by the government. The foreclosure crisis, followed by the Great Recession, created a major new surge in homelessness—and an opportunity for institutional investors to grab newly vacant homes. Private equity is now playing an ever-bigger role in residential real estate. Income inequality, accelerating since the 1980s, has reached extreme proportions.

Without sufficient affordable housing or even emergency shelter, the number of people living in public continued to grow. In response, a destructive new trend gained momentum in the 1990s, championed by the then-mayor of New York City—Rudy Giuliani. Laws and policies that criminalize people for living in public places—despite the absence of alternatives—popped up across the country, like those that Dullanni was experiencing in San Diego and Danny was dodging in Denver.

Predictably, in the absence of housing, encampments of people living in public grew exponentially, dotting streets and woods across the nation. So did laws criminalizing them, which became a primary response to homelessness in red and blue communities alike, triggering an expensive, ineffective, inhumane cycle. Criminalization wastes taxpayer dollars, deepens people's misery, and often creates arrest records that make exiting homelessness even harder, as Dullanni experienced. Kentucky's shocking decision to permit property owners to shoot trespassing homeless people merely takes the trend to its logical next step. In a June 2024 ruling that ignored both the facts and prior precedent, the US Supreme Court opened the way even further to laws that make it a crime for homeless people simply to exist.[5]

Before Reagan's drastic cuts, federal funds had helped ensure housing for lower-income people through initiatives first created in the 1930s as part of President Franklin Roosevelt's New Deal. These included housing programs to alleviate that era's mass homelessness, precipitated by the Great Depression.[6] While the programs were deeply flawed by policies that left out and further segregated Black Americans, Roosevelt made the case for federal aid with a call for social solidarity.

* * *

The harmful narratives Reagan promoted in service of his savage cuts were adopted by many Democrats as well as Republicans. They were given a big boost by Clinton's 1990s campaign to "end welfare as we know it," and the stigmatizing stereotypes it propagated. Now accepting—whether implicitly or explicitly—the Reagan view that people "choose" to be homeless, some state and local leaders claim that criminalizing people for living in public will "help" them get off the streets—ignoring the obvious and enormous lack of housing or even shelter options.

These claims paint a false and damaging picture of the people who are experiencing homelessness, and of the causes pushing them into it. More recently, even more dangerous views are coming to the fore. During his first term in office, President Trump referred to unhoused people as "filth," and his administration proposed banishing them to facilities in remote areas of cities. Template laws to criminalize unhoused people and further restrict funding for housing solutions are being promoted by well-funded interest groups in the guise of "innovative" policy experts; some even claim to be "compassionate." Right-wing ideologues are asserting outright that unhoused people are "not our neighbors"[7]— laying the groundwork for laws and policies that dehumanize homeless people and even invite their murder.

The escalation of large-scale homelessness has been fueled by decades of massive cuts to housing and other social programs, the privatization of public resources, and the conversion of housing from a public good serving a human need to a profitable commodity for the few. On a parallel track, public narratives shifted from the stated commitment to social solidarity as articulated by President Roosevelt to the "bootstraps" ideology of Reagan and the current punitive policies. President Trump's second administration promises to make both the policies and the rhetoric much worse.

For years, advocates in many communities—often led by people who have experienced homelessness—have fought back, helping strike down laws that criminally punish homeless people simply because of their status. These fights will continue, despite the blows dealt by a recent harmful Supreme Court decision and the return of President Trump. But while winning the right not to be punished is critically important, it does nothing to end homelessness. Housing is the essential element needed to end homelessness, and for decades advocates at the local and national levels—with the Law Center playing a leading role—have been calling for the recognition of housing as a basic human right.

The call has gained traction. Over the past twenty years, the movement for the human right to housing has grown, and advocates are now working in communities across the country, and at the national level, for new policies that treat housing as a human right, not just a commodity. This movement is anchored by the UN's guiding proclamation, the Universal Declaration of Human Rights, which reflects President Franklin Roosevelt's 1944 call for a "second bill of rights" recognizing economic and social rights.

Never enshrined in law, Roosevelt's proposal and the social solidarity on which it was premised eroded over time. But for over two decades, our growing movement has been advocating for the fundamental principles of economic justice and fairness underlying it.

Our call gained support—from four presidential candidates in 2020, from the Biden White House, from members of Congress and state legislatures, and from popular cultural figures such as HBO's John Oliver. And, once viewed as politically irrelevant, people who have experienced homelessness are organizing, graduating from colleges and universities, being elected to Congress—and advocating for their own human rights.

These seemingly disparate groups are converging around the idea that to end homelessness we must stop treating housing as a privilege, subject to budget cuts by politicians, or as a profit-generating commodity of the private market. Instead, we must treat it as the fundamental human right that it is. Models from other parts of the world—including Finland and Vienna—are demonstrating that it's possible. And in the

United States, campaigns for the human right to housing—including in Kansas City and Seattle—are notching up victories.

While the return of President Trump is a severe setback to any progress we made at the federal level, it does not preclude advances in state and local battles; indeed, it makes them even more urgent. Nor does it negate the trajectory we've traveled and the trail we've blazed—and on which we can continue to move forward.

* * *

This book traces the evolution of homelessness in the United States and of the movement to end it. It demonstrates how ending homelessness will require fundamental shifts in our society's priorities and beliefs—and that those shifts are possible and in everyone's interest. That's not to say these changes will be easy to make: They require the work of an active, engaged, and large coalition to advance them. It will take more strange bedfellows. Especially now, the fight continues.

The book is organized into three parts. Part I explores the emergence of the crisis in the early 1980s, the causes leading to it, and the early responses that focused primarily on emergency measures like shelter. Part II focuses on the transformation of homelessness from shocking crisis to permanent emergency, the evolution of punitive responses and their accompanying narratives, and the impact of growing up without a stable home on young people. Part III details the growing movement for the human right to housing, showing the work to make human rights a reality in America and internationally. It illustrates the connection between civil and political rights and economic and social rights and argues that ensuring housing for all is essential to democracy, and to our own humanity.

Chapters within each part recount the stories of people experiencing homelessness, activists advocating for rights and solutions, and responses from government and other institutions. The chapters are thematic, each taking on a broad question or issue; each starts close to the present, and then goes back to the start of the issue, before moving forward roughly chronologically.

Key themes recur throughout the book. Racial discrimination is one, as a cause of both homelessness itself as well as its ongoing, deeply disproportionate racial impact. The book puts the growth of homelessness in the context of growing inequality, noting that homelessness is the tip of larger, structural problems—including an affordable housing crisis that is now reaching into the middle class. Throughout, the book highlights the stories and voices of those whose lives have been directly affected by the policy choices leading to this point.

Much of the activism I describe is work I have been personally engaged in, and at times I enter the story, as do some of my colleagues. As the narrative progresses, so does the evolution of my own advocacy and approach. When I first took on the challenge of helping lead a national campaign for a federal response to homelessness, I assumed I would spend a year or two working on it, solve the problem, and return to New York City, my hometown. Over time, it became apparent that ending homelessness would require much more than a couple of years of hard work by an enterprising young lawyer.

Looking back, I don't think my original instinct was naive. Nor do I think I was. While I was new to the issue of homelessness, and never personally experienced its hardship, I had a perspective informed by the suffering and loss of my own family. I had some understanding of oppression and injustice, and some idea about fighting it, and what that might entail.

* * *

I never suffered from material deprivation myself. I grew up in a comfortable apartment on the Upper East Side of Manhattan, during the 1960s and 1970s, a time of social activism. An only child, I often went with my parents and their friends to demonstrations for peace and racial justice. My parents were older White professionals who also happened to be immigrants from another country—and another world.

Almost nightly at the dinner table, I listened as they recounted their experiences in Nazi-occupied Greece during World War II. Food was abundant in the countryside, but Nazi blockades prevented it from reaching Athens, where they were living at the time. Hundreds of thousands of people died of starvation in a single year. Each morning, sanitation workers swept away the emaciated corpses of those who had died during the night.[8] I also heard about the Resistance, which my parents had been part of: the secret organizing, the friends who'd been captured, sent to exile, sentenced to death.

They rarely talked about Nikos, my mother's younger brother, who'd been imprisoned and executed by the Nazis at the age of twenty-three for his resistance efforts.[9] I realize now it was too painful for my parents to talk about, but after they died, I found among their papers six letters Nikos had written from jail. His last one, composed on what he knew was the eve of his execution, was different from the others—a public appeal to the world of which he would no longer be a part. Written on behalf of himself and his cellmate and friend, who was also to die in the morning, it included this exhortation:

Don't cry for us, we are not dying from illness or accident, our fellow human beings will kill us. . . .

We are calm and proud, because we did our duty, and our conscience is clear. Do yours too and light will come to the world quickly.[10]

Many years had passed before I read those words from the uncle I never got to meet. But somehow, they were already in my bloodstream. I wanted to fight the gross unfairness that left so many people struggling just to survive while others had so much more than they needed or could ever use. Thinking that law, which combined the ideals of justice with practical tools for acting on them, might be a way to do this, I headed to law school.

After graduating, I landed a prestigious clerkship. But when it ended a year later, there were few public interest jobs available. It was 1982, the dawn of the Reagan administration, and funding for programs representing poor people was being cut. I accepted an offer from Sullivan & Cromwell, a major Wall Street firm, with the idea that I would work at the firm, make some money, get valuable experience, volunteer for pro bono work, and eventually transition to a career in public interest law.

It was hardly a novel idea. Many students enter law school with idealistic goals, then confront the reality that there are very few jobs for public interest lawyers. Yet, somehow, my plan worked. I had gone with Sullivan & Cromwell without knowing much about it, but I was fortunate to get litigation experience, unusual in a big firm, and I felt lucky in my choice. When the request for pro bono help in Nassau County came into the firm, I jumped on it.

Three years later, I had the opportunity to make the transition to full-time (albeit minimally paid) work as a public interest lawyer fighting a clearly egregious injustice: In a country with so much excess for some, others are going without the basics. I left Sullivan & Cromwell in November 1985, and have spent nearly four decades advocating to end homelessness and protecting the rights of those experiencing it.

Over the years, I've come to understand that our legal system, as currently constructed, is insufficient to truly address the crisis of homelessness and all that drives it. As long as housing is treated as a discretionary privilege instead of as a fundamental human right, its funding and legal protections will remain dependent on the whims of politicians and the moneyed interests influencing them. Securing housing as a human right is a necessary step to end homelessness. It is also essential to ensuring basic civil and political rights. As human rights law recognizes, economic/social rights and civil/political rights are interdependent. Without basic economic and social rights, civil and political rights cannot truly be exercised.

Human rights principles offer more than a legal and policy framework. They outline a worldview that prioritizes social solidarity. Like rights, people are interdependent—no one succeeds or even survives on their own. People form and live in societies for a reason. The critical question is what kind of society we form. Is it one where everyone can have the basics? Is it one where everyone can belong?

In his last letter home, Nikos confronted his impending execution by his fellow human beings. As he wrote to his family, it wasn't illness or accident that would take his life at the age of twenty-three, but the deliberate actions of other people. While the circumstances are different, the essential point remains: Homelessness is not a disease, nor is it an accident, it's the result of deliberate policy choices made by people. We can make different ones.

My early assessment of the time it would take to end homelessness was clearly wrong, but it reflects an underlying truth that remains valid: Poverty as extreme as homelessness doesn't have to exist in a country as rich as the United States. It is a problem that *can* be solved. What I didn't realize at the time was how powerful and deeply embedded the causes behind it truly were. The drive to commodify housing, the policies enabling it, and the simplistic myth of individualism that undermines the very idea of the commonweal have been formidable since the early 1980s—and they've only gotten stronger.

I wrote this book partly to grapple with and better fathom the forces at play in the ongoing surge of homelessness. Having spent the vast majority of my career striving to end it, I wanted to reflect on and describe the larger context that work was operating in. I also wanted to record the stories and amplify the voices of some of the thousands of unhoused people I've worked with over these decades, as well as some I haven't personally met.[11]

Homelessness is indeed a choice, just not the kind that Reagan and his cronies meant. It's a choice our society makes—a choice we collectively make—and it doesn't have to be. A home, that most basic human need, is also a fundamental human right. We know housing is essential for all human beings. Dullanni's wish of housing for all is anything but cheeseball. It's time to make it part of our laws, policies, and national consciousness.

This is not a matter of charity, it's a matter of justice. It's a question of what kind of a society we all choose to be. Ensuring housing for all matters for everyone. Homelessness extracts the biggest price from those it affects most directly: Dullanni, Danny, and millions of others. But by choosing a society that values profit over human beings, we all pay a price.

We need liberty and justice—and housing for all. This book is more than my account of the evolution of homelessness in America. It's a call to action for the human right to housing.

Part I
The Crisis Begins

CHAPTER ONE

Homeless in Suburbia

A Family of Seven Living in Their Truck

In 1982, conspicuous consumption was in vogue and greed was good. Former Hollywood actor Ronald Reagan had won the presidency on his promise to "make America great again" and to end "big government." The White House was hosting celebrities at glittering parties while popular TV shows like *Dynasty* and *Dallas* further glamorized wealth. Leveraged buyouts and junk bonds were fueling the biggest boom in fifty years on Wall Street, and Trump Tower's opulent atrium was about to open on New York City's Fifth Avenue.[1]

Beneath the shiny images and upbeat rhetoric, a very different reality was playing out. Much of the country was still reeling from a deep recession—the second in three years—and unemployment was rising while cuts to social programs removed critical safety nets. Poverty was increasing and inequality was deepening, even as parts of America emerged from the recession.

And homelessness—the most visible sign of dire poverty—was on the cusp of exploding into public view.

For Florence and John Koster and their five children, the explosion had already hit. Native Long Islanders, they'd been renting in Nassau County, a wealthier suburb of New York City. But in June 1982, their landlord told them they had to leave. His daughter was getting married, and the house would be his wedding gift to her. After exhausting options with family and being turned away by the county's social services, the

Kosters eventually moved into their red 1970 Chevy pickup truck. They parked it in the lot of an outdoor shopping mall, just a few miles from their old house. The parents slept in the front and the kids in the covered back, squeezed in with their clothes, food, and three spare tires.

Three years earlier, John had hurt his back working as a chauffeur and Citibank truck driver. Disabled by the injury, he could no longer work. Florence hadn't been employed outside the home of five children, all of whom were still in school. After exhausting their savings, the family went on public assistance. With the monthly welfare check of about $600 and food stamps, they'd barely been able to pay their $440 rent and meet their other basic needs when their landlord gave them notice.

As the surrounding economy boomed, rents shot up and the already severe shortage of affordable housing worsened. The family couldn't find another place they could afford even as they faced eviction. They'd gone to Nassau County's social services office to ask for help, almost daily, for three months. The whole family would wait, often for hours, only to be told again and again that there was nothing the department of social services could do.

Time not spent in waiting rooms went into searching for new housing on their own, visiting real estate agencies in the old pickup truck that would eventually become their home. A few houses were available in their price range, but as soon as the landlords learned they were on welfare, they refused to rent to them. On other occasions, county employees failed to show up for appointments to inspect potential homes—a requirement before the family could rent using their welfare check.

Increasingly desperate, the Kosters had pleaded with their landlord to extend their stay. He did, twice, a month at a time . . . and then told them their time was up, giving them just one more day.

Just before that final day, the Kosters went back to the county to explain they were about to be evicted with nowhere to go. Telling the Kosters this was their "own problem" to solve, the extent of the county's help was to send movers to pick up their furniture and take it to storage.

The family called their church, which arranged for a private charity to pay for a motel for one night. The next day, the whole family was back at the county social services agency, and again they were denied help.

Desperate, Florence called the county executive, the top politician in Nassau County. A welfare worker came out hours later, scolded Florence for "making trouble," and told the family they would be put up in a motel for three nights—Labor Day weekend.

After that, they stayed with relatives—first her mother, then his—splitting up the children and sleeping on couches and floors. Having grown up in the area, they were fortunate to have family nearby. But as often happens, overcrowding eventually made these arrangements untenable. Religious and social services groups paid to shelter the Kosters in a motel, but these private groups soon depleted their emergency funds and couldn't sustain the help.[2] These temporary, makeshift arrangements couldn't take the place of a permanent, affordable home.

While the family bounced from place to place in search of housing, the Koster children—Donna, eighteen; John Jr., sixteen; Helen, thirteen; and the twins, Janet and Edward, eight—missed school, ate poorly, and only had their summer clothes to wear. Years later, the children remembered the experience vividly—and the feeling that few people were willing to help them.[3]

The Kosters were staying in their pickup truck when the local legal aid office—which provided free legal help to low-income people in the area—got involved. The office had been investigating a pattern of the county illegally denying emergency shelter to homeless families seeking help. The legal aid lawyers invited the Kosters to join a lawsuit they were planning with a New York City advocacy organization, the Coalition for the Homeless. This suit would challenge the county's policies and practices and ask the court to order the county to comply with the law.

When the legal aid office and the coalition filed the case in federal court in 1982, the Kosters were among the lead plaintiffs. The case drew national media attention, with the *New York Times* reporting on the surprising appearance of homelessness—then considered solely a big-city problem—on Long Island.[4] Detailing the Kosters' futile efforts to house their family and get help from their local government, the article quoted Florence: "Let the politicians live in the back of a pickup truck with the clothes and food and three tires and five kids. I bet they couldn't survive."

No doubt feeling pressure from the lawsuit and the publicity, the county offered the Kosters a longer stay in a motel. This slightly more stable living situation gave Florence the time to find a house renting for $300 a month. The county inspected and approved it, and by Thanksgiving the family had moved in.

What seemed like a happy ending proved anything but. The house was in such poor condition—with missing windowpanes, mice, and malfunctioning plumbing and electricity—that within three days the Kosters were looking for another place. Later that year, the town condemned the property.

At long last, the family rented a house for $750 a month—well over their entire $600 public assistance check, and 250 percent higher than the welfare office's $300 estimate for rent. Unlike the vast majority of homeless families, the Kosters had family and friends willing and able, at least for the moment, to help make up the monthly shortfall.[5]

HOMELESSNESS GROWS ON LONG ISLAND: SEEKING HELP FROM A COURT

The Kosters' challenges were hardly unique. Thousands of Long Island families were in dire straits, with their ranks quickly growing. A 1983 study conducted by a Hofstra sociology professor estimated that up to six thousand people were homeless in Long Island's Nassau County alone, including more than three thousand families. From 1984 to 1987, the number of homeless families on the island would almost double.[6]

Aware that the problem was widespread, the legal aid lawyers and the Coalition for the Homeless had filed the lawsuit as a proposed class action—a legal mechanism that can extend a case beyond specific individuals to include others in similar situations. Class actions are a powerful tool for changing policies and practices. In this case, the lawsuit was taking on not just how the county responded to the Kosters but other homeless families seeking its help.[7]

Before the suit could proceed, the judge in charge of the case would first have to approve—or "certify"—a class. The legal aid lawyers had to gather evidence to persuade him that the problems faced by the Kosters weren't isolated and were similarly affecting many more families. The county would undoubtedly oppose the request to certify a class, and the lawyers for the families would have to overcome that opposition. Making a strong argument required talking to dozens of other homeless families, taking their testimonies and, eventually, formally adding some of them to the suit. This would take extensive work and resources. In early 1984, the coalition, well-connected to large Wall Street law firms, put out a call for pro bono help. At the time, I was working at one such firm as a litigation associate. The setting couldn't have been more different than the conditions the Kosters were enduring.

Sullivan & Cromwell's main office was downtown, in the financial district. The firm occupied the upper floors of a tall office building, where important partners enjoyed sweeping views of the Statue of Liberty from their private offices. Persian carpets cushioned the floors and Currier and Ives prints adorned the walls. Messengers silently scurried in and out with envelopes and packages. Lawyers in suits, mainly White men, wore serious expressions and spoke in muted voices.

A memo came around the office asking if anyone wanted to volunteer for a pro bono case representing homeless families denied emergency shelter in Nassau County. Only a few months earlier, the firm had held its annual summer "outing" for lawyers in the same county, at a posh country club called Piping Rock. My colleagues and I had traveled there from the office by limousine, for an afternoon and evening of luxury, experiencing what we too could have if we worked hard and made the right moves at the firm. No one mentioned the extreme poverty that coexisted in discrete, isolated pockets alongside the wealth.

I had started at Sullivan & Cromwell with the goal of eventually transitioning to public interest law, and I was especially interested in using the law to fight poverty. The memo caught my attention, and I signed up. Fortunately, Sullivan & Cromwell treated pro bono matters generously. Lawyers representing indigent clients for free could invest the firm's time and resources, so long as we also kept up our work for the corporate clients who paid the hefty fees that made such pro bono work possible.[8] I started going out to Long Island regularly.

ABUNDANCE AND DEPRIVATION

Beth Polner, one of the local legal services lawyers, kept a list of the homeless families who had come to her office seeking help. In the spring of 1984, Beth and I began visiting them, writing up their testimonies, and signing some on as plaintiffs. We also investigated county and state policies and practices, confirming what we had learned from the 1983 Hofstra study of homelessness, surveys conducted by advocates, and the families themselves. Thousands of people were homeless in Nassau County, but the county didn't operate a single emergency shelter.[9] While the county sometimes placed families in motels, this was for a maximum of three days. Many were simply turned away regardless of need, as the Kosters had been at various times.

The county did refer some families in crisis to temporary shelter—at several grossly substandard accommodations. These included rooms in private homes, roominghouses, and even buildings that had been abandoned. Many of these were extremely overcrowded, some with twelve people in two rooms, and conditions were horrific—mattresses without sheets, doors without locks, infestations of rodents and roaches. One house had a family of nine sleeping in the basement with no windows, no toilet, and no water source.

On one of my visits, I met the Myers family—a father, Tony, and his three small children—in the single room they shared in the basement of an otherwise derelict building. I had to step over holes in the floorboards and duck under bare lightbulbs dangling from exposed wiring. The bathroom was down a long hallway, and there were no cooking facilities. Cereal boxes and cans of food were neatly arranged on the dresser top. There was just one bed, a double, and Tony sat on its edge, insisting I take the only chair. The kids played and clowned around for my benefit while their father, a thin, soft-spoken man, looked down at the floor and told their story.

Tony's wife had suffered from depression but couldn't get treatment. She began self-medicating with street drugs, became addicted, and eventually abandoned the family. Tony had juggled taking care of their children while also working as a building caretaker. After arriving late once too often, he lost his job. He couldn't make rent without a paycheck, and he and his children were evicted. Ashamed to seek help from friends or relatives—who were just as broke—he had sought aid from the county. The county put the family up in a motel for three nights, then placed them in what was supposed to be permanent housing—that barren room in the basement of an abandoned house.[10]

Another family, Deborah Dean and her four children—James, fifteen, Lashawnda, thirteen, Cory, seven, and Jamie, seventeen months—became homeless when their landlord evicted them to make renovations to their apartment building. Deborah, pregnant with her fifth child, had turned to the county for help. The Deans were placed in a home rented by an acquaintance of Deborah's, who also had four children. Possibly because of the stress she was under, Deborah gave birth prematurely. Her daughter, Jasmine, weighed only four pounds, and was placed in the hospital's neonatal intensive care unit.[11]

The hospital considered the baby high risk and refused to release her into such overcrowded conditions, so some of Deborah's older children moved in with relatives. Eventually, Deborah found housing through her own efforts, which the county approved. She had moved her family a total of nine times in as many months. During that period, Deborah had been hospitalized, given birth, and temporarily split up her children. She agreed to join our case with her children. The Deans and the Kosters would be the lead plaintiffs for the proposed class-action suit.[12]

The travel time from my office to visit the families in Nassau County was less than an hour, but it was clear I had entered a different world. I would be returning home to my cozy apartment, food in the fridge, cafes around the corner, money in my wallet. But even though they were living in a country with so much abundance, the Kosters, the Myerses, the Deans, and countless other families lacked even the basics for themselves and their children.

Their deprivation struck a familiar chord of grief and outrage. While I had grown up relatively privileged, my parents' dinner-table stories of injustice and suffering in occupied Greece during World War II were never far from my consciousness. Emblazoned in my mind were the images of the emaciated corpses of those who had starved to death while the Nazis prevented food from the countryside from reaching them.[13]

The plight of the families in Nassau County wasn't the same. The country wasn't at war, nor was it occupied by enemy forces. Yet they too were needlessly being deprived in a country that had enough for all. Their suffering too was the result of a man-made disaster.

THE POWER OF THE LAW—FOR SOME

As we prepared our class-action lawsuit, Sullivan & Cromwell's regular corporate clients spared little effort or expense in pursuit of their interests. The disparity felt increasingly jarring as I spent more and more time with my pro bono clients. In the spring of 1984, as I was getting deeper into the Koster case, I was also defending a major car company. The plaintiff had sued virtually the entire auto industry, and Bill, the partner in charge of the case, had arranged for us to organize all the other defense lawyers, with me as the coordinator. The firm was known for taking a sink-or-swim approach with young lawyers, and Bill assigned me the job of taking the plaintiff's first deposition.

I sat across from the plaintiff and his lawyer at a long, oval, polished-wood table in a large conference room at our firm. Some twenty lawyers were lined up around the table, representing about a dozen major law firms. Even back then, before billing rates shot up dramatically, this single deposition added up to thousands of dollars per hour for all the lawyers in the room—simply to listen to the plaintiff's testimony (which would be transcribed anyway), observe his demeanor, and protect their client's interest in case the plaintiff mentioned anything remotely relevant.

This was a nerve-racking, high-pressure experience for a young lawyer. It was also a display of legal might to defend the auto industry from a challenge—considered unlikely to succeed by all—from a single, much smaller, rival company. And it was just one example of the vast resources deployed by "big law" to protect the interests of their corporate clients. These included not just legal talent to argue for them as strongly as possible in court, but also lobbyists to shape the law in the ways most favorable to their interests, public relations professionals to influence public opinion, support staff, and the technology to make it all work.

My firm provided every resource for its lawyers to represent our clients as vigorously and thoroughly as possible: messengers, secretaries, and round-the-clock typists. A "lawyers' dining room" offered free lunches, so we'd have more time to spend on client matters. For dinner, a cafeteria fed all firm employees working late. The expense was more than offset by the savings in billable hours. Rates for corporate clients were already high in the 1980s. As of 2023, some firms topped $1,000 per hour.[14]

The conference room deposition was just a few miles from Nassau County, but the resources devoted to the firm's paying clients were galaxies away from those available to the homeless families of Long Island. Yet the stakes for these families were enormous.

These parents had gone to tremendous lengths to get help for themselves and their children, meeting obstacles at every turn. They had called on family and friends who were often struggling themselves, sometimes at the insistence of the county. They'd split up their children, sleeping on the floors of loved ones who jeopardized their own housing by taking them in. Many resorted to sleeping outside or in their vehicles—as the Kosters had done—risking criminal punishment for loitering or trespassing. They feared permanently losing their children to foster care, and with good reason—some had. As for the kids, they'd been forced to miss school while their parents searched for housing. Some were even denied enrollment because they lacked a permanent address. These children were even more at risk than their parents.

The interests of the Deans, Myerses, and Kosters were at least as important as those of my corporate clients, which typically involved only bottom lines. To me they were clearly much more significant: The lives and futures of human beings were at stake.

Yet those who are poor or homeless are most likely completely on their own, regardless of the severity of their need.[15] If they're lucky, they may be represented by overburdened and underfunded legal aid lawyers. No less zealous or competent than their elite counterparts—sometimes more so—the resources in person power and support they can draw on are orders of magnitudes less.

Pro bono lawyers from big firms can bring additional help, including access to some of those resources, as we were doing in the Koster case. This can make a big difference, bringing a measure of legal power on behalf of those who might otherwise be unrepresented. It's a very important role for firms that take it to heart, as mine did. But in the end, it's not nearly enough to make up for the huge gap in resources facing low-income people at every turn.[16]

Since I first got involved, there's been a growing movement to ensure legal representation for poor people in certain kinds of high-stakes cases, such as eviction. Advocates have achieved important victories in cities and states across the country, starting with New York City. Low-income individuals and families facing eviction in these places—as of December 2024, eighteen cities, five states, and two counties—now have a legal right to be represented by a lawyer.[17]

Because of this, countless families and individuals have managed to stay in their homes, and local governments have saved money they might otherwise have spent on homeless services. Yet while critically important, these initiatives have bridged just a tiny portion of the growing gap. They only come into play to forestall disasters like eviction, not to affirmatively assert rights. And they apply only in a few places—and only when legal aid lawyers are funded.

A WIN ON LONG ISLAND

After months of work, our team of legal aid lawyers, corporate lawyers working pro bono, and coalition staff and volunteers were finally ready. We'd meticulously documented how the challenges experienced by the Kosters, the Deans, the Myerses, and many others were not isolated incidents but part of a much larger pattern, and we asked the judge to let the case proceed as a class action.[18] We summarized the impact of the county government's denial of emergency shelter in our court papers:

> *The families, particularly the children, suffer both physical and psychological harm. Exposure to the cold and denial of sufficient nutritious food are among the most obvious injuries to befall members of a homeless family. Children are separated from their parents or are forced to*

live in dangerous and unhealthy quarters. The children's education is disrupted, incidences of family violence increase, and family stability is undermined—frequently irreversibly—as a result of defendants' refusal to provide homeless families with emergency shelter.[19]

The judge agreed. We were granted our motion for class certification of the Koster case, adding to the earlier victory upholding our right to bring the case in the first place.[20] The county and state were likely looking at a big loss. This made it a good time to open settlement discussions.

After literally years of back-and-forth, in 1987 we entered into a consent decree with Nassau County. The county agreed to provide emergency housing to eligible families the same day the request was made, respond to requests twenty-four hours a day, seven days a week, and ensure that emergency housing met detailed minimum standards.[21]

It made a noticeable difference. Reports of unhoused families being denied shelter and placed into substandard temporary accommodations dropped off in Nassau County. A few months after we signed the settlement, the county announced they would open three new shelters. They also planned to renovate a building to house homeless families, elderly people, and patients released from hospitals with no place to live—as Deborah Dean had been after giving birth to Jasmine, her premature baby.[22]

Meanwhile, both the Deans and the Kosters had at last found permanent homes—largely through their own efforts.

The consent decree changed policy, impacting thousands of at-risk people in Nassau County, and the court decisions set legal precedent that could protect families facing similar challenges.[23] As of 2023, the consent decree remained in effect, although in practice it was still violated. By then, Janet Koster, who had been eight years old when the case was filed, was forty-nine and living in Indiana, where she worked at a fast-food drive-through and struggled to pay the bills.[24] But even when we signed the consent decree in 1987, it was clear that the problems ran much deeper than improved shelter policies could reach.

When our case was filed in 1983, Nassau County welfare benefits provided at most $510 per month to house a family of *eight*, while forty hours a week of work at the minimum wage for a month yielded $580. The cheapest *one-bedroom* apartment rented for $400 per month, not including the security deposit. A single room went for at least $240 per month.[25]

A full decade later, the Nassau Action Coalition (a local advocacy organization) reported that no low-income housing had been built in the county for the past thirty years.[26] Since then, the national gap between the need for housing that extremely low-income people can afford and what is actually available has only gaped wider: In 2023, it was more than seven million units.[27]

The hardships faced by the Kosters and other families were not unusual, in ways that stretched far beyond the bounds of our class-action case. In New York City, the demand for emergency shelter by homeless families rose 24 percent from 1981 to 1982 alone. In 1983, that demand doubled.[28] In 1984, cities including Anchorage, Los Angeles, Seattle, Columbus, Missouri, and Tucson saw dramatic increases in homelessness over the previous year.[29] The media started covering this sudden eruption of extreme need more frequently, and stories recounting the suffering of desperate families and individuals were landing on front pages. Homelessness was becoming a national crisis, but communities were left to fend for themselves. There was virtually no response from Washington.[30]

In fact, federal policies were fueling much of the crisis.

NOT AN ACCIDENT, NOT A "CHOICE"— FEDERAL POLICIES DRIVE THE CRISIS

It may have seemed to appear suddenly, but homelessness did not come out of nowhere.

During the Great Depression, which began in 1929, millions of Americans lost their jobs and their homes, and homelessness became a mass phenomenon in the United States for the first time in the modern era.[31] Hoovervilles—shantytowns named after then-president Herbert Hoover—sprang up around the country. Their makeshift dwellings were constructed of cardboard boxes, discarded bricks, and other salvaged materials, much like the encampments proliferating today.[32]

President Franklin D. Roosevelt's 1932 election brought the New Deal, his response to the chaos and suffering of the Depression. Creating dozens of new social programs, the initiative addressed the urgent needs of the time, including housing. The new programs alleviated much of the crisis—at least for White Americans. Black Americans and other minorities were largely excluded, entrenching racial segregation and inequality, and contributing to the disproportionate racial impact that is very much present today.[33]

Military spending in the lead-up to World War II helped shore up the economy and reduce unemployment. Those not absorbed by the war effort tended to be elderly or disabled, and this limited population began to constitute the "typical" homeless person on the skid rows of major cities after the end of the war.[34]

Beginning in the 1960s, the failure to fully fund President John F. Kennedy's initiative to reform mental health care in America pushed a new population into homelessness—those with psychiatric disabilities. JFK had argued for people with mental disorders to be treated in their communities instead of the often-inhumane state mental institutions. But while the state-run sanitoriums were indeed shuttered, not enough community mental centers were funded to replace them. In the 1970s, changes in the real estate market made cheap housing increasingly scarce, and many former residents of mental institutions had nowhere to go but the streets.

By the early 1980s, homelessness was growing dramatically. While the estimated number of homeless people was—and still is—a matter of heated debate, most everyone agreed that whatever the number was, it was rapidly going up. Many experts believed that more people were homeless in the 1980s than at any time since the Great Depression. Annual surveys, initiated in 1984 by the US Conference of Mayors—a group representing big-city mayors—documented a soaring demand for emergency shelter in major metropolitan areas around the country, coupled with an inability of local authorities and private charities to meet it.[35]

The populations affected by homelessness were also quickly changing. Families with children became the fastest-growing group. Homelessness among racial and ethnic minorities also grew, forming a disproportionate percentage relative to their representation in both the population at large and stably housed low-income people in particular.[36] Younger working men and women were affected as well.

Geographically, homelessness was no longer limited to large urban areas. From suburban neighborhoods to rural communities, the impact was everywhere. What the Kosters, Deans, and other families on Long Island had experienced—suburban family homelessness—was becoming the rule, not the exception.

Several developments had converged to drive this larger trend. Starting in 1981, his first year in office, President Ronald Reagan led a successful campaign to reduce federal funding for social safety net programs. Housing took an enormous hit, with funding cut by 50 percent—literally shrinking available new housing to less than 1 percent of what it had been.[37] In 1979, federal low-income housing programs funded over *347,000* new units of rental housing affordable to impoverished Americans. By 1982—just three years later—that number had been slashed to *2,630*.[38] While the following decades saw some increases in funding for low-income housing, the huge gulfs left by Reagan's cuts were never filled. According to the most recent data, only *one in four* of those poor enough to be eligible for housing assistance receives it—and this is directly due to funding shortfalls.[39]

In 2025, the lack of affordable housing remains the leading cause of homelessness.

Income is the other side of the coin. No housing is affordable if the money you have coming in keeps going down. And even as Reagan was promising the return of American greatness, plants were closing all over the country. The steep decline in relatively high-paying manufacturing jobs left many people unemployed, underemployed, or with sharply diminished incomes.[40]

Finding new work was also taking longer. By 1982, the number of Americans who were unemployed for longer than twenty-six weeks had shot up to 1.4 million—a 300 percent increase in only three years.[41] In early 1983, after reaching a high of almost 11 percent, unemployment finally began to fall, but many of the new jobs were in the poorly paid service industry.[42] The federal minimum wage, which had gone up every single year since 1974, froze after the Carter administration's final increase in January 1981. The next bump in the minimum wage wouldn't arrive for almost ten more years, in 1990.[43]

Countless Americans were clearly struggling to make ends meet. Instead of helping, the Reagan administration pushed to cut federal income support programs and tightened eligibility standards.[44] Public service employment was eliminated, extended unemployment benefits were reduced, welfare eligibility requirements for poor mothers and children became more onerous, and disability payments for elderly and/or disabled low-income Americans were reduced.[45] States followed suit, cutting or eliminating "general assistance" programs that provided very modest cash aid to single people who were down on their luck.[46] Financially at-risk individuals lost this public income support just as their job options in the private market were drastically dwindling and housing costs were climbing.[47] Legal services programs, targeted for elimination by the Reagan administration, also took a hit, leaving the most vulnerable people even more exposed.[48]

A Right to Shelter—Not Housing

Even before Reagan's drastic cuts, homelessness had become more visible on city streets around the country. Starting in the 1970s, privately owned forms of cheap housing were targeted for redevelopment by profit-driven entrepreneurs, displacing their former residents. Nonprofit groups were offering shelter, meals, and other direct emergency help. Some organizations were secular, others faith-based, including several inspired by Dorothy Day and her Catholic Worker movement. Often staffed only by volunteers and operating with few resources, they were on the front lines.[49] Seeing the need firsthand, many became advocates and activists.

By the end of the 1970s, activism to demand a government response was growing. Litigation filed in 1979 by legal aid and pro bono lawyers on behalf of a group of homeless men in New York City proved one notable example. The lawsuit, *Callahan v. Carey*, asked the court to require the city and state to provide shelter and meals to the men, arguing that failure to do so would cause them irreparable harm, including possible death from exposure. That December, relying on a provision of the New York State constitution that said that "the aid, care and support of the needy are public concerns and shall be provided by the state," along with state and local laws implementing it, the court issued a preliminary ruling that the unhoused men were entitled to "Board and lodging."[50]

Following that ruling, in 1981 New York City entered into a consent decree—a legally binding settlement, signed by the judge—in which the city agreed to provide overnight shelter to every eligible homeless man.[51] (It would take two subsequent cases to extend the obligation first to women and then to families.[52]) Notably, the right created by the settlement was to emergency shelter—not permanent housing.

The consent decree set detailed shelter standards, including specifying minimum bed dimensions, toiletries to be supplied, and minimum hours of recreation provided.[53] The terms, eerily reminiscent of prison condition settlements, were clearly meant only to address the immediate crisis. The sole provision arguably aimed at helping people transition out of homelessness was a requirement that the city provide written notice of other aid for which they might be eligible.[54]

New York City was already facing an affordable housing crisis, meaning that any assistance it might offer to homeless people in finding a permanent place to live would be very limited.[55] In the years that followed, the housing crisis only intensified as rents skyrocketed, wages stagnated, and assistance plummeted.

While the consent decree didn't address these bigger problems, it did spur the creation of a massive shelter system that, as of December 2024, accommodated over 124,000 people—men, women, and children.[56] But despite the decree's detailed requirements, the obligation to provide decent shelter was often violated, and over the decades advocates returned to court repeatedly to enforce its terms.[57] When an influx of financially desperate migrants began arriving in the city in 2022, many without resources and needing shelter, Eric Adams, the City's Democratic mayor, claimed there was no room and sought to overturn the decree. Already homeless New Yorkers had been languishing in the city's shelters for years due to the lack of affordable housing.[58]

In the 1980s, right-to-shelter litigation had secured a modicum of emergency aid for homeless people in the country's largest city. But without also requiring housing, it couldn't bring a more permanent solution to the burgeoning societal crisis. Instead, it may have influenced the short-term, shortsighted nature of government response for years to come. The 1979 litigation did, however, bring tremendous public attention to the issue, and often public sympathy.[59] The case also spurred the founding of the Coalition for the Homeless in New York City,[60] and inspired similar coalitions and litigation in other communities.[61] In some cities, activists began holding demonstrations and staging sit-ins to draw attention to the growing numbers of people in need—and to demand government aid.

As homelessness grew, activists in communities across the country came together to coordinate their efforts. This led to the formation of the National Coalition for the Homeless (NCH) in 1983. Sharing space and staff with the established but locally focused Coalition for the Homeless, the national group was also based in New York City. As the need for a federal response became increasingly clear, so too did the need for action in Washington, D.C.—the government wasn't going to act on its own.

I was still at Sullivan & Cromwell at the time, working on the Koster case pro bono with the coalition, when NCH approached me in 1985. They wanted me to go to Washington, D.C., to organize and lead a national campaign pushing for federal action. The resources for the campaign were slim. Relying on donations, with no government grants or paying clients, NCH would fund an office—with me as the sole, minimally paid, staff member.[62] To me, it seemed like an exciting opportunity, and I agreed.

A NATIONAL CAMPAIGN

By the early to mid-1980s, it was clear to anyone paying attention that homelessness was a national crisis. To many, including me and other activists, it also seemed obvious that a federal response was not just "necessary and proper"—in the language of the law—but urgently needed. The federal government had to act—now. Case closed.

Needless to say, this view was not shared by the Reagan White House. The administration responded to the growing calls for action by first denying that the problem even existed, and then by shifting the blame to homeless people themselves. In 1982, while the Kosters and thousands of others were struggling without housing, an official of the Department of Housing and Urban Development (HUD) had claimed, "No one is living in the streets."[63] Two years later, President Reagan gave a speech referring to "the people who are sleeping on the grates, the homeless who are homeless, you might say, by choice." He repeated this characterization on national TV, calling homelessness a "lifestyle choice."[64] Shelters were available in "virtually every city," Reagan claimed, but people chose not to use them. Help was available, but people in need rejected it.

According to the Reagan administration, with few exceptions, homelessness was not an issue for federal action.[65] It was a matter to be addressed by private charities or, at most, local government. This view held sway with many in Congress, too. As homelessness swept across the country in the early 1980s, virtually the only federal response, beginning in 1983, was a series of ad hoc appropriations for emergency food and shelter through the Federal Emergency Management Agency— the agency responsible for aiding victims of natural disasters such as hurricanes.[66]

The Reagan administration's dismissal of a federal response was not surprising, given that its aggressive attacks on social programs—with eviscerating cuts to low-income housing—had massively exacerbated the crisis. The reach of this austerity stance may be less obvious. While funding for low-income housing programs has increased in the decades since, the Reagan cuts have never been restored to their original numbers—while the affordable housing crisis has deepened. This yawning chasm in funding has yet to be filled, and the administration's rhetoric that blamed poor people for their own plight has proved at least as harmful and long-lasting as their policies.[67]

The false narrative that people choose to be homeless—and willfully reject readily available help—is an invidious legacy of the Reagan administration. As of 2025, this rhetoric is still prevalent—and, with the advent of the second Trump administration, destined to intensify. Sometimes couched in more benign-sounding terms—such as "helping" people get assistance and not "enabling" their homelessness—it's a narrative that is surging across the country, advanced by Democrats as well as Republicans. Politicians claim that laws that criminally punish homeless people for sleeping outside—even in the absence of any alternative—are necessary to prod people to seek help, even when help is not available. It's the story the Democratic leaders of Denver used to justify their horrifying sweeps of unhoused people in the snow. During the pandemic, as people who had gratefully accepted placement in empty hotel rooms were tossed back out into the streets—by political leaders of every party—the lie behind the narrative became even clearer.

But in the 1980s, as homelessness was first exploding across the country, these battles were still in the future.

CHAPTER TWO

Reagan's America

"No One Is Living in the Streets"

Half a mile from the Capitol building—an eleven-minute walk—over a thousand men lived in a gray, dilapidated, formerly abandoned federal building. A few dozen women lived in a separate wing of the building. The Community for Creative Non-Violence (CCNV), a nonprofit collective, had converted the building into a shelter. When I arrived in D.C. in the mid-1980s, it was by far the largest shelter in the country. The interior consisted of a warren of long hallways and dorm-like rooms lined with bunk beds. Cots had been set up in some of the hallways. CCNV operated the shelter with zeal and compassion, but it felt crowded and depressing.[1]

Many of the residents were veterans with honorable discharges, mostly from the Vietnam War.[2] Robert, who slept in a hallway on the second floor, was a vet who'd become a federal employee. Health problems had forced him to retire after over nineteen years of work. He'd gone to the Department of Veterans' Affairs (VA), the federal agency charged with caring for veterans, but was turned away for benefits because his disabilities were not "service related."[3] Robert received a monthly federal retirement annuity of $557 but had no other income. He had no savings and had become homeless when his girlfriend, a chronic alcoholic, had kicked him out.

James, also a veteran with an honorable discharge, was disabled and receiving $187 monthly from the VA; he also got federal disability benefits through the Social Security Administration (SSA).[4] His previous month's checks had been stolen and cashed by someone else. With no savings and without the checks, he'd been unable to pay his rent and been evicted. James had written to the VA to try to get his check reissued but hadn't heard back. With nowhere else to turn, he'd moved into the shelter.

Not all the residents were veterans, of course. A couple, Jeff and Mary, arrived at the shelter when an unscrupulous landlord took their rent for a month and evicted them after a week. They were living in separate parts of the shelter, which didn't have the capacity to house couples or families together.

Robert, James, and Jeff and Mary were clients at the makeshift legal clinic a few volunteer lawyers and I had organized inside the shelter. We'd set up a card table in a hallway—there was no other space to spare—and taped a handwritten "legal clinic" sign on the wall behind our chairs. We volunteered in the evenings to accommodate the many residents who worked day jobs, as well as our own schedules.

Many of the people who came to us wanted help with evictions. Some worked as day laborers and were being mistreated by the agencies that employed them. Charged for uniforms, tools, van rides, and more, they often took home much less than the minimum wage (at the time) of $3.35/hour at the end of a long shift.[5]

Some of these problems we could address by making calls or writing letters. Some were potential court claims that we could refer to other volunteer lawyers.

But many of the clinic's clients simply wanted help finding a place to live that they could afford. Our clients had assumed a lawyer could help them find housing. But the frustrating reality was that in most cases there was little we could do beyond referring them to housing programs with long waiting lists.

Under US law, there is no right to housing.[6]

A NATIONAL CRISIS AND A CALL FOR ACTION

Legal aid offices (like the one I had worked with on Long Island) were increasingly seeing homeless and near-homeless clients. Funded since the 1970s by the federal government—this support would soon be drastically cut at Reagan's behest—these local offices responded to the urgent legal needs of poor people in their communities. They also documented the needs they saw and funneled their findings to the small network of national legal aid organizations that supported them. Working on different aspects of poverty, a loose coalition of the national groups compiled a long list of problems and potential solutions.

Arriving in Washington, D.C., in late 1985, I joined them to help turn the list into a three-part proposal to Congress. This became the Homeless Persons' Survival Act,[7] which spoke directly to the problems faced by unhoused individuals and families.[8]

Part 1 addressed the immediate needs of those already experiencing homelessness. It would provide emergency shelter and remove barriers (such as address requirements) to existing anti-poverty programs like Medicaid, disability benefits, job training, and welfare. Part 1 also sought to ensure homeless children received the public education to which they were entitled.[9]

Part 2 aimed to prevent those on the edge from falling into homelessness. This would be accomplished by offering temporary aid to people who were about to be evicted, lose their homes to foreclosure, or discharged from hospitals and other institutions. A little bit of help at a critical moment might keep them from ending up in a shelter or on the streets in the first place.

Part 3 increased funding to the low-income housing programs that had fallen victim to Reagan's cuts. This was the most expensive phase of the plan, and therefore fated to be the most contentious. But it was essential to begin to close the gap opened by the Reagan cuts that had sent more Americans plummeting into homelessness.

The Homeless Persons' Survival Act was an ambitious national agenda based on clear needs reported by communities across the country. It directly addressed many of the problems that Robert, James, Jeff, and Mary, the Kosters, the Deans, and millions of others were experiencing. Much of the proposal aimed to reverse the policies and funding cuts that had fueled the crisis in the first place. The estimated cost of the whole thing was about $4 billion—what would be $11 billion today.[10]

Our proposal faced an uphill battle. Reagan's popularity was high, and his views dominated much of Washington.[11] In Congress, many Democrats had joined Republicans in embracing the view of government as the problem, not the solution, and argued that social programs should be cut, not expanded.[12] Party affiliation, it turned out, was hardly determinative of any given congressperson's position on this point. The influence of money in politics was growing, and our most immediate constituents were, by definition, totally destitute.[13]

We planned to call on activists in communities across the country to help push for our proposal. They could press their representatives and senators to support it. We'd simultaneously work on Capitol Hill to get pieces of the Homeless Persons' Survival Act passed incrementally, step by step. But to even begin this effort, we first needed to find a member of Congress willing to take the lead by sponsoring our proposal and introducing it as draft legislation.[14]

"THE HOMELESS DON'T VOTE"

Homelessness was spreading at an alarming rate, but our campaign for a federal response faced daunting odds.

This became clear as soon as I began visiting the Hill. I started with a short list of liberal Democrats, mostly from New York, that my organization had deemed "sympathetic" to our cause.[15] Staffers repeatedly assured me that what my organization was doing was very important and that the congressperson fully supported it. *However,* I was invariably told, he— or, less likely then, she—was facing an election in the fall, the proposal was expensive, and "the homeless don't vote." Every congressperson on our list would love to help, if only they could—but none were willing to sponsor the proposal.

Others were ideologically opposed. In lockstep with the Reagan philosophy, their goal was to shrink the federal government, not expand it. Some just laughed: To them, homelessness didn't rise to the level of a national political issue appropriate for congressional action. And even if they personally felt that it should, this was the Reagan era. Did I seriously think such an effort was possible? How terribly naive I must be![16]

After months of meetings with dozens of legislative offices, what was beginning to seem like a miracle happened: Representative Mickey Leland expressed interest. Leland was a respected Democratic congressman from Texas and a former anti-poverty activist.[17] In Congress, he chaired the Congressional Black Caucus, as well as the House Select Committee on Hunger, which he'd helped create by crossing the aisle to work with Representative Ben Gilman, a Republican from New York.

Once Leland agreed to serve as lead sponsor of the Homeless Persons' Survival Act, securing a second sponsor was a tiny bit easier,[18] the third slightly easier still, and so on, until we had sixty sponsors. All were Democrats except for a lone Republican—Representative Gilman.[19]

The Senate was then controlled by Republicans and getting support there proved even harder. An unexpected turning point arrived in the form of the Congressional Wives for the Homeless, a group that had come together out of concern for the growing crisis. They invited me to speak at an event for their members. The setting seemed incongruous with the topic: We sat in plush armchairs covered in floral fabric in an ornate drawing room, sipping tea from fancy china. But it turned out to be a pivotal event. The group's founder, Tipper Gore—wife of then-senator Al Gore—had begun volunteering in a shelter in 1984. Tipper felt strongly about the need to address homelessness and, after hearing me describe our challenges in finding support in the Senate, she promised to speak to her husband.[20]

I'd already met with Gore's office, without success.[21] But Tipper Gore's passionate interest apparently made a critical difference, and Senator Gore agreed to be our first Senate sponsor.[22] That June, some six months after we'd begun working on it, the Homeless Persons' Survival Act of 1986 was introduced in both the House and Senate.[23]

DEFINITIONS, NUMBERS—AND POLITICS

Reaching this point had required more than securing congressional support. Getting Leland and Gore on board as lead sponsors had been hard enough. But then we had to translate our proposal into legislative language, turning it into a bill that Congress could consider and act on.[24] One element of the proposal was especially challenging and critically important: defining homelessness. This would determine who would be eligible for and protected by the programs our proposed legislation would create. But the definition of homelessness was—and remains—far from straightforward.[25]

At a basic level, homelessness is the lack of housing. People who are living on the streets, in parks, or other public places are clearly homeless. So are people living in shelters. But what about a family living in a single, rundown room without a kitchen or bathroom, like the Myers family on Long Island? What about a family who couldn't find an affordable place after being evicted and ended up sleeping on another family's couch or kitchen floor, like the Kosters? What about someone who rents a weekly room for part of the month, but must move to a shelter or the street when the disability check is spent?

Two years earlier, in 1984, the Reagan administration had published a controversial report that claimed that the size of the homeless population was a fraction of what many advocates had estimated.[26] When the report was released, activists were warning that between 2.5 and 3.5 million Americans were without a place to live. The Reagan administration's report asserted that only 250,000 to 350,000 Americans were experiencing homelessness—one-tenth of what advocates estimated.

The report was roundly criticized by experts, with advocates attacking it for being politically motivated. Much of the critique centered on the seemingly intentional sloppiness of the methodology. Indeed, within a few years rigorous studies would back up the advocates' estimates and point to even larger numbers.[27]

Beyond its methodological flaws, the Reagan administration's report used a narrow definition of homelessness, which further minimized the numbers. According to the administration, homelessness consisted of two categories: people living in public or private emergency shelters[28] and people living in the streets or other public places.[29] This definition would exclude people like the Kosters during the period when they had split up their children to move in with family, sleeping on the floor. It would leave out the Myerses, temporarily placed in a single basement room with missing floorboards and no bathroom, cooking facilities, refrigerator, or running water.

People who lose their homes typically move through stages, or in and out of them. Often, they double up with friends or relatives, but these arrangements usually can't last long. Family and friends are often stretched thin themselves; conditions are overcrowded, and food and other resources very limited. Doubling up may also jeopardize the host's own housing by violating the lease. Bouncing around from host to host—as the Kosters and Deans had done—is common. When these options run out, a person will likely seek emergency shelter if it's realistic and available, or live in a public place if it's not.

How do you translate this reality into legislative language? To define homelessness in our bill we had to capture the fluidity of lived experiences while also providing the specificity needed in a statute. In the end, the language we proposed included people living in temporary shelters of various kinds, as well as people living in a public or private place "not designed for or ordinarily used as a regular sleeping accommodation for human beings." But it also included a broader formulation that would include the Kosters, Deans, and Myerses: those who lacked a "fixed, regular, and adequate nighttime residence."[30]

Later, after the law was enacted, federal agencies would interpret this formulation in dramatically different ways, leading to controversies that have persisted into current debates.[31] Some agencies, most notably the US Department of Housing and Urban Development (HUD), construed the statutory language narrowly, limiting its scope. Other agencies, like the US Department of Education (ED), interpreted the language broadly, including the children of families living doubled up with others due to economic necessity.[32]

Differing definitions are part of the reason that the seemingly simple question—how many people are homeless?—is still so difficult to answer. Include people who've lost their housing and doubled up with others, moving from place to place, and you get a much bigger number. Only count those in shelters or public places and the figure is much smaller.

The other reason the question is hard to answer is that, regardless of the definition used, there is no accurate count. Lack of resources, inconsistent methodologies, stigma, and fear contribute to the difficulties.[33]

As of 2025, each definition has its own proponents, and disagreement is fierce. The main controversy is between those who think it's better policy to "target" limited resources to a smaller group of people, as the narrower HUD definition would do, and those who prefer a definition that better reflects reality, as the ED definition does.

While there's a certain pragmatism to targeting, I advocate for the broader approach. The argument for targeting assumes limited funding, and that is our current reality—existing resources are woefully inadequate. But that reality just underlines the urgency of advocating for more funding and building a broad coalition to do so effectively. Recognizing that homelessness is part of the much larger problems of housing instability, extreme poverty, and inequality expands the potential for such a coalition. It's a way to challenge and *change* the current reality—not just accept it.

UNLIKELY ALLIES AND A FIRST VICTORY

In 1986, adopting a false—not just restrictive—definition was one of the ways that the Reagan administration tried to avoid the responsibility of responding to homelessness. Minimizing its extent, denying its existence, and even claiming it was a "choice" all furthered the excuse that homelessness did not require a federal response. This was an issue for charity to address, the argument went, or, at most, local government. But we were working very hard to get the idea of a significant federal response taken seriously.

So far, we'd relied on the strength of the evidence and the logic of our arguments to gain enough political support to get our bill introduced. It soon became clear, however, that getting the legislation *passed* would require much more. In the US political system, major industries and corporations rely on high-powered lobbyists to further their interests in Congress—and to benefit their bottom line. Our most directly affected constituents were totally destitute, and while our arguments were strong, we lacked money and the other trappings of power.

Another early hitch was that, trained as a litigator, I had little knowledge of the legislative process. We would need help to gain access to key players, and the expertise to use it effectively.[34] One way to do this was by marshaling some of those same high-powered resources to help us pro bono—just as my old firm had done back when I first got involved.

Covington & Burling was a major global law firm with a commitment to public service (a reputation that continues to this day).[35] I made a cold call to their pro bono coordinator and heard back almost immediately. Rod DeArment, a partner in the firm's legislative practice, had volunteered and was putting together a team to work with me. Soon we were meeting at the firm's offices, sitting around a polished-wood table in a conference room decorated with Currier and Ives prints. Covington & Burling had the same conservative, understated décor as Sullivan & Cromwell, and I settled into the familiar surroundings as we talked.

A self-described conservative Republican, Rod had arrived at the firm right out of law school. Covington & Burling had an innovative program that offered its new attorneys a chance to be paid by the firm while working at Neighborhood Legal Services, a local nonprofit providing free legal representation to poor people in the city.[36] Rod signed up for a six-month stint, which gave him a firsthand look at the challenges of poverty. A few years later, he left the firm to work on Capitol Hill, eventually becoming chief of staff to the powerful Republican Majority Leader, Senator Bob Dole.

While a seemingly unlikely ally, Rod was deeply religious and felt a connection to issues of homelessness and poverty through his early legal aid work. He'd recently returned from the Hill to become a partner at Covington & Burling, as well as cochair of their legislative practice.[37] With the Senate controlled by Republicans, Rod's connections, experience, and knowledge would be critical to our efforts on Capitol Hill. We began paying calls together in search of support.

One of our visits was to the office of Republican Senator Pete Domenici of New Mexico, chair of the powerful budget committee. Domenici was Catholic and, like Rod, strongly in touch with his faith. One of his daughters had mental health issues, and as a significant minority of unhoused people also experience mental disorders, Domenici had associated the two and taken a personal interest in homelessness.[38] Rod and I began regular communication with his staff, and eventually they arranged for us to meet with the senator himself.

In person, Domenici was warm and engaging as we sat in his spacious, imposing office. Listening to our pitch for the Homeless Persons' Survival Act, Domenici was skeptical about the link between cuts in federal funding for housing and the growth of homelessness. He also thought that, in any case, the Senate didn't yet see that connection. "Maybe," he allowed, there was a link between cuts in welfare payments and homelessness.[39] We didn't come away optimistic, but after the meeting, his staffer called to say that the senator wanted us to prepare a "Domenici package" made up of low- and no-cost items from our larger proposal.[40] These would be easier for him to help us pass—the ones that would cause fewer ripples with his constituents and fellow Republicans.

These were mostly modest changes to existing law, such as making it easier for homeless people to apply for and receive certain federal benefits for which they were already eligible, even if they lacked the permanent address that was typically required. There was also a provision to allow people to apply for food stamps and disability benefits while they were in institutions such as hospitals, jails, and prisons. Having these resources as soon as they got out could prevent them from becoming homeless.[41] The Congressional Budget Office (CBO), a nonpartisan congressional entity, was in charge of estimating how much each of these proposed changes would cost to implement.

Here the Reagan administration's reluctance to acknowledge homelessness as a major problem worked in our favor. CBO had gone to each of the federal agencies administering the benefits programs and asked them how many homeless people were denied benefits due to lack of a permanent address. In each case, the response was that the number was negligible—because the official government tally of homeless Americans in general was grossly underestimated and also because the agencies did not want to admit to denying benefits to people without homes. That implied the cost of removing barriers would also be negligible, and CBO assigned zero cost to the proposal—just as they did for the provision to let those in institutions apply for aid, and for similar reasons. Domenici put the pieces together in a package called the Homeless Eligibility Clarification Act.

Pragmatic politician that he was, Domenici found a way to fast-track our proposal through the often sluggish legislative process. An antidrug bill was moving quickly through Congress in the fall of 1986, with both sides of the aisle joining the president's push for immediate action.[42] By noting a connection between drug use and homelessness—again relying on prevailing stereotypes—Domenici was able to attach our amendment to it. Because Domenici was the lead sponsor, other Republicans, including archconservatives such as Jesse Helms, signed on as cosponsors. On October 26, 1986, the Anti-Drug Abuse Act of 1986 passed with strong bipartisan support. President Reagan signed it into law the next day— and the Homeless Eligibility Clarification Act of 1986 was included.

Just months earlier, the Reagan administration had disavowed responsibility for homelessness, denying its very existence as a social problem. Many in Congress, including liberal Democrats, wouldn't even acknowledge it as an issue for federal legislative action. Our three-part Homeless Persons' Survival Act had laid out an ambitious national agenda and local groups had organized around it, as we'd hoped they would. Activists had called, written, and visited their representatives in Congress, showing the passion of people who clearly voted. And now, thanks to "inside the beltway" lobbying and the personal interests of powerful key players, we'd successfully pushed Congress to implement the first small pieces of our agenda.[43]

It had been an improbable victory, and I invited congressional staffers, Democrats and Republicans alike, to my cramped apartment in a questionable part of town to celebrate. We were all jubilant that our long-shot effort had paid off. One committee staffer confided that when we'd first met, he thought, "This is a nice lady, but she's not going to get anything done." I was used to being underestimated because of my small size, youth and, of course, gender. Sometimes this disarmed potential adversaries, and maybe it had also helped here.

Regardless, it was an important victory. We had definitively affirmed that Congress had a role to play in addressing homelessness. And if the federal agencies had vigorously implemented our new law, it could also have made a critical difference in people's lives.

Sadly but predictably, the Reagan administration was hardly eager to do this. In fact, it had been ignoring another law that was already on the books.

SUING THE REAGAN PENTAGON

In 1983, as the homelessness crisis was intensifying, Congress enacted a law giving the Department of Defense (DoD) authority to use vacant military property for shelter. The following year, it appropriated $8 million for this purpose. This action came after four people died on the streets of Washington, D.C., in as many days, followed by advocates' public demands—widely publicized in the press—for the federal government to open unused buildings to homeless people and prevent more deaths.[44] By the time we were lobbying Congress in 1986, the earlier law had been in place for three years. But the DoD had done nothing with it. There was simply no process for anyone to apply to use vacant properties or access the allocated money.[45]

In New Haven, Connecticut, Columbus House was turning people away from its emergency shelter nightly, unable to meet the growing need. Having heard about the DoD program, the shelter director tried to find out how to apply to use one of two nearby vacant military installations. Her efforts led nowhere. One military official replied that there were no military facilities in the area, while a different official wrote that there *were*, but no funding existed for the necessary modifications to make the facilities usable.[46]

The story was the same in Washington, D.C. A shelter provider was promised trailers by the DoD, to be received by Christmas 1983. But after repeated delays, DoD officials informed the group that they did not think it was appropriate for the military to get involved in the shelter business.[47] Had the DoD made good on its promise, it could have helped people like Barry Bruce. Barry couldn't find steady work and had been homeless for six years. With local shelters already overcrowded, he was living on the street near Washington Circle, a few blocks from the White House.[48]

Such examples were legion around the country. In Washington State, a local shelter wanted to use a vacant military site to house fifty women and children. The facility needed renovation, and military officials rejected the request, claiming no funding was available for rehabilitation. Since no rules had ever been created to formalize the process for handling renovations, the DoD simply determined that it couldn't spend money on them. In Fort Monmouth, New Jersey, an unused military warehouse stood empty but the county, fearing the cost of opening a shelter—and having no way to apply for the funding allocated by Congress—didn't utilize the property until after a homeless man froze to death outside. And in Alameda County, California, the DoD refused to meet its obligations to prepare a facility for use by the Salvation Army. The site had previously been used to test radioactive materials, contained exposed asbestos, and had mercury in the water, but the DoD claimed it was safe and would not pay for further rehabilitation. The director of the Salvation Army decided she could not in good conscience use it for a shelter with so many obvious safety hazards.[49]

Working with service providers in parts of the country with vacant military property, I documented these and other examples. A pro bono law firm team and I petitioned the DoD to implement the program. Collectively, we publicized the DoD's failures. It was all to no avail.[50] Our options exhausted, the pro bono law firm team and I filed suit in federal court. We asked the judge to order the DoD to issue regulations as soon as possible, and to direct military officials to identify vacant spaces and make them available for use as shelters beginning that winter. The court ruled in our favor, and the victory was covered in the national media, drawing attention to the administration's responsibility to act— and its failure to do so.[51]

Three years after it was legally required to go into effect, the Pentagon's program to provide emergency shelter began to operate in 1987.

We'd won this battle, but it was just one of many. While we were going up against the DoD, we'd also been fighting on other fronts.

A WINTER CAMPAIGN

Our victory over the DoD came shortly after the Homeless Eligibility Clarification Act—the Domenici legislation—had passed. I knew we needed to follow up to hold the impacted agencies accountable, but my attention became diverted by another urgent initiative.

Activists around the country had been agitating in their communities for years, pressing local leaders to provide aid to homeless residents. Many advocates provided shelter, food, and other critical aid themselves. Washington, D.C., was home to one of the most active and prominent advocacy groups, the Community for Creative Non-Violence (CCNV).[52] In addition to running the largest shelter in the country, CCNV was passionately committed to activism.

Founded by a Paulist priest in 1970, CCNV had started out working on a range of social justice issues. By the early 1980s, their focus had tightened on homelessness, initially taking on the local government and later engaging with the Reagan administration.[53] Their tactics included hunger strikes, civil disobedience, and other forms of public protest that brought media attention and, sometimes, public action.[54] Mitch Snyder was the group's most visible member,[55] often appearing on TV and in the newspapers. Some regarded Mitch as a saint, others were put off by his confrontational style, considering him a showman.[56] Regardless, there was no denying his dominant presence and personality.[57]

In the fall of 1986, as the National Coalition for the Homeless, Rod, and I were winning passage of the Homeless Eligibility Clarification Act, Mitch proposed working together on new federal legislation that would allocate $500 million in aid to homeless people.[58] He considered this sum very ambitious but not impossible, and wanted to push Congress to pass it that winter.[59] To do this, we would mount a campaign that put the urgency of cold weather front and center.

This approach risked furthering the prevailing view of homelessness as a temporary crisis that could be addressed through emergency measures, not as a systemic problem with deeper causes.[60] It was a shift from the strategy behind the Homeless Persons' Survival Act, our comprehensive three-part plan that aimed to keep the focus on bigger, longer-term solutions while incrementally advancing smaller pieces. But Mitch was adamant, and he had a point.

We'd just experienced the enormous difficulty of finding support for the mere *introduction* of the Homeless Persons' Survival Act. Getting Congress to commit $500 million for *anything* would be a huge challenge, and emphasizing the emergency nature of the need would surely help. Political and strategic calculus is complicated, and eventually I deferred to Mitch. NCH and CCNV would join forces and make an all-out effort that winter.

I also thought that we might be able to have it both ways. While the collaborative effort would focus on getting $500 million that year, we could draw on the specific legislative proposals in the Homeless Persons' Survival Act to shape the programs receiving this funding. I would also try to keep a focus on the longer-term issues. If we succeeded in securing emergency aid, it would be a first step toward the bigger goal. At least I would try to frame it that way publicly.[61]

STRANGE BEDFELLOWS?

As activism spread around the country in 1986, attention on homelessness was also rising dramatically.[62]

Martin Sheen starred as Mitch in *Samaritan*, a made-for-TV movie about his work with CCNV. It premiered in Washington, D.C., with celebrities and politicians in attendance.[63] Hollywood comedians and HBO teamed up to raise money for aid to homeless people.[64] Hands Across America, a highly publicized event with millions of people joining hands in a single line across the country, also boosted awareness and funds.[65] Mayors convened to strategize on addressing homelessness, and a new advocacy organization of homeless and formerly homeless people, the National Union of the Homeless (NUH), was founded.[66]

That fall, over five hundred activists from around the country came to Washington for a conference hosted by the National Coalition for the Homeless (NCH). Many attendees had helped put pressure on their congressional representatives to support the Homeless Persons' Survival Act. Our event coincided with the Senate voting on the Homeless

Eligibility Clarification Act, electrifying the group, who was seeing a tangible result of its efforts.[67]

On Thanksgiving Day, Mitch announced he would set up camp outside the Capitol until Congress passed the new proposal for $500 million in emergency aid. The vigil included a daily meal served to homeless and low-income people, dramatizing the extreme need that our legislation was meant to address—and that Reagan and his allies denied existed.[68] In January, the incoming Speaker of the House, Jim Wright, toured the CCNV shelter. Soon after, he announced plans to support our proposal, a commitment that would be instrumental to our efforts.[69]

Our new bill was introduced by the new House Majority Leader and the bill's primary Republican sponsor, Stewart B. McKinney.[70] The Urgent Relief for the Homeless Act consisted of most of Title I of the Homeless Persons' Survival Act—the emergency relief part[71]—and authorized $500 million. Speaker Wright promised to fast-track its passage.

At the same time, Representative Mickey Leland, reintroduced the complete Homeless Persons' Survival Act.[72] My pro bono team and I were still pushing to sign on cosponsors for the full proposal, even though we had agreed to focus our work on the joint $500 million proposal with CCNV. We could use that support to bolster our efforts to actually pass the $500 million measure that winter. In a promising sign of bipartisan support, Senator Domenici agreed to keep working with us, supporting mental health services and housing for homeless people with mental disorders.[73] We were off to a promising start, but to maximize our collective chances of passing the new bill, we needed to coordinate closely with Mitch.

Nervous about bringing together people who were so dramatically different, I arranged a meeting with Rod DeArment, Mitch, and myself on a Saturday at the offices of Covington & Burling.[74] Rod drove in to the firm in downtown D.C. from his suburban home in Virginia. Mitch came over from his usual heat grate, dressed in the clothes he lived and slept in. I arrived from my modest downtown apartment. Despite my anxiety, the meeting went well. Rod seemed to relish the experience, or at least not be put off by it. Mitch was very reasonable—not always a given. We agreed to start going on lobbying visits together.

The three of us were an odd group: Rod and I in suits, looking like lawyers, Mitch looking like a homeless person, carrying along his notoriety in lieu of a briefcase. We certainly made an impression, and this may have helped us. Despite our wildly different backgrounds and appearances, we delivered the same message. Homelessness was a national crisis, and the federal government had to act. The Urgent Relief for the Homeless Act was a much needed first step, and we wanted their support.[75]

The House scheduled an early hearing on the measure, signaling the urgency and seriousness with which it was moving.[76] Governor Mario Cuomo of New York, a powerful moral voice who had lent his name to an important report on the issue, testified.[77] So did Mayor Raymond Flynn of Boston, bringing to bear his Catholic faith, as well as his leadership of the Task Force on Hunger and Homelessness of the US Conference of Mayors, another important lobbying group.[78] Speaker Wright added his voice, showcasing the House Leadership's commitment.[79]

Our efforts were also beginning to be taken seriously in the national media. Days after the hearing, both the *New York Times* and the *National Journal*, a publication influential in policy circles, ran stories.[80] And on March 5, 1987, the Urgent Relief for the Homeless Act passed the House of Representatives with a large, bipartisan majority.[81]

But the version of the bill that passed the House was missing a critical section.[82]

FIGHTING FOR HOMELESS CHILDREN'S RIGHTS

As initially passed by the House, the Urgent Relief for the Homeless Act left out the portion designed to ensure access to education for homeless children.

When the bill was first being discussed, influential education groups had objected. The crux of the problem they identified was that addressing the educational needs of homeless children would require money—and the funding proposed in the bill was miniscule. But instead of advocating to increase the amount, the groups were trying to kill the proposal. To overcome their objections, the lead committee staff person working on this part of the bill needed to bolster the case for safeguarding education for unhoused children. He called asking for data on the problems homeless kids faced.[83]

The harms homeless children suffer were already well documented. Due to their precarious living conditions, they experience higher rates of infectious diseases, depression, and anxiety.[84] They also have trouble keeping up academically, without a quiet—or any—place to do homework while living in a crowded shelter, car, or tent, often suffering from hunger. Compared to their housed peers, they're more likely to repeat a grade or drop out of school.[85]

Unhoused kids could also be denied access to school by the public education system itself. School enrollment is based on residence, which is based on address. Homeless children staying somewhere other than their original school district were no longer considered "residents" of that district. And since schools didn't typically consider a shelter, much less an outdoor location, to be a fixed address, they weren't residents of their current location, either.

This is what had happened to Iraida Delgado's two children. The family became homeless in October 1986 in Freeport, Long Island. They'd successively been placed in shelters in three different neighboring towns, ending up in Roosevelt. Iraida wanted her children to keep attending their school in Freeport, so they could stay with their teachers and friends in familiar surroundings despite the turmoil of homelessness. But the education agency said the children were no longer Freeport residents, so they didn't have the right to go to school there. Nor could the kids enroll in school in Roosevelt, since that school district didn't recognize their homeless shelter as a legitimate address. The result was that these two children missed months of school.[86]

The section of the Urgent Relief for the Homeless Act that was stirring up controversy was designed to address exactly this problem.[87] It said that school districts had to ensure that homeless children could enroll in either their original school or a school in the district where they were currently living—and that the choice was up to the parent. School districts would be required to pay for transportation back to a kid's original school, if necessary, as well as making records immediately available for transferred children and taking other steps to guarantee these kids got their education. The proposed legislation authorized a small amount of federal funding to help cover increases in the school districts' costs.

The resistance to these seemingly commonsense provisions proved fierce. Why were education groups, generally Democratic, opposing this effort to help vulnerable children?[88] Anticipating that homeless children would need more time and attention from educators, they objected to being required to take on this added challenge. We spent months organizing meetings with the key players to try to hash out the differences,[89] while also calling on local groups to contact their representatives in Congress.[90] The National Education Association ultimately agreed to remain neutral, neither supporting nor opposing the bill. The School Board Association opposed it but agreed not to actively work against it.[91]

We had to give some ground, but we still managed to agree on strong and specific protections. Eventually, these were included in the final version of the Urgent Relief for the Homeless Act.[92] This would pay off later, when we filed litigation to enforce the law—and the degree of specificity in the statute was critical in establishing our ability to sue.[93]

But while there was agreement on all sides on the need for increased funding—lack of enough money was the stated basis for the education groups' opposition—we were far less successful on that point. Even with a Democratic Congress and supportive leadership, the lobbying might of the education establishment had been able to water down our language—but not to increase funding for public schools to educate poor children. This experience proved an object lesson in the difficulty of building political support for impoverished children.

WHERE'S THE MONEY?

Despite the obstacles, we'd managed to get the House to pass our bill. But we still needed the Senate to introduce and pass a counterpart to the Urgent Relief for the Homeless Act—before they can become law, bills need to clear both houses of Congress and be signed by the president. Our proposed legislation was asking for new funds that went over the existing federal budget, which meant we'd need sixty votes in the Senate.

Getting those would require bipartisan support.[94] Thanks to our earlier work on the Homeless Persons' Survival Act and Rod's connections, we already had strong relationships with influential Republicans. Our bill was introduced with the support of ten Republican sponsors, including Dole and Domenici.[95]

Just before the Easter recess, the Urgent Relief for the Homeless Act passed the Senate eighty-five to twelve.[96]

But it turned out we were hardly done fighting yet. We still had to spend months persuading Congress to actually *fund* the bill. All our work so far had been to get the Urgent Relief for the Homeless Act "authorized." Getting money "appropriated" was a totally different matter, which required additional legislation in both the House and Senate. We had had to get agreement from both houses of Congress to waive budget limitations simply to pass a law *authorizing* Congress to appropriate funds.[97]

We had just gone through this incredibly arduous effort to get Congress to pass our authorizing legislation, and it might be almost completely meaningless. There were important sections that didn't depend on funding, of course, such as the provisions that protected children's right to attend school, and another that gave service providers a right of first refusal to use vacant federal property to help homeless people. But most of our new law created programs to distribute federal funds for shelter, housing, health care, and other services. Without the actual funding these parts of the Urgent Relief for the Homeless Act would provide no relief at all, just empty promises. The harsh truth was that just because Congress had authorized a certain amount of funds didn't mean it would appropriate the same amount. The authorization was a *ceiling*, not a guarantee.

While Congress was mired in this maddening political process, Ned had a far more urgent problem. A day laborer who lived at CCNV's massive shelter half a mile from the Capitol, Ned had been in a car accident while working an overnight janitorial job at Dulles Airport (one of the D.C. metro area's biggest hubs).[98] The labor pool company had sent a van to pick up Ned and his fellow day laborers at Dulles after their shift ended at 6:30 a.m. and take them back to the shelter. The van driver had been putting in eighty to ninety hours a week, and his previous pickup that day had been at 3:30 a.m. He must have dozed off on his way back to the shelter, crashing the van.

Ned hadn't been wearing a seat belt—not because he'd been careless, but because there were literally no seats in the van. The labor pool company had removed them to cram in more people, a way to save on transportation costs. Luckily, Ned's injuries weren't life-threatening, but he was in a great deal of pain and wouldn't be able to work for some time. He came to the makeshift legal clinic at the CCNV shelter where I still volunteered with other lawyers in my scant free time. Ned wondered what he could do, if anything. I referred him to a colleague to investigate possible legal claims.

Before his injury, Ned had made $28.46 a day working eight-hour shifts for the labor pool company, lunch not included. The paltriness of this sum and the dehumanizing conditions Ned had endured were heartbreaking—and enraging. Maybe our free legal counsel could help him a little. But Ned's horrifying experience certainly helped me stiffen my resolve.

We had to keep pushing Congress—and navigating its Byzantine rules—to fund our bill.

A PARADIGM SHIFTS—SORT OF

Finally, in June 1987, both houses of Congress passed the final version authorizing our bill—and a separate bill funding it.[99] Large bipartisan majorities supported authorizing the bill: 301 to 115 in the House, and 65 to 8 in the Senate.[100] What had started out as the Urgent Relief for the Homeless Act was renamed in honor of Stewart B. McKinney, its chief Republican sponsor, who had died of AIDS in May.[101] Thirteen years later, the name of another key leader, Bruce Vento, was added after his untimely death in October 2000. To minimize confusion, I'll hereafter only refer to the legislation by that name: the McKinney-Vento Homeless Assistance Act.

On July 10, our authorizing bill landed on the desk of President Reagan. Under the Constitution, he had ten days—not including

Sundays—to sign or veto it. If he took no action, the bill would automatically become law.[102]

On July 22, at the end of the very last day that he could do so, President Reagan signed the McKinney-Vento Homeless Assistance Act into law. There was no signing ceremony, and Reagan only picked up his pen that evening. According to an anonymous White House official, the unusual timing was intended to signal Reagan's "lack of enthusiasm" for the bill.[103]

Presidential enthusiasm or no, the enactment of the new law made the front page of the *New York Times*.[104]

The McKinney-Vento Homeless Assistance Act authorized over $1 billion in federal aid for homeless people over two years, with Congress appropriating just over 72 percent of the funds it had authorized.[105] The law created twenty new programs to fund shelters, transitional housing, and a very modest amount of permanent housing, as well as physical and mental health care, food, and drug abuse treatment. Most of these programs operated by funneling federal funds to states, local governments, and private nonprofits. The Act also protected the right of homeless children to a public education and gave groups serving the homeless first dibs on using vacant federal properties for free.

Just as consequentially, the McKinney-Vento Homeless Assistance Act affirmed the federal government's responsibility to address homelessness. Small wonder Reagan had balked at signing it, when it directly refuted the very paradigm he'd help define. The Act explicitly stated that homelessness is a national crisis and that the federal government has a responsibility to address it. It also created a new independent agency, the US Interagency Council for the Homeless (USICH), to coordinate the federal response to homelessness, defining a central point for federal accountability.[106]

Touching on many of the issues included in the original Homeless Persons' Survival Act, the McKinney-Vento Homeless Assistance Act suggested what a comprehensive solution might look like. Embedded in the law were amendments to larger social programs, such as job training, designed to ensure that homeless people could and would benefit from them. "Demonstration" programs were also created—such as one for adult literacy—with small amounts of funds attached to them.

Yet at $720 million over two years, appropriations were significant but short of authorizations. In some cases, the discrepancies between authorized and appropriated amounts were enormous. For the Emergency Shelter Grants program, of the $120 million authorized for 1988, only *$8 million* was appropriated. For the 1988 Section 8 single-room-occupancy (SRO) program, no funds were appropriated at all. More importantly, even had the programs been fully funded, they were far from enough to meet even the immediate needs of people who were homeless. Applications for the 1987 funds exceeded availability tenfold, despite the newness of the programs.[107]

Funding shortfalls weren't the only problem. The McKinney-Vento Homeless Assistance Act mainly focused on emergency relief, like shelters. We knew that at best this approach would ameliorate the problem, not solve it. Longer-term measures were essential, and we made sure to have key supporters make statements to that effect. Speaking on the floor of the Senate when the bill was first introduced, Senator Gore said: "[This legislation] is an essential first step towards establishing a national agenda for action to eradicate homelessness in America. . . . No one in this body should believe that the legislation we begin considering today is anything more than a first step towards reversing the record increase in homelessness."[108]

Pushing Congress to move beyond that first step would become an ongoing challenge.

For me personally, it became even more of a challenge in the immediate aftermath of the enactment of the McKinney-Vento Act. Less than two weeks after Reagan signed the bill into law, I received a diagnosis of Hodgkin's lymphoma, a type of cancer. I was very fortunate to have good medical coverage through the coalition, and to receive a temporary bump up in my minimal salary. An additional lawyer joined my office to help, providing a major boost, and I continued to work during the nine months of chemotherapy. I couldn't help but wonder what would have happened to me had I been uninsured and unhoused—and without a network of family and friends with resources.[109]

A MUCH DEEPER CRISIS

Even as homelessness was first exploding in the 1980s, it was obvious that stemming it would take much more than emergency shelter and aid. A Columbia University study published just a few years later showed that from 1985 to 1990, well over five million people had experienced "literal" homelessness—sleeping in a shelter or in a public place—at some point in those five years. Individuals and families who were doubling up with others because they'd lost their housing and could not find another place they could afford increased that number to over eight million people. Perhaps most shockingly, the study found that 13.5 million people— 7.4 percent of American adults—had been literally homeless at some time in their life. Including those who were doubled up pushed the lifetime estimate to nearly 26 million. The researchers cautioned that the difficulty of collecting this data meant these numbers were likely *under*estimates.[110]

A far worse crisis was brewing than what was visible on the streets and in shelters. A bed for the night might help the few who were able to get it, but it wouldn't address even the immediate needs of everyone caught up in the expanding maelstrom of homelessness, much less stem its growth. Over the coming years and decades, funding for the McKinney-Vento Homeless Assistance Act would increase, and some funds for low-income housing would be restored. But Congress still wouldn't close the yawning gap opened by the Reagan cuts or make good on the promise of long-term solutions.

In the absence of those solutions, homelessness continued to increase, becoming a seemingly permanent part of the American landscape and pointed to as an "intractable" problem. Almost thirty years after the McKinney-Vento Homeless Assistance Act was first passed, the CCNV shelter at Second and D Streets in northwest D.C. was still overcrowded most nights. By 2016, a Hyatt hotel opened across the street in a swiftly gentrifying downtown. Over a thousand people still lived at the shelter, in an area that had once been an urban wasteland.[111]

Ali was one of them.[112] He'd been living there for years, working odd jobs as a day laborer, never earning close to enough to afford stable housing. At least this particular shelter was open 24/7, meaning he could come and go as needed whenever he could find work. Ali could even leave his few personal belongings, including documents like his birth certificate, in a locker—a luxury in the shelter system. His application to the city for housing assistance had been languishing on a waiting list for years, and it felt like he might never escape the shelter. Like most of his fellow residents, what Ali wanted most was help finding jobs and job training, which he viewed as critical to securing his own housing.[113]

Around the same time that Ali was marking time in the D.C. shelter, in Boise, Idaho, Lawrence Lee Smith was living in a tent he'd set up deep in the woods, near a river. Lawrence had become homeless after his degenerative joint disease progressed to the point where he could no longer work his construction job. He'd been able to get disability, but the check wasn't enough to cover a month's rent plus other necessities. The shelters in Boise were so overcrowded that the few times that he'd been able to get in he'd slept on a mat on the floor.[114] All told, Boise's three shelters at the time had 354 beds and 92 floor mats. According to the official count—likely a gross underestimate—there were almost nine hundred homeless individuals. Given these odds, Lawrence had eventually given up and pitched his tent outside.

Across the country, between 2017 and 2020, an average of 908,530 people became homeless each year—and 900,895 people exited homelessness that same year. These numbers obviously represent good news for those who are no longer homeless, and they make clear that ending homelessness is possible. But the figures also show that *each year more people enter homelessness than leave it*. Crunching these numbers, that's 7,635 more people entering homelessness each year than leaving it, for three years in a row. And that's according to conservative definition and estimates from the federal government—the actual number of people entering homelessness was almost certainly much larger.[115]

This was *before* the economic collapse of 2020, when the COVID-19 pandemic suddenly and drastically increased the need.

With nowhere to isolate or even regularly wash their hands, people experiencing homelessness were much more likely to contract the virus than the housed population. Researchers estimated that when they did contract it, homeless people were twice as likely to be hospitalized, two to four times as likely to require critical care, and two to three times as likely to die.[116] We and other advocates pressed for action, and new federal guidelines laid out recommendations to protect people experiencing homelessness from COVID-19. Shelters were advised to cut their numbers to allow for more space between beds and some semblance of "social distancing," both to protect the people using them and to prevent the spread of the virus. A federal eviction moratorium temporarily banned most evictions for non-payment of rent.

In 2021, federal pandemic relief added $4 billion to the main emergency shelter program, increasing funding more than tenfold.[117] The new federal funding also allowed local governments to move people from crowded shelters and encampments into vacant hotel rooms, a welcome respite for those who got them—as well as to a hotel industry decimated by the pandemic's effect on tourism.

Interfaith Sanctuary in Boise, Idaho, was one of the city's three overnight shelter providers. It placed needy families into empty rooms at one hotel, prioritizing those whose medical needs made them especially vulnerable. Soon it had a waiting list of about 180 families. Some of those families wound up living in tents in the woods, while those who still had their cars used them to sleep and store their belongings. April Kuper, her husband, and their four children were among the lucky ones who received temporary help from the new hotel program.

The Kupers had been renting a three-bedroom house in Boise when their landlord gave them thirty days to leave. April's husband worked nights for a health care provider, making fifteen dollars per hour—a decent income. But this was in June 2021, when housing prices had almost doubled, and the family couldn't find a new place they could afford. Fortunately, April's mother lived close by, but her house was small: two bedrooms, with April's sister already living in one of them. For a while the Kupers split up their family between April's mother's house and a friend's spare room, sometimes paying to stay in hotels or motels while they fruitlessly hunted for housing.

Just before their eviction, April had been diagnosed with stage 2 breast cancer. When they reached out to Interfaith Sanctuary, the group prioritized the family for their hotel shelter program. April, her husband and their three youngest children moved into a room with two beds.

Despite the cramped conditions, April told a local TV station that she counted herself grateful, because "I look around and I could be sleeping in our little tiny car . . . or sleeping in a tent somewhere."[118]

But even with the stability of a room at the hotel-cum-shelter, the family couldn't find permanent housing they could afford.

Forty years after the Kosters had to sleep in their pickup truck after their pleas for help proved futile, people like Lawrence and hundreds of thousands of others were being denied emergency help. Even those who were able to get emergency shelter, like Ali and the Kupers, often languished there, financially unable to move on to more secure housing. And the people who were able to exit shelters for permanent housing were replaced by even greater numbers of those who had lost their homes.

Meanwhile, emergency systems meant to respond to immediate crises became increasingly complex, governed by hundreds of pages of regulations. Case managers began compiling lists of unhoused people by name, assessing their degree of vulnerability, and prioritizing their needs through "coordinated entry" systems. Much more was known about how best to provide services, and much more data were collected documenting the need. While emergency systems may have become more efficient, desperate people seeking emergency shelter were still turned away. People in dire need were still being "diverted" to stay with overcrowded and impoverished family and friends or even placed on long waiting lists for *emergency shelter*.

HOUSING OR HANDCUFFS?

The federal eviction moratorium expired in 2021, along with those adopted by some state and local governments. Without tenant protections in place, evictions were higher than they'd been *before* the pandemic. By 2023, federal pandemic funds had run out.

At the end of that year, the annual "point-in-time" count, administered by the federal government since 2007, reported a 12 percent increase in people living in shelters and on the streets in just twelve months. This was surely an underestimate: Even the federal government has acknowledged its data collection methods regularly miss large numbers of people. And because it uses a narrow definition of homelessness, the HUD count only includes those living in shelters or on the streets, excluding anyone living doubled up for financial reasons.[119]

During the pandemic, increased federal funding helped increase the number of available shelter beds people who were sheltered by almost 19 percent between 2000 and 2023. Tens of thousands of homeless people had been temporarily housed in vacant hotel rooms, including whole families such as the Kupers. But the expanded funding still didn't keep pace with the expanding need, and as the funding ran out, the growth in needed capacity slowed. By 2023, the federal government estimated the shortfall at just over 200,000 beds. The real deficit was surely much larger.[120]

Even before the pandemic, though, the situation had become increasingly bleak. In the absence of even sufficient emergency shelter, let alone affordable housing, outdoor encampments of homeless people proliferated, increasing by over 1,300 percent from 2007 to 2017.[121] Across the country, many city mayors—Democrats and Republicans alike—responded not with new low-income housing or even shelters, but with laws making it a crime to live outside, despite the absence of alternatives. Many repeated the false narrative that help was readily available but people just preferred to be homeless. The "blame the victim" view promoted by Reagan returned—or maybe it had never really gone away.

The extreme shortage of affordable housing, decades in the making, was thrown into sharp relief by the pandemic—which only made it worse. But while the crisis in the United States was deepening punitive and destructive government policies, other countries were embracing the view that housing is a basic human right. Enshrining this right in their constitutions, they were reducing or even eliminating homelessness. Inspired by these successes, activists were increasingly calling for the human right to housing in the United States, and some were notching up victories.

A new coalition, including many who had personally experienced homelessness, was growing.

CHAPTER THREE

Broken Promises

"I'm Not Getting Nothing"

On a sidewalk in Berkeley, California, in view of an upscale neighborhood in the hills above, Star lived in a tent. Fifty-five years old, mentally disabled, and unable to hold down a regular job, she'd been on disability for years. In 2022, Star told the local street newspaper she used to make a little money doing odd jobs before the pandemic made that impossible. The $1,100 she received in disability benefits each month was barely a third of the average $3,000 rent for a one-bedroom in the area. Even before you factored in the security deposit and other incidental costs of moving into a new place, Star never had a chance of finding secure housing.[1]

In Upstate New York, Bob hadn't been able to make much money even before he injured his back and could no longer work at all. He did manage to qualify for disability benefits, but they weren't enough to cover housing, leaving him to rely on family and friends. After outliving his siblings and most of his friends, he piled his few belongings into his new home—a beat-up old car. His monthly disability check covered car insurance and gas; for food, he relied on soup kitchens, food pantries, and whatever his meager food stamp allotment allowed. Bob had never suffered from depression, but by 2022, at the age of seventy-eight, he'd started thinking about ending things. He knew how he'd do it, too—by taking all his prescription medications with a bottle of whiskey.[2]

In Kalkaska, a village in northern Michigan, "Three-fingered Jim" had been living outside for ten years when the organization Invisible People interviewed him in 2017. He'd been a certified Harley-Davidson mechanic until an accident mangled his right hand, making it impossible for him to do his job. He applied for disability five times, and he was turned down each time. Jim lost his house, his vehicles, and his tools. He started drinking too much. Camping in a wooded area with a handful of friends in similar circumstances, he suffered through a decade of brutal Michigan winters. A few months after his interview, Jim was finally placed into housing. Three months later, he died of pneumonia.[3]

Star, Bob, and Jim each have their own stories, but their experiences are hardly unusual.

Visit virtually any American city and look around you. You'll see people in wheelchairs, on crutches, with walkers, begging for spare change. You'll see elderly people, bundled up in blankets or sleeping bags, curled up on park benches. You'll see people in apparent mental distress wandering the streets, sometimes speaking animatedly to no one—or anyone who will listen. Unless you look closer, you may not notice the people living in their cars, nursing coffees by day at McDonald's, entering shelters in the evening.

And this isn't just in cities. You'll also see people camped out or sleeping in their vehicles in suburban communities, in rural communities. Anywhere there are people, there are unhoused people. You just have to look.

How can this be happening in the richest country on earth?

For years, conventional wisdom held that most homeless people had mental health issues—and that a major cause was the closure of state mental hospitals, commonly known as deinstitutionalization. Some politicians still embrace this view, like New York City mayor Eric Adams and California governor Gavin Newsom, who have called for addressing homelessness by involuntarily committing people—in 2024.

Yet, while a significant number of unhoused people do suffer from mental disorders—they are certainly the most visible homeless individuals to the public eye—they are by no means the majority.[4] And while there is an element of truth to the theory that deinstitutionalization contributed to homelessness, it leaves out the most important part: Less than half of the promised community supports were funded. The theory also doesn't account for the wide diversity in the homeless population, which includes people with other forms of disability, and many with no disabilities at all.

The real story is much more complex—and disturbing. It started decades ago.

Abandoned to the Streets

In 1955, more than half a million people lived in state mental institutions. Populated by those who couldn't afford private care, these facilities were often overcrowded, understaffed, and offered little treatment. Many not only warehoused vulnerable individuals, but kept them in straitjackets, fed them starvation diets, and subjected them to physical and sexual abuse.[5] Public outcry converged with state concerns over rising costs to create pressure for change. With the advent of new psychiatric medications in the 1950s, many states created small community programs for patients who responded well to the drugs. Moving slowly, states discharged about 54,000 people to these programs from 1956 to 1962.[6]

President Kennedy strengthened this push with a major national initiative in 1963. This urged Congress to create and fund comprehensive programs for people with mental illness to live and receive treatment in their communities. Kennedy called for 2,000 new community mental health centers, including day treatment and hospital care. Beds in state mental hospitals were cut by more than half, from over 500,000 in 1963 to just over 200,000 in 1974.[7]

Yet fewer than half of the 2,000 promised community mental health centers were ever funded.[8]

Even the best plan is doomed if only half of it is implemented. While state institutions were indeed closed, the critical second part of the initiative—the creation of community supports—never materialized. The federal government's failure to follow through with the promised community care left those released from state hospitals with few options. Unlike people with mental illness who could afford private care, many of those in public institutions had very limited resources.[9]

In 1972, a new federal program was created as part of the Social Security Act; it would be administered by the Social Security Administration (SSA). Signed into law by President Nixon, this program was intended to help low-income individuals who were elderly or disabled—physically, mentally, or both—with a modest cash benefit.[10] Those discharged from state mental institutions were eligible for this aid, known as Supplemental Security Income (SSI), if they could prove they were poor enough and too disabled to work. Recipients could then use the monthly check to pay for inexpensive lodging, such as a room in a boardinghouse or a single-room-occupancy (SRO) dwelling.[11] Consisting of single rooms with shared kitchens and baths, SROs were a form of inexpensive, dormitory-like housing then prevalent in cities around the country.[12]

Sometimes the SSI check wasn't quite enough to last until the end of the month, and many precarious lodgings charged by the week or even the night. No longer able to pay for their housing, recipients had to find somewhere else to go until the next check arrived. In New York City, "Alvin" arranged to be admitted to a psychiatric hospital when his funds ran out, then checked himself out on the first of the month to pick up his SSI check and return to the SRO. "Joseph," ninety-two years old and also in New York City, lived on the streets when his SSI money ran out, checking back into a hotel when the following month's check arrived.[13]

Even as the new SSI program offered a potential, albeit often inadequate, income source, inexpensive lodging was fast disappearing. Fueled by government incentives, gentrification was reshaping neighborhoods, with upscale housing replacing SRO units. Developers were eager to buy the properties, often resorting to harassment to force SRO tenants out so they could convert the property into more lucrative use.[14] A New York City employee recounted one incident where developers walked into a rundown Manhattan hotel carrying sawed-off shotguns, ordering everyone out. Dogs were used to threaten residents early in the morning.[15] Around the country, a million SRO units were lost to development in the 1970s alone, leaving many of their former tenants with mental disabilities with nowhere to go.[16]

Coming into office in 1977, the Carter administration launched an initiative to finally follow through on Kennedy's promised resources for those discharged from state hospitals. New legislation enacted by Congress in 1980 planned to increase funding for community mental health centers, and to provide more comprehensive support for patients discharged into community settings—including housing.[17] But when Ronald Reagan became president in 1981, his administration scrapped those plans in favor of destructive new policies that hurt not only poor, mentally disabled people, but poor, disabled people in general. As part of his agenda to shrink the federal government, Reagan took aim at the federal disability benefits that impoverished elderly and disabled people relied on to survive.[18]

These new policies directly contributed to the explosion of homelessness that began in the early 1980s.[19]

DROPPED FROM THE ROLLS, FOILED BY INSURMOUNTABLE BARRIERS

The Social Security Act was designed to protect people who, because of disability or age, are unable to support themselves. It's the essence of the social contract: the promise of help to those who find themselves in need through no fault of their own. Monthly benefits could be used to pay for basic needs, like housing. If the recipient isn't able to manage their finances, someone can be appointed to manage the disability benefits for them. This could be a family member, case worker, social worker, or other trusted individual—or it could be a community organization, social services agency, or state or local government office.[20]

For many people, receiving SSI benefits also means automatic eligibility for health coverage through Medicaid. Health coverage is important for everyone, but especially for disabled and elderly individuals.[21] Those who had worked before becoming disabled—and thus paid into the system through their employment—could apply for a related benefit, called Social Security Disability Insurance (SSDI), which paid a somewhat higher benefit.[22]

Crucially, SSI benefits are an "entitlement." Unlike other programs—notably housing—your right to these benefits doesn't depend on how much, if any, money Congress chooses to allocate each year. Funding expands to meet the need. If you meet the eligibility requirements, you are "entitled" to the benefit. In theory.

In practice, while funding for an entitlement isn't subject to direct cuts, there are more subtle ways to accomplish the same result. Eligibility standards can be tightened. The application process can be made extremely onerous. Agency staff can be cut, causing backlogs and delays in processing applications. Individuals who have already been deemed eligible and are receiving benefits can be required to re-prove their eligibility.

The Reagan administration tried all these tactics and more.

In the early 1980s, the administration began a program of so-called "re-examinations" of people who were already entitled to and receiving benefits.[23] In a shift from prior policies, the burden was placed on the recipients to prove their continued eligibility—a difficult, sometimes costly process, especially for indigent people who were elderly or physically or mentally disabled.[24] It was part of an overall effort by the Reagan administration to cut spending on safety-net programs for poor people.

Many of those thrown off SSI were still disabled, still unable to work, and still legally entitled to their benefits. But under Reagan's initiative, proving eligibility had been made much harder. Appealing required tremendous effort and skilled assistance. It often meant going through multiple levels of review within the agency, and, if those were unsuccessful—which they often were—filing a lawsuit in federal court. All of this took persistence and access to help, including a lawyer. Many of those who were wrongly terminated simply lacked the wherewithal to fight back.

By 1985, almost 500,000 people had been dropped from the disability rolls.[25] A disproportionate number were mentally disabled. While they accounted for just 11 percent of all disabilities, about a third of those kicked off SSI had mental disorders.[26] People who had been able to avoid homelessness with the help of these benefits were now thrust into it. New York City, Denver, Colorado, and Columbus, Ohio, all cited a direct connection between disability terminations and increases in homelessness in their cities.[27]

Of those who were able to appeal, more than 200,000 had their benefits reinstated. Eventually. The hundreds of thousands who couldn't appeal were left with nothing. And even for those who could push their cases forward, the Reagan administration made sure to limit the impact of their successful appeals, through an aggressive policy of "nonacquiescence." This meant that if an applicant challenged her denial in federal court—even up to the federal appeals court—and the court agreed that the agency had misinterpreted the law, the agency would follow the court's decision *in that case only*.[28]

Other applicants with the exact same issue were out of luck unless they could marshal the resources to go through the same arduous process. This amounted to an outright refusal by an executive agency to recognize the authority of the federal courts to interpret the law—an affront to the rule of law. Nonacquiescence continued through the early 1990s, until a series of court rulings and public outcry forced the SSA to modify its position.[29]

Meanwhile, as hundreds of thousands of people who had wrongly been thrown off the rolls struggled to get back on, others had never been able to get on SSI in the first place. The Byzantine eligibility process implemented by the Reagan administration had effectively prevented countless entitled candidates from ever receiving assistance.

Even those who qualified were subjected to rules chipping away at what little they'd been able to get. One particularly egregious policy, adopted by the Reagan administration in 1987, counted emergency shelter stays, soup kitchen meals, and donations from food pantries as "income" when calculating federal disability benefits. For every bag of groceries a food pantry gave a poor, elderly, or disabled person, the federal government would reduce that person's already paltry check even further. A payment of $340—the maximum *monthly* benefit at the time—could be cut by as much as $113.[30]

SHELTER AT NIGHT, LOCKED OUT DURING THE DAY

By December 1989, Yvonne had been living in a mass shelter in Detroit for five weeks. It was the third time she'd been homeless in the past two years.[31] The first time she'd stayed at the Salvation Army shelter for twenty or thirty days, she couldn't remember exactly. After that she'd stayed in a room at the Roosevelt, an old hotel in Detroit that, having seen better days, had been turned into a shelter.

Yvonne's mental health had been deteriorating for years. Over the course of the previous decade, she'd been hospitalized at several state mental health institutions. She hadn't been able to work since her mental health issues began and relied on a small state welfare grant of about $130 a month. This didn't include medical coverage. Yvonne couldn't afford treatment or medicine. As she described it, "I get very agitated and can't concentrate without medication."

A few years earlier—she couldn't recall when—she'd applied for federal disability benefits, newly available under the Social Security Act. At the time, the average amount of these benefits was $368,[32] more generous than the state welfare grant. Unlike her state grant, it included medical coverage for treatment and medications. But she'd never heard back on her application. She put it plainly: "I have no idea how to follow up to see whether I might be eligible."[33]

Twenty-two-year-old Timothy was living at the same shelter in Detroit. He wanted to move out but, he said, "I have no income and no money to rent a place." Timothy heard voices and had been hospitalized twice in a state mental health hospital. After receiving federal disability benefits, he'd been cut off several months earlier. He didn't know why, or how to get back on.[34]

During the day, neither Yvonne nor Timothy had anywhere to go. The Detroit/Wayne County Union of the Homeless, an organization of and for homeless people, operated a drop-in center for those who were locked out of shelter during the day. On an average winter day, between 70 and 100 people crowded into the center. But more than 27,000 people were homeless each year in Detroit, and many had no option but to spend their days, as well as their nights, on the streets.[35]

Most shelters required people to leave in the morning, sometimes very early—many still do. That meant that Yvonne and Timothy often spent their days in public. Without health insurance to pay for medications or treatment, symptoms of their mental disorders were on full display. Without access to a place to store their belongings or wash their clothes or themselves, they likely appeared dirty and unkempt. Being on the street itself would likely worsen their agitation. Speaking to imaginary companions, they might attract attention, informing public perceptions of "the homeless": people who have mental health conditions, "others," not like "us."[36]

Around the same time in Washington, D.C., Frank had become homeless. His father could no longer pay the bills and had put the family home up for sale. Frank had been working two jobs to help support his family. But then a severe asthma attack at work landed him in the hospital, and he was fired. He found other jobs, but, as his asthma worsened, he couldn't keep any of them.

Frank tried staying in shelters, but, he told me, "the smell was so bad I couldn't breathe." He bounced from shelter to shelter, always encountering the same problem. Eventually, he slept on the street—"that was the only way I could breathe." Only later did he find a shelter with a ventilation system where he was able to stay despite his asthma.

Frank had heard about disability benefits, and went to the Social Security office. He filled out the fifteen-page form by himself. A month later, he got the letter that his application had been denied. He couldn't understand why and didn't know he could appeal. With no money, he again found a job. But his asthma made him repeatedly miss work and his boss told him to leave. He hadn't worked since.[37]

A large man with a gentle demeanor, Frank had no visible disabilities. The ventilated shelter he'd finally found allowed residents to stay during the day, and to store their belongings there, so he didn't have to carry them around when he left. He was able to shower and keep his clothes clean. You might pass him on the street and not realize he was homeless. His presence would do nothing to counteract the images forming in the popular consciousness.

"A LACK OF INTEREST IN THE PLIGHT OF THE HOMELESS"

To those paying close attention, it was clear that countless people who were impoverished, elderly, disabled, or all of the above were being denied the help they were entitled to by law. They were being thrown off the rolls, unable to apply, or foiled by insurmountable barriers. At a time when benefits could still be enough to cover modest accommodations, they instead found themselves in shelters or on the streets. Any meaningful federal response to homelessness had to include them.

That's why as we were planning our campaign to force the federal government to address homelessness, we included a special focus on federal disability benefits. At the same time we were pushing the McKinney-Vento Homeless Assistance Act through Congress, we also worked to make it easier for eligible homeless people to get federal disability benefits through the Social Security Act. Congressman Fortney "Pete" Stark, a California Democrat, spearheaded the bill, called the Homeless Outreach Program. In December 1987, just months after the McKinney-Vento Homeless Assistance Act was signed into law, Stark's bill was enacted as a "demonstration program," authorizing funding of up to $4 million over two years.

Lack of information and inability to navigate the complicated application process were the main problems for most, if not all, homeless applicants—like Yvonne, Timothy, and Frank. The "demonstration" meant that the agency would offer grants to a few of its local offices to reach out to disabled homeless people who might be eligible, explain the benefits and, crucially, help them apply. It was modeled on a New York City program that had shown a 62 percent approval rate for homeless participants who were offered this help—much higher than the 10 percent average of the time.[38]

The new program never had a chance. In March 1988, just months after the law was enacted, the SSA commissioner—the top Reagan administration official charged with implementing it—instead recommended its repeal. But higher-ups in the administration worried that advocating for repeal would be "politically untenable" and could be "interpreted as a lack of interest in the plight of the homeless." This, they feared, could open up the "Administration to strong criticism of a politically sensitive and visible issue in an election year."[39] While Reagan's second term was coming to an end, his vice president, George H. W. Bush, would be on the ballot that November.

Ultimately, instead of seeking repeal, SSA pursued more subtle forms of sabotage. After considering "somehow 'complying' with [the Act] by expanding activities already under way," the agency simply decided not to request any funds to implement the new program, a position it thought it "could easily justify" by claiming that the program was duplicative since the agency was already helping homeless people apply for benefits.

Except, of course, that it wasn't. By the end of the 1980s, fewer than one in five eligible homeless individuals were receiving benefits.

"REPEATEDLY DENIED": FIGHTING A BROKEN SYSTEM

While the Social Security Administration (SSA) was finding creative ways to evade its responsibilities, Ramon Willis was trying to find a way to survive in Washington, D.C.

In 1988, at thirty-three years old, Ramon had been diagnosed with HIV by a blood test at So Others Might Eat, a local soup kitchen. Ramon wasn't homeless at the time, but his dishwashing job at a local deli didn't bring in enough to both house and feed him. He supplemented his food budget by eating at soup kitchens. This remains a common scenario today, even as 38 percent of the nation's food supply is wasted and CEOs are paid 344 times as much as workers, a ratio that has increased exponentially over the past six decades.[40]

As Ramon's condition worsened, he could no longer work. Physically weak and psychologically distraught, by December 1989 he'd been unemployed for six months; his first experience with joblessness since graduating from high school. Unable to pay the rent, he became homeless. Ramon sometimes stayed in a set of trailers that the local government had converted into a makeshift shelter in the northwest quadrant of the city. But there were only ninety beds, and these filled up very quickly. If he couldn't get a bed there, he'd hike over to a shelter in the southwest quadrant. If that too was full, or if he lacked the energy to keep walking, he slept outdoors on heat grates or in doorways. He had no permanent address and no telephone.

Ramon received $258 each month from D.C.'s general assistance program—a welfare program for needy individuals then operated by the local government—as well as food stamps and health benefits. But the cash assistance was not enough to rent an apartment or even a room. He used it to pay for food, cigarettes, and to launder his clothes. Cutting his smoking habit might've improved his health, but it would've added to his stress while hardly making a dent in his financial issues, certainly not enough to afford housing. Nothing was left over.[41]

A social worker told Ramon his HIV diagnosis might make him eligible for SSI benefits. He was very interested but knew nothing about the program. Ramon couldn't imagine how to even begin to go about finding out about its requirements, much less apply. His life, as he put it, "is such a shambles now that it would be really difficult for me to take even the first step in applying by myself." Without an address or a phone, it might be impossible.

Earlier that year, I'd left the National Coalition for the Homeless (NCH). I'd felt increasingly unhappy at NCH but was determined to continue the work I'd begun.[42] In June 1989, I founded a new organization, now known as the National Homelessness Law Center (the "Law Center").[43] The Law Center would focus on using the power of the law to advance our goal of ending and preventing homelessness, serving as the legal arm of the growing national movement working toward that goal. We'd continue to recruit pro bono lawyers from big firms to help, building on the earlier strategy. One of the first issues we took on was removing barriers to disability benefits for homeless people.

In December 1989, Ramon became one of several plaintiffs in a lawsuit filed by the Law Center. The case aimed to force the SSA to comply with the 1987 law that created the Homeless Outreach Program. Even though plaintiffs included two states—Michigan and Massachusetts—and a major law firm was working on the case pro bono, we knew it wouldn't be an easy fight. Congress had authorized funds—promised them, in theory—but had not appropriated them (that is, made them available in fact, specifically for this program).[44]

The SSA had other funds it could use, but without mandatory language and a specific appropriation, we faced an uphill battle. The judge, Gerhard Gessell, knew something about political machinations: He'd presided over the Watergate case in the 1970s. But even with the damaging internal agency memos that we had uncovered and included, Judge Gessell threw our case out, noting that "political posturing is not illegal."[45] Indeed.

Nevertheless, the case—and the publicity it helped generate for the plight of disabled homeless people—precipitated action by the SSA.[46] The administration said it would make up to $1 million available to fund programs to conduct outreach to homeless people. They even published a formal notice saying they were soliciting "ideas" on how to conduct this outreach.

Obviously, this wasn't enough. Even if the SSA did solicit ideas, there was no reason to believe that the agency would act on any of them. We could keep some pressure on the agency by continuing our court case with an appeal. But the real problem was that the legislation we had won in 1987 was too weak. We would have to go back to Congress.

A HOMELESS GO-GO DANCER FINDS A HOME—AND ADVOCATES IN CONGRESS

A few key members of Congress—like Congressman Stark, who was "disgusted" with the SSA—were determined to keep up the fight.[47] As the new George H. W. Bush administration was coming into office, a congressional hearing was scheduled to investigate the problem and consider the need for stronger legislation to address it. I was invited to testify to represent the Law Center's position.

The report I presented on April 5, 1990, included testimonies from state officials and homeless individuals who'd been hurt by the failures of the SSA. We cited studies showing that fewer than 20 percent of homeless people who were eligible for disability benefits received them—and in some places fewer than 9 percent did. Our report also outlined changes we wanted Congress to make and called on them to pass a new bill that addressed these concerns, introduced by Stark and some of his colleagues in the House in the Homeless Outreach Act of 1990.[48] Perhaps most importantly, I brought someone to testify with me.

Then sixty-three years old, Mary Rose Gerdes was slim and elegant, with an air of fragility. A recovering alcoholic and substance abuser, she had worked for years as a cocktail waitress and go-go dancer in

Washington, D.C. Eventually she'd become so ill with pancreatitis and severe depression that she could no longer work. Unable to make rent, she moved in with an alcoholic man until, fearing she might start drinking again, she left his apartment for a shelter.

Mary Rose spent a year there before a welfare worker told her to go to the Social Security office to apply for SSI benefits. She filled the complicated form out by herself, even though she couldn't understand it. "I was very frightened," she recalled. But, she said, "I filled [the form] out the best I could." Her application was denied. She tried again, this time with the help of a social worker. Again, she was denied. They appealed—and were denied.

In 1987, another social worker, Julie Turner, took the case. Affiliated with a Presbyterian church group in downtown Washington, D.C., Julie tracked down extensive medical records and submitted another application. This too was denied. But Julie appealed—and prevailed.

Finally, after three tries and two appeals over three years, Mary Rose got her disability benefits: $412 per month.[49] At the time, this was enough to rent a small efficiency apartment. She left the shelter, putting a little aside each month until she built up $400 in savings—her sole financial backup.

Sitting at the witness table in the imposing hearing room, looking up at the members of Congress seated on a dais in front of her and shaking as she spoke, Mary Rose described the life-changing impact of these very modest Social Security benefits: "For the first time in my life, I feel sort of secure."

Testifying right after Mary Rose, Gwendolyn King, the newly appointed head of SSA, admitted that as many as 50 percent of financially insecure individuals who were eligible for benefits—due to disability and/or age—were not receiving them. She was candid about the reasons, describing the application process as "more than a little hard," adding that "it boggles the mind." She vowed that the SSA would "take any and all measures necessary to ensure that SSI benefits are paid to those who should be receiving them."

For all her seeming sympathy, King argued that eligible applicants could not be signed up without "a large infusion of money." Instead, volunteers—whom she called the "thousands of caring, compassionate people out there"—could be engaged to help. Basically, she was opposing the core proposal of the Homeless Outreach Act, which would require SSA to visit shelters to explain benefits, help homeless people apply, and speed up the appeals process for those cut off from aid.

Julie Turner, the tenacious Presbyterian church social worker who had helped Mary Rose, was outraged: "I'm not here to push the papers for the federal government, and I'm not trained to do Social Security's job for them."[50]

Coming into office, George H. W. Bush had pledged that his administration would be "kinder and gentler" than Reagan's. The Bush administration might have *sounded* better than Reagan's, but the bottom line was the same. Apparently, the plan was to turn the federal government's responsibilities over to volunteers—or, as Bush put it, the "thousand points of light."

HELP, SABOTAGED

Between 1989 and 1992, Congress appropriated a total of $15 million for the SSA, to be used to award grants to its local offices to reach out to potentially eligible applicants—including homeless individuals. The agency spent just half that amount and awarded only two small "demonstration" grants for outreach to homeless people specifically.[51] Intended to test innovative models that, if effective, could then be replicated, the two "demonstrations" were showing success by simplifying the application process and modifying the SSA's complex bureaucratic rules. One was the New York City program on which the Homeless Outreach Act had been modeled—the tremendously successful initiative that had helped up to 62 percent of disabled homeless applicants be approved. Given their "implementation" of the Homeless Outreach Act, it wasn't too surprising that SSA chose not to continue funding the demonstration programs once they were complete. Nor did SSA revise its policies to reflect what the taxpayer-funded projects had demonstrated.

Obviously not much had changed at SSA, despite Commissioner King's promises to correct course at the agency so it could better help disabled homeless people. The new "kinder and gentler" Bush administration was continuing the sabotage of the Reagan administration, in practice if not in rhetoric.

This was just one of many broken promises.

Congress had passed numerous laws aimed at helping impoverished and homeless people get the disability benefits they were entitled to and desperately needed. One of these was intended to help financially precarious individuals in institutions—like hospitals, other medical facilities, and prisons—who were typically cut off from benefits during their stay.[52] To ensure they wouldn't be penniless upon discharge, the law required SSA to let those who were eligible for benefits apply up to thirty days before their release. And in a familiar pattern, the law was often ignored.

Many local SSA offices had never even heard of the requirement. One agency staff person told our organization he thought applications before release were actually *prohibited*.[53] This wasn't really their fault. We can blame the lack of priority given by SSA—and the Bush administration overseeing it—that meant frontline staff were most likely not provided the training or tools to carry out the law. The rule was on the books, but those in charge of implementing it simply chose to ignore it.

How could these government officials—charged with helping people like Yvonne, Frank, Timothy, and Mary Rose, their fellow human beings—instead inflict so much needless suffering on them? I doubt the people in charge of the agency *consciously* intended to harm them. But it would have taken deliberate effort for them *not* to realize the impact of their actions—and inactions. Maybe they were under orders from higher up. Whether cognitive dissonance or willful mistreatment was at play, no explanation can excuse their failure to carry out their duty to the vulnerable people they were sworn to help.

Not all challenges were external during this time. In July 1990, my cancer recurred, distracting and partially disabling me for the next year while I underwent treatment. I spent over six weeks at Memorial Sloan Kettering Cancer Center in New York City, followed by several months of recovery at my parents' home in the city, then worked part-time from my apartment in D.C. Again this time I was extremely fortunate to have insurance, access to top medical care, and a strong and well-resourced support network. I was also lucky to be able to hire an excellent interim director, Patty Mullahy Fugere, to run the National Homelessness Law Center, which I had founded just a year earlier, in my absence. July 1990 was also when Mitch Snyder took his own life; though we had not been working together at the time, his suicide obviously affected me, and dealt a major blow to our movement.[54]

A $300 MILLION INJUSTICE

By March 1992, our legislative proposal to require comprehensive national outreach by SSA—the latest version of the Homeless Outreach Act—had not gained much traction. We were stymied by an official estimate that put the cost of the bill at $1.4 billion over five years.[55] Instead of including only the cost of the outreach—which was much lower, less than $50 million a year—this estimate included the collective cost of the SSI benefits *themselves*, even though the would-be recipients were already entitled to them.[56] This artificially inflated cost effectively turned our otherwise modest proposal into a legislative nonstarter. It also illuminated the huge injustice being perpetrated on disabled homeless people: The federal government was wrongly denying them almost $300 million (in 1992 dollars) *each year*.

Some of this was their own money that now-unhoused individuals had paid into Social Security when they were still able to work—and that they were being denied in their time of need.

Larry Melton, an honorably discharged Vietnam veteran, had worked all his life: first in the textile mills of Georgia, then managing a grocery store. A high school graduate, he'd moved to Washington, D.C., and worked construction and other manual labor jobs. An injury left him with degenerative disk disease, restricting his ability to stand, walk, and even sit for extended periods. Carrying more than minimal weight was unthinkable. He felt it was "degrading for a man not to be able to work," but despite his efforts, he just couldn't.

Over his twenty years of work, Larry had paid plenty into the Social Security system. After his injury, he'd applied for disability on his own five separate times. Each time he'd been denied. He'd been homeless for five years, living in the shelter on Second and D streets, which fortunately didn't impose time limits on stays. In the meantime, he'd met Julie, the church social worker, and she had taken up his case. Julie helped him fill out forms, collected the many documents he needed to submit, arranged appointments with doctors to substantiate his disability, and provided bus tokens to help him get to the doctors' offices.

Larry recounted this experience to a congressional committee in 1992. Congress held this hearing specifically for our Homeless Outreach Act, which had been reintroduced. Larry told the committee he was still waiting to hear back on his sixth application. With the help of his social worker, who understood the system, he had a chance.[57] But, he said, summing up the problem concisely: "The people who need the benefits the most are the very ones being repeatedly denied because they do not understand the system."[58]

The congressional committee seemed interested in Larry's plight and our proposed legislative solution. But Congress moves slowly, at least where poor people's needs are concerned, and November 1994 arrived without any substantive action. That midterm election transferred control of both houses of Congress to Republicans and gave impetus to the "Contract with America." Cowritten and championed by Newt Gingrich—a proponent of extreme right-wing ideas, scorched-earth tactics, and obstructionist politics—this austere legislative agenda took its cues from the Heritage Foundation, a conservative think tank that promoted large cuts to social programs.

Two years later, this agenda—coupled with a promise by then-president Bill Clinton to end "welfare as we know it"—resulted in further restrictions. Up until this point, some impoverished people disabled by addiction to drugs or alcohol had been able to receive federal disability benefits. To qualify, individuals had to participate in treatment programs, and benefit payments were made to a responsible designated representative. But in 1996, along with eliminating welfare for financially at-risk families, Congress decreed those disabled by addiction were now ineligible for SSI and SSDI. Between March 1996 and December 1997, over 100,000 people had their benefits terminated as a direct result.[59] The Reagan legacy of slashing the federal safety net continued.

In this climate, the already daunting prospects for passing our bill for comprehensive outreach dimmed further.[60]

A Promise to End "Chronic" Homelessness

Perhaps surprisingly, when George W. Bush came into office in January 2001, his administration declared ending "chronic homelessness" a priority. Their definition included people who were mentally or physically disabled. Increasing access to federal disability benefits—SSI and SSDI—fit with this goal. Suddenly, the SSA became interested in helping eligible homeless people get financial assistance. But after decades of systematically erecting hurdles, they had little idea how to do this. Starting a process that would take years, the law center and another group agreed to produce a training manual for how the SSA could do its job.[61]

An already challenging undertaking became even harder after the 9/11 attacks, when enhanced security measures—such as requiring identification to enter government buildings, including Social Security offices—made it even more difficult for homeless people to apply for disability benefits. Legally recognized forms of ID and other critical documents often went missing during evictions or in the chaos of life in shelters or the streets.[62]

Around the same time, we were able to push through a congressional directive to SSA. This required the agency to develop a plan to improve services to homeless people.[63] In 2003, Congress approved $8 million in funding for a new round of "demonstration" grants to reach out to unhoused individuals and assist those eligible in applying for SSI benefits.[64] And in 2005, SSA finally published the manual we produced to train their employees to help homeless people get their disability benefits, launching the start of a promising new program: SOAR.[65]

Based on the lessons of the early "demonstration" projects, SOAR spelled out how to help unhoused individuals overcome the barriers to receiving disability benefits. The federal agency that funded our manual also funded a course to train caseworkers on the model and supported them with free "technical assistance" to help implement it. Following advocacy to increase funding for SSA, in 2009 they created a national "technical assistance center" that offers support to service providers across the country.

But Congress didn't fund additional staff to *implement* the program. This critical task fell to already overburdened existing employees at organizations working with homeless people. Not surprisingly, only 13 percent of the service providers trained in the method actually used it to complete applications—many simply didn't have time, given their other responsibilities. Nor did SSA make systemic changes to modify or remove the barriers that make getting benefits so hard. According to the most recent evaluation of the program, each application takes twenty to forty hours to complete. A caseworker who spent all their time helping homeless individuals apply for disability benefits using the method would complete only fifty applications per year.[66]

Our training manual couldn't do anything to simplify the time-consuming application process, nor could it change the structural barriers erected by SSA. All it could do was show people the straightest path through the obstacles. And within these big constraints, the method worked. In 2021, 65 percent of those helped by the program received their benefits either on first application or on appeal—compared to just over 30 percent of those who applied without help.[67] From its inception in 2006 to 2023, SOAR has helped over 65,000 unhoused and at-risk individuals receive their federal disability benefits.[68]

This is significant—but it's still only a tiny fraction of those who could benefit from it. In 2023, SOAR reached—at best—*2 percent* of eligible individuals.[69] The overwhelming majority of people in need most likely didn't receive the modest benefits to which they were *already entitled*, benefits that could potentially prevent them from becoming homeless or help them if they did.

These figures didn't stop then-president Trump from trying to roll back even this slight bit of progress. In late 2019, his first administration proposed a new rule to review disability benefits for recipients—potentially terminating their already inadequate support. Fueled by an ongoing right-wing narrative that disability fraud was rampant—and the old myth that people would rather receive a check than work—the Trump administration attempted a replay of the odious Reagan-era policies that threw hundreds of thousands of disabled people into homelessness from 1982 to 1984.[70]

Within weeks of coming into office in 2021, the Biden administration rescinded the proposed rule.[71] But while welcome, it was not nearly enough.[72]

ON DISABILITY, IN A SHELTER

As housing costs have shot up, disability benefits have lagged far behind; even those who've managed to receive them are often unable to afford necessities. In 2023, the *maximum* federal SSI benefit for an eligible individual was $914 per month, or $10,968 per year—only 75 percent of what the federal government itself set as the poverty level for that year.[73] The national average rent for a one-bedroom apartment at the end of 2023 was $1,149—or *over 125 percent of* average monthly SSI payments.[74] This leaves hundreds of thousands of vulnerable people living on the streets or in shelters,[75] including fifty-five-year-old Margaret Davis.

In September 2022, Margaret was staying in a shelter in Charlotte, North Carolina. She had diabetes that required dialysis three times a week, making it hard to hold a steady job. Every month she received a $750 disability benefit and $150 in food stamps. But average apartment rents in Charlotte had reached $1,500—a jump of about 70 percent over the past decade, when she first started getting disability.[76] Over that same timeline, her monthly benefit payment had gone up just $60. After two months in the shelter, finding housing she could afford seemed increasingly out of the question. As her diabetes worsened, she faced the prospect of having one of her legs amputated.

Around the same time, Cori was sitting on a sidewalk in LA, her infant daughter in a stroller next to her. She had set up a table where she displayed donated jewelry and her own art, selling a few pieces for a dollar or two while also soliciting donations. Diagnosed with autism at the age of three, she was unable to work, and the disability benefit she received—$795 per month—was nowhere near enough to rent even a room. She slept in a shelter with her baby, the ninety-day limit on their stay looming. Neither she nor the shelter had been able to find housing for the small family. Cori kept a tent under her bed at the shelter, preparing for the worst for her and her baby.

Disability benefit levels clearly need to be raised significantly. The Biden administration had proposed adjusting them, as had some members of Congress, notably former Ohio senator Sherrod Brown, who chaired the Senate committee overseeing the programs.[77] But after the November 2024 election, these proposals are unlikely to move. Regardless, any real solution must also address the larger affordable housing crisis.

STIGMA, VISIBILITY, AND A BROKEN SYSTEM

Rough estimates hold that about a third of the homeless population is living with significant mental health conditions.[78] The popular stereotype that all or most homeless people are mentally ill is simply not true. But people in mental distress who are living in public places—either all the time or just during the day, like Yvonne and Timothy—stand out and attract attention, contributing to public perceptions that drive the misleading narrative that equates homelessness with psychological disabilities.

Many Americans face mental health challenges—and other disabilities—without having to live in shelters or on the streets.[79] The inability to afford housing is the critical underlying factor that forces some into homelessness. The denial or outright removal of essential income support—like the disability benefits to which people are entitled by law—makes the gap in affordable housing that much more acute. Without a safe place to live, existing health problems, be they physical or mental, almost inevitably deteriorate. There is a shortage of mental health care in the United States, and for people living in poverty it's especially severe. In New York City, where a centerpiece of the mayor's proposal to address the crisis is to involuntarily commit homeless people with mental illness, only 2.3 percent of those voluntarily seeking help were able to receive it.[80] Even if treatment options are available, sustaining them without stable housing can be impossible.

That's one of several catch-22s at play. People with mental or physical health issues face multiple obstacles to critical support—including education, employment, and housing—that make them more likely to be poor.[81] They also face bureaucratic red tape to gain access to potential help such as disability benefits, and the very disabilities that make them eligible make it extremely difficult if not impossible to overcome those barriers. The inevitable result is that such individuals are far more vulnerable to homelessness. These are not personal failures—they are societal ones.

As the crisis of modern homelessness first exploded, an influential book claimed that advocates had misled the public into thinking that homeless people were just like anyone else. *A Nation in Denial: The Truth about Homelessness* argued that, in fact, "they" were not like "us," but rather people suffering from deep personal problems—and that's why they were homeless.[82] Something was wrong with *them*, and not with our social and economic structures.

This perception has persisted for decades, and it disconnects homelessness from the bigger picture of rising housing costs, falling wages, slashed social services, and pervasive discrimination. These are problems that also affect many people who are *not* homeless, potentially creating a bridge for that larger, more secure group to care about those who fall into homelessness. Misdirecting public attention to problems defined as personal—whether mental illness, drug addiction, or even family conflict—allows for the distance to view people experiencing homelessness as different, "other."

Reminiscent of the Reagan administration's "blame the victim" philosophy, such thinking is still very present and, increasingly, independent of political party. It featured prominently in Bill Clinton's campaign to "end welfare as we know it and break the cycle of welfare dependency," reinforcing the view promoted by Reagan that people would rather "depend" on welfare than work.[83] In the 1990s, the same mischaracterization was a theme of then–New York City mayor Giuliani's campaign to "crack down" on unhoused residents, which helped launch decades of laws and policies that criminalize homelessness.[84] President Trump was even more explicit, referring to homelessness as "filth" that needed to be "cleaned up"—he proposed forcing unhoused people into tents and banishing them to the "outer reaches" of cities.[85] The demonization of unhoused people continues to this day, with New York City mayor Eric Adams stepping up police sweeps of homeless encampments even as already miniscule affordable housing options shrink and shelters overflow.[86]

A MORE NUANCED PICTURE

The reality is that homelessness is part of a much larger continuum.[87] It's both the last stop on a long downward spiral and an early sign that something is going very wrong in our society. Forty years ago, when private development converted inexpensive SRO housing to luxury units, the former residents of state mental institutions—the most fragile, at-risk tenants of that housing—started appearing on streets and in shelters. A few years later, a president heralding a new "Morning in America" decimated federal low-income housing programs, thrusting a far larger and more diverse group of Americans into homelessness. Some of those who were most directly affected entered the public eye, living in streets and shelters, but many more remained hidden, doubled and tripled up, moving from place to place with no home of their own.

Over the ensuing decades, such bursts of visible, extreme poverty have served as largely ignored canaries in a deepening coal mine. The foreclosure crisis starting in 2007 forced many formerly middle-class Americans from their homes and into homelessness, a dramatic spike almost rivaling that of the early to mid-1980s. In the late 2010s to the early 2020s, as the cost of housing steadily skyrocketed, more and more middle-class people are feeling the pinch. In March 2021, only a year into the pandemic, Gallup reported that hunger and homelessness topped the list of national issues Americans worried about—the first time in twenty years of measurement.[88]

The promise of help to those who are unable to support themselves through no fault of their own is fundamental to any civilized society. Our country has a responsibility to fulfill this promise to Yvonne, Timothy, Frank, Ramon Willis, Mary Rose Gerdes, and the untold numbers of other people in similar situations. It's a promise not only to those who now happen to be labeled "other," but to all of us—and on which we should all be able to depend in times of need.

In the early 1980s, this promise was broken—not by accident, not even through simple negligence, but deliberately. And the false narrative that those most hurt were somehow to blame helped obscure that breach.

It has yet to be repaired.

PART II
A PERMANENT EMERGENCY

CHAPTER FOUR

"Move Along to Where?"

Mid-pandemic, Miranda fell behind on rent in Monterey, a small town east of Nashville, Tennessee. Her boyfriend had moved out, and she couldn't swing the payments on her own.

Sending her children to live with her parents, Miranda applied for government aid. Unlike many, she received it—but it still wasn't enough to get her back into stable housing. Receiving a housing voucher felt like winning the lottery, but she couldn't find a landlord willing to accept it. Miranda got married in the midst of her struggles, and together she and her new husband had been able to finance a car. They used it to work as delivery drivers, saving money for an apartment where her children could move back in with them. In the meantime, Miranda and her husband lived in the car, parking it overnight in the nearby town of Cookeville.

Then the car broke down. Miranda was terrified they'd lose that, too. Shelter options in Cookeville were very limited, as they were statewide: Tennessee had one of the highest numbers of unsheltered homeless people in the country.[1] Miranda feared they'd have to pitch a tent in a state that had just made it a felony to do that.

Tennessee made shameful history in May 2022, becoming the first state to make camping on public property not only illegal, but a *felony*.[2] Miranda and other unhoused people could face up to six years in prison if they were caught in a tent on a sidewalk or in a public park. Conviction would mean the loss of voting rights, and a criminal record that would make finding housing even harder. The state was already 128,000 units short of the amount of affordable housing that Miranda and other extremely low-income people needed.[3]

As the Tennessee State Senate voted on the new law, one vocal proponent of the anti-camping bill made international headlines by pointing to Adolf Hitler as a role model. State Senator Frank Niceley noted the fascist dictator had once been homeless, "and then went on to live a life that got him in the history books."[4] Less shocking but even more telling was the comment from the bill's sponsor, State Senator Paul Bailey: "I don't have the answer for homelessness."[5]

Apparently, Tennessee's main goal was not to solve homelessness. The State Senate just wanted to remove people experiencing it from sight.

MORE PEOPLE OUTSIDE, MORE LAWS CRIMINALIZING THEM

If you live in America, you've seen people living outside in tents, makeshift shacks, cardboard boxes, or other temporary structures. Much of the increase in homelessness is reflected in the growth of these encampments, sometimes called tent cities. Since at least 2007, their numbers have grown exponentially across the country. A 2017 survey by the National Homelessness Law Center found an increase in documented encampments of *1,342 percent* over the previous ten years; they're in every state, as well as the District of Columbia.

The number of unsheltered people is still rising. In 2023, the US Department of Housing and Urban Development (HUD) estimated homelessness was up a record 12 percent. Shelter beds were also up, but only 7 percent, the increase far outstripped by the numbers of individuals needing them. This national shortfall of over 200,000 beds[6] meant that at any given point in 2023, nearly 250,000 people had nowhere to sleep—or sit, or lie down, or use the bathroom—except in public. And that's based on the federal government's very conservative estimate. The real numbers were certainly much larger.

The flaws in HUD's methodology for accurately counting people experiencing homelessness are only part of the problem. Regardless of how many people are unhoused, emergency shelter is just not a long-term solution. Most shelters have barriers that prevent them from even effectively serving as stopgap measures, including curfews, religious requirements, restrictions on personal property, and forced separation of families and pets.

Between the massive, indisputable shortfall in emergency shelter options and the myriad issues with those that are available, people end up scrambling to survive as best they can. Those who have cars—like Miranda—move into them. Others seek refuge in abandoned buildings, like John-Ed Croft, who squatted in New York City.[7] Desperate people take shelter in bus terminals, subway stations, and tunnels. They set up camp along river embankments, dig caves, pitch tents in woods, parks, under bridges, on sidewalks. This is how encampments of all sizes form—unhoused people coming together for safety, community, resource-sharing, or other forms of support.[8]

As encampments have become more common, so too have laws like Tennessee's that criminalize "camping" in public. This is typically defined as sleeping with a blanket or tent, sometimes just sleeping, period. Cities have used these laws to conduct "sweeps" of encampments, targeted enforcement to force people to leave, often with little or no notice. In addition to having to find another place to live, residents may lose whatever belongings they have—including medications, IDs and other critical documents, and essential protection from the elements such as extra clothing, bedding, sleeping bags, and tents.[9]

Often citing a need to "clean up" the area, the police carrying out these sweeps may simply scoop up such items and toss them in the trash. These aren't just unattended personal effects that could easily be mistaken for abandoned, either. In a sweep that was later challenged in court by homeless people and their advocates, a disabled veteran watched police trash his wheelchair, military records, identification, and photographs of his family. Unable to stop the destruction, he was "forced to stand and watch as his and others' belongings were thrown away like garbage into city trucks."[10]

For people living outside, the loss of survival gear can also be deadly: In 2023, between 15,000 and 40,000 unhoused people died preventable deaths.[11]

A BAN ON "URBAN CAMPING"

The video is grainy, shaky, hard to follow. But it clearly shows a small group of homeless people sleeping outside on a frigid November night.[12] Snow is on the ground. Several police cars are already there, and more arrive during the less-than-nine-minute clip. Armed police officers approach the homeless people and literally snatch the blankets they are using to protect themselves from the cold. After carefully shaking out, folding, and stacking the blankets, the officers place them in their patrol cars. They explain that the blankets are "evidence" that they must confiscate to prove that the group is in violation of the city's "Urban Camping Ban."[13]

The Urban Camping Ban is the law the Denver Police Department (DPD) uses to justify their sweeps. This particular law defines "camping" to include using a blanket, sleeping bag, or "any form of cover or protection from the elements other than clothing." Sleeping uncovered is legal in the Mile High City, sleeping with a blanket is not.[14]

Jerry Burton, a Marine Corps veteran, lost his home after he became disabled and could no longer work. He appears on the now-infamous video, the police taking his blanket during the sweep and ordering him to move under threat of arrest for violating the camping ban.[15] Rousing himself, Burton observed, "This isn't camping. Camping you do for fun—this you do to survive to the next day."[16]

The video had been recorded by a local business owner, horrified by what he was seeing. The images of police snatching blankets off people sleeping outside with snow on the ground were shocking, and the video went viral. It even made the front page of the *New York Times*.[17] Denver activists and allies organized a public forum that drew hundreds of in-person participants and thousands of virtual attendees on its live Facebook feed. A big coalition of faith leaders, activists (many unhoused themselves), and a few sympathetic business owners came together to denounce the sweeps and call for housing instead.[18] I flew in from Washington, D.C., to offer a national perspective.

By the time I landed in Denver it was too late to even think about looking for a hotel shuttle. I jumped in one of the cabs waiting at the airport stand. After winding through dark abandoned streets, we eventually pulled up to what looked like an old warehouse. The driver was skeptical that this could be my destination, but I recognized a few of the people milling around outside and waved him off. For advocates fighting homelessness, money for events is often tight.

Inside, the cavernous space was dark and crowded, anticipation in the air as the final touches were put on the makeshift stage. Boxes of pizza were brought in and set at randomly arranged tables. They'd been donated by the owner of a popular pizza joint—the same man who had shot the viral video of police snatching blankets.[19] Without it, it's unlikely the police's actions—which were hardly unusual—would have received the attention that they did.

The forum was aptly named "Move Along to Where?" For years, the DPD had relied on the Urban Camping Ban to force people living outside to "move along," usually trashing their belongings in the process. But where were those affected supposed to go?[20] At the time of the November 2016 sweep, the city estimated there were 3,456 people experiencing homelessness in Denver on a single night and, at most, 1,500 emergency shelter beds. As with the federal government's annual counts, Denver's official numbers were widely considered to be a gross underestimation. Even setting aside all the reasons that shelter is not a real solution or even available for many people, the arithmetic simply didn't add up.

Denver had passed the Urban Camping Ban in 2012, as an increase in local encampments (following the national trend) led to business leaders putting pressure on city hall. Promoted by newly elected city councilman Albous Brooks, a Democrat whose district included downtown, it was signed into law by Mayor Michael Hancock, also recently elected and also a Democrat. In the first year of the ban, some 83 percent of homeless residents reported being required to move by police sweeps enforcing the new law.

The mayor and the city council president were major proponents of the Urban Camping Ban. Insisting that shelter was plentiful and available to all who needed it, they claimed that those sleeping outside simply chose to do so. Speaking at the 2016 forum, Albus claimed that repealing the camping ban—one of the event's two prime goals—would not help put homeless people in a better position. He simply ignored the event's other central demand: alternative housing solutions.[21] Over thirty years later, both Albus and Hancock were channeling Ronald Reagan and his claim that homelessness represents a "lifestyle" choice.

In 2022, local advocates named the ten years of the ban's enforcement the "decade of doom." That grim assessment remains relevant in 2024, a new mayor, Mike Johnston—also a Democrat—vetoed a law passed by the city council that would have prevented sweeps in freezing temperatures.[22]

A NEW TWIST ON A LONG HISTORY

They've taken new forms, but these kinds of laws have a long, ignoble history, tracing back centuries. As feudalism was breaking down in England, early precursors to vagrancy laws sought to control the movements of laborers and force them to work at specified wages. Later, with the advent of Elizabethan poor laws, local authorities relied on vagrancy statutes to discourage entry or expel poor people who might seek their support. Imported into colonial America, these laws also kept out unemployed laborers who might compete for jobs with local residents. Following the Civil War, "Jim Crow" laws specifically targeted newly freed slaves, imposing a regime of racial segregation as well as exclusion.[23]

By 1949, every state had anti-vagrancy laws.[24] Some of their broadest, most egregious formulations were limited by the US Supreme Court in 1972, in a decision striking down an ordinance that criminally punished "vagabonds," "habitual loafers," those "wandering . . . without any lawful purpose," persons "neglecting all lawful business," and people who were deemed guilty of similar offenses. The decision did not, however, invalidate vagrancy and loitering laws in general.[25] Many cities simply amended their ordinances to make them more specific.[26]

Over time, laws regulating the use of public space evolved to target homeless people specifically. By the early 1990s, laws criminalizing the public presence of people without housing became a major form of local government response to homelessness. Cities across the country enacted bans on camping, sleeping, vehicle habitation, panhandling (aggressive or otherwise), public urination and defecation, and property storage—as well as "sit-lie" bans, and many more. Municipal governments also began regulating would-be helpers, restricting their ability to offer food to needy people in public places, among other restrictions.[27]

Go Directly to Jail

Laws criminalizing homelessness were increasing with alarming speed, and at the National Homelessness Law Center we pondered how to respond. No national reports had yet documented the trend, and we initially hesitated to do so, fearing that drawing public attention to the laws might encourage their growth. But it soon became clear that we had to act. For one thing, local media reports on the new laws were repeating the Reagan-era narrative that help was available but that people chose not to use it. We had to refute this false picture that hundreds of thousands of Americans were voluntarily losing everything and rejecting all aid.

In December 1991, the Law Center published "Go Directly to Jail," our national report on the trend. Looking at nine cities around the country, we examined the new laws, as well as the lack of resources for unhoused people in each city. Focusing on shelter, housing, wages, and disability benefits, we found they were all grossly inadequate.[28] Help was *not* available, and people were not living outside by choice. They were living outside because they had no other options.

We released the report on a cold December day, at an outdoor press conference in Lafayette Park—outside the White House. The *Washington Post* featured our report, and the publicity helped to mobilize some allies.[29] A year later, the national association of big-city mayors officially condemned the criminalization of homelessness. A major law enforcement group called for police to better coordinate with social service agencies. But as the affordable housing crisis deepened, wages stagnated, and the safety net frayed, people remained on the streets—and criminalization continued to spread across the country.[30]

In 2019, the Law Center published our thirteenth report on the topic. We'd surveyed 187 cities across the country, large and small, urban and rural. In the twenty-eight years since our initial report had first warned against the push to criminalize homelessness, the trend had only increased. Over 70 percent of the cities had made it a crime to "camp" in public, often defined as sleeping with "camping paraphernalia" such as a blanket, or even just sleeping outside. Of those, over half prohibited camping *anywhere* in the jurisdiction. Over half of all the cities we looked at prohibited simply sleeping in public—and over 20 percent of all cities prohibited sleeping *anywhere* in the city.

We'd begun surveying these same 187 cities in 2006, to better analyze and respond to trends. Some of the increases between 2006 and 2019 were especially striking. The biggest was a 213 percent spike in laws banning sleeping in vehicles. Citywide bans on loitering, "loafing," and vagrancy shot up 103 percent, while citywide bans on "camping" increased by 92 percent.[31]

None of the laws explicitly state that it's illegal to be homeless. On the contrary, cities defend the bans by saying they apply equally to everyone—no one is allowed to sleep in public places. This is debatable. A middle-class White person napping on a picnic blanket in a park is highly unlikely to be disturbed by the police, much less cited, fined, or arrested. Nor are laws against "loafing" in public places typically enforced against anyone who isn't poor, homeless, Black, or Brown.

Selective enforcement aside, more to the point is the reality that only those without reasonable indoor alternatives regularly seek refuge in public places.

The trajectory of these laws mirrored that of homelessness itself: Over this same period, tent cities had snowballed across the country. And while there isn't yet reliable national data, recent local studies show that the numbers of people living in their cars or other vehicles has also risen dramatically.[32] Instead of offering solutions like housing and social services, many local governments simply tried to outlaw homelessness in all its forms, old and new.

While punitive laws grew exponentially, resources to prevent people from having to live outside shrank. Nationally, in 2024 there was a shortage of over seven million units of housing affordable to extremely poor people.[33] In only 7 percent of the nation's counties can a full-time minimum wage worker afford a one-bedroom apartment; in no state, city, or county can they afford a modest two-bedroom rental.[34] These statistics are based on the federal government's own affordability guidelines, which stipulate that rent should be no more than 30 percent of income, so that there is enough to meet other basic needs. And as previously mentioned, our country is hundreds of thousands of shelter beds short of the number of people who are already outside and need a safe place to sleep for even a night.

When we published our first report in 1991, we included the experience of Arnold, a homeless man in Washington, D.C.: "One night when the shelters were full, and I couldn't find a place to sleep, I went to Lafayette Park across from the White House. But an officer woke me up and said, 'Not in my park . . . get up and move on.' I had to walk around the rest of the night."

Dennis, also in D.C., told us: "The police tell people they will spend the night in jail if they don't stop begging. . . . Since I'm trying to get a job, I can't risk getting an arrest record. So I have to beg where the police don't patrol as often and watch for their cars."

Their stories and words still reverberate today.

"Continually Removing Them"

Early on in this trend, some local officials explicitly stated their intent in enacting the laws: They wanted to drive homeless residents out of the city.

Santa Ana, in California's Orange County, provides a brutal early example. In August 1990, the city essentially carried out a sting operation on its homeless residents. As described by the police, five "two-man arrest teams" descended on the civic center plaza and arrested dozens of homeless persons who'd been living there. They were taken to an athletic field for booking, chained to a fence, marked with numbers, and held for as long as six hours.

The criminal charges included dropping a match, a leaf, or a piece of paper, and jaywalking. The city was carrying out a policy aimed at "cleaning up its neighborhoods and forcing out the vagrant population" by following a policy of "continually removing them from the areas they are frequenting."[35] Two years later, Santa Ana formalized this policy by enacting a law banning "camping" in public.

The ban was challenged in court by legal aid lawyers representing a group of homeless people. Among them was Mildred, a thirty-five-year-old woman with schizophrenia who lived in the civic center plaza because the police were always nearby—they made her feel safe. Sheltering in a tunnel one rainy night, she was approached by ten police officers and two men in civilian clothes. They cited her for violating the camping ordinance. After they left, she said, she decided to stay there. "It was pourin' down rain. I didn't have anywhere to go."[36]

At the time Mildred and others were being cited, Santa Ana had only 332 shelter beds for its 3,000 homeless residents—this according to the city's own, inevitably low estimates. The city's ban was eventually struck down in 1994 by a panel of state court judges who labeled it "constitutionally repugnant." But the following year, the California Supreme Court reversed that ruling. The law had only been challenged based on its language—and by its terms, it was neutral. The city's clear intent to drive its homeless residents out didn't matter, the court said. The ban applied equally to everyone.[37]

Years before the court ultimately upheld the law, the city's police chief had clearly conveyed his goal to remove homeless people from downtown, using very carefully crafted language that didn't quite say the quiet part out loud. This was a campaign to establish "order" and to prevent crime. It was based, he said, on the "visceral intuition" that "when we allow unruly conduct to flourish severe crime problems quickly ensue."[38] In his telling, people trying to survive outside in the absence of other options were being "unruly." Restoring "order"—and preventing "serious crime"—meant driving them out.

To bolster his argument, the police chief cited a theory developed in the early 1980s by two conservative social scientists. First articulated in a 1982 article in the *Atlantic*, the "broken windows" theory of policing held that allowing minor crimes to go unchecked created a climate of "disorder" that then invited more serious crimes. The analogy is that a broken window in a house, if left unrepaired, supposedly signals that no one cares, which leads to more broken windows not just in the house but in the broader community.[39] The theory was gaining popularity in Santa Ana and other places seeking to push homeless people out of their downtowns, if not their city limits altogether. Homeless people were like broken windows, the argument went, and first criminalizing and then removing them was necessary to their cities' crime prevention efforts.[40] The article's authors had said it directly: "The unchecked panhandler is, in effect, the first broken window."

This argument got a big boost in public attention in the 1990s from the then-mayor of New York City.

BROKEN WINDOWS: MAYOR GIULIANI LEADS THE CHARGE

Long before he disgraced himself as Trump's lawyer, and before he was lauded for his response to the September 11th attacks, Rudy Giuliani was making a national name for himself in a fight against poor and homeless people in New York City, where he was mayor from 1994 to 2001. Giuliani's very public campaign sought to crack down on minor, "quality-of-life" offenses, such as sleeping, begging, and urinating in public. Seizing on the "broken windows" theory, Giuliani and his police commissioner, William Bratton, argued that this would deter more serious crimes.[41]

Promoting anti-homeless laws, Giuliani and Bratton tied the public presence of unhoused people to increased crime. When crime rates went down, they credited their harsh new policies. Over time, however, the theory has been criticized. Scholars have noted that crime rates declined nationally during this same period, not just in New York City, and for a variety of reasons, undermining Giuliani's claims.[42] The "broken windows" theory has also been called out for its inherent racism in promoting policies that target minoritized, poor, and homeless people.[43] Not surprisingly, further studies have undermined its claims that associate homelessness with serious crime.[44]

In fact, homeless people are more likely to be victims of crime than perpetrators. Violence against unhoused people—including murders—has been rising since 2010.[45] And at least some of this violence by private citizens correlates to the increasingly harsh government policies that criminalize homelessness and the demonizing rhetoric that often accompanies them.[46] The killing of Jordan Neely—an unhoused Black man suffering from mental disorders—on a New York City subway car came in the midst of the current mayor's campaign to conflate homelessness with criminality. Jordan, who was Black, had been asking his fellow passengers for food and water when he became upset, raising his voice—and that was enough for a twenty-four-year-old White man to tackle Jordan and strangle him to death. Witnesses agreed Jordan hadn't physically threatened anyone, but his killer claimed he was defending himself and other passengers before Jordan could attack them.[47]

Even some police departments and officers question the wisdom of deploying their resources to cite or arrest homeless people. John Tharp, an Ohio sheriff, argued in an op-ed that police responses to social problems like homelessness are expensive and ineffective. Also, he wrote, "It saps officers' morale to spend their time prosecuting the downtrodden rather than preventing real crime."[48]

While Giuliani's high-profile "crack-down" on his homeless constituents may have done little to actually curb crime, it undoubtably fueled the trend toward criminalizing the unhoused—not just in New York City, but across the nation.

HOMELESSNESS GROWS—AS DOES ITS CRIMINALIZATION

Housing costs climbed in the 1990s. Predictably, so did the number of extremely poor people who couldn't afford housing. By 1999, HUD reported that there were only forty-two affordable units for every one hundred extremely low-income households.[49] Even emergency options were in short supply, with shelters across the country turning away rising numbers of people seeking help for lack of space. As homelessness grew, more and more people had no other option but to live on the streets and other public places, and laws criminalizing their presence proliferated.[50]

By 2001, laws criminalizing homelessness were ubiquitous. As previously discussed, the George W. Bush administration put enhanced security measures into place after 9/11 that further marginalized people without homes, who often also lacked IDs. IDs were sometimes lost during evictions or while people were living in shelters or on the streets, and they were sometimes confiscated during sweeps. Lack of ID could mean that eligible applicants couldn't even enter government buildings to apply for benefits to which they were entitled. In a vicious cycle, lack of ID also could become further grounds for harassment from police demanding identification.[51]

Even emergency shelter resources failed to keep up with demand as homelessness increased, sending more people to the streets. As housing costs skyrocketed, the George W. Bush administration championed cuts to funding for low-income housing and other social welfare programs. From 2004 to 2008, low-income housing programs lost almost $2 billion in funding.[52] Meanwhile, the administration loosened regulation of the housing finance industry, laying the groundwork for the foreclosure crisis that would soon follow.[53]

Needless to say, homelessness and tent cities increased sharply after the foreclosure crisis and Great Recession. In response, cities accelerated their enactment of laws restricting homeless people's public presence.[54]

"COMPASSION FATIGUE"?

Crime prevention was a big part of the rationale cities used to justify their draconian laws. But an additional justification they gave—and still give—for criminalizing homelessness was public demand. This justification is often highlighted in news stories, as if it's a given, further amplifying it.

Media reports of "compassion fatigue" were already prevalent in the early 1990s. When visible, large-scale homelessness first began appearing across the country in the 1980s, it had spurred much public concern, and largely sympathetic media coverage. But as the issue persisted unabated—even in the face of what seemed to be ameliorative efforts like emergency shelter—it was increasingly described in the press as part of a landscape to which the public had become accustomed and with which it had lost patience.[55] Having tried to help and failed, the idea seemed to be, an otherwise compassionate public had grown exhausted and was clamoring for sterner measures.

This may not have originated in media descriptions—it's certainly a rationale promoted by cities themselves to defend laws criminalizing homelessness. But regardless of how it started, waning public sympathy quickly became a common explanation for the trend. And while compassion fatigue became a popular catchphrase, public opinion polls paint a more nuanced picture. From the 1990s to 2016, public opinion surveys consistently showed public compassion and support for more government funding for the unhoused—and structural solutions such as more affordable housing and a higher minimum wage.

During the pandemic, with sharpened public attention on the plight of people with no home in which to isolate or even wash their hands, polls showed even more support. Of those surveyed, 93 percent favored emergency rental assistance for people struggling to afford rent or at serious risk of eviction, and 90 percent favored expanding funding for homeless assistance.[56] In a 2021 Gallup poll, hunger and homelessness topped the list of issues Americans were concerned about, a first in twenty years of measurement.[57] Tellingly, a 2021 CBS News poll found that 28 percent of Americans feared not having a place to live, and 41 percent reported knowing someone being evicted or losing their home—if not experiencing it themselves.[58] This kind of personal experience—"proximity"—increased compassion and support for government response.[59]

Studies also show diminishing public support for laws criminalizing homelessness.[60] In the early 1990s, the public already ranked homelessness as a very important problem and supported increased federal spending for low-income housing, as well as increased taxes to pay for it and other social supports—but a majority of the public also supported restrictions on panhandling and sleeping overnight in public places. A significant minority also viewed homeless people as lazy and irresponsible.[61] By 2016, these attitudes had shifted, with the majority opposing restricting the rights of homeless people. A 2020 California poll found that only 28 percent supported banning encampments without first establishing housing.[62] By 2022, a full 65 percent of Americans said they opposed arresting homeless people as a response to the problem of homelessness.[63]

This doesn't mean that most Americans support just leaving people with no options but to live in public places—the public wants government to do *something*. Polls show that over 60 percent of Americans think that government can do a lot to address homelessness. And what they want government to do is to address the structural *causes* of homelessness, like high housing costs, low incomes, and lack of social services.[64] Instead, many local and (increasingly) state governments, led by Democrats and Republicans alike, are promoting further measures to criminalize people for their homelessness.[65]

The claim of compassion fatigue may be a case of a vocal minority getting outsized attention. Even more insidious—and dangerous—is the role of money in magnifying its voice. Consider the misleadingly named Cicero Institute, a well-funded right-wing organization founded by venture capitalist Joe Lonsdale that promotes itself as a "nonpartisan public policy organization" developing "innovative" policies.[66] These include model state laws that criminalize survival activities that homeless people must perform in public in the absence of other alternatives.[67] This is the group behind the law that made camping a felony offense in the state of Tennessee, which terrorized Miranda when her car broke down and she feared she and her husband would have to move into a tent.[68]

Cicero promotes these harmful laws while also claiming that widely accepted, evidence-based approaches have failed to solve homelessness. Among its chief targets is the Housing First approach, which makes providing housing the top priority and *then* offering other needed services, like mental health care. The theory is that without a stable place to live, other services have a poor chance of working. The effectiveness of the approach is backed by mountains of evidence, and most Americans support it. But while countries such as Finland have already implemented Housing First with remarkable success, the critics are right that it hasn't made much of an impact on homelessness in America.

That's because it's never been funded at anything close to scale.

In 2022, nearly three in four Americans said they viewed housing as a basic human right.[69] Yet housing hasn't been enshrined in our constitution or our laws, and it's certainly not funded at levels that come anywhere close to meeting the need. Despite some important progress during the Biden administration, basic economic and social rights—like housing—remain largely absent from our laws or policies.

Sadder still and despite the polls, such basic rights aren't even clearly articulated or fully embraced as commonly accepted and understood national values.

A Short-Lived Pandemic Reprieve

As the pandemic spread across the country in early 2020, and in a victory for advocates and the unhoused, the Centers for Disease Control and Prevention (CDC) issued guidance urging cities to protect homeless people and prevent community spread of the virus. These were the governmental recommendations that led to vacant hotel rooms being made available to homeless families, such as the Kupers.

If such individual housing options weren't feasible, the CDC guidance encouraged cities to provide encampments with port-a-potties and handwashing stations, and to refrain from carrying out sweeps. These would only force their residents to move elsewhere, increasing the likelihood of community spread. While cities carrying out sweeps often cite concerns about public health, the CDC guidelines expressly stated that public health concerns militate *against* sweeps.

These new recommendations made a difference in many important cases. In New Orleans, local advocates like Martha Kegel used the CDC guidelines to convince the city to offer hotel rooms to unhoused people. Some two hundred individuals and families living in an encampment moved into a hotel that was largely vacant due to the pandemic.[70]

Other cities, like Denver, rejected the CDC guidance, continuing their sweeps during the pandemic. In October 2020, local advocates filed a federal court case to stop them. Three months later, on January 25, 2021, the judge ordered the city to give seven days' notice before a sweep. He allowed a limited exception in the event of a public health or safety emergency, but even in that case he required at least forty-eight hours' notice. The city appealed, and the order was overturned.[71]

That November, the city council approved a new "safe camping" site for the city's homeless residents. Such sites—also called "sanctioned" encampments—are growing in urban areas around the country. Local governments "allowing" people to keep living outside so long as they do so in designated zones may seem preferrable to citywide bans—and sometimes it may be. But sanctioned encampments also further entrench laws criminalizing the unhoused from staying elsewhere and may divert energy and resources from permanent housing.

Frankie was living in one in Missoula, Montana, on a snowy January day in 2022. Called "Temporary Safe Outdoor Space," nonprofits had created it with help from local government. The temperature was ten degrees, but the twenty tents in the encampment were equipped with propane heaters. Frankie had spent most of her previous two years living in cars, unable to afford housing in Missoula's tight market, where the vacancy rate for rentals was below 1 percent and the median home price had topped half-a-million dollars. Her tent in the city-sanctioned space offered security, a makeshift shared kitchen and bathrooms, proximity to public transportation, and regular visits by city case managers. For Frankie, the tent gave her enough stability to hold down a steady job. Eventually, with the help of a case manager, she was able to secure a small apartment.[72]

Frankie's tent in the sanctioned encampment had been a lifeline. But twenty tents couldn't stem the homelessness crisis engulfing Missoula or even begin to address its acute housing shortage. Like Denver and a growing number of other cities, Missoula was bowing to the reality that people had to be *somewhere*—and unless the city provided housing, then that somewhere would be outside. While not meeting the deeper housing need, the safe, heated tents undeniably helped those who were lucky enough to get one. But without a commitment to create permanent affordable housing, they were also another stop in a race to the bottom. Some have compared them to concentration camps.[73]

The High Cost of Punishing Poverty

With the pandemic over (at least on paper), the CDC guidance expired. Federal funds for hotel rooms were spent and the tourism business roared back to fill them. Cities that had temporarily let up on criminalizing their homeless residents resumed their prior practices. But forcing people to move from place to place when they have no permanent place to be does irreparable harm. Difficult lives are made more miserable, with innocent people given a criminal record that makes finding housing and employment that much harder. Cruelest of all, it just doesn't work. People need to be somewhere, and if they are pushed out of one location, they will move to another. And the cost is high—not just to the people, but to the city.

It turns out criminalizing unhoused people isn't cheap.

Denver police spent over 6,000 hours in 2018 arresting and issuing warrants to homeless people for offenses related to their lack of housing.[74] But when the city instead provided permanent housing with supportive services like health care, it *saved* $6,900 per person. This approach also solved homelessness for most of the people it served—over three-quarters were still stably housed three years later.[75] Providing housing and any needed services is often demonstrably *less* expensive than trying to sweep people away.

Take Los Angeles. In 2022, the city spent an estimated $70 million to criminalize and exile homeless people from its public places. One sweep, which targeted people living in vehicles parked on a public street, was documented on video. The operation mobilized fourteen sanitation workers (not including the drivers of the garbage trucks), three police officers, parking enforcement officials, and a few city social services employees to monitor everything.[76] After it was over, the people targeted just moved to another street—now missing many of their belongings. All the time and money that went into the sweep had done nothing to solve the problem. It merely made life worse for vulnerable people who were further traumatized and robbed of their few possessions.

Cities often try to have it both ways: offering housing and services—though not on a sufficient scale to meet the need—while *also* criminalizing anyone still forced to live in public places. Houston, despite some success in housing former residents of the encampments it closed, still has its camping ban—now augmented by a statewide ban that cities are required to enforce. Houston spent more on encampment "cleanup" in 2019 than on permanent housing for those who had once lived there.[77]

In 2023, the state of California allocated $750 million to cities to "clear" their encampments and move the residents either into housing or temporary shelter with "a clear pathway" to permanent housing. But over a year after the first grants went out and the cities had commenced their "clearing" operations, only a small fraction of impacted homeless people had found permanent housing—even as new residents moved into the encampments. Given the extreme shortage of affordable housing, it was completely predictable.[78]

As the trend of criminalization developed and spread, homeless people and their advocates mounted legal challenges. By 2021, the National Homelessness Law Center reported wins in a significant majority of challenges to such laws.[79] One of the most important early cases was launched in 1988.

"[They] Literally Have Nowhere to Go": Court Wins and Their Limits

Peter Carter and Michael Pottinger often slept in downtown Miami's Bicentennial Park, choosing the location for its restroom and running water. Part of a group of fifteen to thirty people who came together for community and greater safety, they were asleep one night in 1988 when police officers arrived around midnight with patrol cars and a paddy wagon. Peter and Michael were among the fifteen or so people arrested, taken to the station, then put in jail while the police checked for outstanding warrants.[80]

The group wasn't released until around 4 a.m. They were returned to the park, but all their belongings were gone. Peter spent about three weeks reassembling all his personal documentation. Without identification in the interim, he was unable to get a job. He did eventually land one, as well as a place to live, but the arrest had prolonged his homelessness.[81]

Peter and Michael became plaintiffs in a class-action lawsuit filed in federal court by a volunteer lawyer for the local ACLU. The 1988 case, *Pottinger v. Miami*, challenged the city for criminally punishing homeless people for "innocent, life sustaining" conduct such as sleeping in public, despite the lack of indoor alternatives for thousands of homeless people. Some six thousand men, women, and children were unhoused in Miami, yet there was little affordable housing and fewer than seven hundred emergency shelter beds.

"The majority of homeless individuals literally have nowhere to go," the judge concluded.[82]

Ruling in favor of the homeless plaintiffs, the judge agreed that the city's arrests and repeated "move on" orders violated their rights under the US Constitution.[83] A key issue was whether the city was punishing status or conduct. The city argued that it was merely punishing the plaintiffs for their conduct—sleeping—and that no one was allowed to carry out said conduct in public. With complete seriousness, they were repeating the observation made ironically in 1894 by French writer Anatole France: "In its majesty equality, the law forbids rich and poor alike to sleep under bridges, beg in the streets and steal loaves of bread."[84]

Fortunately, the judge didn't buy this. Because human beings cannot survive without sleeping, and because they had nowhere to sleep but in public, Peter, Michael, and the thousands of others living on the streets were essentially being punished for their status—simply for existing as homeless people. The judge applied earlier US Supreme Court precedent to conclude that this violated the prohibition on cruel and unusual punishment under the Eighth Amendment to the Constitution.[85]

Around the same time *Pottinger v. Miami* was being litigated, another federal court case, *Joyce v. San Francisco*, yielded a different result. Again there were more homeless people than shelter beds, and again the city punished sleeping in public.[86] San Francisco's ominously named "Matrix" program, designed to remove homeless people from downtown, had led to over three thousand issued citations in the first three months alone.[87] Despite the city's aggressive actions, the court ruled against the unhoused plaintiffs, arguing that homelessness is not an immutable characteristic, like race, and therefore not a legitimate status. Homeless people didn't have to be homeless, so punishing them for sleeping in public—even though they had no other choice—was simply punishing conduct, not status. This was the law in its "majestic equality."

Even the favorable *Pottinger* decision brought problems. What was the remedy? The ideal solution, according to the judge, would be to provide housing and services to the homeless city residents. But, he said, this was up to other branches of government, not the courts. The plaintiffs had simply asked the court to order Miami to stop arresting and harassing homeless people, but the judge apparently wanted to somehow balance the interests of each side. He ordered the city to work with the plaintiffs' lawyers to create two "safe zones," public spaces that would be arrest-free. Until the city did that, it was not to harass or arrest homeless people for carrying out necessary, innocent life-sustaining activities in public.

The decision in *Pottinger* and several similar cases was based on the complete lack of options available to homeless people. Miami had banned sleeping anywhere in the city—and so had Dallas, Huntsville, Alabama, and other cities where challenges to sleeping bans had found success. The unconstitutionality of the laws hinged on the argument that making it a crime to sleep in public anywhere, anytime, amounts to criminalizing simply existing.[88] As a result, many cities simply narrowed their laws. Instead of banning sleeping citywide, at all hours, they banned sleeping downtown, or sleeping between the hours of 7 a.m. and 9 p.m., for example. Sleeping was still theoretically possible—and successful challenges would be harder.

Some cities tried a similar approach with laws banning begging. Because the First Amendment strictly limits bans on speech, and several court cases had applied this protection to begging—speech requesting help—cities began trying different strategies to reach the same end. Bans on "aggressive panhandling" were one such tactic. This included measures such as banning requests for "immediate" donations within five hundred feet of an ATM, laws they would argue banned dangerous conduct, not speech.

Seattle was among the first to try this narrowing strategy, with a law banning sitting and lying prone downtown during certain times, as well as aggressive begging. Enacted in 1993, just a year after the court first ruled in *Pottinger*, the law was challenged by a group of local homeless people and advocates. The court upheld the law, basing its decision on its relative narrowness.[89] Seattle's city attorney, Mark Sidran, became a well-known proponent of so-called "civility" laws. The Alliance for Rights and Responsibilities, a nonprofit organization formed in 1989, helped cities draft laws that could withstand court challenge—just as the more aggressive Cicero Institute would do decades later.

Another method certain cities employed was to create special "pods" or "pavilions" in remote sections of parks where homeless people could sleep without being subject to arrest—forcing them to remain there. By providing such "safe zones," a city could then freely arrest people sleeping outside of them while dodging legal challenges that used arguments similar to those in *Pottinger*.[90] Of course, narrowing the language of anti-homeless laws didn't slow the rise of homelessness, nor was it designed to. The only goal was to make anti-homeless laws harder to challenge.

With different courts adopting different approaches, cities didn't limit their efforts to trying to evade lawsuits by narrowing their laws. Municipal efforts to criminalize unhoused people—including broad bans on sleeping or "camping" anywhere in a city—increased dramatically, regardless of the availability of housing or shelter.[91] Unsheltered homelessness was expanding everywhere, and cities wouldn't be deterred from criminalization by the possibility of court challenges. Homeless people and their advocates continued to file litigation, with mixed results. It would be years before court decisions would begin trending in favor of upholding the challenges.[92]

CRUEL AND UNUSUAL

Lawrence Smith, a construction worker in Boise, Idaho, became homeless after his arthritis got so bad he couldn't work. No longer able to make rent and with no emergency shelter available, he had nowhere to live but in public places. He was arrested, first in April 2007 and again in May, for camping in public. During his one hundred days in jail, he lost his tent, his stove, and the fishing equipment he relied upon to live—leaving him with nothing upon his release.

A 2009 court case filed by Lawrence and five other homeless or formerly homeless people challenged Boise's laws and policies criminalizing the unhoused. *Martin v. Boise* was tied up in the courts for years. In the final decision, the federal appeals court noted that as of 2016, by the city's own count, there were 867 homeless people in the county on a single night—and that Boise's three homeless shelters only contained a total 354 beds and 92 overflow mats.[93] The court ruled the city's laws were unconstitutional and struck them down.

This proved an unusually strong decision. The city had argued that two of its shelters never reported being full and turning people away due to lack of space. But rather than accepting this claim at face value, the court probed further. The plaintiffs had shown that the two shelters, both rescue missions—one only for men, the other only for women and children—limited their stays. Women and children had a thirty-day maximum; men were only allowed seventeen days at a stretch. After reaching your time limit, you had to wait at least thirty days before coming back. The only way you could stay longer was by entering the "Discipleship program," described as "an intensive, Christ-based residential recovery program." This requirement conflicted with the First Amendment's guarantee of religious freedom.[94]

Considering all this, the court ruled that shelter was not practically available in Boise. The city's laws were unconstitutional, and the court struck them down. It was a major decision: The federal appeals court's ruling set precedent for all federal courts in the nine states in the ninth circuit.[95] The city tried to overturn the decision by the three-judge panel, seeking review by all the judges in the circuit. To bolster its case, the city mobilized cities and states to submit friend-of-the-court briefs supporting its position. When that failed, and the full court of appeals affirmed the panel's decision, Boise sought review by the US Supreme Court. Advocates around the country breathed a collective sigh of relief in December 2019 when the high court declined review. The decision would stand.

Our relief would be short-lived. Just over four years later, in January 2024, the US Supreme Court agreed to review a similar case from Grants Pass, Oregon.

There was a slight difference. In the new case, *Johnson v. Grants Pass*, the city had tried to get around the *Martin v. Boise* ruling by initially imposing a civil penalty for sleeping in public, as opposed to a criminal penalty. The city was trying another version of earlier efforts to circumvent court rulings by revising the form criminalization took. Even though the punishment was initially civil—a fine instead of jail time—by the law's terms it could turn criminal. Violate the public camping ban too many times—which you almost certainly would, since Grants Pass had zero shelter beds—and you would be subject to arrest and jailing. The appeals court didn't buy the city's efforts to sidestep established law and held that the *Martin* precedent applied.

The city had also tried arguing that this case was different because their law didn't prohibit simply sleeping—it prohibited sleeping with a blanket or other protection from the elements, such as a cardboard box. Sleeping uncovered was perfectly fine. Again, the appeals court saw through this: Sleep could well be impossible without basic protection from the elements.

The reasoning of the appeals court seemed logical and the result hardly expansive: It was still a very narrow decision. Both this and the earlier *Martin* ruling were based on US Supreme Court precedent from the 1960s. There was no fight among the federal appeals courts—no "split in the circuits," typically a reason for the high court to issue a rare decision to grant review. There was even a case from another circuit that agreed with the Ninth Circuit decisions.[96] Why was the Supreme Court taking *Grants Pass v. Johnson*?

A BIPARTISAN ATTACK

A seemingly unusual coalition had come together to file amicus—friend-of-the-court—briefs to support the city of Grants Pass in its quest to punish its unsheltered homeless residents.

Democratic California governor Gavin Newsom, the Democrat-led cities of San Francisco, Los Angeles, and Honolulu, and conservative Arizona lawmakers and right-wing organizations all joined in. Newsom argued that the court ruling in Grants Pass, like the earlier Ninth Circuit decision in *Martin v. Boise*, prevented cities from "clearing encampments" and addressing the "dangerous and unhealthy conditions" they fostered. Citing accumulating garbage and feces, Newsom and his allies blamed the court rulings for depriving them of "a vital tool for helping to move people off the streets, to connect them with resources, and to promote safety, health and usable public spaces."[97] Allowing states and cities to criminally punish unhoused, unsheltered people was apparently necessary to ensure standards of sanitation and public health.

It's an interesting argument, to say the least. Of course, public health and sanitation must be protected—for housed and unhoused city residents alike. And it's true that trash can accumulate around encampments and, even worse, so can human waste. But it's hardly surprising, in the absence of trash pickup and public toilets. The same would happen with any community of people, housed or unhoused, without these basic services.

Instead of providing trash cans and public bathrooms, or at least port-a-potties, cities leave people without homes no other option but to use public places to perform basic bodily functions. To then claim that the ability to punish people for living outside—in the absence of other alternatives—is a "tool" you need at your disposal is, at best, disingenuous and hypocritical. At worst, it's cruel and unusual. But then so is the lack of housing that forces people to live outside in the first place.

Theane Evangelis, a partner at big law firm Gibson Dunn and the lead lawyer for Grants Pass, made an even more cynical argument, claiming that "the tragedy" was that rulings were actually hurting unhoused people.[98] This was another spin on Newsom's claim that the threat of arrest and incarceration was necessary to "help people move off the streets." Left unexplained was *where* exactly they would move to, in a state with one of the biggest shortages of affordable housing in the country and a city where emergency shelter is far outstripped by need.

That didn't stop a six-justice majority of the Supreme Court from siding with Grants Pass. In a June 2024 opinion written by Justice Neil Gorsuch, the majority said that the city law was not punishing status, which would be unconstitutional under earlier precedent. Instead, the opinion said, the city law was targeting unhoused people's "actions": camping outside for "the purpose of maintaining a temporary place to live." And, it noted—without irony and certainly without reference to Anatole France—the city's prohibition applied equally to everyone, covering traveling backpackers and student protestors, as well as homeless people.[99]

Of course, "actions" like sleeping outside in the absence of a home are part of the *definition* of homelessness. Penalizing them punishes homelessness—the *status* of homelessness—itself.[100] Unlike backpackers and students, unhoused people have no out-of-town home or dorm room to go back to. But the high court dismissed the yawning gap in the city—and across the country—between the numbers of homeless people and the number of shelter beds, not to mention affordable housing units.[101]

In a powerful dissent, Justice Sonia Sotomayor put it simply: "Sleep is a biological necessity, not a crime." All human beings must sleep, and those without an indoor place have no choice but to do so outside—and face arrest. The ban on "camping" doesn't just punish their status, it makes it a crime for homeless people simply to *exist*.[102]

BEGGING FOR CHANGE

As if bans on sleeping or even sitting in public weren't dehumanizing enough, some laws also make it a crime to ask for help. Often laws that restrict requesting assistance—"begging" or "panhandling"—are used together with sleeping and "camping" restrictions.

In Montgomery, Alabama, Jonathan Singleton had experienced both. He'd been homeless since 2014, after kidney failure and uncontrolled diabetes made working impossible. Unable to afford health insurance or care, he was trapped in a cycle of homelessness, asking strangers on the street for help meeting his basic needs. Sometimes he just held a sign: "HOMELESS. Today it is me, tomorrow it could be you." When police saw him, they told him to rip up the sign. By 2020, he'd been arrested or cited six times.

Jonathan slept under a bridge, but police would often run him off, telling him it was illegal to be homeless. Every time he saw them approaching, he'd get anxious and scared, and he preemptively moved around to avoid them. When Jonathan could collect enough money, he'd pay someone ten dollars to crash on their porch.[103] At least that way he might get some sleep.

Laws targeting begging have been on the rise for years; they more than doubled between 2006 and 2019. As of 2019, 83 percent of surveyed cities had at least one law restricting begging in public.[104] These are sometimes based on the claim that people in need are merely con artists trying to avoid work, or the fear that any direct donations will be used for drugs, alcohol, or other potentially harmful purposes.

Some cities, like Pocatello, Idaho, have set up "donation meters" downtown, urging passersby to feed them their spare change instead of giving it to people begging on the street. Rapid City, South Dakota, installed "giving meters," serving much the same purpose. The names may vary, but the idea is the same: Instead of providing direct aid to people in need, dropping change into meters will ensure that the money is used responsibly.[105]

In reality, most people asking for help on the street are simply trying to survive. Jonathan was collecting cash to finance a night on a porch instead of the street. Others are trying to buy food, hygiene products, toiletries, and other necessities.[106] Andrew, a homeless vet who'd done two tours of duty overseas, ended up asking strangers for help on a downtown sidewalk in Harrisburg, Pennsylvania. He said he'd much rather "get up and go to work every morning," but had a hard time finding a job.

On average, panhandling in the United States brings in about $300 per month—hardly enough to discourage work.[107] Pilot programs offering employment and support services to people asking for help on the street found that virtually all who were offered jobs accepted them. Yet despite their successes, many of these local programs were terminated and replaced by bans.[108]

While the stereotype that most people begging for money are addicts is false and hurtful, no one would argue that drugs aren't an issue for some unhoused individuals. Overall, about 26 percent of people experiencing homelessness suffer from addiction. This isn't much higher than the approximately 19 percent of all Americans aged twelve or over who used illicit drugs or misused prescription drugs—not including alcohol and tobacco—in 2021.[109]

Addiction can be both a cause and a symptom of homelessness. For some formerly housed individuals, substance abuse cost them their job, family ties, and relationships, leading to homelessness. For others, it was the pain and hardship of homelessness itself that led them to start self-medicating. Overcoming addiction is challenging under the best of circumstances, and without a safe, stable place to live it's that much harder.

Andrew, the veteran in Harrisburg, had suffered from addiction. Treatment for a wartime leg injury had hooked him on opiates, and he'd lost his job and become homeless. Maybe the drugs had also helped him cope with his memories of war and the difficulty of readjusting to civilian life. Unlike many, Andrew had managed to overcome his addiction while on the streets, and he'd been sober for seven years. His most immediate challenge as he sat on the sidewalk was assembling enough cash to replace his worn-out shoes.[110]

PLEASE DON'T FEED THE HOMELESS

Advocates have invoked the First Amendment to challenge bans on publicly asking for help, arguing that such requests are protected speech.[111] This argument was strengthened when a 2015 decision from the US Supreme Court made First Amendment challenges easier in general.[112] While that case didn't involve a begging ban—*Reed v. Town of Gilbert* concerned an effort to ban a sign erected by a church—the implications were clear.

When the 2015 decision came down, we already had a case in front of a federal appeals court challenging a law in Springfield, Illinois that banned "vocal solicitations of cash donations." Based on the new Supreme Court decision, the court in our case invalidated Springfield's law, setting a precedent that we and other advocates then used to strike down scores of similar bans around the country. Among our victories was the repeal of the Alabama law that the Montgomery Police Department had used against Jonathan Singleton.[113]

Punitive laws don't just target homeless people, they can also go after those trying to help. Some take aim at charities offering food to poor people in public places. In one particularly blatant example, Las Vegas passed a law in 2006 that made it a crime to offer food to anyone who looked as if they might be eligible for public assistance. The city was just unabashedly saying what's at the heart of such bans: that we should remove visibly poor people from sight. Sharing food with someone who didn't look hungry enough to really need it was fine—what had to be banned was helping the people who *did* need it. Advocates challenged this especially egregious, odious law.[114] While it was struck down, other subtler bans remain in place around the country.[115]

A case that gained worldwide notoriety involved ninety-year-old veteran Arnold Abbott, who was arrested in Ft. Lauderdale for violating the city's feeding ban in 2015. Photos of the slight, elderly man handcuffed and being led away by police for his act of charity made international headlines. Recounting his arrest, Abbott told a local TV station that "one of the police officers said, 'Drop that plate right now,' as if I were carrying a weapon." Threatened with jail time, Arnold, a World War II veteran who had defied the Ku Klux Klan to help Black people register to vote in Mississippi in the 1960s, vowed to keep offering food to those in need. He explained that he was "not trying purposefully to aggravate the situation." Arnold simply believed that "any human has the right to help his fellow man."[116]

The local Food Not Bombs collective brought a case the following year that ultimately succeeded in striking down Ft. Lauderdale's law.[117] Although generally conservative, the federal appeals court nevertheless ruled that the act of providing food also carried a message. By offering meals in a visible, public place, Food Not Bombs was calling attention to its belief that access to food is a basic human right. Coupled with the group's message, sharing food with destitute neighbors was more than just an act of charity—it was "expressive conduct" protected by the First Amendment.[118]

The US Constitution protected the organization's right to convey the message that food is a basic human right. That's obviously important. But did the hungry and destitute people participating in the food sharing events also have a right to sustenance? All human beings need to eat, and human rights law recognizes the human right to food. But US law doesn't, at least not yet.[119]

The Right to Sleep under a Bridge? Maybe . . . but No Right to Housing

Food isn't the only basic human need overlooked by US law. The human right to housing is also unprotected.

Just as people begging for help would rather have a job, virtually all encampment residents will choose stable housing over living outdoors. In a 2022 survey of almost one thousand unhoused Denverites, between 93 and 99 percent said they wanted housing.[120] Yet the city continues to respond with sweeps instead of providing the housing that human beings need and want.

The June 2024 Supreme Court decision in *Grants Pass v. Johnson*, bad as it is, does not preclude *all* legal challenges to laws criminalizing homelessness. The immediate impact is on challenges to laws prohibiting "camping" in public under the "cruel and unusual" punishment clause of the Eighth Amendment. But arguments can still be made under other provisions of the US Constitution, including other parts of the Eighth Amendment itself, other federal law and some state constitutions and laws.[121] In fact, some successful cases brought on such grounds have led to important safeguards, like requiring a city to give advance notice of sweeps, and to protect and store the property of encampment residents instead of just trashing it.

Some have also led to new resources for unhoused people. Successful challenges to bans on "vehicle habitation"—aimed at the growing numbers of people living in their cars, like Miranda and her husband in Tennessee—are spurring some cities to create "safe parking lots." The idea is the city won't enforce prohibitions on vehicle habitation in the lots, allowing those living in their vehicles to park safely without fear of being ticketed or towed. Some lots also offer basic services, such as port-a-potties, security, and access to social workers. Many are run by faith-based groups whose volunteers offer additional support, including food and warm clothes.[122]

But just as with emergency shelter, there aren't nearly enough legalized encampments and safe parking lots to meet the demand. Also like emergency shelters, they cannot replace adequate, affordable housing as a true long-term solution.

Why couldn't the judges who struck down various anti-homeless laws just order cities to provide housing and social services, which would have solved the problem? Because while the Constitution protects the right to not be subjected to cruel and unusual punishment, it doesn't protect the basic human right to housing.

Every human being needs a place to live. But while housing, like food, is recognized by the world community as a basic human right, it is not recognized as a right under the US Constitution.

CHAPTER FIVE

"This System Is Rigged"

Property Rights and Wrongs

In Indianapolis, Indiana, Akiela, Johnny, and their one-year-old baby, Ajhonaiste, huddled together in the front seat of their Ford Fusion, struggling to stay warm as summer was ending in 2022. They were parked overnight in a friend's yard, trying to sleep in the fifty-eight-degree chill. After the baby was born, they hadn't been able to find affordable childcare, and Akiela had to quit her job to take care of their child. Johnny worked at a plastic recycling factory, but even with overtime and donating plasma, it hadn't been enough. They'd missed a rent payment, been evicted, and moved into their car.[1]

Federal rental assistance, allocated to help people during the pandemic, had stopped. So had the eviction moratorium, and eviction filings by large corporate landlords, like the one that had been renting to Akiela and her family, were rising. Indiana had landlord-friendly laws and corporate owners like Akiela's landlord were using them to force tenants out as soon as rent was delayed. Akiela had applied for housing assistance over two years earlier and was still on the waiting list when the family got the eviction notice.[2]

Akiela had repeatedly called government offices for help but got nowhere. She'd been turned down for public assistance and never heard back from agencies she'd begged for aid or advice. Receiving only $310 a month in food stamps for her entire family, she often went hungry to feed her baby. Fighting back tears, she told a local newspaper reporter she'd tried everything, but "this system is rigged."

Around the same time, in Oakland, California, sixty-seven-year-old Lilian had been sleeping outside at a bus stop, where she suffered through the cold every night. She'd ended up there after being kicked out of the hotel room the city had put her in during the pandemic. Funding for the COVID-19 hotel program had run out and caseworkers hadn't been able to find Lilian permanent housing. Thanks to a nonprofit housing provider, she was eventually able to move from the cold bus stop into temporary "respite housing." But the nonprofit's funds were limited, and she would only be able to stay for six months. As of April 2023, she was still on a waiting list for housing for low-income seniors, with no idea how long it would take for her number to come up.[3]

Marcus was on a Washington, D.C., waiting list for housing assistance for *fifteen years*. In 2022, he finally got into permanent supportive housing through a specialized program for people experiencing long-term homelessness. His name still hadn't been called on the regular list for housing assistance, where some 40,000 people were waiting.

It's no exaggeration to say Marcus had spent his whole life waiting for stable housing. Growing up in foster care, he'd aged out of that system when he turned eighteen. Struggling to find a place he could afford, he'd applied for housing assistance, and was placed on a list that already had 58,000 applicants ahead of him. As the months and then years dragged by, he was homeless, his mental health deteriorated, and he sold drugs to supplement what little he was able to earn working odd jobs. He acquired a criminal record and was never able to complete high school—leading to ongoing struggles finding work.[4]

"A Decent Home for Every American Family"

First enacted during an earlier crisis of homelessness, federal low-income housing programs were meant to ensure that poor and middle-income Americans had safe, decent, affordable housing—even when the private market did not. But over the intervening decades, while housing costs skyrocketed and incomes fell or stagnated, the programs had their funding slashed. In the face of dramatically increasing need, they remain grossly underfunded.

After millions of Americans lost their jobs and their homes during the Great Depression, leading to mass homelessness, President Franklin D. Roosevelt's New Deal created dozens of initiatives to address the crisis. These included early measures to create low-cost housing, as well as efforts to stem foreclosures and make homeownership more affordable.[5] Later programs created public housing, which was initially aimed at middle and lower-middle class Americans. FDR promoted the New Deal with a vision that emphasized unity,[6] asserting that "the test of our progress is not whether we add more to the abundance of those who have much; it is whether we provide enough for those who have too little."[7]

FDR warned that, "as a nation, we all go up, or else we all go down, as one people." Yet despite this message of unity, the New Deal embedded explicitly racist and segregationist policies, promoting homeownership for White people while excluding Black Americans, and created racially segregated public housing.[8] By the time the Fair Housing Act of 1968 outlawed such blatant discrimination, more middle- and lower-middle-class White people—along with industry—had fled cities for the suburbs. This "White flight" consisted of many who had previously benefited from the homeownership programs. Public housing was no longer primarily for middle and lower middle-class White people, but for low-income Black Americans.[9]

While deeply flawed, the New Deal programs demonstrate the federal government's critical role in ensuring affordable housing. Building on what FDR started, the Housing Act of 1949, part of President Truman's Fair Deal, set a new national goal: "a decent home and suitable living environment for every American family."[10] But this ambition was never enshrined in the law itself, meaning that the programs the 1949 Housing Act created remained subject to spending cuts.[11]

A notable shift in the federal role in housing began in 1974, when President Nixon halted government spending for public housing. Congress created a new subsidy program aimed at making private market housing affordable, essentially subsidizing landlords. Now known as the housing choice voucher program, it pays the difference between rent charged by the landlord and what is affordable for a low-income tenant.[12] Despite this move toward privatization, the federal programs continued to make housing more affordable for extremely poor people, funding 347,600 new low-income housing units in 1979, and continuing the implicit social contract launched by Roosevelt.[13]

President Reagan broke this long-standing commitment. Coming into office pledging to shrink the federal government, Reagan promoted private enterprise and glorified "entrepreneurial genius," ignoring the government subsidies and tax breaks, not to mention publicly funded infrastructure, that made it possible. With thinly veiled and sometimes overt racism, Reagan didn't stop at alleging people were homeless by choice, he also portrayed impoverished mothers as lazy, devious "welfare queens" looking to cheat the government.[14]

As previously noted, these false narratives helped rally political support for harsh cuts to the fraying social safety net that had been in place since the New Deal. Reduced spending was supposedly necessary to protect taxpayers, prevent fraud, and even to "help" recipients better themselves by pulling themselves up by their bootstraps. Reagan's cuts decimated housing programs, triggering the explosion of modern homelessness—still surging in communities across the country—and all it has led to, from inadequate, overflowing shelters to increasingly punitive laws that are becoming the dominant response to people living outside.

While the criminalization of homelessness primarily unfolded at the local level, this trend paralleled the growth of harsh and punitive federal responses to poverty launched by Reagan in the early 1980s. Over the coming decades, as criminalization displaced unhoused people from even public spaces, housing in America increasingly became a vehicle for private profit.

Kinder and Gentler?

George H. W. Bush campaigned on a promise of a "kinder, gentler" nation. In stark contrast to Reagan, he acknowledged homelessness as a national crisis and promised to make addressing it a federal priority. Whereas Reagan had signed the McKinney-Vento Act into law with reluctance, Bush promised to fully fund it. Much to the surprise of advocates at the Law Center and elsewhere, he even referred to the act by name as he made this promise in a televised pre-election debate.[15]

It was a marked and welcome shift in rhetoric. With the end of the Cold War, Bush also promoted the prospect of a "peace dividend" that could help support domestic programs. But despite the administration's lip service, even its promise to fully fund the McKinney-Vento Act fell short.[16] The administration's budget proposal for low-income housing— just over $2 billion spread across three years—hardly made up for the $24 billion cut by the Reagan administration. Bush soon abandoned any notion of a federal anti-poverty agenda in favor of addressing the needs of poor people through the volunteers he called "a thousand points of light."[17] The new HUD secretary, Jack Kemp, a self-proclaimed "bleeding heart conservative" who vowed to "end the tragedy of homelessness," championed an initiative to privatize public housing.[18]

The gap between rising housing costs and stagnant incomes was widening. Federal low-income housing assistance programs, decimated by the Reagan-led cuts, stretched ever thinner. Restrictions on private housing built for low-income communities with government funding in the 1960s—and subsidized by rental assistance—were expiring, making it eligible for sale or conversion to upscale market-rate developments. Public housing, starved of funding, was in a state of increasing disrepair.[19] To bring attention to the crisis, and to pressure the Bush administration and Congress,[20] advocates organized a march on Washington.

Tens, maybe hundreds, of thousands of people marched to the Capitol, politicians, religious figures, labor leaders, and Hollywood celebrities among them. The call was for "Housing Now!"[21] The event received major media coverage,[22] and just over a year later, the Democrat-controlled Congress approved new housing legislation. The new law forestalled some of the feared conversions—although this would change a few years later. But funding for low-income housing remained virtually the same. The new legislation even incorporated some of Kemp's plans to privatize public housing, which resulted in a net loss of units.[23]

Meanwhile, Congress had allocated billions in response to the savings and loan crisis, the first big bank failure since the Great Depression. Congress created a new agency, the Resolution Trust Corporation

(RTC), to take over and dispose of the failed banks' assets. These assets included single-family homes and apartments. In a small concession to advocates for poor and homeless people, Congress also created a program to make some of these otherwise vacant properties available at a discount for affordable housing. Nonprofit housing groups and impoverished people were eager to acquire such properties, and the Law Center and other advocates pushed to implement and expand the new program.

For those who managed to acquire them, the properties made a life-changing difference. Eddie Sockbeson, a thirty-four-year-old Native American man in Lawton, Oklahoma, had done some time and couldn't land a job after getting out of prison. Homeless, he found refuge at a local shelter, which eventually hired him to work there helping others. With the shelter director vouching for him, Eddie was able to get the promise of a mortgage from a local bank, bid successfully on a property at an RTC auction, and buy a modest home for $12,000.

Converting vacant federal properties into housing for people who didn't have any seemed like a no-brainer. It made sense on paper: Congress had bailed out the banks with taxpayer dollars, taken over their assets, and directed that some of these be used for a public purpose: affordable housing. But whether intentionally or not, the RTC made little effort to publicize the properties to the people who needed them. By 1994, about 22,000 properties had gone to low- or very low-income people through the program—a significant number, yet still just a tiny drop in an ocean of need. Many properties that could have helped poor people were auctioned off to private speculators instead.[24]

It turned out to be an early sign of what was to come.

THE "PEACE DIVIDEND" THAT WASN'T

The end of the Cold War also meant that some military bases were no longer needed.[25] Local redevelopment authorities were created to plan their closure and conversion to civilian use. City governments, real estate developers, and other business groups were keen to acquire these valuable public properties. But there was, for them, a problem: Once fully or partially vacant, the bases would fall under Title V of the McKinney-Vento Act.

Title V gives nonprofit groups serving homeless people a "right of first refusal" to acquire vacant federal property. Eligible groups are nonprofits, both public—state and local governments—as well as private. The law gives them first dibs on properties the federal government deems "suitable" for programs to help homeless people, and nonprofits can apply to use them for shelter, housing, job training, day care, food banks, and the like. The federal government deeds or leases the properties to successful applicants for free; they then take over utilities and maintenance costs. Property falling under Title V can be a piece of vacant land, an unused warehouse, an empty office building—or former military housing.

Military base closures were especially well-suited for the Title V program, and there were a lot of them. In 1994, over 50,000 family housing units in good condition were on bases slated to close over the next five years.[26] These properties were part of what Congress, in passing the McKinney-Vento Act just a few years earlier, had called the "existing capacity" of the federal government. Congress had specifically directed that such existing public resources should be deployed to meet the critical needs of unhoused men, women, and children.

By the early 1990s, though, Congress had other ideas.

As Senator Mark Pryor, an Arkansas Democrat, put it: "Local communities that are working diligently to bring new businesses to town are repeatedly finding their efforts disrupted by the so-called McKinney Act legislation."[27] Pryor and his Democratic colleague, Senator Diane Feinstein, proposed a bill to exempt military bases from Title V and create a new process that "emphasizes the importance of weighing economic development plans with the local needs of the homeless." Of course, Pryor insisted, "the authors of this bill are not suggesting that the needs of the homeless in America are not a high priority."[28]

The closed bases represented a potential bonanza for developers: the opportunity to convert previously public property to private, profit-generating use. Powerful interests were pressuring Congress to repeal or at least weaken the law, putting the property interests of large developers over the rights of people who had no property at all.[29] At the time, however, Senate Republicans, still in the minority, were using procedural maneuvers to prevent Democrats from scoring any victories whatso-ever—and for any legislation to pass, it had to garner "unanimous con-sent." This put the Law Center in a good bargaining position since any objection by one of our allies in Congress would jeopardize passage of the bill. After months of meetings and negotiations on the Hill—and the pro bono help of our high-powered lawyers and lobbyists at Covington & Burling—we reached a deal.[30]

In exchange for giving up the right to first refusal, we won the right to be part of the process. Homeless people or their representatives had to be included on the planning bodies for base conversions, and the needs of homeless community members had to be addressed. Long-standing rules that had prevented use of the properties for permanent housing—as opposed to shelter—were eliminated.[31] To ensure compliance, redevel-opment plans would have to be reviewed and approved by HUD.[32]

Another victory, of sorts, extracted from the jaws of defeat.[33] But it would be no match for the growing privatization of these public resources—and the continued deepening of the affordable housing crisis.

The only option for most people losing their homes were shelters or the streets.

STUCK AT THE SHELTER: THE "PERMANENTIZATION" OF HOMELESSNESS

Larry Presher, a Vietnam veteran, had been living under a bridge in Baton Rouge and contemplating suicide. Searching for work, he made it all the way to Washington, D.C., where he found refuge at a shelter—a bed and three meals a day. Finally, he felt his life "was turned around." Unlike many, the shelter didn't require him to leave during the day or participate in religious programs. He still couldn't find permanent hous-ing, though. Larry just couldn't secure a job that paid enough to afford an apartment of any size in D.C. Emergency shelter had saved his life—but it wasn't enough for him to move forward.[34]

The McKinney-Vento Act had only ever been intended as a stopgap—and it proved a very inadequate one at that. Annual national surveys of cities around the country consistently reported that emergency shelters were still turning away significant percentages of people. The legislation had made a difference, but nowhere near enough to meet the emergency need—let alone end the crisis or even address its causes. From the late 1980s to the early 1990s, funding for the McKinney-Vento Act tripled—yet this was nowhere near enough to offset the decimation of funding for low-income housing.

A cottage industry of service providers had grown alongside—and from—the federal funding. Once the fiercest advocates, their voices were increasingly muted by the fear of losing the government support on which they now depended. In the coming years, Congress would move to make that threat explicit, with a series of proposed measures designed to severely limit the ability of nonprofit organizations to use even private funding for advocacy.[35] The service providers whose activism had helped the McKinney-Vento Act become law were now threatened into silence lest they lose the vital (if woefully inadequate) funding that the legislation provided.

Henry Gonzalez, the Democratic San Antonio congressman who was the powerful, longtime head of the House Housing Committee, called it the "permanentization" of homelessness. Gonzalez feared that "instead of attacking the root causes"—the lack of affordable housing chief among them—Congress would stop at emergency responses. Stuck in a kind of suspended animation, shelters would become the permanent and only response.[36]

We were witnessing the beginning of the institutionalization of homelessness: what had once been seen as an urgent crisis now becoming accepted as a permanent feature of American life. What made it even worse for advocates and activists was wondering whether our hard-fought victory—enactment of the McKinney-Vento Act—was driving this trend toward acceptance. Invariably, though, we concluded that the problem was not the McKinney-Vento Act, which demonstrably provided lifesaving aid to people like Larry. The true culprit was the failure to follow up on emergency response legislation with long-term solutions.

The only thing to do was to keep pushing those solutions forward. This would be a huge challenge under any circumstances. Without a fearless, vocal coalition, it would be an even bigger one.

"Everything I Felt Being Put into Words"

Craig Champ wound up homeless in Washington, D.C., after getting divorced and losing his job. He finally managed to move into a city-owned trailer, one of several that D.C. had temporarily placed in Foggy Bottom, a neighborhood near the State Department. When the city decided to close the trailers, displacing their residents to the streets, they resisted, organizing a group they called the Foggy Bottom Family. Craig became one of the leaders.[37]

Craig also became a key part of a new effort the Law Center launched with other advocates. Called "Beyond McKinney: Policies to End Homelessness," it aimed to make Congress keep its promise that the McKinney-Vento Act would just be a first step, to be followed by long-term solutions. Speaking at a national meeting we convened to flesh out the proposal and plan strategy, Craig described his own experience, emphasizing the complete lack of help for able-bodied, single homeless people. He stressed that unhoused people want to work but can't afford to pay 70 percent of their income for housing. Craig also talked about the ability of homeless people to organize themselves, citing his group's resistance to the shelter closing. Beyond McKinney, Craig said, was "everything that I felt being put into words."[38]

Beyond McKinney had an ambitious agenda, even more so than the Homeless Persons' Survival Act. We wanted to capture the range of system failures that thrust people into homelessness and elucidate its connection to poverty. Our principles were straightforward and comprehensive: "Permanent solutions to homelessness must address its fundamental causes: the shortage of affordable housing, inadequate income to meet basic needs, the lack of social services, and political disenfranchisement." We called for specific policies to increase affordable housing, provide adequate income and social services, and end discrimination.[39]

The idea was to address the reality faced by people experiencing homelessness, like Craig, Larry, and so many others. We would have to confront the political constraints of the moment, but we also wanted to try to influence—not just accept—the politics to meet the need. With the weakening of service providers' ability to advocate, we'd need a big coalition to have any hope of doing so. A proposal connecting homelessness to the larger issue of poverty—and spanning the multiple issues poor people faced—would not only reflect the truth, but also give us a fighting chance to build support.

At least we hoped it would.

"A HIGHEST PRIORITY"

The Clinton-Gore victory in November 1992 brought a sense of excitement and opportunity. As a senator, Al Gore had been the lead sponsor of the Homeless Persons' Survival Act, the ambitious bill that had included not just the emergency relief later enacted by the McKinney-Vento Act, but also prevention and long-term solutions focused on low-income housing. Henry Cisneros, the former San Antonio mayor who became Clinton's HUD Secretary, quickly proclaimed homelessness, "a highest priority." Touring streets and shelters, he promised there would be "fewer homeless people on the streets when we are finished."[40] Andrew Cuomo, who had founded an organization serving unhoused people in New York and was considered by some to be an advocate, joined Cisneros as an assistant secretary, becoming the HUD point person on homelessness.[41]

Homelessness was rapidly increasing in communities across the country—affecting families in particular—and members of Congress were showing more interest. Clinton asked House Speaker Tom Foley to appoint a Task Force on Homelessness, and Foley named our close ally, Bruce Vento, to chair it. Influential groups like the US Conference of Mayors—who had supported us before—signed on to endorse the Beyond McKinney agenda. We scored our first legislative victories, securing refundable tax credits to supplement the incomes of working homeless people. Clinton's Justice Department appointed a senior official to work with us to fight the growing criminalization of homelessness.

The White House also issued an executive order on homelessness, signed by Clinton in 1993, which included a directive to the US Interagency Council for the Homeless (USICH)—the independent agency created by the McKinney-Vento Act in 1987—to develop a plan to "break the cycle of homelessness."

Intended to lead the federal government in addressing homelessness, the agency brought together the heads of over a dozen federal agencies with some connection to homelessness, with the HUD secretary initially acting as chair of the council and providing much of the staff. USICH had been criticized by the Law Center and other advocates for failing to perform a sufficiently active role in promoting federal policy change.[42] The previous administration had also developed a federal "plan" to address homelessness. (And, it turned out, so has every administration since.)

But Clinton's executive order seemed to signal a new level of attention. Prospects for moving forward were looking up.

GROWING ALARM

Over the coming months, hope for the new administration turned to concern, then alarm.

While the Clinton administration proposed modest increases to funding for the McKinney-Vento programs, it simultaneously proposed cuts to low-income housing programs. Months after ordering USICH to create a plan to address homelessness head-on, the administration failed to advocate in Congress to fund USICH at all, allowing the agency to die. Mysteriously, though, the following month, USICH was resurrected as part of the White House's Domestic Policy Council, essentially unchanged, still primarily led and staffed by HUD, with Cuomo playing the key role.[43] Maybe it had just been a power play, but eliminating the only independent federal agency charged with addressing homelessness seemed like a dangerous price to pay, even if it did come back as part of the White House

Titled "Priority, Home! The Federal Plan to Break the Cycle of Homelessness" and published in 1994, the Clinton administration's plan for tackling homelessness contained a spot-on analysis detailing the structural causes of the crisis. For the first time, a presidential administration was recognizing the systemic causes of homelessness. Unlike Reagan, this was not putting the blame on homeless people or calling homelessness a lifestyle choice. Unlike Bush, this was not putting hope in the charitable efforts of "a thousand points of light." This was recognizing the reality of homelessness, naming it as an extreme form of poverty, and affirming the duty and role of the federal government in solving it. The plan called for increased funding for the emergency assistance of the McKinney-Vento Act, and also recognized the need to move beyond it, including with more funding for housing.

But while the administration's proposed budget included a slight increase in overall funding for housing—about $1 billion—it also proposed *cutting* funds for public housing and elderly poor people. In a sleight of hand, the plan claimed it would provide an additional 15,000 housing units for homeless people, but the actual budget only proposed to "set aside" this amount—out of *already allocated* funds—for this purpose. In other words, rather than fund new units, it gave homeless people priority in getting into the same number of existing units. This meant other poor people had to wait even longer—and possibly fall into homelessness while they did so. The biggest increases in the proposed budget were for emergency shelter and housing under the McKinney-Vento Act.[44]

The Clinton administration also launched a plan to reorganize and "streamline" the McKinney-Vento Act shelter programs into a "continuum of care," the brainchild of Andrew Cuomo. A flowchart illustrated how it would work: A homeless person or family would enter the system—through an emergency shelter, a separate intake center, or street outreach—and have their needs assessed, then be sent on to either permanent or transitional housing. If they went to transitional housing, they would receive supportive services, typically for two years. In theory, they would then "graduate" to permanent housing or, if they needed ongoing services, to permanent supportive housing.

In theory.

Implementing the model relied on there *being* housing—and without adequate funding, there wouldn't be. And the assumption that people had to enter the shelter system and then "graduate" was contrary to what was known even at the time about offering permanent housing as a necessary first step, not a final one. Even worse, it was not only patronizing, but it also suggested that homelessness was a personal failure instead of a structural one—contrary to the administration's own analysis of the problem. With government policy still largely focused on reforming the existing aid provided by the McKinney-Vento Act instead of driving new efforts to prevent and end homelessness, the institutionalization of the crisis was now official.[45]

The downward slide wouldn't stop there.

"Ending Welfare as We Know It"

Clinton's 1992 presidential run had tried to attract a broad swath of voters, and one of his rallying cries was to "end welfare as we know it." As the slogan was developed into proposed policies, it became increasingly clear that this wasn't just an empty campaign promise. Clinton fully intended to institute harmful policies and continue the racist, punitive narratives of Reagan.

Framing government aid to low-income Americans as a "way of life," Clinton claimed welfare supported "a culture of dependence," discouraged work, and undermined the traditional two-parent family. In 1996, Clinton signed welfare reform into law, repealing the New Deal–era program that had provided aid—albeit extremely miserly—to poor families. The new law, explicitly titled the Personal Responsibility and Work Opportunity Act, not only dismantled FDR's safety net for at-risk Americans, but it also reinforced the idea that poverty came from personal shortcomings.[46] With less fanfare and public attention, Clinton also repealed benefits for people disabled by addiction, leaving them with no means of support.

Welfare wasn't working, it's true, but not because it fostered a culture of "dependency." Families—like the Kosters, the Deans, and the Myerses—had done everything they could to care for themselves and their children. Despite their best efforts, they were trapped in a system that drove them into homelessness and prevented them from escaping it. Public assistance—welfare—levels were so low that rent was often more than an entire monthly check. Likewise, full-time employment at the minimum wage was not enough to allow workers to cover housing costs, much less meet other needs on top of rent. Subsidized childcare, which was supposed to make work possible for poor families, was underfunded, resulting in long waiting lists where many never received the help they needed. Under such conditions it was often literally impossible for families to make it.[47]

Driven by rising housing costs, gutted low-income housing programs, a low minimum wage, and pitifully inadequate public assistance levels, family homelessness became an epidemic in the 1980s. By the early 1990s, 72 percent of shelters surveyed around the country reported turning families away nightly because they simply didn't have the space for the growing influx. To cope with the mounting need, overcrowded family shelters set rules: Two-thirds wouldn't accept men or "older" male children, sometimes as young as twelve.

By the time a family seeks shelter, it's already exhausted its support networks, who are often living in poverty themselves and can't accommodate more people for any extended period. That meant when a husband or son was turned away from a family shelter, they probably wouldn't be able to make other arrangements with friends or relatives. Fathers and boys had to stay in men's shelters or on the streets.

The inadequacy of both welfare benefits and wages to meet housing costs was shoving poor families into homelessness, and *that* was leading to family dissolution. The government's own standards were out of whack with each other: Full-time work at the government-set minimum wage wasn't enough to pay for what the government said was "fair market rent." Nor was the minimum wage enough to cover what the government said was a reasonable childcare rate, never mind other basic needs like food, utilities, diapers, and clothes. It just didn't add up—and families were becoming homeless as a result.

Once a family was unhoused, the pressure only mounted. Overwhelmed shelter systems were turning away whole families and separating the ones that made it in—if they hadn't already split up before arriving at shelter intake.[48] The disconnect between housing costs and income—whether from welfare *or* work—was making families homeless, and the inadequate shelter system was pushing them to separate.[49]

"Dependency" wasn't causing family breakdowns, as Clinton alleged. The lack of affordable housing and a livable income were to blame.

A "CONTRACT WITH AMERICA"

Part of the impetus for repealing the already modest welfare benefits was the shift in power in both houses of Congress after the 1994 midterm elections. Right-wing ideologue Newt Gingrich became Speaker of the House, and his new "Contract with America" focused on conservative priorities such as shrinking government and cutting taxes. Gingrich and his supporters pushed for "welfare reform" and cuts to other anti-poverty programs—including major reductions in funding for the McKinney-Vento Act—and increased funding for law enforcement and prisons.[50]

Many state and local governments followed the federal lead. At the state level, limiting or outright repealing "general assistance" programs for poor individuals severely eroded an already limited and inadequate source of aid. At the city level, time limits and other restrictions on shelter—including the repeal of an individual's right to shelter in Washington, D.C.—removed even that emergency support. These cuts further shredded the already weakened safety net, while the rhetoric of personal responsibility further shifted the blame to those hurt by them.[51]

Given the cuts and absence of alternative solutions, it's hardly surprising that homelessness continued to grow. Nor was it unexpected, given the victim-blaming narrative, that laws criminalizing unhoused people became even more popular.[52] By 1999, bans on sleeping, sitting, or lying in public had nearly tripled from the previous five years, and sweeps had doubled.[53]

"ONE OF THE BEST THINGS TO EVER HAPPEN"

Clinton and his backers argued that increasing the incomes of low-wage workers would at least partially offset the impact of the repeal of welfare and promote an alternative, more positive narrative about poor people. The centerpiece of their approach was a significant expansion to a refundable tax credit, known as the Earned Income Tax Credit (EITC). Basically an income supplement for low-wage workers, this would rise to a certain threshold as wages went up, then gradually phase out after a worker reached their maximum payout.

In 2020, the average annual amount for families was $3,099.[54] But in the early 1990s, unhoused families were excluded from receiving this help, which was only available to families with homes. Maybe it was intentional, or maybe no one had been thinking of the possibility of working families being homeless. Either way, opening eligibility was one of the demands of our Beyond McKinney agenda, and in 1993 that particular demand succeeded. Our victory was again thanks again to our high-powered pro bono lobbying team who, while advocating for tax benefits for their corporate clients, also included our request.[55]

Studies at the time indicated that significant numbers of homeless people worked but didn't earn enough to pay for housing. Few of them knew about the tax credit or had the wherewithal to apply for it. The Law Center organized a national outreach campaign aimed at service providers, advocates, and homeless people themselves, with posters designed pro bono by a marketing firm.[56] We conducted trainings on how to apply, offered support to local groups, and published informational materials. For those who were eventually able to get it, the credit made a sometimes-critical difference.[57]

A homeless mother in Muncie, Indiana, had been living in shelters with her three toddlers because she lacked access to private or public transportation. "Without a car, I could not take my children to daycare, go looking for a job, or even get food or needed supplies easily. When I received my tax check [for $3,676], I was able to buy a very dependable vehicle, get insurance, title, and plates, with still enough money for other needed items. With a car, I was able to obtain employment, get groceries and needed items timely and give my children a better life. This credit is one of the best things to ever happen to low-income single parent families."[58]

The program offers much less aid to childless adults, but in the 1990s what help it did offer could make a difference. In a suburb of Washington, D.C., a man who had been homeless for three years and had an adjusted gross income of $6,229 received $584. This may not sound like much, but according to him it changed everything: "I am very happy with the 'EIC' which help[ed] me pay back taxes and still leaves me with some money! I am now working a full-time job and [a second] part-time [job]. I have been staying in Arlington, VA Emergency Winter Shelter. This moneys will help me secure a permanent place to live—although not a lot of money—I've paid a debt to IRS and still get some cash to help me out of the 'shelter cycle.'"[59]

Over 50 percent of people living in shelters work, according to recent national studies. And over 40 percent of those living unsheltered—on the streets or in other public places—also work.[60] But many eligible unhoused workers don't claim their EITC simply because they don't know how to get it or even that it exists.[61] And while it can help families—and make a big difference for some—for most it's not nearly enough to overcome the high cost of housing.[62] For childless adults, single or married, the help is negligible.

From the beginning, the EITC offered much less to individuals or couples than to families with children. The amount it paid out didn't significantly go up until 2021, as part of the American Rescue Plan— President Biden's pandemic aid package—and that increase was only for the year. In 2023, a qualifying, full-time, minimum-wage worker without kids could only receive $200; not enough to offset income and payroll taxes, much less make a dent in housing.[63]

The EITC has been criticized for essentially subsidizing low-wage employers, enabling them to continue paying unlivable wages. Instead of changing the broken system to help workers, it puts downward pressure on wages overall, especially since not everyone is eligible to claim the credit. A better, more direct response to inadequate income would be raising the federal minimum wage and empowering labor unions.[64]

PLANNING TO END "CHRONIC" HOMELESSNESS

A year after he entered office in 2001, George W. Bush announced an initiative to end "chronic" homelessness in ten years.[65] But when his administration left office eight years later, his policies had not only increased the privatization of housing and precipitated the foreclosure crisis, but they'd also forced a new wave of Americans into homelessness.

Starting in the 1980s, some researchers and service providers had begun using the term "chronically homeless." The phrase referred to people who were disabled or who'd been unhoused repeatedly or for long periods of time.[66] Over the coming years, studies showed that while they made up about 20 percent of the homeless population, chronically homeless people accounted for about 50 percent of shelter use. In other words, spending on homelessness (much of it public) was disproportionately being used to help a relatively small part of the overall unhoused population.[67]

The point was famously made by Malcolm Gladwell's 2006 *New Yorker* article detailing the story of "Million Dollar Murray"—a man who lived, and ultimately died, on the streets of Reno, NV. The costs of his ambulance rides, ER visits, and hospital and jail stays were estimated to total $100,000 a year, or $1 million for the decade he was on the streets.[68] Ending chronic homelessness, as Bush pledged, would save money that could then be used to address all homelessness.

But the administration's initiative turned out to be a case of one hand giving and the other taking away.

Bush had campaigned as a "compassionate conservative."[69] He'd promised deep tax cuts, and these were enacted early in his administration as the country entered a recession. Primarily benefiting affluent Americans, these tax breaks sharply increased inequality over the coming years. More immediately, as the deficit predictably increased, Bush and Congress axed funding for domestic programs—including low-income housing—pushing more people into homelessness.[70]

The post-9/11 heightening of security measures and identification requirements made it harder for the unhoused to secure public benefits, housing, or employment, as previously discussed.[71] This also intensified the criminalization of homeless people, who were even more likely to be forced to "move on" or arrested by police.

Nonetheless, the Bush administration promised to end chronic homelessness, making the commitment in an obscure budget document. The surprising pledge owed much to the work of the National Alliance to End Homelessness (NAEH), founded in 1983 as the Committee on Food and Shelter. A cofounder and board member of the group was Susan Baker, wife of Jim Baker, a former cabinet member in both the Reagan and first Bush administrations. The organization's board also included other members with good access to Republican, as well as Democratic, policymakers. These ties helped open the door to the administration of the second President Bush.[72]

Following this commitment, however, the administration threw the responsibility for meeting its goal to local governments, challenging them to develop plans to end homelessness in ten years. In a flurry of activity, communities across the country gathered stakeholders to create local plans. A small amount of federal funding, $35 million scrounged from unspent funds versus new resources, was allocated to a handful of communities to implement portions of their strategies.[73]

Phillip Mangano, the Bush administration's new head of USICH, traveled the country hailing these local efforts with much fanfare, and they were often covered in the press. A former Los Angeles music agent turned self-described crusader for the poor, Mangano embraced and promoted the Housing First model as key to ending homelessness in America. Advocates had long been pushing for this programmatic approach, which starts with providing housing first—then offering health care, addiction treatment, and any other needed services. It's a departure from the idea that people need to first solve problems like addiction or mental disabilities before "graduating" to housing. It's a highly effective approach, as demonstrated by multiple evidence-based studies. Its success, however, depends entirely on the availability of housing.[74]

By 2009, some 234 local plans had been created, calling for the creation of over 375,000 total units of affordable, permanent, supportive housing for homeless people.[75] Many plans included cost studies, showing how much money would be saved if people were housed.[76] But while Mangano tirelessly promoted the need for these plans to local communities and the press, the Bush administration continued to cut federal funding for low-income housing—the very resources the local plans were calling for.[77] To the public, it may have *appeared* that solutions were being put in place, but the reality was trending in the opposite direction—dramatically so.

To be fair, the Bush administration also modestly increased certain funding for homeless assistance. More notably, it endorsed and promoted Housing First, a major shift from previous administrations on either side of the aisle. In 2007, HUD reported a 12 percent decline in the unhoused population since 2005. Mangano hailed this as the "largest documented decrease in homelessness in our nation's history."

These numbers may or may not have been accurate, as they still relied on HUD's "Point-in-Time" count and its questionable methodology. The administration's increased focus and funding, albeit for emergency shelter, may have helped with the documented decline.

So did HUD's narrow definition of homelessness: The official government counts didn't reflect increases in people living doubled up. The data from schools—which do include those doubling up—showed a 17 percent *rise* in homeless students during the 2006 to 2007 school year alone., and a 20 percent increase the following year. By the end of 2009, the increase over the three-year period from 2006 would reach 41 percent.[78] Beneath Mangano's rosy announcement, a grimmer reality was playing out.

While the head of USICH was promoting ending homelessness with housing, his boss's administration was cutting federal funding for low-income housing.[79] This undermined any effective implementation of the Housing First model it had publicly embraced, as well as any prospects for succeeding in its stated goal of ending chronic homelessness. Even worse, while the Bush administration called for an "ownership society" and promoted homeownership for minoritized communities,[80] it pushed to deregulate the subprime mortgage market. Continuing the trend toward deregulating the banking industry that had begun in the 1980s enabled lenders to develop risky products, like low-interest loans with surprise balloon payments. Seeking new markets, banks targeted low-income and minority communities. And with easier access to credit, speculators increasingly bought and then sold affordable properties that might have otherwise gone to lower-income buyers, "flipping" them for profit. By the mid-2000s, private equity firms began buying rental properties, initially focusing on apartments.[81]

Deregulation also fueled the unchecked growth of the mortgage-backed securities market, which pooled mortgages, packaged them, and sold them to investors, including private equity firms. Often based on predatory loans, subprime mortgages paid high interest rates and could be quickly generated and "securitized." Their popularity helped inflate the swelling housing bubble.[82] Wealthy individuals also bought US properties as "safe" places for their capital, regardless of whether they planned to use them or not. American real estate increasingly became an investment vehicle for corporations and the superrich around the globe.[83]

When the bubble burst, it triggered rampant foreclosures and evictions. An average of ten thousand American households lost their homes every day in 2008. Minoritized communities, targeted by the drive to expand the subprime mortgage market, were disproportionately hurt. By 2009, as Bush left office and Obama took over, the immense surge in the unhoused population rivaled that of the early 1980s when modern-day homelessness first appeared.[84]

SO MUCH FOR THE AMERICAN DREAM

In New Hampshire, Jane and her husband, Bill, an electrician, had been living what they considered a middle-class life. As Jane put it, "We had two cars, money in the bank and a reasonable mortgage." Then, she said, "On September 12, 2008, my husband's company sent everyone home. The company could no longer afford to pay their employees. We have had no money coming in since then and absolutely no prospects. Our savings is all gone . . . our home is being auctioned off. So much for the American Dream."[85]

Cities and states around the nation were reporting startling increases in homelessness, including among people experiencing it for the first time. In Denver, nearly 30 percent of the homeless population was newly homeless in 2008. In Massachusetts, the number of families living in shelters rose by 33 percent that same year. In Concord, New Hampshire, a church food pantry reported serving four thousand meals to over eight hundred people each month, around double the rate from 2007. Economic inequality widened further, with disparate racial impact.[86]

With already inadequate and insufficient emergency housing, more people were on the streets. Communities of people living outside grew exponentially across the country: A 2017 national report by the Law Center conservatively estimated that in the ten years since the recession had started in 2007, encampments increased by over 1,300 percent.[87] Two-thirds of this spike occurred *after* the recession was officially declared over in 2012, suggesting its continuing effects. Many cities responded by doubling down on criminalization. From 2006 to 2008, laws prohibiting "camping" went up 7 percent.[88]

Some relief arrived in 2009 with the enactment of the Obama administration's economic stimulus package, called the American Recovery and Reinvestment Act. Included in the law was the Homelessness Prevention and Rapid Re-housing Program (HPRP). Providing $1.5 billion in aid over three years, the HPRP supported people teetering on the verge of homelessness with temporary assistance for rent, utility payments, and other services. Funds were also included to help already homeless people find housing. The program ultimately helped more than 1.3 million people exit or avoid homelessness.[89]

Soon after, Congress also revised the McKinney-Vento Act to incorporate some of the measures from the stimulus bill.[90] The biggest change was shifting the McKinney-Vento Act programs away from emergency shelter and toward preventing homelessness through housing— essentially pushing the federal government to adopt Housing First. While these changes remained after the end of the three years, the extra funding did not, and the one-time aid wasn't enough to solve the problem over the longer term. Once again, the federal government had shown that making progress toward ending and preventing homelessness is possible—when the right approach is properly funded. And once again, after the stimulus money ran out, funding fell back to the previous inadequate levels.[91]

Not that the stimulus program alone was sufficient. While it offered housing assistance, the amount of that assistance was still limited, and it wasn't tied to need. It still didn't even come close to a right to housing.

Up for Grabs: Homes for Corporate Profit

Millions of households had been forced from their homes by 2012, leaving behind vacant properties in neighborhoods across the country.[92] Many of these had mortgages insured by Fannie Mae and Freddie Mac, private entities sponsored by the federal government. The government had taken over both entities in 2008 in response to the financial crisis, and now the hundreds of thousands of foreclosed houses in their portfolios had become federal liabilities, too. To get them off the federal government's books, the Obama administration launched a program incentivizing private equity firms and other institutional investors to buy the properties. This loosening of regulations allowed investors to snap up single-family homes. The result was a massive transfer of wealth away from the former homeowners—disproportionately members of minoritized communities—to private equity.[93]

By 2013, investors had converted the expected rents from the properties into securities—"securitizing" them—and creating Real Estate Investment Trusts (REITs), financial instruments traded on the stock market. While private equity owned just a fraction of total homes, by concentrating on specific types of properties in targeted geographic areas, it was able to dominate those markets, driving up home prices and rents. To maximize profit, investors-turned-corporate landlords began systematically raising rents, adding fees, cutting costs (including by not making needed repairs), and quickly evicting tenants who fell behind. They also politically organized to defeat proposals that would have protected tenants' rights. This was a full-on effort to bend housing in America to the aims of Wall Street.[94]

Coming into office in 2017, the Trump administration didn't just promote cuts to funding for low-income housing, they pushed for measures to further deregulate the housing market.[95] At this point private-equity groups, hedge funds, and other large investors had spent some $36 billion buying more than 200,000 homes.[96] By 2018, they owned more than 300,000. Many were in the low-income, minority communities hardest hit by the subprime mortgage crisis. When COVID-19 arrived, the pandemic helped investors further expand their real estate holdings—as homeowners lost their jobs and their homes, private investors seized the opportunity to acquire more foreclosed properties. By 2022, 18 percent of homes in the United States were being bought by investors.[97]

Deregulation by successive administrations wasn't the only factor driving purchases. New landlord software also made it easier for institutional investors to manage rental properties from a distance—and to evict tenants remotely and efficiently.[98] During the pandemic, moratoria on evictions and foreclosures had provided protections. But as these safeguards expired, along with funding to help cover rent, the rate of evictions shot up, in some cases over 50 percent higher than before the pandemic.[99]

That was how Akiela, Johnny, and their one-year-old baby found themselves sleeping in their car in Indianapolis in September 2022. They had been evicted from their private-equity-owned apartment after missing a single month's rent. Unlike the Kosters in the 1980s, who got several extensions from their landlord, Akiela and her family received no grace from the corporate owner.

A First Step and a Broken Promise

Over thirty-five years have passed since Congress promised that the 1987 McKinney-Vento Homeless Assistance Act would only be a "first step," to be followed by long-term housing solutions. That promise has long since been broken, our early hopes dashed by both Republican and Democratic administrations. Not only have Congress and the White House failed to significantly increase aid for low-income housing programs, but they've also often cut funding further. In 2023, only one in four of those poor enough to be eligible for low-income housing assistance received it. Waiting lists for help remain years long. In many communities they've grown so long they've closed, taking no new names.

The national shortage of affordable and available rental housing was over seven million units in 2024, affecting every state in the country. The poorest Americans are hit hardest, especially Black, Latinx, Indigenous, and other people of color. Among "extremely poor" renters—a technical term meaning they're at or below the federal poverty line or 30 percent of the area median income, whichever is greater—more than 70 percent pay over *half* of their income on housing. Little is left over to meet other needs, like childcare, transportation, diapers, clothes, or food.[100]

Funding cuts aren't the only federal cause. The loosening of regulation and oversight has unleashed the full force of the private market to profit from housing. Increasingly, housing is treated as a lucrative investment opportunity rather than as a fundamental good that all human beings need and deserve. Housing is a commodity rather than a basic human right. Often hidden from broader public view, investors have been transforming the landscape of privately owned housing.

Public property, by contrast, is shrinking. While the federal government was inviting private equity firms to buy properties it had acquired through foreclosure, it was also selling off public property it owned directly. Already, in 2012 the Obama administration had issued a directive to its agencies to "freeze the footprint"—to stop expanding their property holdings. By 2015, the Democratic administration commanded them to "shrink the footprint." Agencies were directed to consolidate their use of real property and sell the excess.

The government still had to first offer "suitable" properties to groups serving homeless people before looking for more profitable buyers; despite multiple efforts in Congress to undermine Title V of the McKinney-Vento Act, it remained the law of the land. But this didn't stop agencies from doing everything possible to get around the requirement.

In downtown Seattle, a former federal reserve building stood vacant while people camped on the sidewalks. By the federal government's own count, there were at least 9,000 unhoused residents in the city, and a coalition of service providers had developed a 400-page application to use the property to meet some of the rising need. Blatantly disregarding Title V's mandate, in 2015 the federal government auctioned off the building for $16 million to a real estate developer, who turned it into a "Class A" office building.[101]

The harsh reality is that the Obama administration was determined to sell off federal assets for maximum profit instead of helping its neediest constituents. While we could stop some of it, we couldn't reverse the trend. All the while private investors were snatching up foreclosed properties and transforming what had once existed to meet human need into profit-generating machines. And as more people were squeezed out of their homes, many onto the streets, even that little bit of public space was increasingly off-limits.

Criminalization was only part of it. Public space was also being privatized, as business improvement districts (BIDs) popped up in communities across the country. Funded by businesses in individual city neighborhoods—usually downtown—BIDs often function as private security agencies. Roaming city blocks, their paid guards may encourage unhoused residents to move along, calling in police as necessary.[102] Even more significantly, BIDs lobby for laws further criminalizing homelessness. A 2018 study found a strong correlation between the growth of BIDs and the increase in punitive laws.[103]

Some businesses, as well as cities themselves, install physical deterrents to push homeless people out. Known as "hostile architecture," these manifest as spikes on building ledges and sidewalks, particularly in covered areas where unhoused people might seek shelter. When you see multiple armrests on public benches, they're intentionally placed there to prevent people from lying down to rest. In liberal cities that don't want to be perceived as uncaring, municipal deterrents can be more covert to prevent public outcry, such as Seattle installing bulky bike racks under a bridge immediately after sweeping the encampment that had been there. Hostile architecture takes many forms, but the goal is the same.[104]

In spite of all the efforts by powerful private interests and local, state, and federal governments, low-income communities and their advocates are fighting back fiercely. Sometimes the fights are against our purported "friends." When the Obama administration tried to overturn the court order we'd already won requiring agencies to make vacant federal properties available to help homeless people—as stipulated in Title V of McKinney-Vento Act—we battled them in court. With the help of our pro bono law firm partners, we not only resoundingly defeated their gambit, but we also won a new order further requiring their agencies' compliance.[105]

Yet our wins, no matter how hard earned, haven't been enough to overcome decades of funding cuts and the tsunami of global capital seeking profit at all costs. Nor have they been enough to counter the demonizing narratives and punitive policies that punish people for the sole crime of lacking housing. Adding insult to injury, decades of successive administrations of both parties have announced ambitious plans to end homelessness and seemingly innovative "demonstration programs" to do so, lending the appearance of action. In 2022, the federal government reported, using its own stingy numbers and definitions, that

908,530 new people entered homelessness—and only 900,895 people exited it.[106]

Despite all the rhetoric, plans, and promises, our leaders in government have yet to protect, much less put in place, housing as a basic right for all human beings.

CHAPTER SIX

"They Should Help Us Go to School"

As COVID-19 swept the country in early 2020, Esther found herself living in a Harlem shelter with her four children. She had fled domestic violence in her home, taking the kids with her. Two of them were enrolled in the New York City public school system. The others were still too young for school.[1]

New York City was an early epicenter of the virus, going into lockdown in March 2020. Its vast public school system moved to virtual instruction, affecting more than a million schoolchildren. Students logged on to computers, entering "virtual" classrooms with their teachers and classmates, accessed school resources online, uploaded their homework, and participated in class discussions. Because many did not have computers, the city bought and distributed iPads enabled with cellular plans to low-income schoolchildren—including the estimated 114,000 school-aged children who were experiencing homelessness. Among them were Esther's two school-aged girls, Anna and Lily.

Unfortunately, the cell connection didn't work consistently at the shelter, and the girls were often unable to get online with their school. Esther called the city's technical support office repeatedly, to no avail. She tried using her own cell phone as a hot spot, but its signal was too weak to allow both girls to connect. The shelter gave her its Wi-Fi password, but it didn't extend to the family's living space. Esther's daughters missed so much school their mother worried they would have to repeat fifth and sixth grades, respectively. Even worse, despite her constant communication with them, the city threatened to take Esther to family court over the girls' repeated absence.[2]

The family's experience was not unique. Homeless children across the country were shut out of school during the height of the pandemic by poor or no internet connections. Many didn't even have tablets or computers. In New York City, internet service across the city's sprawling family shelter system was spotty, leaving many homeless children without access to online learning. Advocates filed suit on behalf of Esther's kids and other unhoused students. Within a few months, the city had entered a legal settlement, agreeing to provide in-room Wi-Fi in every city shelter and to ensure each child could connect.

Critical to the case and the settlement was Title VII of the McKinney-Vento Homeless Assistance Act.[3] Titled the Education for Homeless Children and Youth (EHCY), this part of the legislation almost didn't get enacted in 1987, when we were first working to pass the McKinney-Vento Act.[4]

AN ONGOING STRUGGLE FOR BASIC RIGHTS

The impact on children of missing school was widely documented during the pandemic, and the effects are still being felt. Even for children who could attend remotely, missing in-person schooling was often detrimental, affecting their ability to learn, their social development, and their mental health. For low-income children, many of whom relied on school for meals, the harm was magnified. For homeless children, the damage was even greater.[5]

Compared to even low-income housed peers, homeless children are more likely to suffer from hunger, malnutrition, depression, and anxiety—and all their negative effects on health.[6] School can help mitigate some of these immediate harms of homelessness, serving as a source of regular meals and basic health care, sports and other extracurricular activities and, potentially, a link to other social services. School can also offer a sense of stability amid the chaos of homelessness through the continuity of teachers, classmates, and place. Longer term, school gives kids a chance for a better future, helping to interrupt the cycle that makes childhood homelessness a strong predictor for adult homelessness.[7]

Esther's girls were shut out of virtual school during the pandemic by a faulty internet connection. But both before and after the worst of COVID-19, when in-person instruction returned, many unhoused children still couldn't go to school. Lacking a permanent address—typically the basis for school placement—may result in denied enrollment, but it's not the only barrier. Some literally can't get there—the school bus doesn't come to their shelter or car or tent—and their parents can't afford transportation. Others are forced to transfer from school to school as they move to different shelters or makeshift arrangements, doubling up with friends or family, all but ensuring academic setbacks and emotional harm.[8]

That's why in 1987, when we were pushing Congress to pass the McKinney-Vento Act, we insisted Title VII make it into the final legislation. Title VII's Education for Homeless Children and Youth ("EHCY") program was the only thing ensuring access to education—including school continuity—for these kids. That part of the law had been met with surprising opposition, as mentioned earlier, and getting it enacted turned out to be much harder than we imagined. Even getting the federal education department to launch the education program after the McKinney-Vento Act became law had taken a lawsuit.

This turned out to be just the beginning of a struggle to make real the law's promise of an education for homeless children. It's a struggle that continues to this day. It's also one that may be showing signs of slow but meaningful progress.

"Education Is the Only Way"

In 1990, three years after the McKinney-Vento Act went into effect, a national survey showed that despite the law's requirements homeless children *still* faced high barriers to education, often missing school for weeks at a time. Lack of transportation to school was a significant problem in 75 percent of the states, as well as in Washington, D.C.[9] The study was carried out by the National Homelessness Law Center, the organization I had founded the previous year in D.C. After reviewing compliance nationally, we took a closer look at our home community, where we could more easily interview families and get their perspectives directly. More than half of the families we spoke with told us their children regularly missed school because they couldn't afford transportation.[10]

One such family was the Ivys. They'd become homeless when both parents lost their jobs, could no longer afford rent, and were evicted. The Ivys were placed in a shelter far away from the school that all four kids had attended for many years. Not wanting to further disrupt the lives of their children, the parents tried to keep them enrolled. They couldn't always afford the bus fare to get them to school, however, and two or three times a week the children had to stay home. Their older son, Albert, sixteen, had fallen behind and was preparing to enter ninth grade for the third time. He'd tried to catch up in summer school, but was expelled when he missed three days—again because his parents didn't have the money for bus fare.[11]

The Rileys had a similar story. Shirley, mother of eleven-year-old Antwaun, wanted her son to stay at his old school, even though it meant traveling at least forty-five minutes each way from their shelter: "I don't want him to have to adjust all over again at a new school—he's happy at his school. Living in a shelter is a living hell, with feeding schedules and other people telling you what to do with your children."

Antwaun missed nine days of school in one month alone because his mother couldn't afford transportation. The impact was obvious, Shirley noted, "Antwaun was a straight 'A' student until we moved here. He gets 'Cs' now."

For a dedicated student like Antwaun, not always being able to make it to school was frustrating: "I might miss a critical skill, like exponents in math."[12]

Some families went to extreme lengths to ensure their children's education. Gregory Mitchell, a twenty-five-year-old single father, felt so strongly that "education is the only way" that when he didn't have money for bus fare, he walked his ten-year-old son, Stanley, to school and back—four miles each way. It was a lot, but Gregory wanted to give his son the best chance possible. Because Stanley was involved in many extracurricular activities, he often stayed late, and father and son would sometimes miss the 6 p.m. evening meal at the shelter.[13]

"I Want My Kids to Get an Education"

Brenda Lampkin, the twenty-nine-year-old mother of three little girls—Jessica, five, Christine, three, and Ashley, two—became homeless in 1991. A resident of the District of Columbia, Brenda would play a pivotal role in securing the education rights of unhoused children, both in D.C. and nationally.

Before her younger daughters were born, Brenda lived with her mother, who watched Jessica while the single mom worked as a cook and waitress at a Pizza Hut. Brenda had previous experience as a nurse's aide at two different nursing homes, and as a cook and cashier at Holly Farms restaurant. In 1989, after Brenda became pregnant with Christine—and even though little Jessica was already living there—the landlord told them children weren't allowed in the building. Brenda and her children had to leave.

With no one to help her care for her two little girls, Brenda had no choice but to give up her Pizza Hut job and go on public assistance. She and her daughters moved in with Christine's other grandmother, but only for a month while Brenda looked for her own place. Finding a room for rent, she and her girls moved in right away, but it turned out the landlord didn't have a license to operate a roominghouse, and they had to move on again.

Brenda got them into an apartment next, where the family lived for almost a year, growing a little bigger with the birth of Ashley. Then a fire destroyed their home and all their possessions. Ashley, still an infant, was badly burned and had to be hospitalized for over a month. Overwhelmed, desperate, and afraid, Brenda went back to her mother, who had since moved into her boyfriend's apartment. They all lived there for nine months, until the landlord told them there were too many people in the one-bedroom apartment. Feeling she had exhausted all her options, Brenda finally sought help from the District government in September 1991.

Brenda and her three young daughters waited together at the shelter intake center for nine hours.[14] They were then taken to the Budget Motor Inn, a motel the District was using to shelter unhoused families. The Budget Motor Inn was on a busy street on the other side of D.C. from the school that Jessica had recently started attending. No one at the shelter intake center had discussed Jessica's schooling with Brenda, nor did she think to raise it herself. Reasoning it would be more manageable because of distance and cost, Brenda transferred Jessica to a school near the Budget Motor Inn and enrolled Christine in a Head Start program at the same school.

Brenda took both of the older girls to school herself. When she had the money, they rode the bus. Sometimes, when the weather was good, they walked. She never considered letting them walk or take the bus alone; they were too young, and it was too dangerous.

Bus fare cost Brenda $4 a day, so $20 a week, $80 a month. This was a lot for someone without a job, but if she started working again who could take her older girls to school or watch Ashley? Bus fare had to come out of Brenda's $499 monthly public assistance check, which she also used to cover clothes, laundry, diapers, personal items, and food. The motel shelter only provided one serving of milk per person per day, and the last meal offered ended at 6 p.m., but her children needed more milk, and they got hungry after six.

Predictably, Brenda couldn't always afford the bus fare, and the girls had to miss school two or three times a week. Jessica, who Brenda said was very bright, didn't like this. As Brenda explained, "Even the days she has to stay home she likes to look at books. I think she can really be somebody and do something with her life. I want my kids to get an education, so they don't have to go through what I did."

The Education of Homeless Children and Youth program—Title VII of the McKinney-Vento Act—laid out very specific requirements for cities and states to follow when children entered the shelter system. None of these had been followed when Brenda Lampkin and her daughters went to the D.C. shelter intake center seeking help. No one at the center had even asked Brenda where Jessica went to school, much less whether it would be in the girl's best interest to continue at that school or transfer to one that was closer. Even though they were placed in a shelter far from Jessica's school, Brenda wasn't offered transportation assistance.

The problems the Lampkins, the Mitchells, the Rileys, and the Ivys encountered getting their children to school were exactly those that the McKinney-Vento Act's Education of Homeless Children and Youth program was meant to address. The law not only says that state and local education agencies must remove barriers to education for homeless kids, but it also spells out how they must do so. The EHCY program requires education agencies to consider what would be in the child's best interest: continuing at their original school or transferring to a school closer to where they currently reside, while also taking into account the preference of the parents.[15] The agencies must ensure that children can *get* to school as a practical matter—including helping with transportation, usually the biggest hurdle.

The federal law had been in effect for three years, but these families in the District of Columbia weren't getting the help that it guaranteed. Instead, parents were having to choose between spending their meager funds on food or bus tokens.

Intentionally or not, the District of Columbia was clearly violating the legal rights of its homeless residents.

"Please Don't Take Our School Bus Away"

Litigation is typically a last resort. Even with pro bono help, going to court takes time and effort, and there's always the risk of losing. Trying to get voluntary compliance makes more sense, so we sent letters and met with local officials. When that went nowhere, we wrote a report detailing the obstacles that the families and their children faced, the requirements of the law, the District's failure to comply with them, and our proposals for compliance. To make sure we were heard, we held a press conference to publicize the report.

In her official response, Beverly Wallace, the D.C. official responsible for homeless children's education, claimed that the barriers we addressed were "very minimal."[16] Her office had been discussing the issue of transportation but had not reached any decisions. They had, however, prepared four hundred "back-to-school packets" for homeless children—to be distributed a month after the start of the school year—and created a data-base to track the children.[17] This was all too little and too late.

A coalition of advocates, service providers, and faith-based groups came together to press the school district to run buses between schools and shelters.[18] The D.C. superintendent of education agreed to designate a public school bus to take the homeless children staying at the Budget Motor Inn—including Brenda's daughters—to school and back, and to provide a little money for bus tokens for children in other shelters to use on city buses. But the day before the program was to start, the Board of Education raised concerns. They were especially worried that by pro-viding transportation to one group of homeless children they might be required to serve all of them. The result was that the plan was delayed for months.[19]

As we were taking on the District, thirteen-year-old Aubrey Powell was struck by a car and seriously injured right in front of the same shel-ter that housed Brenda and her daughters. Aubrey had been coming home from school when his nine-year-old brother darted into the street. Aubrey was running to protect the younger boy when he was hit by oncoming traffic.[20]

Aubrey and his family had become homeless six months earlier. His mother lost her job as a nurse's assistant, exhausted her savings, and fell behind on rent. After the family was evicted, they were placed at the Budget Motor Inn. This was six miles away from the boys' school, which had been across the street from their former home. For Aubrey and his brother to get to school, they had to take two, sometimes three, buses each way—and to do that, they had to cross the busy thoroughfare in front of the shelter where Aubrey was eventually hit.

Maybe this tragedy spurred government action. Almost five months after first agreeing to do so, the District began a "pilot program" to bus children back and forth from the Budget Motor Inn to their schools.[21]

The new bus meant that Nicole, a six-year-old, could finally go back to school. She'd already missed the first five months of first grade and would have to repeat it. Her mother explained, "There was no way for Nicole to get to school because I didn't have the money to get her there;

I didn't want her walking alone because she's too young, and since I'm in a wheelchair, I couldn't go with her."

Nicole reported that she liked the bus because she liked going to school every day.[22] Another six-year-old, Quenisha Hollowell, said that she liked taking the bus to school with her friends, "because it's fun."

But perhaps sensing that the arrangement might be temporary, Quenisha added: "Please don't take our school bus away."[23]

Little Quenisha's worry proved prescient. The bus ran through the end of the school year, in June 1991. The next month, the District released an "evaluation" of the pilot program, claiming that even though school attendance had improved at every grade level, this result was not "statistically significant." Later, Beverly Wallace elaborated in comments to the press: "We looked at the cost, and we would have to pay additional drivers and purchase a minimum of two buses at $32,000 each."[24]

Money, not the well-being of children, was the more important concern. This according to the D.C. Coordinator of Education for Homeless Children and Youth.

STANDING UP FOR THEIR CHILDREN'S RIGHTS

The District of Columbia had abandoned its responsibility to transport homeless students to school. In response, ten families stepped forward to put their names on a legal complaint. This was no small matter: They might have to be questioned under oath by the city's lawyers, face retaliation, and be interviewed by the press. The Law Center would of course do everything we could to protect them, but we couldn't guarantee anything. Our case would only seek to change the city's policies, not ask for money.[25] Still, these families were willing to take the chance. Brenda Lampkin, on behalf of herself and her three minor children, would be the lead plaintiff.

Litigation is expensive, and the only way we could file suit would be with pro bono assistance. King & Spalding, a global law firm headquartered in Atlanta with a commitment to pro bono work, quickly responded to our request for help. Jim Miller, a serious, courteous man who looked to be in his early to mid-forties, was a litigation partner in

King & Spalding's D.C. office. When we met he'd already assembled a small team, and they were eager to get started. We gathered in a conference room, sitting around a polished wooden table. There was nothing on it except for pens and stacks of yellow legal pads embossed with the name of the firm. Refreshments were laid out on a side table.

We went to work. It didn't take long to find an expert who easily discredited the District of Columbia's "evaluation" of the pilot bus program and the claim that the children's improved attendance was not "statistically significant."

The firm made maps showing the locations of shelters used by the city for families and the locations of each school. These clearly demonstrated that there were already shelters near the schools our plaintiffs' children were attending, but apparently no one had bothered to consider this when deciding which shelter to place them in. This seemed to be part and parcel of an utter disregard for the well-being of the families. Like the Nassau County office where the Kosters and their children had waited for days more than ten years earlier, the District also required families to wait with their children at the shelter intake office to be placed at all. That's why Brenda Lampkin had been stuck keeping her three little girls busy and quiet over the nine hours they waited for placement. Forcing children to be present for intake assessments and other social services could make them miss days of school, sometimes more, all just waiting around.[26]

Our case faced an early setback. The US Supreme Court had just handed down a decision in a case involving the federal Adoption Assistance and Child Welfare Act. Like the Education of Homeless Children and Youth program that was at the heart of our case, the adoption-related legislation gave federal funds to states that submitted "plans" promising to take certain actions. The Supreme Court had ruled that the Adoption Assistance and Child Welfare Act had not actually created enforceable rights. In a departure from precedent, the Supreme Court had made it much harder to sue to enforce federal funding statutes.[27]

We still filed our case, *Lampkin v. District of Columbia*. As we'd predicted, the District asked the court to throw it out based on the new

Supreme Court case. Unfortunately for us, Judge Royce Lamberth, a Reagan appointee, agreed.

After all this effort, two months after filing our case, we were out.

"A Mix of Large Visions and Gritty Detail"

Having our case dismissed was beyond frustrating.

So much work had gone into getting Congress to pass the McKinney-Vento Act and its education provisions, and we'd worked harder still to get them to appropriate funding. We'd filed an early lawsuit against the federal education department that had forced it to distribute those funds on the expedited timetable specified in the law, so that children wouldn't miss even more school.[28]

Now a federal court was saying that the McKinney-Vento Act's Education of Homeless Children and Youth program hadn't created enforceable rights? That these unhoused kids had no legal right to an education, even though they could be labeled truant for not going, even though their parents could be held accountable for not sending them? Even though Congress had expressly recognized the difficulties they faced and tried to remedy them? Even though we'd done everything possible to make sure the language in the law was clear and mandatory?

We were determined to fight this. We appealed the ruling in *Lampkin v. District of Columbia*, arguing that the McKinney-Vento Act's education law was different from the adoption legislation at issue in the recent Supreme Court decision. Our case would be heard by a three-judge panel of the federal appeals court, and the judges randomly assigned to our case did not bode well: Only one was liberal; the other two very conservative. We argued the case, and waited.

Finally, the ruling came down: It was a split decision, 2–1. But we'd won.[29]

Calling the Education of Homeless Children and Youth provision of the McKinney-Vento Act "a mix of large visions and gritty detail," the federal appeals court said that it *had* created enforceable rights. That "gritty detail" had made the difference between meaningless language and legally protected entitlements. The care we had taken in 1987 when we were developing the McKinney-Vento Act had also made a difference. Anticipating that we might need to go to court to enforce the law, we'd made sure to use "shall" instead of "may" wherever possible. This careful word choice made clear that the obligations on state and local governments were mandatory, not discretionary ones that "may" be honored—or not. The "best interests of the child" language I had inserted when working on the legislation, relying on a dim memory from a law school class, also turned out to be both familiar and acceptable to the court.[30]

We were all elated by the successful appeal. All but the District, of course—they petitioned the US Supreme Court to reverse our victory. More legal briefs followed. Supreme Court review is typically discretionary, so we knew D.C.'s request was a long shot. Still, we waited anxiously. Finally, just after Thanksgiving 1994, the Supreme Court declined review.[31] The appeals court ruling would stand. We had won.

This was huge—but the fight wasn't over. Our victory meant that the law could be enforced, but the case still had to be sent back to Judge Lamberth to tell the city specifically what it had to do to meet its legal obligations. This time around the language the judge used was more expansive. Citing *Brown v. Board of Education*, Lamberth called his new opinion a "modest step" toward realizing the ideals expressed in that historic decision over forty years earlier. This felt especially fitting: Virtually all the children in our case, and millions more who would be affected by it, were Black or Brown. While Lamberth may or may not have noted the intersection, the judge certainly saw the parallels between excluding children based on their race and excluding them based on their lack of housing.[32]

True to his word, Judge Lamberth's remedy was indeed modest. Rather than ordering the District to reinstate the bus program, he offered an option: provide free buses *or* tokens that homeless students and a parent or other adult escort could use for public transportation. And in another modest win, unhoused students would now have to be identified by shelter intake staff and referred for educational services within seventy-two hours of being put on a waiting list for shelter.[33]

And that was about it for the District's obligations. It was almost three years to the day since we'd first filed our case.

Mild though the court's order seemed to us, it was still apparently more than city officials could stomach. Less than two weeks later, they withdrew from the Education of Homeless Children and Youth program, returning the federal funds.[34] They would rather forgo the admittedly small federal grant than be told how to spend it by a judge. We tried to argue that they still had an obligation, but without federal funding we had lost the basis for our legal case to force them to comply.[35]

When we first filed the case, we had argued that the US Constitution required equal access to education for homeless children. But after our complaint had initially been dismissed, we hadn't appealed the dismissal of that part of our case, focusing only on the Education of Homeless Children and Youth program created by the McKinney-Vento Homeless Assistance Act as the basis for our claims. And the Act's mandate applied only if the state (or in this case D.C.) took the federal money.[36]

Around the time we were litigating *Lampkin* in 1992, the Chicago Coalition for the Homeless (CCH) filed a similar case in Illinois state court on behalf of local homeless children. They were facing the same counterargument, based on the adoption-related Supreme Court case, that the McKinney-Vento Act's education provisions were unenforceable. When we won our appeal two years later, the advocates at the Chicago Coalition for the Homeless were jubilant—and they used it to leverage a favorable settlement with the city.[37] Because Chicago was much larger, its federal grant to implement the Education of Homeless Children and Youth program was more substantial, and they avoided our fate in the District.[38]

This was the first example of the legal precedent set by *Lampkin* yielding real dividends. D.C. may have given back their funding to avoid complying with the ruling, but the federal appeals court's decision interpreting the meaning of the law still stood. Over the coming years we were able to point to that precedent again and again to help homeless students around the country assert their rights under the law.

Almost a decade later, after another alarming US Supreme Court decision in 2002,[39] we filed a new federal case in New York that ultimately reaffirmed the *Lampkin* precedent. Better still, in the judge's 2004 decision he agreed with our argument that denying homeless children access to education violated not just the McKinney-Vento

Act's education provisions, but also the Equal Protection Clause of the US Constitution.[40] This meant that children had a right to go to school regardless of whether the state accepted federal funds—a measure of protection against the politics we had encountered in the District of Columbia. Subsequent cases brought by the Law Center and other advocates continued to affirm these rights. The precedents set by *Lampkin*, the later New York case, and others like them—when followed—remain powerful legal tools to protect the education rights of children experiencing homelessness.

Topping it all off, the District of Columbia reentered the Education for Homeless Children and Youth program in 2006.[41] The retirement of Beverly Wallace, the District of Columbia official who had resisted the law's requirements, may have helped.

"THEY SHOULDN'T TRY TO RUIN THE ONE CHANCE WE'VE GOT"

Before we even fought our first court battles to get state and local education agencies to carry out the McKinney-Vento education provisions, Congress had already weighed in again, beginning long-running efforts to correct the noncompliance we were seeing. At a Senate hearing in 1990, Kendrick Williams, a formerly homeless boy, gave a firsthand account of his experience missing school when his mother didn't have tokens or money to pay for transportation. Worse yet, he said, was the time the school couldn't find his records and he had to miss almost a month of classes:

> *I love to read and learn, so that month was really hard on me. I really missed school. They shouldn't do that. They should be on our side and try to help us by sending a bus to the shelters, and once we are in, not kick us out halfway through because they can't find our records. They shouldn't try to ruin the one chance we've got.*[42]

Later in 1990, Congress addressed the issue by strengthening the McKinney-Vento education law. Further amendments—and improvements—were added over the years to come.[43] We began seeing progress. In 2000, the US Department of Education reported that 77 percent of homeless children regularly attended school, a significant improvement over 1987, when only an estimated 57 percent were regular attendees.[44] The percentage was clearly inadequate, but it was progress.[45]

Congressional updates to the Education of Homeless Children and Youth program had improved things, as had the successful litigation to enforce the law. But these weren't the only factors helping more unhoused children attend school. Getting the word out that homeless kids had a right to their education also made a difference.[46] The National Homelessness Law Center and other organizations published reports, guides, and fact sheets. We reached out to teachers, school administrators, parents, shelter providers, and families and children themselves. Often the issue was simply that key people didn't *know* about the law and how to put it in place—or claim its protections.

Early on, soon after the law was enacted, the director of a family shelter in California called the Law Center with an all-too-familiar problem: The local school wouldn't accept the shelter as a permanent address, so the kids staying there weren't allowed to attend. We faxed her our fact sheet— that's how we worked in those days—summarizing the rights of homeless schoolchildren. The shelter director took the fact sheet to the school district and based just on that piece of paper (with our letterhead) she was able to get the children enrolled. The word "law" in our name no doubt helped.

SEPARATE AND UNEQUAL

Significant improvements notwithstanding, compliance with the law continued to be uneven across the country, and children were still being denied access to education through the 1990s.[47] An alarming new trend appeared: Separate schools were being created for homeless children. In 2000, our report *Separate and Unequal* identified forty such schools.[48] These varied greatly: The largest, in Maricopa County, Arizona, served some eight hundred elementary and high school students. Others resembled "one-room schoolhouses," combining multiple grades and ages, and sometimes operating in shelters or community centers. Many lacked certified teachers and didn't follow standard curriculums. Some were part of the public school system, some received private funds, and some were taking funding directly from the McKinney-Vento Act.

Many of these programs had been founded by well-meaning people who wanted to help homeless children who were being excluded from regular public schools. Placing "schools" near or in shelters would eliminate the biggest barrier that was keeping kids out: transportation. Proponents of the programs also argued that separate schools allowed children to be with others in similar circumstances without fear of ridicule or shame. At first glance, these might seem like good points. But it soon became clear that these schools hadn't just been developed in response to the exclusion of homeless children—in violation of their rights under the law—they also constituted a *further* violation of those same rights.

These children had a right to equal access to public school. The families, the Law Center, and other advocates had fought for that right for a reason. In a democratic society, education is fundamental to participation, to opportunity, and to a chance for a productive future. And that right is a right to equal access, not to some different version apart from others. The law doesn't just ensure access, it includes a right to not be stigmatized—and there's an obligation on schools to ensure this.

Separate schools were a red flag indicating noncompliance with the law protecting these basic rights. Much as emergency shelters signal a lack of housing, separate schools indicated a deeper problem. The shelter system now constitutes a cottage industry with its own infrastructure, and this model of schools was threatening to do the same. Our report and others called attention to this dangerous new development and made clear that these schools not only *indicated* an underlying violation of the law—a lack of access to public schools—but that they also *were* a violation of the law, which specifically required that homeless children not be isolated or stigmatized. We urged Congress to make even more explicit that this approach to serving the educational needs of unhoused children was prohibited.

This proved to be a controversial position on Capitol Hill.[49] The new schools had a financial stake—they wanted to remain eligible for federal funds under the McKinney-Vento education program—and their lobbyists made their case to Congress. We countered by citing test scores that demonstrated the schools provided inferior education, and that they segregated children. In a reference to *Brown v. Board of Education*, we called our report *Separate and Unequal* to emphasize that not only were homeless children being treated differently but that most were children of color.

Congress acknowledged our argument—for the most part. Despite adding language to the McKinney-Vento Act that explicitly prohibited separate educational institutions, five of the schools were grandfathered in and allowed to continue operating. Their lobbyists had won that concession. But as of 2023, only one remained in operation.[50]

"SO POOR, SO BLACK"

The subtext of race underlying homelessness became even clearer when Hurricane Katrina struck in 2005. Like most people, I was safe and dry at home as I watched the shocking footage of desperate people marooned on rooftops, in boats, surrounded by water, pleading for help. As the disaster continued to unfold day after day, images of unbelievable hardship filled the media. I remember scrutinizing them, hoping to see any evidence that what was becoming increasingly obvious wasn't actually true: The people who were suffering were virtually all Black. Eventually, CNN's Wolf Blitzer blurted out what it seemed no one wanted to say: The most hard-hit victims were "so poor, so Black."[51]

Of course this was true, and the reasons for the disproportionate racial impact were crystal clear: The hardest-hit areas were the poorest and most segregated.[52] These people were living in the cheapest, least-protected housing, in the most exposed, defenseless parts of the city, the places White residents avoided if they could and the places where discriminatory laws and practices had pushed people of color. Imagining it could be otherwise meant overlooking the racist structures and inequities deeply embedded in this country. My hopes early in the disaster had been born of my own White privilege.[53]

Katrina caused a huge increase in homelessness. Hundreds of thousands of extremely poor people had nowhere to go and no way to meet their basic needs. Many hadn't been able to leave before the storm hit, lacking a vehicle or other means of escaping on their own.[54] Evacuated after the fact by the National Guard and other agencies, with all their possessions destroyed, survivors were dispersed across the country. They typically didn't even know where they were being sent, ending up in Red

Cross shelters or trailers provided by the Federal Emergency Management Agency (FEMA) or temporarily placed in motels or hotels.[55]

Three months after the hurricane, many were still stuck in their motel or hotel rooms, never having received the housing assistance that FEMA was required by law to provide disaster victims.[56] Just before Christmas, FEMA announced it would evict the evacuees from their motels and hotels. Advocates were ready.

A coalition of groups had already filed a class-action suit against the agency on behalf of the evacuees. Having prepared in advance, we were able to quickly stop this additional disaster in federal court.[57] FEMA was ordered to process the pending claims for housing assistance. Not only that, but the court agreed with us that FEMA's duties were not discretionary, nor was the agency shielded from judicial review, as it had argued. The agency was accountable, and it had to comply with the law.[58] While disaster response remained—and still is—inequitable, we'd won some measure of federal assistance to meet the housing needs of the evacuees.

"NOT THE TYPICAL HOMELESS CHILDREN"

Housing may have been the most obvious need for the Katrina survivors, but it certainly wasn't the only one. Many families—including some 372,000 children—had been evacuated to communities across the country. They were suddenly showing up in Utah and Texas, and there was an immediate and pressing concern: How and where would the children go to school?

Just south of Salt Lake City, around six hundred evacuees had arrived at Camp Williams, a National Guard training site near Bluffdale, Utah. The local school district made plans to bus the displaced children to school and many volunteers mobilized to help.[59] But at the last minute, the governor's office intervened. According to a special advisor to Governor Jon Hunstman Jr., sending the recently displaced children to school away from their families wouldn't be wise, given their recent trauma.[60] Instead, the advisor said, a special "one room schoolhouse" should be set up at the base where they and their families were being sheltered. This raised an obvious problem: the McKinney-Vento Act's ban on separate schools for homeless children.

There was no question that the children were homeless—fortunately, no one disputed this. But according to Senator Orrin Hatch of Utah, "These displaced and homeless children are not the typical homeless children."

The governor's office had contacted Hatch and he, in turn, had asked the US secretary of education, Margaret Spellings, to seek a waiver of the law. Apparently by way of explanation, and either not understanding or willfully misrepresenting the reality that *most* homeless children live with their families, Hatch wrote, "Nearly all of them are with their families. It is important to keep families together as the [Katrina] victims receive aid and support."

A waiver would require congressional action, but a request from the secretary would presumably help spur it along.[61] Spellings assured Hatch that she would not enforce the law while they waited for Congress to make the exemption official.[62]

Why the urgent, high-level push to suspend the McKinney-Vento Act's education protections? If anything, this was the moment when they were *most* needed.

"This law has helped evacuees to enroll in schools without red tape," noted one Mississippi education official. She went on to say, "If there were no McKinney-Vento prior to the hurricane, surely the hurricane would have created it."

At a Senate hearing addressing the needs of children made homeless by Katrina, Democratic Connecticut senator Chris Dodd noted his gratitude that the law had recently been strengthened and its funding increased.[63] Everyone, regardless of party, seemed to agree that getting children back to school was critically important not just for their education but for restoring some sense of stability to their lives.[64]

One potential factor in Utah was that the school district near the military base housing the evacuees was overwhelmingly White. Literally 1 percent of their students were Black. Most likely, someone had raised a concern about enrolling the unhoused children, who were almost all Black.[65]

Advocates organized to fight the waiver request. Together with Rod DeArment, the well-connected Republican lobbyist whom I'd first worked with to get the McKinney-Vento Act passed, I asked for a meeting with Secretary Spellings. Aside from Rod's skills as a lobbyist, he would have more clout than I would with a member of the George W. Bush administration. By the time the date of our meeting arrived, the Education Department had backed down in the face of our opposition, giving up its waiver request. We'd won another battle, safeguarding critical legal protections for the children displaced by Katrina, and preserving the right to equal education for all homeless children—and, hopefully, those who might one day be displaced by future disasters.

But despite this success, racial discrimination and racism in responding to the education needs of disaster survivors continued.[66] In South Carolina, a Greenville college official resigned after referring to Katrina-displaced children waiting to be picked up by school buses as "yard apes."[67] St. Augustine, Florida, provides a more recent odious example. In the wake of 2017's Hurricane Irma, locals who had been homeless before the storm were given yellow wristbands to demarcate them from newly unhoused individuals. Those with yellow wristbands—who were disproportionately people of color—were separated from the others seeking help, and left to spend the night on concrete floors without cots or blankets.[68]

The problems are systemic, not isolated incidents. Federal relief for disaster victims is heavily weighted toward whiter, more affluent communities versus the poorer communities of color that need it most, perpetuating and deepening inequality. Reforms supported by the Obama administration helped somewhat.[69] In 2024, the Biden administration made further changes to strengthen federal disaster response and to make it more equitable for minoritized and low-income communities. The administration also adopted the first national climate resilience strategy, but stopped short of a comprehensive plan.[70]

As climate change intensifies and disproportionately affects poor and minority groups, communities and advocates will be watching to see the impact of these reforms—and the need for more.

"The Jobs That Pay Decent Salaries"

A different kind of disaster swept the country in 2020: COVID-19. In New York City, as Esther was struggling to get her two daughters remotely connected to their middle school, Jose, a student at Columbia College, was facing a different set of challenges. A first-generation college student who'd been homeless when he entered college, Jose had been relieved to be able to live in the dorms. Then his school abruptly announced it was closing student housing due to the pandemic. He had just forty-eight hours to pack his things and leave.[71]

Jose was lucky: His sister lived in the city, and he could crash on her couch. Through a special pandemic program, he was able to get extra data on his cell phone to use as a hot spot. Jose was emphatic about needing to continue college: "Higher education is extremely important. It opens up a lot of opportunities. It means you qualify for the jobs that you want. The jobs that are going to be paying decent salaries."

Extremely stressed out by his situation, Jose reached out for help from his school's mental health services, which were still operating. Thanks to his sister's assistance, the extra cellular data, and ongoing mental health support, Jose was able to continue his classes remotely. Others were not so fortunate.

In the fall of 2020, some 14 percent of college students were experiencing homelessness in America. By late 2021, nearly one-third of college students were missing a meal at least once a week.[72] Almost half experienced housing insecurity, meaning they struggled to cover rent, had to move frequently, or otherwise faced challenges staying stably housed.[73] The invisible storm had been building for years: Nine percent of college students were homeless as early as 2019, with one-third already housing insecure.[74] The pandemic made it worse, but also brought it into the open.

As campuses shut down and dorms and dining halls closed, students like Jose scrambled for new sources of housing and food. Likewise, with restaurants and other businesses shuttering, many also lost the full- or part-jobs that helped them pay for college—and life. Shelters cut capacity to allow for "social distancing," and soup kitchens scaled back or shut down for want of volunteers. As businesses closed, unsheltered people—including students living in their cars or couch surfing—had even fewer resources to draw on. Where could they go to study or rest, or even wash up or use the bathroom?

In California, where housing costs are especially steep, by 2013 more than two hundred campuses had food pantries for needy students (often also used by staff and some poorly paid faculty). Experiencing hunger typically accompanies homelessness and is often its precursor. Ten years later, virtually every public college and university in the state had some kind of student food pantry. California also approved funding for "basic needs" programs at all its community colleges, which offer help with food, mental health support, and, crucially, connections to housing.[75] The need is acute: A 2019 survey of California public community colleges found that 19 percent of students had experienced homelessness in the past year.[76]

In the fall 2021 semester, Long Beach City College (LBCC), part of the California state university system, identified 225 students as "literally homeless." That same semester, 1,200 students requested housing support from the school to pay rent or other bills. LBCC partners with a nonprofit organization that helps get homeless college students into transitional housing, at an annual cost of about $10,000 per student. Some of their applicants were already living outside, like Fifonsi Jenkins, an international student who found herself without a place to live after leaving her abusive husband and their home. Fifonsi was living in a makeshift shelter she'd constructed on campus, literally sleeping in the bushes, eating out of garbage cans, and washing up in restrooms. Frustratingly, the LBCC program doesn't have enough funding for every student who needs it—not even the majority of them. As of 2022, only about thirty students had been housed through the program.[77]

For those it does help, the results can be life-changing. Leeann, a twenty-one-year-old nursing student, had spent months couch surfing to save on rent after cutting her work hours. She lived with constant anxiety and no quiet place to study. Having grown up financially insecure, sharing a room with four family members, Leeann saw a nursing degree as her route to a more stable future. She didn't consider dropping out an option, even as her grades plummeted mid-pandemic. Through the LBCC housing program, she was able to move into an apartment near campus in 2022, sharing it with three other students grappling with housing instability. After three months of chaos, Leeann was able to once more concentrate on her studies, dramatically improving her classwork.[78]

Fifonsi had a similar experience. An LBCC trustee helped her get a housing voucher and financial aid, which allowed her to move from her makeshift hut on campus into an apartment. Once settled, Fifonsi was able to focus on her coursework, receive her diploma, and make plans to become a pharmacist.[79]

Dozens of LBCC students were sleeping in their cars, and in November 2021 the school launched a "safe parking" pilot program for students. As with similar initiatives in other cities, this provides a desig-nated place for students to park overnight without having to worry about being ticketed by police or other harassment. It offers access to Wi-Fi, bathrooms, and nearby showers. But this program is also extremely limited, accommodating only about eight students at a time. Still, those who have gotten in have benefited from the increased stability. Some have made the dean's list for their academic performance, and a few have transitioned to the housing program.[80]

On the other side of the country, Osemenga Celey-Okogun, a freshman in New York City's public university system, was about to drop out in the fall of 2022. The friend she'd been staying with could no longer host her and, without other options, she was facing homelessness. Osemenga was preparing to put her dream of becoming a doctor on hold and withdraw from school.[81]

But then she applied for help through a new pilot program for stu-dents at risk of homelessness. The program, run by a nonprofit housing organization and funded primarily by an affluent church group, subsi-dized Osemenga's move into a shared apartment. As of late 2023, the program housed twenty-three students in the city university system who would otherwise be living in shelters, sleeping overnight in their work-places, living in their cars, or dropping out, as Osemenga had planned to do.[82]

This critical support annually cost about $25,000 to $30,000 per stu-dent in 2022, covering shared housing, a food pantry, an on-site social worker, and academic and employment help. Compared to the estimated cost of providing emergency shelter for a year—about $52,000—it seems like a no-brainer. With a stable place to live and support for other basic needs, students have a chance to break the cycle of homelessness and poverty. Students who receive college degrees through the city's public system earn 40 percent more than those with just a high school educa- tion.[83] As the country was recovering from the Great Recession, over 95 percent of newly created jobs went to those with at least some college education.[84]

Yet despite its promise, New York City's program is just a drop in the bucket. In 2019, over three thousand students were homeless in the city university system, and more than ten thousand worried about secur- ing food and other necessities. These pre-pandemic figures don't include students who have since dropped out or would-be students who haven't enrolled at all. In the fall of 2020, national enrollment for first-year col- lege students went down 13 percent. This decline was even steeper for those facing challenges in meeting basic needs like housing and food, and especially so for Black and Native American students.[85]

As of 2023, several states have enacted laws that waive tuition and/or fees for unhoused students at their public colleges and universities. Some offer lower "in-state" tuition to these students or provide other supports, including requiring schools to designate homeless liaisons on college campuses (like those required for secondary education by the McKinney- Vento Act). Three states—California, Minnesota, and Washington— have allocated funds to help homeless students with housing.[86]

What more and more university systems are learning is that students are more likely to drop out due to an inability to afford housing and other basic living expenses than due to tuition costs.

HOMELESS TO HARVARD
Khadijah Williams grew up homeless on the streets of Los Angeles, graduated from Harvard, and is now a national leader advocating for solutions to homelessness. She was interviewed by Oprah Winfrey on her show, and Khadijah's story received national attention. She is surely uniquely talented, but she's by no means alone.

Many homeless students manage to enroll in and finish college, and some go on to obtain graduate degrees. While there's currently no way to know for sure, anecdotally, at least, it appears their numbers may be increasing. That's certainly been my impression, based on my own experiences over the past decade or so. In 2018, I began teaching a seminar on homelessness law and policy at Columbia Law School, together with noted scholar Kim Hopper (who helped us with the language defining homelessness in the original McKinney-Vento legislation in 1986). Every year, at least one of our twenty or so students has confided that they had experienced homelessness as children. A few years ago, a UCLA graduate student writing his doctoral dissertation on the McKinney-Vento education program contacted me. As we discussed the program, he too revealed having experienced homelessness as a child. Now he's a professor, teaching and writing on the issue.[87] In Bastrop Texas, Norma Mercado, the local liaison under the McKinney-Vento Act'seducation program, was unhoused as a child. She is currently writing her PhD dissertation on the program she now helps implement.[88]

These are just a few examples of the highly accomplished people I've happened to meet who experienced homelessness as children—an unscientific and selective sample. There are countless others, including, of course, many whom I don't know and will never meet. Are they exceptional outliers? Or, as seems much more likely, do they just prove how much talent is unfulfilled when homeless children are denied the most basic right to an education? Are they further indication that homelessness is affecting more and more people? Or is something changing? Is access to education for unhoused children improving, albeit much too slowly? Maybe all of the above. Young people who succeed at such high levels in the face of tremendous barriers deserve enormous credit for overcoming them, and their success is testament not only to their abundant talent and hard work, but also their perseverance and strength.

Making an Impact?

Early on there was some indication of the impact that the Education of Homeless Children and Youth program can have—when the law is followed. In 1987, the year the McKinney-Vento Act went into effect, a survey by a national advocacy group found that 43 percent of unhoused school-aged children were not attending school regularly.[89] By 2000, the US Department of Education (ED) estimated that number was down to 23 percent.[90] Subsequent reports by the federal education agency didn't attempt to gather this critical information, focusing instead on numbers of homeless students *identified* by schools. But since reliable data on total numbers of homeless school aged children are lacking, the number of homeless students found *in* school says little about how many were *not*.

Then, in 2016, the ED began collecting data on "chronic absenteeism" for homeless students. During the 2018–2019 school year, 37 percent of homeless students met this definition, missing 10 percent or more of school days.[91] The agency cautioned that the numbers may be inflated—some students who changed school may have been double counted. But the number had been trending up for the previous two years before that.

Then came the pandemic, and all bets were off.

Up to that point, as homelessness in general increased, the numbers of homeless students reported by schools also shot up, reaching a high of over 1.5 million in the 2018–2019 school year.[92] When the pandemic started and schools moved to remote instruction, the numbers dropped precipitously: During the height of the pandemic in 2020, that number went down to just under 1.2 million. But while at first glance that might seem like good news, in fact it means that these children were unaccounted for by schools.[93]

Despite the drop in the "official" count of homeless students, the need for education support for these children was increasing, not falling. Many—like Esther's girls—were unable to attend class remotely, and schools had a harder time identifying them.[94] The inability—or failure—of schools to even identify them made it very unlikely they were receiving the support they needed and had a right to under the law.[95]

By the 2022–23 school year, the numbers of homeless school-children identified had gone back up to almost 1.4 million.[96] But that same school year, the Education Department reported that about 48 percent of homeless students had been "chronically absent"—defined as missing 10 percent or more of school days.[97] That's much higher than the 28 percent national average for all public-school students during this time. And given the difficulties in identifying homeless schoolchildren, even before the pandemic, the real numbers are almost certainly much higher.[98]

The American Rescue Plan, championed by the Biden administration in response to the pandemic, helped: Congress appropriated an additional $800 million for the McKinney-Vento Act's Education of Homeless Children and Youth program in 2021. While very substantial, this was a one-time boost. To make a real and lasting impact, ongoing increased funding is needed.[99] And while regular annual funding for the McKinney-Vento education program has increased, reaching just over $129 million for 2023, so has the need. In 2023, after the artificial pandemic drop, the numbers of homeless schoolchildren increased by 10 percent over the previous year.[100]

Currently, fewer than one in four local districts receive funding from the McKinney-Vento Act's Education of Homeless Children and Youth program.[101] So while each school district is required by law to designate a special "liaison" to address the needs of unhoused students, this person will most likely already be doing at least one other job—maybe many of them.[102] Increased funding, sustained over time, is urgently needed.

This is especially true in the aftermath of the pandemic. School closures set back academic progress for many schoolchildren around the country; for poor and unhoused students in particular, the impact was devastating. The long-term effects on any gains these students had been making pre-pandemic remains to be seen.

Not all improvements require money, and some can save it. Coordinating the temporary and long-term housing placement of families to put them closer to the schools their children are already attending would go a long way. The amount saved on transportation alone would be significant, and it would remove one major hurdle to keeping kids in school. As illustrated long ago by our maps in the *Lampkin* case, planning family placement based on schools can be fairly easy. Some communities have taken this simple and obvious step, but by no means all.[103]

Of course, the obvious, most effective solution here is the same one that would fix all the other issues facing homeless families and individuals: permanent housing.

When the law works to help unhoused kids go to school, families like the Ivys, the Rileys, the Mitchells, and the Lampkins don't have to choose between food and bus fare. Their children—and other young people, like Esther's two daughters and Kendrick—have a shot at a better future. But the need for the law's protections—and the harms that come from not having adequate housing—would be greatly reduced if these families had homes.

Students experiencing homelessness graduate from high school at significantly lower rates even as compared to other poor students. Without a high school degree, they are less likely to find employment that pays enough to afford housing—increasing their risk for homelessness as adults.[104] In fact, not having a high school degree or GED is the single greatest risk factor for homelessness for young adults.[105] Receiving an education, as guaranteed by the McKinney-Vento Education for Homeless Children and Youth program, not only helps the well-being of children as they experience homelessness, it also helps *prevent* future homelessness.

And yet the law enshrining this fundamental, life-changing right is still being violated.[106] It needs to be strengthened, funded, and enforced vigorously.[107] This requires committed advocacy and much greater political support.

This should not be controversial. Every state's constitution guarantees every child the right to a free public education. Even so, it took a new law, McKinney-Vento Act and its Education of Homeless Children and Youth program, for homeless children to even start equally enjoying that right. And it has taken—and is still taking—lawsuits, advocacy, and outreach campaigns to implement the law. Rights are essential, but they can be meaningless if they aren't protected and enforced.

One hopeful sign is that more people who've experienced homelessness are entering politics and other public arenas. Currently or previously unhoused individuals seem to be increasingly earning degrees from colleges, law schools, and graduate programs. As some, like former Democratic

Missouri congresswoman Cori Bush, go on to run for office and gain influence in the political sphere, they offer hope and the real possibility for positive change.[108]

Repairing these broken systems shouldn't require those who've personally suffered the consequences to also fix these systems themselves. Political leaders of any background or party affiliation *can choose* to hear the simple plea of homeless children like Kendrick Williams to be "on our side" and not "ruin the one chance we've got" for a better life. But while a few have, most American politicians can't be counted on to listen to the voices of people lacking money and other traditional forms of power. Increased political pressure from a broad coalition of allies—and the leadership of political advocates with lived experience, like Congresswoman Bush—is needed to spur action.

Making even fitful progress has required decades of vigorous advocacy and relentless pressure, including lawsuits, legislative efforts, and public outreach. Meanwhile, another generation of unhoused children is growing up, and the people most directly affected can't afford to wait. Increasingly, people who have experienced homelessness themselves are organizing for change.

PART III
HOUSING FOR ALL

CHAPTER SEVEN

"Housing Is a Human Right!"

When Dominique Walker returned to Oakland, California, she was amazed by the transformation. Thousands of people, mainly Black and Brown, were without housing—couch surfing, living in shelters, camped out in public places.

Born and raised in the city, Dominique had gone to college in Jackson, Mississippi, and ended up staying. In April 2019, fleeing domestic violence, she came home, bringing along her two young children. She found a full-time job, and then a part-time one too. But she still couldn't afford to rent a place in Oakland for her small family.

At first, Dominique stayed with family members, sleeping on couches, sometimes in a spare room with her kids. But much of her family and community had been displaced from the city by escalating housing costs—some to neighboring towns up to two hours out, some to the streets. Moving from couch to couch with her children, Dominique spent hours commuting from these temporary living arrangements to her jobs and to day care. The hardest part, she told a reporter, was not being able to give her kids the stability of home: "My children weren't able to be really free."[1]

Dominique reached out to the city for help, to no avail. City programs had exhausted their resources. By the fall, with no end in sight, she was ready to try a different approach. Seeing what had happened to her home city in her absence, she said, "changed everything for me."

Dominique met Carroll Fife, a local community organizer, and, through her, other mothers facing similar hardships. Calling themselves Moms 4 Housing, they banded together to help themselves and protect their children.[2]

A house on Magnolia Street had been sitting vacant for almost two years. Painted white, it had a front porch, a backyard, two stories, and three bedrooms. But it had been abandoned—roof leaking, bushes overgrown on either side—and as it fell into disrepair, neighbors worried it would become a base for drug dealers. The mothers decided they had to act. On November 18, 2019, Dominique, two other mothers, and their children moved into the vacant house.[3]

The moms had done their research, finding that the house was owned by Wedgewood Property Management, a self-described "leading acquirer of distressed residential real estate." The house was one of hundreds of vacant properties across the city, many in newly built highrises towering over streets dotted with encampments. As early as 2016, Wedgewood claimed it was the largest "fix and flip" company in the country, buying some 250 homes that had been foreclosed on (or were about to be) each month.

The company's CEO considered the market for "distressed" properties "hot and sexy," and Wedgewood operated on a model of buying properties cheaply, evicting their tenants, renovating the homes, then selling them at much higher prices. The process often kept homes vacant for months or years—as they had done with the house on Magnolia Street, waiting for the market to go up—directly contributing to the rapid rise of housing costs and the shortage of affordable housing.[4]

Wedgewood called the mothers criminals for taking over the property, but Walker countered that "the true crime lies in this society that we live in that can normalize people living in the street."[5]

Describing Moms 4 Housing's takeover as "an answer to a desperate need," Dominique neatly summarized their position: "It should be illegal to have vacant houses and have people sleeping on the streets."[6]

Sameerah Karim, another Moms 4 Housing member, noted that there are "four times as many empty homes in Oakland as there are homeless people. . . . Why should anyone—especially children—sleep on the street while perfectly good homes sit empty?"[7]

Taking over the property was "coming out of a necessity between life and death," according to Sameerah, "born out of the human right to housing."[8]

Separated at Birth: Economic and Civil Rights

"The human right to housing" captures perfectly what Sameerah and the other Moms 4 Housing members were feeling—and what they were claiming. But while virtually the entire world acknowledges this basic human right, at least in theory, the United States has not done so. Nor has it recognized other economic and social rights. The United States *has* adopted civil and political human rights, albeit with reservations, claiming that these rights are "primary." Over the years, US resistance to economic and social rights has yielded increasingly untenable results— including, as Dominique noted, normalizing people living in the street. Some, like President Reagan, have even called it a choice, as if homelessness were itself an exercise of personal freedom.

It wasn't always this way.

Decades ago, the United States helped lead the world in defining human rights as embracing *both* economic rights *and* civil rights. In 1941, as the country was coming out of the Great Depression and on the brink of entering World War II, President Franklin D. Roosevelt set out a vision for democracy centered on freedom of speech, freedom of religion, freedom from want, and freedom from fear. Articulated in what is now known as his "four freedoms" speech, it informed the joint vision of the United States and the United Kingdom for a postwar world that held civil and economic rights to be as inseparable as they were fundamental.[9]

FDR reiterated the interdependence of these rights in his 1944 State of the Union address. Noting that civil rights were inadequate "to assure us equality," he called for a "second bill of rights" that also protected economic rights, including the "right to a decent home."[10]

Just before World War II ended, FDR died unexpectedly, but many of his views are reflected in the founding documents of the United Nations.[11] Created in June 1945, a few months before the war's official end that September, the UN's mission was to help prevent future wars, protect human rights, and promote international collaboration.[12] Eleanor Roosevelt, FDR's widow and a political leader in her own right, chaired the UN committee charged with drafting the new organization's foundational document, the Universal Declaration of Human Rights, which bears the marks of US leadership.[13]

Beginning with the assertion that "all human beings are born free and equal in dignity and rights," the Declaration lays out a broad vision encompassing civil, political, economic, social, and cultural rights, including passages that recall FDR's "second bill of rights."[14] Article 25, Section 1 specifically provides that "everyone has the right to a standard of living adequate for the health and well-being of himself and of his family, including . . . housing . . . and the right to security in the event of unemployment, sickness, disability, widowhood, old age or other lack of livelihood in circumstances beyond his control."[15] Also included are personal responsibilities, and the obligation to respect the rights and freedoms of others. Placing individuals squarely within their community, with duties to it, the Declaration exhorts all people to "act towards one another in a spirit of brotherhood."

The UN General Assembly adopted the Declaration on December 10, 1948, with the details to be spelled out by treaty. The goal was for a single accord, but Cold War politics interfered: The Declaration's civil and political rights were identified with the West, while its economic, social, and cultural rights were associated with the East, and drafting a single treaty that combined both sets of rights became fraught with that tension. The result was two separate treaties, adopted by the UN in 1966, to implement the Declaration.[16] The International Covenant on Economic, Social and Cultural Rights covers a full range of economic, social and cultural rights, such as the right to food, health care, and adequate housing.[17] The International Covenant on Civil and Political Rights includes protections like the right to vote and to be free from arbitrary arrest and detention.[18]

The treaties became effective in 1976, after thirty-five nations had ratified them. President Jimmy Carter signed them both the following year.[19] Noting that "these covenants express values in which the people of my country have believed for a long time," Carter seemed to have little interest in distinguishing between the two sets of rights.[20]

The Senate saw things differently: It ratified the covenant on civil rights in 1992, making it officially part of US law, albeit with "reservations."[21] The Senate has not yet ratified the economic rights treaty, instead promoting the view that civil rights are primary.

But it's a key human rights principle that all these rights are indivisible and interdependent.[22] Civil and political rights cannot be freely exercised when basic material needs are unaddressed, and economic, social, and cultural rights cannot be fully realized without civil and political rights. FDR had made exactly this point in his 1944 State of the Union address when he argued that "necessitous men are not free men" and emphasized that "true individual freedom cannot exist without economic security and independence."[23]

The Reverend Martin Luther King Jr., while widely known for his calls for racial justice, consistently linked civil rights to economic justice.[24] In a 1967 address calling for "genuine equality," he argued that "we have moved from the era of civil rights to the era of human rights."[25] In a speech delivered weeks before his assassination in April 1968, he was clear about the difficulty of achieving that genuine equality: "It's much easier to guarantee the right to vote than it is to guarantee the right to live in sanitary, decent housing conditions."[26]

Sometimes called "positive" rights, economic rights impose an affirmative obligation on governments to act. This action need not be immediate—economic rights are supposed to be realized "progressively" according to a country's abilities. A wealthy country such as the United States should be able to realize basic economic rights much more quickly than a less affluent nation. Civil and political rights, in contrast, protect individuals from arbitrary government action. Sometimes called "negative" rights, they proscribe action and are supposed to be implemented immediately. Whether these rights are actually different is debatable: It may simply be a matter of semantics. FDR made that point with his formulation "freedom from want."[27]

Decades later, Dominique Walker saw the link clearly. When they were homeless, she said, "my children weren't able to be really free."[28]

Once they moved into the house, "they were always smiling and running around and being free."

Letting their imaginations roam, Dominique's kids decorated a shared room with drawings. "And that's how all parents want their children to be," she added, "just to be children and to have some sort of stability and everyday structured environment where it's not changing every single night."[29]

"Is Housing a Human Right?"

In 1993, the UN explicitly affirmed the indivisibility and interdependence of all human rights in a new declaration adopted by consensus.[30] Civil and political rights could not be separated from economic and social rights—they were all "interdependent," in the language of human rights law—and all had to be honored. Bill Clinton had just taken office that January, and the United States was among the nations affirming this commitment.

Despite this seemingly auspicious start, just a few years later the Clinton administration actively sought to undermine a key economic right—the human right to housing. For US advocates working to end homelessness, fighting the administration's efforts would be the start of our ongoing campaign to win recognition of this right here at home.

In the early 1990s, housing as a human right was a new idea to many US advocates. Then, in 1995, a small group of advocates were invited to a European conference on homelessness in Madrid, where we spoke about the US situation and learned about the issues in Europe. Posted outside a door in the conference venue was a sign asking: "Is housing a right?" It was for a session on the topic.

Our international colleagues were well-versed in making the case that housing is a right. To us the idea was intriguing—and exciting. The biggest cause of homelessness was—and still is—the lack of affordable housing. The biggest obstacle to ending it was that the resources to fund housing assistance were dramatically insufficient to meet the need. Funding for low-income housing has always been "discretionary," as in subject to the annual whims of Congress. It's explicitly *not* tied to people's needs for housing, no matter how dire. Aid can be cut at any time and competes with many other more powerful interests jockeying for congressional funding. Advocates representing poor people often lack the traditional tools of political power—such as money—which makes winning sufficient increased resources a steep, almost insurmountable uphill battle. A human right to housing, if we could make the case for it in the United States, could add important leverage.

American advocates had argued for a right to housing for years, looking to existing federal statutes and other US laws for a way to piece one together, never finding a fully satisfactory solution. But framing housing as a *human right* brought in an entire legal system—international human rights law—that embraced this right, as well as other economic rights, including work, food, and health. This framework explicitly cuts through the binary of positive and negative rights, asserting that all rights are indivisible and interrelated. It posits that ensuring people's economic and social rights is essential to the exercise of their civil and political rights, and to their ability to contribute to their community.

In the human rights framework, housing is not primarily a commodity from which a few can profit regardless of the impact on the larger community. Housing is instead viewed and prioritized as serving a universal human need. Human rights concepts are based on a worldview that centers human dignity, treating all people as worthy, and makes a commitment to meet their needs.

Housing as a human right was part of the worldview embedded in FDR's proposal for a "second bill of rights" in 1944, which fused civil and political rights with economic and social rights. Yet while FDR's formulation laid the foundation for international human rights law, it wasn't enshrined in US law. FDR himself claimed that the nation had already accepted the principles he articulated, and his New Deal programs reflected some of them. Years later, President Carter explicitly recognized them as basic American values. But they were never legally defined as rights in this country.[31]

Of course, when Ronald Reagan entered office in 1981, he put forth a radically different worldview: People had to pull themselves up by their bootstraps, even if they couldn't afford boots. His administration drove policies to enact that philosophy, cutting funding for social programs.

By 1996, many of Reagan's ideas had been accepted and become mainstream. President Clinton himself played a central role in entrenching them with campaign promises to reverse "dependency" by "end[ing] welfare as we know it."

So it was disappointing but not too surprising to advocates that the Clinton administration continued that legacy by fighting to remove recognition of the human right to housing in a UN conference on the topic.

"THE RIGHT TO ADEQUATE HOUSING SHOULD BE DELETED"

The UN headquarters in New York City were buzzing with activity in early 1996. Preparations were underway for Habitat II, an upcoming international conference with two themes: "adequate housing for all" and "sustainable human settlements." A small group of US housing and homelessness advocates had been invited to participate.

This would be the second UN conference on housing. Habitat I, held in Vancouver in 1976, had brought together government officials from around the globe. Decrying then-current living conditions in many parts of the world, the conference concluded by calling on all governments to take action, including fulfilling the human right to adequate housing.[32] Twenty years after this first step, Habitat II would be held in Istanbul, Turkey, in June 1996. This conference would be different: In addition to governments, it would also include nongovernmental entities. Advocacy groups—such as the National Homelessness Law Center— could participate.[33]

That's how we found ourselves at the New York headquarters of the UN in February 1996, at the start of round three of a lengthy process leading up to the conference itself. Our small group of housing and homelessness advocates had come to participate—and to hold our government accountable. We soon discovered that the United States was creating a major controversy at the gathering. Our first order of business would be to protest our own government's position.

At issue was the phrase "human right to housing" in the draft document to be presented for adoption at the world conference. While many of those involved considered the right to housing *the* most important issue to be addressed at Habitat II, the United States was insisting that *no language* be included suggesting that housing was a human right. A coalition of groups, including ours, held a press conference to highlight a joint public letter to President Clinton. We asked how the United States could "maintain its credibility as a defender of international law if it rejects a right that has been recognized since the 1948 Universal Declaration of Human Rights?"[34]

We were new to international human rights advocacy, but we'd teamed up with established human rights organizations, including Amnesty International, Human Rights Watch, and the National Council of Churches, to protest the administration's efforts to undermine the right to housing. The larger groups knew the human rights world—but we knew the reality on the ground. Homeless and poor Americans urgently needed to have their human right to housing recognized by their own country.

The UN had spelled out the key elements of the right to housing in 1991.[35] One of the most important factors was affordability: Housing is not actually adequate if it costs so much that it compromises your ability to enjoy your other human rights. If you are paying so much for housing that you can't afford food, health care, childcare, or other basic needs, one of your basic human rights is being violated.[36] By that measure, millions of Americans were—and are—having their human right to housing infringed daily: They are homeless or on the brink, skipping meals or medications to make rent. In 1996, over 17 percent of all renters spent *50 percent or more* of their income on rent.[37] By 2022, the figure had climbed to nearly 25 percent of all renters.[38]

Instead of working to address this obvious unfolding crisis, the United States was trying to erase even the words "right to housing" from the document to be discussed at a world conference *on the right to housing*. At an earlier meeting, the Clinton administration had made clear that while it "endorsed the goal of shelter for all and rights of nondiscriminatory access to housing, financing and other conditions that support adequate housing, the right to adequate housing should be deleted."[39] By the time we arrived in New York in early 1996, pressure from the UN and advocates had pushed the administration to budge—a little.[40]

The United States was now willing to include the words "right to housing" in the official conference document—with two-and-a half pages of caveats. Our government apparently acknowledged that housing was included in the "right to an adequate standard of living," recognized by the Universal Declaration of Human Rights, but denied it had any independent meaning itself.[41] Debate raged in the windowless rooms and corridors of the basement of UN headquarters as an informal drafting committee considered revisions and compromises. We crafted language and arguments, confronted our government officials, and lobbied for the right to housing . . . but by the end of almost two weeks, no agreement could be reached.

Then, less than a month before the start of the global conference, came a breakthrough.[42] In the face of continued pressure from the EU, as well as our group of American advocates, the administration agreed to include in the official conference document a call for "the progressive realization of the right to adequate housing as a component of existing rights." It also explicitly recognized that "all human rights—civil, cultural, economic, political and social—are universal, indivisible, and interdependent and interrelated."[43]

Not only had the right to housing *not* been deleted—it had been affirmed.[44] This gave us hope.

A Global Call to Action—an Opening for US Progress?

At the conference itself, the action centered on finalizing the "Habitat Agenda," the document to be discussed and adopted by the national governments that gathered at the June 1996 conference in Istanbul—including the United States. The final version endorsed the human right to adequate housing and issued a global call to action: In line with the right itself, the agenda urged governments to implement it progressively, over time, by adopting policies to protect and promote.[45]

In keeping with the US position, the text stated adequate and affordable housing was to be achieved mainly through market forces. But thanks to advocates, it also affirmed the need for governments to *regulate* markets, and to assist vulnerable groups who were often excluded from them. We managed to include language demanding attention be paid to the needs of inadequately housed and homeless people, including supportive services in addition to housing.

The agenda also included a prohibition on laws penalizing homeless people for their status. This provision was sponsored by the US delegation at the request of advocates, with a goal of addressing the growing criminalization of homelessness in the country.[46] The agenda isn't legally binding, but it is a statement of global consensus—a kind of "soft law"—that can influence policies and even be cited by courts. The US delegation's push for the provision rejecting the criminalization of homelessness was the first time the federal government had taken such a public position on the issue. It seemed like an important, albeit small, step forward.[47]

Returning home from the UN conference, we saw an opening for further progress. Despite the spread of municipal laws criminalizing homelessness, some major cities had held back, and we hoped to reverse the trend in those that were enforcing them.[48] Riding the momentum of the Habitat II conference, four national advocacy groups, including the Law Center, created an initiative to follow up on the Habitat Agenda in the United States. Funded by HUD, for over a year the initiative—called Meeting America's Housing Needs—brought together key organizations across the country, including local governments, to develop strategies to implement the goals embraced at the gathering.[49]

Closing the Door: Cuts, Criminalization, Don't Say "Right to Housing"

The post-conference opening for reform proved to be short-lived.

Newt Gingrich's Contract with America, first introduced in 1994, had continued to gain steam, dominating national policy debate. Cuts to social welfare programs, including aid to homeless people, advanced as part of the Gingrich plan to shrink the federal government. Clinton's campaign to "end welfare as we know it" at best gave cover to right-wing ideologues and at worst reinforced their rhetoric.

Either way, after two failed veto attempts, in August 1996 Clinton signed legislation that repealed the long-standing federal cash assistance program for poor children and families. It had been in place since the New Deal. The program—whose paltry benefits had scarcely been updated to conform to rising costs—had at least created legal rights for low-income families. Cuts to housing programs continued apace, public housing was increasingly privatized, and low-income units were demolished. Two years later, new federal legislation prohibited the construction of any new public housing and eliminated the requirement that any destroyed units had to be replaced. The surge of demolitions of public housing launched in the 1990s would result in the net loss of some 250,000 public housing units by 2018.[50]

Federal cuts and policy changes meant fewer affordable housing options and shrinking income sources, putting more people out on the streets around the country. The response of cities was to enact laws forcing them out of sight—instead of creating housing.[51] By 2002, a Law Center survey of fifty-seven cities found that every city, without exception, had *both* some type of public space restriction *and* insufficient shelter or transitional bed space to meet the need. As detailed earlier, people were increasingly—and literally—pushed out of both indoor and outdoor options, their very existence made illegal, and after 9/11 the situation only deteriorated further.[52] Dialing up security measures and the police presence on the street meant more harassment, move-along orders, and arrests, while increasing identification requirements even as unhoused individuals were more likely than ever to have lost their IDs in a sweep or eviction made it even harder for people to claim what little assistance they were lawfully entitled to.[53]

Nevertheless, when the United States had to report, along with other countries, on its progress toward meeting the Habitat Agenda goals, the George W. Bush administration was upbeat. At Istanbul +5, the UN meeting held five years after the Habitat II conference, the administration focused on increases in homeownership. It claimed this as progress, even while also noting the parallel and "exponential" growth of predatory lending and consequent increase in foreclosures. Over the same period, the administration boasted, federal funding for shelter and other services had increased by about a third, from $823 million in 1996 to $1.12 billion in 2001.[54] Apparently, the Bush administration felt that emergency shelters were an appropriate solution for people who had lost their homes. The administration made no mention of the over one million families on waiting lists for HUD-assisted housing, with an average wait time of nearly three years.[55]

Ahead of the Istanbul +5 meeting, Miloon Kothari, a housing rights expert, had been appointed the first UN Special Rapporteur on the Right to Adequate Housing.[56] Created in 2000 by the UN Commission on Human Rights as an unpaid position, the Special Rapporteur serves as the top UN official on the human right to housing. As reported at the time, a senior US State Department lawyer approached the new Special Rapporteur at a meeting during the Istanbul +5 review and "told him bluntly that the US government would prefer it if he did not mention housing as a right, let alone as a human right, in his address to delegates."[57]

Whatever progress we had extracted from the Clinton administration, modest though it was, seemed to be lost. Our government was doubling down on its effort to undermine the human right to housing.

A Movement for the Human Right to Housing Grows in the United States

George W. Bush was in the White House and Republicans held sway in both houses of Congress. Clinton's anti-welfare campaign had narrowed any difference between the parties, at least on issues of economic justice. Prospects for reform seemed bleak. But with criminalization expanding, housing shrinking, and even shelter insufficient, we needed bold action.

Advocates from around the country gathered in 2003 in Washington, D.C., to debate the possibility of a national campaign for the human right to housing here in the United States. The Law Center had joined with an international housing rights group to convene the meeting, and the dozens of groups that came included those that had traveled to Istanbul in 1996.[58] In many national policy circles, the idea was met with skepticism if not outright derision. The notion of a human right to housing in America seemed quixotic, even laughable. But people who were or had been homeless knew firsthand that their human rights had been violated, and to them the idea that housing is a fundamental human right made immediate sense—just as it would make sense, years later, to Dominique Walker and her fellow Moms 4 Housing.

By the time of our 2003 national meeting, grassroots groups in various parts of the country had already begun advocating for economic human rights, including the human right to housing. Our gathering spoke to a need that was already evident—and growing. After much discussion, the participating groups resolved to continue working together. A new national campaign would support local initiatives and help catalyze more of them. We were part of what was then a burgeoning movement.[59]

In Philadelphia, a formerly homeless mother and other grassroots advocates had launched the Poor People's Economic Human Rights Campaign in 1998 to advocate for those rights in the United States. In Los Angeles, the LA Community Action Network (LACAN), a group of homeless and formerly homeless people, had come together in 1999 to fight criminalization, the most immediate issue facing its membership. By 2002, they'd added the human right to housing to their mission. Like others, LACAN saw the need not just to fight being penalized for living on the street, but also to demand an alternative place to be—housing.

Members of the Chicago group that had traveled to the Habitat II conference—the Chicago Coalition for the Homeless—helped fuel the national campaign we launched in 2003, taking the fight for the human right to housing to their community. More than 6,000 people were estimated to be homeless each day in the Windy City at that time, according to official estimates. Local experts calculated the true *daily* number to be over 20,000—which, given the fluctuating nature of homelessness, came to more than 70,000 who were homeless at some point over that year.[60] The entire county surrounding Chicago was facing an affordable housing crisis, with almost 200,000 residents who were both extremely poor and paying over 35 percent of their income in rent, putting them at high risk of homelessness. Any unexpected expense could tip them over the edge.[61]

Advocates were pushing a proposal in the Illinois legislature to levy a ten-dollar state tax on real estate filings, hoping to fund subsidies for 1,600 to 2,000 units.[62] A modest request, given the enormity of the need, but it faced opposition from major political players. Armed with an understanding of international human rights, the Chicago group and their allies convinced the Cook County Council to pass a resolution affirming its commitment to the human right to housing and supporting the proposed state housing subsidy program.[63]

The 2004 resolution helped bolster support for the proposal, which passed the state legislature the following year, creating an important new program to help low-income people afford to rent housing in the private market. Given the scale of the crisis, it was just a thimbleful of water dripped on to a raging housefire. But it helped strengthen the call for the human right to housing.

"WHAT ARE POOR PEOPLE TO DO?"

While advocates were fighting for subsidies that would help them rent private housing, residents of Chicago's remaining public housing were fighting to stay in their homes. In late 1999, Mayor Richard M. Daley had launched a "Ten Year Plan for Transformation" to demolish public housing and develop new mixed-income housing. Decaying after years of neglect and funding cuts, the public housing at issue was downtown—a prime area for developers—driving the city's rush to tear it down. Cabrini-Green, a large public housing project, was among those on the chopping block.

Carol Steele and other Cabrini-Green residents formed the Coalition to Protect Public Housing to fight the demolition. When American officials refused to listen, they invited Miloon Kothari, the recently appointed UN special rapporteur for the right to housing, to visit Chicago, tour public housing, and meet with residents. As Carol put it, "Mr. Kothari told us that people around the world have perceptions of America that there is no hunger, no homeless, no poverty here. Yet, when he was in Chicago, Mr. Kothari told us that at Cabrini he saw first-hand that we have the same problems he sees around the world. Forced evictions. Huge housing shortages. A rollback of government services."[64]

A few months after the special rapporteur's visit, the coalition and its allies made a formal request to the Inter-American Commission on Human Rights for a hearing on US policies that contravened the human right to housing. The commission held its first hearing on the right to housing the following March, in 2005, at its headquarters at the Organization of American States in Washington, D.C., Carol Steele testified, as president of the Coalition to Protect Public Housing Residents, along with the Law Center and other members of the national campaign.[65]

Carol described the impact of demolishing public housing in a city with a severe affordable housing crisis. By 2005, some 16,000 public housing units had been taken down—and fewer than 1,500 replacements built. More than 90 percent of those displaced were Black, mostly women and children. Once forced out, they had few options. The Chicago metro area had a shortfall of over 153,000 low-income housing units. The waiting list for public housing was so long—more than 57,000 people—that it had been closed to new applicants since 2000. Few landlords accepted vouchers, especially in the high-opportunity neighborhoods touted by Mayor Daley. Carol asked the commission: "What are poor people to do?"[66]

Instead of landing in newly built units or "better" neighborhoods, some former residents were showing up at shelters. One study had found that from January to June 2003, 172 families moved directly from public housing to shelters. Carol told the story of one displaced woman, whom she called Mary, who was given vouchers to find replacement housing for herself and her children. Unable to find stable, safe housing in the gentrifying city, she moved twelve times. Mary had a hard time getting and maintaining work, while her children changed schools seven times.[67]

A few months before the hearing, on December 10—the anniversary of the 1948 signing of the UN's Universal Declaration of Human Rights, commemorated globally as Human Rights Day—Carol's group held a rally outside their building calling for the human right to housing. Kothari had sent the coalition a statement of solidarity, warning that what was taking place in Chicago was also happening across the country and the world, as governments dismantled publicly supported affordable, nonmarket housing—often called "social housing" in other countries—and cut housing subsidies in favor of the market and privatization.[68]

Chicago's public housing residents knew the odds were against them, according to Carol, and their assessment proved accurate. Announcing his plan to the residents of Cabrini-Green in 1997, Mayor Daley had promised that all the families living in the public housing complex's 3,606 apartments would be moved into brand-new units. But as late as 2021, fewer than 1,000 of the demolished units had been replaced, and many of those were single-room studios, too small for families.[69]

The hearing, and the activism of Carol's grassroots coalition, were part of growing efforts by US advocates to invoke human rights norms. In our increasingly hostile political climate at home, engaging international human rights bodies to pressure our own government seemed like a strategy worth pursuing. It would be a long game—one that's still playing out.[70]

HOUSING RIGHTS ARE CIVIL RIGHTS ARE HUMAN RIGHTS

National groups such as the Law Center were supporting grassroots activists while also reaching out to human rights leaders.

A key figure was High Commissioner on Human Rights Louise Arbour, who was the top UN official overseeing the organization's human rights program. Appointed to her UN position in 2004, she'd been a Justice on the Canadian Supreme Court. Arbour had also served as chief prosecutor for the International Criminal Tribunals for the former Yugoslavia and for Rwanda. She was used to seeing human rights violations.

In June 2006, Arbour was in Washington, D.C., and met with a small group of US advocates working to hold our government accountable to its human rights commitments. We were sitting around an oval table in a downtown conference room, afternoon sun streaming in through the large windows, and we went around the table introducing ourselves and our organizations, briefly describing our work. A range of activists were in the room, working on issues like prisoners' rights, conditions at Guantanamo, and the juvenile death penalty.

When my turn came, I described the rise of the criminalization of homelessness across the country. I gave examples of what was then a troubling new trend: laws targeting not only homeless people but also those who were trying to help them. In Las Vegas, almost 15,000 city residents were homeless, with only 400 available emergency shelter beds,[71] and only 5 percent of homes affordable—using federal guidelines—for *working professionals*, let alone extremely poor people.[72] The mayor of Las Vegas, who seemed determined to wage war on the city's unhoused and poor residents, had just signed a new law that made it a crime to offer food to "the indigent."[73]

Hearing this, High Commissioner Arbour put her head in her hands and laid it on the table in disbelief.

A few weeks later, we made our case more formally. The UN Human Rights Committee was reviewing US compliance with the International Covenant on Civil and Political Rights, which the United States had signed and ratified in 1992. Like all countries that have ratified the treaty, the United States is reviewed every four years and must submit a report as part of the review. The George W. Bush administration's most recent report at the time—submitted seven years past the due date—had included only two passing mentions of homelessness, with no discussion.[74]

Fortunately, we had an official way to challenge it. After a government submits their mandatory report, the UN Committee holds a hearing to review it with a representative of that government. Ahead of this hearing, the process allows nongovernmental organizations (NGOs) to submit their own presentations, known as "shadow reports," to give the Committee more context and information. The Law Center was one of some 140 NGOs that submitted shadow reports to the UN, detailing our concerns about the human rights of homeless and poor Americans.

During the July 2006 hearing, a member of the committee used our report to ask the US representative about the deleterious, sometimes fatal, impact of homelessness on health. The committee member cited twenty-one homeless people who had died during a heat wave in Arizona the previous year. Failing to prevent these deaths, he said, was a violation of article 6 of the covenant on civil and political rights, which provides that "no one shall be arbitrarily deprived of his life."[75]

The US representative, Wan Kim, assistant attorney general for civil rights in the Department of Justice, may have been caught off guard. He replied that "housing rights are basic important rights guaranteed at both the state and federal level," and that, "every person is entitled to shelter as a basic need."[76]

Kim went on to qualify his remarks, saying that "obviously we cannot house every single person. But we are taking steps toward that goal."[77] Apparently, even the official US representative found it hard to imagine that his government failed to protect the basic right to housing—or at least shelter. But, of course, his statement wasn't true.[78]

Nor was the UN Human Rights Committee convinced by the US response. Its final report zeroed in on a particularly stark fact: While Black Americans constituted just 12 percent of the population, they represented 50 percent of homeless people. Citing articles in the International Covenant on Civil and Political Rights that prohibit discrimination, the Committee admonished the United States to "take measures, including adequate and adequately implemented policies, to bring an end to such de facto and historically generated racial discrimination." It was the first time the Committee has directly addressed the problem of the discriminatory impact of homelessness in the United States.[79]

US advocates were obviously encouraged by this. As conditions continued to deteriorate at home, we increasingly used human rights arguments and UN mechanisms to put pressure on our government.

Homeless While Black

The following year, 2007, the Bush administration submitted another report to a different UN committee. The Committee to Eliminate Racial Discrimination was reviewing US compliance with the Covenant to Eliminate Racial Discrimination, signed in 1966 by President Lyndon B. Johnson and ratified by the Senate almost thirty years later, in 1994.[80] The US report painted a sunny picture of the administration's efforts to fight discrimination, including in the sale and rental of housing and in mortgage lending. It also touted its "announcement" of $1.27 billion in "homeless assistance." The report didn't mention that almost all of these funds had been previously authorized by Congress as part of the long-standing McKinney-Vento Homeless Assistance Act. Only $35 million came from a new initiative of the administration, and even that wasn't new money—the entire $35 million had been cobbled together by three agencies out of unused funds to provide housing and social services toward the official goal of ending "chronic homelessness" in ten years.[81]

Also not included in this feel-good report was the true magnitude of the need that this initiative was supposed to address. In the previous year alone, over 70 percent of major US cities had reported a 6 percent increase in requests for emergency shelter. On average, 14 percent of all requests were going unmet—for homeless families, the figure was 32 percent.[82] This left many people with no option but to live in public places. Because Black people were disproportionately represented in the homeless population, as the UN's Human Rights Committee had noted just the previous year, those forced to live on the streets were also likely to be people of color.

While the Bush administration was crowing about its progress, Otis Howard, a homeless Black man living on the streets of Los Angeles, was smoking a cigarette as police officers watched him from across the street. When he tapped his ash onto the sidewalk, the officers rushed over, handcuffed him, and ticketed him for littering.[83] Around the same time, Leonard Woods, a poor Black man who used a wheelchair, was waiting to cross a different LA street. Once on the other side, he was cited for jaywalking—because he'd waited on the street for the light to change, just off the curb. Almost certainly unable to pay the fines they received or appear in court to contest them, Woods and Howard would risk jail time as the unpaid citations turned into warrants for their arrest.[84]

And in the background, cuts to funding for low-income housing programs, pushed by the Bush administration, meant even fewer options for people like Otis and Leonard.[85]

FORECLOSED: NO HOME, NOT EVEN A STREET

In 2007, the foreclosure crisis and concurrent recession were well underway, and the racial disparities were clearer than ever. Just as those who had been targeted for predatory subprime mortgages were disproportionately Black, so too were those then forced out of their homes by foreclosure. Homeowners weren't the only ones affected. Many renters were living in properties that, often unbeknownst to them, were being foreclosed on.[86] As people lost their jobs to the recession and their homes to foreclosure, many became unhoused, fueling a tidal wave of mass homelessness to rival the initial explosion of the early and mid-1980s.[87]

Desperate people scrambled for help, but long-inadequate shelters and other support systems were overwhelmed, driving more people to the streets. Encampments, already on the rise by the mid-2000s, grew faster and faster. A national survey by the Law Center conservatively estimated that from 2007 to 2017 encampments grew by over *1,300 percent*.[88] Expelled from their homes, people were setting up tents on sidewalks, parks, and other public places. Many cities responded by doubling down on criminalizing the public presence of homeless people.

Public housing was being destroyed to make way for more profitable luxury developments. Homes bought with federally insured mortgages were being foreclosed on and sold to investors looking to flip them for a profit. Public space too was increasingly regulated to benefit private businesses, and more and more business improvement districts (BIDs) cropped up to lean on local governments. Privately funded but publicly sanctioned, BIDs encouraged cities to pass laws to keep their unhoused residents out, claiming they drove off customers and were bad for business. As laws making it a crime for homeless people to live in public multiplied exponentially, otherwise public spaces—such as sidewalks, parks, and plazas—were increasingly forbidden to people with no other place to be.[89]

Emboldened by their successes and the increased criminalization of homelessness, some businesses simply took matters into their own hands.

In Atlanta, one notorious effort surfaced in 2008. Rufus Terrill, owner of a downtown bar, built a three-hundred-pound remote-controlled machine to patrol nearby streets and alleys. Dubbed the "bum bot," it included a water cannon, spotlight, and a loudspeaker that Terrill used to shout at people sleeping or resting in public: "You're trespassing. That's private property. Move on." Blasts from the water cannon would emphasize the message as needed.[90]

Previously public space was increasingly under the control of private interests. This was just one horrific result.

"Simply Unacceptable"—or Is It?

In this bleak time, the historic inauguration of President Barak Obama in January 2009 inspired millions with excitement and hope for the future.

Among them was Edgar Auld, a resident of the Next Step Shelter in Honolulu. He'd never voted before, but a voter-registration drive—as well as Obama's candidacy—had spurred him and some forty other shelter residents to do so. Thirty-seven years old at the time, Edgar had been laid off months earlier by a stonework company and, unable to find another job, he'd sought refuge at the shelter. He and his fellow residents weren't necessarily expecting anything from the president-elect. But they felt it was important that their voices be heard. And, Edgar said, Obama's election gave him strength during a difficult time: "It inspires me to have hope that you can never give up, just keep trying and trying and eventually something has to turn over."[91]

Obama's election had also given hope to activists championing many different issues. Those of us working for the human right to housing had taken special note of Obama's comment that health care should be a right, not a privilege, during the second presidential debate in October 2008, just before the election. We were further heartened during the first meeting of the US Interagency Council on Homelessness under his administration, when Obama issued the statement that "it is simply unacceptable for individuals, children, families, and our nation's veterans to be faced with homelessness in this country."

It seemed like a promising sign.[92]

The following year, 2010, the United States was reviewed by the UN Human Rights Council for compliance with a full range of human rights obligations, in a process known as the Universal Periodic Review (UPR). Every member country in the UN is subject to the UPR every four years. The review evaluated compliance with the Universal Declaration on Human Rights—including the right to adequate housing, as part of the right to an adequate standard of living. The US government had to prepare a report assessing its compliance, the creation of which required formal "consultations" with NGOs to inform the report. The UPR Planning Committee, formed by US NGOs to coordinate our efforts, prioritized including people who were directly affected.[93]

More than one thousand community members, spanning multiple issue areas, participated in ten consultations in cities around the country. The country was in the midst of a housing crisis caused by predatory mortgages, foreclosures, attacks on public housing, and the Great Recession. By this time, the Law Center and our allies had trained many US homelessness and housing advocates in using international processes to advocate for the human right to housing, and they came out in force.[94] One key government official remarked, "We have heard more about housing in these sessions than you would believe. If I had to pick the number one issue brought to the US, it would be housing."[95]

Despite all the community input they received, the government's official report to the Human Rights Council included no recognition of the right to housing. Instead, it repeated its ambiguous commitment to ending homelessness and the "great progress" it was making. Citing questionable numbers from the most recent HUD count, it claimed homelessness was declining for veterans, families, and disabled people. The report pointed out that homeless children's right to education was protected by federal law—but failed to mention that the law, the McKinney-Vento Act, had been passed in 1987 and still wasn't consistently enforced over twenty years later. The government also noted that the then-new National Housing Trust Fund was expected to begin distributing funds—six years later, in 2016. The National Housing Trust Fund was supposed to increase and preserve affordable housing for very low-income and homeless individuals, but the year it finally went into effect it only offered $174 million in funding, a small fraction of what was needed.[96]

It was a disappointing showing by the Obama administration. A week later, it offered a tiny bit more: A top administration official, speaking at an event commemorating the seventieth anniversary of FDR's Four Freedoms speech, included this comment in his remarks: "As Martin Luther King once noted, an integrated lunch counter doesn't help the person who can't afford to eat there. Therefore, we will work . . . to adopt . . . resolutions at the UN that speak to the issues of economic, social, and cultural rights and are consistent with our own laws and policies."[97] Hardly a ringing endorsement; it was a careful, caveated, and less-than-official hint at possible future acceptance of economic rights.

But the consultations had led to much more organizing for the human right to housing, and laid the groundwork for future advocacy.

PROFIT OVER PEOPLE: HOUSING IS COMMODIFIED

For all their early rhetoric, the Obama administration was moving backward.

As people lost their jobs to the recession and foreclosures swept the country, private equity saw an opportunity for profit. The trend, already well underway, gained greater momentum as the White House created incentives for institutional investors to buy foreclosed properties that had been insured by the federal government; they had become unwanted federal property after the banks foreclosed on them. Between 2011 and 2017, private equity firms and other large investors would spend $36 billion to acquire more than 200,000 homes in ailing markets across the country.[98] The result was a massive transfer of wealth away from the former homeowners—disproportionately members of minoritized communities—to private equity.[99]

While private property was shifting from individuals to for-profit investors, a parallel trend was affecting public property. A new administration directive to "freeze the footprint" of federal property ownership morphed into a commitment to "reduce" it. The federal government officially entered the game of selling off public property—acquired with taxpayer dollars—to private developers. Just like that, instead of being used to meet urgent public needs, public resources were converted to private profit.[100] The selloff was despite—and often in blatant violation of—Title V of the McKinney-Vento Homeless Assistance Act, the law that gave a right of first refusal to nonprofit groups who could use vacant federal properties to house and serve homeless people.[101]

The contrast between rhetoric and reality, politics and human need, was not lost on Deborah Burton, a Black mother and grandmother who had experienced homelessness in Los Angeles. After losing her job and then her home, Deborah considered herself fortunate to have spent only a little over a year living in shelters before finding a subsidized unit. She knew many others were unhoused much longer. The experience led her to activism with LACAN, the grassroots organization formed by directly impacted and allied city residents. In 2010, it inspired her to go even further—Deborah went to Geneva, Switzerland, where the United States was being reviewed by the UN Human Rights Council for compliance with its human rights obligations. She presented testimony on behalf of LACAN.[102]

At the time, between 50,000 and 80,000 people were homeless in Los Angeles. Black residents were by far the most impacted—1 in 18 Black residents was homeless, compared to 1 in 270 White residents. In the middle of this housing emergency, Deborah noted, the local public housing authority had just introduced a plan to sell every unit of public housing in the city. As she explained in her testimony to the human rights body, Deborah had come to Geneva because "it is urgent that more people understand that the US is *not* a model for the right to housing and that our government is doing everything it can to remove itself even more from their obligation. I also want people to know that thousands like me are fighting every day to push our local, state, and federal governments to acknowledge our rights to housing."[103]

Traveling to Geneva to testify is just one example of how US advocates were becoming more adept at using human rights arguments and processes. We were also increasingly urging human rights monitors to visit and see US violations for themselves—and publicize their findings to the world. It was another way to exert pressure on our own government.

In 2011, Catarina de Albuquerque, a UN special rapporteur, visited the United States on an official mission to assess compliance with the human right to water and sanitation.[104] As she noted in her report on the visit, in the United States there is near-universal access to clean drinking water. However, she emphasized, a human rights analysis must include the poorest, most marginalized and excluded. Among those she visited were homeless residents of an encampment in Sacramento, California.[105]

Tim, a member of the group, called himself their "sanitation technician." There were no public restrooms nearby, so Tim created a contraption with a seat and a two-layered plastic bag underneath. Every week,

Tim collected bags full of human waste—weighing from 130 to 230 pounds—and carried them on his bicycle to the nearest public restroom, several miles away. There he waited for a toilet to become available, emptied the bags, put them into another bag, then tied it off before throwing them all into the garbage. He cleaned his hands with water and lemon.[106]

The special rapporteur's report included a detailed description of the process. It also included Tim's rationale for doing work he acknowledged was difficult. He did it for the community, he said, especially the women. In her report, the UN expert called out the "remarkable contribution of this single human-rights defender," while emphasizing that it in "no way reduces the responsibility of public authorities."

Tim was embodying the essence of what a commitment to human rights means.[107] The contrast with prioritizing profit—at all costs, and despite human need—couldn't have been starker.

"What Happens When Property Rights Conflict with Human Rights?"

Picture the Homeless (PTH), a grassroots group in New York City, followed a similar trajectory to Los Angeles' LACAN. Anthony Williams and Lewis Haggins Jr. had founded PTH in 1989 to fight the city's growing efforts to criminalize the unhoused for living in public places. Composed primarily of homeless and formerly homeless people, the organization soon expanded its mission to embrace the human right to housing.[108] PTH trained its eye on the thousands of properties that were standing vacant across the city while people slept on streets, in shelters, and on the floors and couches of friends and family.

Early on, PTH launched a campaign to force New York City to conduct a census of vacant units. After the city refused, the group did it on their own. They partnered with experts at Hunter College, using Freedom of Information Act requests to gather data from over a dozen city agencies and walking block by block to survey property. PTH was able to cover just one-third of the city in its count but turned up over 3,500 vacant buildings and almost 2,500 vacant lots. In 2012, they published their findings in a report.[109]

All told, the group estimated these unused resources could house just shy of 200,000 people—more than enough for the 40,000-some people then counted as homeless by the city. Most of these properties were privately owned—taxes paid—but kept vacant as investments, waiting for prices to rise or neighborhoods to gentrify to maximize profits. The PTH report often found a ground-floor storefront would be rented for commercial use, bringing in income, while upper-floor residential space was held vacant.[110]

National census data proved the situation in New York City wasn't an anomaly. The researchers confirmed that there were 18.6 million vacant homes around the country. This isn't just enough to house the country's entire unhoused population—it amounts to *five* vacant homes for every homeless person. In New York City, the report noted, the budget for housing was just 63 percent of what it spent on emergency shelter. PTH argued that landlords should not be allowed to keep housing vacant during a housing crisis with people living in shelters and on the streets. Instead of spending money on emergency shelter, which *nobody* thinks can end homelessness, the group asked, why not create a program that combined jobs and housing? Why not hire homeless people to help rehabilitate vacant properties that could then also house them?[111]

But landlords were allowed to leave their properties vacant—even *rent-stabilized* apartments, meant to help keep housing affordable. Not only that, but beginning in 1997, an exception to state laws governing rent-stabilized apartments *encouraged* landlords to do so.[112] Rent stabilization laws limited rent increases, but after a vacancy, landlords were allowed to raise the rent above and beyond those limits, and even to remove them from regulation altogether. These were not mom-and-pop landlords: Most of the city's rent-stabilized units were owned by landlords holding one thousand or more units.[113]

The "vacancy bonus" exception was finally repealed by a change to the law in 2019. Landlords could no longer use a vacancy to raise rents past the limits, but they *could* still keep rent-stabilized units vacant.[114] New York City's big landlords responded by challenging the entire rent stabilization law in court.[115] They argued that it amounted to an unconstitutional "taking" of their property. Basically, they claimed they had an unfettered right to extract as much money as possible from their property—regardless of the impact on their community.[116] The landlord groups claimed they were losing money on the rent-stabilized units. Government data showed this simply wasn't true. Adjusting for inflation, their net operating income had increased 46.6 percent since 1990. On average, an owner of a rent-stabilized property netted over $6 million in 2020 alone.[117]

Two federal courts rejected the landlords' private property–based challenge to the city's rent stabilization law, noting that this law has regulated the otherwise "unforgiving" housing market for over a century. The US Supreme Court let those decisions stand, denying the landlords' request for review.[118] But their challenge crystallized the question: When housing is so unaffordable that people are sleeping on the streets and in shelters, and many more are at risk, what kinds of limits can—and must—be put on private property rights?[119]

"What happens when human rights are in conflict with property rights?" That was how Picture the Homeless framed the dilemma in their report. Underlying it is the question of whether housing is a commodity like any other, to be exploited for maximum profit, as private equity and other institutional investors are increasingly doing. Or is housing a human right—a social good that addresses the universal human need for shelter, that must be protected and regulated to ensure everyone has access to it?

This only raises more questions. If the human right to housing isn't protected by one's government, can those left out on the street while homes stand vacant act to take them over, as Dominique Walker and the other Moms 4 Housing had done? How can our laws and policies be changed to align more closely with human rights norms? Should they protect economic and social rights as well as civil and political rights?

How we choose to answer these questions speaks, ultimately, to what kind of country we want to live in.

"RIGHT TO LIFE WITH DIGNITY": BRINGING THE RIGHTS BACK TOGETHER

Danny said that during the winter of 2023 he'd felt "forgotten. Just brushed aside." He'd started to notice the frostbite in January. Danny was living under a tarp in Denver. He didn't feel safe in the city's congregate shelters, but in any case, they weren't an option. His part-time job cleaning and stocking shelves at a local convenience store kept him at work until midnight, but the shelter required everyone to be in by 5 p.m.

The city opened cold-weather shelters when the temperature dipped to ten degrees or below, and these were open twenty-four hours a day. Danny stayed at them when they were open and he could find a way to get there; volunteers with Denver Mutual Aid were sometimes able to help. Otherwise, he was outside under his tarp. By February, he said, his foot "progressively got worse and worse."

Danny knew the dangers of frostbite and went to urgent care multiple times. He was repeatedly turned away without treatment or medications, other than Oxycontin for the pain. Only when he developed gangrene did he receive lifesaving medical attention—his right leg was amputated below the knee and his left foot had all five toes removed.[120]

Amy Beck, a volunteer with Denver Mutual Aid, helped Danny get to his medical appointments and advocated with the city to connect him to housing. She accompanied him to the hospital to get his stitches removed, and she filmed him on her phone as he sat on the exam room table. He had a hard time speaking, his voice catching as he tried to describe his ordeal over the previous few months. But asked about solutions, Danny was clear and his voice firm. "The solution is housing. . . . Housing will remedy this whole epidemic that we have right now of homelessness that you see everywhere. Housing is the number one solution."[121]

A native Denverite, Danny became homeless after his parents died and he had to leave the apartment they'd lived in for thirty years, the place where he'd grown up. Danny had been on his own for a long time but moved back in with them after his marriage of ten years collapsed. It was nothing acrimonious, he said, it just hadn't worked out. They'd had their own home, he'd had a full-time job, and he supported his wife and her daughter. But he hadn't been able to save much after the separation, so he moved back with his folks. And since his name wasn't on the lease,

Danny became homeless when his parents died—along with his mentally disabled brother, who'd also lived there.[122]

Danny wanted to get his story out, so Amy gave her video from his hospital visit to the local ABC TV station, which did a segment including the clip.[123] The station also interviewed a Denver employee identified as the "encampment response executive" for the city, a position created the previous year. He was responsible for removing what he called "encumbrances." These were the tents, tarps, blankets, and other belongings that people living outside rely on to protect themselves from the elements. The city targeted these critical possessions for removal during its near-constant sweeps.[124]

With a concerned look, the city official said, "Every person on the street has a different need, a different story. . . . There's also the need for the addressing of public health and safety issues that these camps can pose."

According to him, the city had removed almost three tons of trash.[125] He didn't mention that the city provides no trash pickup service, port-a-potties, or security to the site—simple steps that could address the concerns that were urgent for everyone involved. Nor did he mention that the city doesn't provide housing for the encampment residents, which would solve the issues entirely.[126]

The official "encampment response executive" didn't even seem aware that much of what the city considers "trash" is private property, however meager, that serves as essential survival gear.

Following an earlier sweep, in November 2022, a different Denver Mutual Aid volunteer had filmed an interview with Malaki Walker, another unhoused city resident. Malaki stood on an icy sidewalk describing how it felt for him and his partner to repeatedly—systematically—lose virtually everything they owned to sweeps.[127] In the past two weeks, he said, their possessions were seized and trashed eight or nine times—including their tent, essential protection from the bitter cold of the Mile High City. After some of these raids, they were able to get a new tent donated by Denver Mutual Aid. When the advocates were stretched too thin to help, Malaki and his partner had to buy a new one for $200 at Walmart. Going without is not an option in autumn Colorado, with average lows in the twenties and harsher weather always looming.

At the time of the interview, Malaki and his partner had finally lined up housing—but the most recent sweep had robbed them yet again. With the added expense of replacing what the city had stolen, they'd have to wait at least another month to save up Malaki's disability checks to afford the security deposit. Malaki summed up the impossible situation the city had put them in: "They're getting on us for being homeless, and we were about to not be homeless, but now we are because of them."[128]

Malaki's property had been considered "trash" and thrown out by the city—simply because he had no home in which to store it. Even personal property rights are dependent on housing rights.

"DIRECT THREATS TO LIFE"

The International Covenant on Civil and Political Rights, adopted by almost all countries and ratified by the United States in 1992, protects the human right to life. In a human rights context, the "human right to life" includes the duty of nations to "take appropriate measures to address the general conditions in society that may give rise to direct threats to life or prevent individuals from enjoying their right to life with dignity." Listed among the specific examples of such general conditions are "extreme poverty and homelessness." [129]

It's hard to imagine that Danny—and the hundreds of thousands of others who have succumbed to the dangers of living outside on Denver's streets and elsewhere—don't deserve protection under this provision.[130] Sameera Karim, one of the Moms 4 Housing in Oakland, called taking over the vacant house on Magnolia Street "a matter of life or death." Her fellow Mom, Dominique Walker, observed that without a home, her children couldn't really be free.

FDR used the term "freedom from want" to illustrate the interconnection between civil rights and economic rights. Unfortunately, this part of his vision has yet to be adopted. While the lived experience is often wildly different, our country at least theoretically protects civil rights for all or most people. But it very explicitly only protects economic rights for some—such as property owners—*not* for all. Even personal property rights, enshrined in the Constitution, are honored selectively—as Malaki learned when the gear he relied on to stay alive was confiscated and thrown out on orders from his local government.

The world community—including the United States—has endorsed the interdependence of rights.[131] But to date, the International Covenant on Economic, Social and Cultural rights, signed by Jimmy Carter and submitted to the Senate for its advice and ratification in 1977, is still pending there nearly fifty years later.[132]

Under US law, until June 28, 2024, someone living outside without access to adequate shelter had a fighting chance to win legal protection from being criminally punished for sleeping in public. In theory, Robert Anderson could lawfully sleep on the streets of Boise, Idaho, in the absence of adequate shelter, thanks to the 2018 federal appeals court decision in *Martin v. Boise*—before it was overturned in 2024. Challenges may still be available after the Supreme Court's ruling in Grants Pass v. Johnson. But even if so, the harsh reality is that under our current legal system, Robert had no right to a safe, permanent place to live—a home.[133]

Likewise, the civil and political human rights that the United States has endorsed—and promotes to the rest of the world—protect Danny's right to be free from "direct threats" to his life and to enjoy it with "dignity." But the United States has so far refused to endorse the economic and social human rights that would make that possible—in particular, the human right to housing. The inevitable result is that Danny was not only "brushed aside," he was left to lose his limbs on Denver's freezing streets. Proving the interdependence of rights, this also violates the very civil and political rights the United States has agreed to uphold.

Rob Robinson was homeless for almost three years, first on the streets of Miami and then in the New York City shelter system. His experiences inspired him to become an activist. In 2022, reflecting on the years he'd spent fighting the criminalization of homelessness, Rob admitted that he sometimes felt a tension between that fight and his belief in "the right to a home."

Which makes perfect sense. The best-case scenario in combating criminalization typically means preventing someone from being punished for being unhoused—not getting them into a home. But on reflection, Rob concluded that "those two things aren't mutually exclusive."[134]

In a country as wealthy as the United States, it shouldn't be hard to both protect homeless people from being criminally punished for living outside when they have no other option *and* ensure that they have a home to go to instead. There's no question that it's possible for our country to honor and protect civil and political rights *and* economic and social rights. So far, it has chosen not to.

There's a glimmer of hope that this could change.

Housing Is a Human Right

In the run-up to the 2020 presidential election, four candidates, all Democrats, called for recognizing housing as a right, not a privilege. After his election, Joe Biden repeated that statement, which he'd made as a candidate, the first time since FDR that a US president had done so.[135] His HUD Secretary, Marcia Fudge, affirmed her commitment to the human right to housing,[136] as did the US Interagency Council on Homelessness.[137] Biden's "Build Back Better" proposal put specifics on the concept, including making federal low-income housing vouchers an entitlement. This would have meant that anyone poor enough to qualify for this form of housing assistance would receive it. As of 2024, funding remains discretionary, subject to cuts by Congress, and only a quarter of eligible applicants actually receive it.[138]

What's so frustrating is that the proposal, had it been implemented, would have profoundly shifted federal policy and gone a long way to ending homelessness, as well as the widespread housing precarity that typically precedes it.[139] Build Back Better was first watered down, then torpedoed by two recalcitrant senators.[140] But the once-considered-laughable concept of housing as a right, not a privilege, has now entered mainstream policy discussions.[141]

Most likely, it has a long way to go before it's adopted. Attacks on the fundamental idea of housing as a solution to homelessness, always present, gained visibility during the first Trump administration. Promoted by right-wing ideologues, this pushback gathered momentum after Trump left office—and will likely only gain more force during his second administration. Yet while the work is ongoing, and more urgent than ever, the human right to housing has come a long way since the Clinton administration tried to delete it from a world conference *on the human right to housing.*

The bottom line is that there's a growing movement for housing that puts human needs before profits. Dominique Walker and the other Moms 4 Housing were able to stay in the Magnolia Street house thanks to a community land trust. This homeownership model is designed to protect affordability. It's just one example of what the human right to housing could look like here in America.[142]

And there's growing support for the right—including inside government, thanks to activists who are entering public office. In 2020, Dominique ran for and was elected to the Berkeley Rent Stabilization Board,[143] and Carole Fife, the community organizer who'd worked with her and the other Moms, was elected to the Oakland City Council.[144] In 2024, in coalition with other grassroots groups, the local ACLU chapter, the National Homelessness Law Center, and progressive elected officials, they were pushing for an amendment to the California Constitution that would add the right to housing.[145]

Ultimately, it did not go forward; it remains for another day. The advent of a Trump presidency and a Congress poised to do his bidding may delay it further. But the movement we have been building is here to stay—and continues pushing for housing for all.

Chapter Eight

Human Rights in Action

"Seeing Housing as a Human Right"

Before the foreclosure crisis and recession, Tom lived in a nice apartment in Minneapolis and ran a successful business.[1] The economic downturn hit him hard in 2009, and Tom feared he wouldn't be able to recover, certainly not quickly. He researched opportunities in Finland, his father's native country. Seeing a potential a market for his business there, Tom moved to Helsinki. He got his business up and running, found an apartment, and bought a car—but then the global financial crisis hammered Finland, too, and his business foundered. When it went under, Tom couldn't make rent and was evicted. He moved into a hostel and temporarily stored his belongings with a former employee, an experience that "felt like a nightmare."

Tom's former secretary told him about the Y-Foundation, a Finnish nonprofit that develops affordable housing. Tom couldn't just take the first place available, either, since an old back injury left him with very specific housing needs—a place on the bottom floor in a building with an elevator. The Y-Foundation found him a suitable apartment within a month and a half.

According to Tom, his new place "had everything." It was in an "incredibly sedate" neighborhood with the "nicest, quiet" neighbors. He called it "a salvation out of the blue."

Tom didn't regret leaving the United States. He missed the food, but overall felt much happier in Finland because "I don't have to worry about ending up on the street." He noted that after he left the United States, rents had skyrocketed and tent cities were everywhere, with even veterans out on the street. Contrasting what he'd left behind to his new home, Tom remarked that "Finns would never let that happen to their own."[2]

Tom may not have realized it, but his instinctive understanding of Finnish reality—and its contrast to that of the United States—reflected the difference in the two countries' legal and political systems. Unlike the United States, Finland enshrines the right to housing in its constitution, and backs it up with national legislation and affordable, social housing— publicly supported affordable, nonmarket housing.[3] The country also has a national policy, supported by funding and affordable housing, to address homelessness.

What may be at least as important as the policies is the sense of community—or commonweal—captured in Tom's assessment that "Finns would never let this happen to their own."

Finland's approach has received global notice, for good reason: It's significantly reduced homelessness and plans to end it by 2027. And there's nothing mysterious about it. Finland is implementing Housing First—the same model that's now embedded in American federal policy. The critical difference is that Finland carries out the program in a context that not only ensures housing as a right to the country's constitution and national legislation, but it also *funds* it—along with social housing and social welfare programs in general.[4]

Juha Kaakinen is the recently retired longtime head of the Y-Foundation, the group that helped Tom before he ever ended up on the streets. The Y-Foundation is the main nonprofit organization implementing the Housing First approach in Finland. Juha, a key proponent of the model, explained in a 2019 interview that small-scale "pilot" programs—popular with US policymakers—serve little purpose: "We know what works. You can have all sorts of projects, but if you don't have the actual homes. . . . A sufficient supply of social housing is just crucial."[5]

The Nordic country took some time to adopt Housing First as national policy. In 1987, pronounced the "International Year of Shelter for the Homeless" by the United Nations, Finland set an official goal to end homelessness. They adopted the "staircase" approach to make it happen. Unlike Housing First, the staircase approach requires homeless people to first address whatever problems they might have—such as mental health or addiction issues—through social services. Only *after* individuals have resolved any other issues are they granted access to housing. This resembles the approach prevalent in America through the 1990s, before the Housing First model began to be more widely adopted in the 2000s.

Initially, Finland's staircase method seemed to work, with the country's homelessness halved by 1994, at least according to available estimates. But then progress stalled, the numbers of unhoused Finns started going up, and eventually researchers concluded that the "treatment first" approach only worked for a limited subset of people.[6] As study after study confirms, it turns out most people need the security of a permanent place to live before they can address whatever other problems they may have.

In 2007, an influential Finnish report presented Housing First as a more effective alternative, and the following year Finland adopted it as its national policy for addressing homelessness.[7] Housing First reverses the staircase approach: People are given a stable place to live up front and *then* are provided with any needed social services to address other challenges.

These services are voluntary—the model prioritizes respecting people's dignity and autonomy. And it works: Four out of five people remain housed permanently.[8] As the American expat Tom put it, "Having this apartment has provided me the ability to return to normal life and start planning the future again."[9]

Housing First functions within Finland's broader societal and governmental context, which considers housing to be a human right—serving primarily to meet human needs, not to generate profit.[10] What that means in practice in Finland is that when new housing is developed, 25 percent of the units must be social housing—which means it must be affordable.[11] Unlike some forms of social housing, which explicitly define it as including a range of incomes, in Finland it is aimed at people most in need—a qualification that has been criticized by some commentators as undercutting the principle that housing is a universal need.[12] Nonetheless, compared to the United States, it is—currently at least—successfully addressing homelessness.

Juha Kaakinen, the former head of the Y-Foundation, pointed out that "this [requirement] has kept the supply to a reasonable level. This has been probably the main reason why we don't have the kind of housing crisis that most European countries have at the moment." People with the lowest incomes are prioritized for social housing.[13]

Finland also offers a range of other social supports. Its constitution includes a right to subsistence for "those who cannot obtain the means necessary for a life of dignity."[14] The country provides health care, childcare, support for unemployed people, disabled people, and senior citizens—and a housing benefit for those who need it. As of 2023, the benefit covered up to 80 percent of housing expenses. For those with very little or no income, there is a social welfare benefit to make up the remaining costs.

Having helped develop and implement Housing First in Finland, Juha considered affordable social housing and housing benefits to be the "cornerstones" of his country succeeding in the fight to end homelessness.[15] All these social supports may seem expensive, but Juha noted that ending homelessness *saves* money, citing the many studies that show that allowing people to remain homeless is more expensive than providing housing. In 2023, Finland spent an estimated 9,600 euros (about $10,000) less per homeless person than it did before adopting Housing First. These savings come from reduced health care, police, and shelter expenses.[16]

American studies yield similar results. As of 2022, Housing First nets an average annual savings of $25,000 per homeless person.[17] But a critical difference between Finland and the United States—in addition to laws, policies, and funding—may be what Juha called "a political understanding and political consensus: This is a national problem that we should solve together. . . . It demands politicians who have an understanding of human dignity."[18]

The "main thing," in Juha's view, is "treating homeless people like everybody else—people who have the same rights and seeing housing as a human right."

Embedding the human right to housing in a country's constitution makes its centrality clear and provides legal grounding for the right.[19]

As of 2023, Finland has virtually eliminated family homelessness, with only about 150 families living doubled up with friends or relatives or in temporary accommodations. The country hasn't yet eliminated other forms of homelessness—single men make up the bulk of the remaining population—but given its track record so far, Finland's goal to do so by 2027 seems realistic.[20]

To paraphrase Tom, having a common understanding of what members of a society owe one other is essential—and attainable.

Housing First Started in the United States—as a Model

By most accounts, the Housing First model originated in the United States.[21] But unlike Finland, our country hasn't provided anywhere near the necessary funding to implement it nationally, nor has it embedded the model within a larger framework of social housing or support. Housing First hasn't even enjoyed the broader societal understanding or support of the importance of housing that has been crucial to Finland's success.

And during the first Trump administration, it came under increased attack.

A New York City program called Pathways to Housing pioneered the Housing First method in 1992, focusing on individuals with mental disorders. Beyond Shelter, a program serving homeless families in Los Angeles, initiated a similar approach in 1998. Over time, both showed remarkable success, with numerous evaluations demonstrating high rates of housing stability for those in the programs.[22] After five years, 88 percent of tenants in the New York City program remained housed, compared to 47 percent of those who were in residential treatment centers in the city during the same time.[23] The successes in NYC and LA led to other programs around the country implementing the Housing First model. In 2009, the federal government adopted the approach and, as of 2024, it's still the model it prioritizes.[24]

Yet while the United States officially championed Housing First, it never provided the legal and policy foundations for the programmatic approach to work at the national level. Nor did it adopt the larger housing and safety net structure that the program needs to succeed. And it certainly never provided the *funding*. Instead, the primary source of federal funding for the model is—still—the McKinney-Vento Homeless Assistance Act. The legislation we fought so hard to get enacted in 1987 as a "first step" toward ending homelessness remains one of our federal government's *only* steps.[25]

To be fair, funding for the McKinney-Vento Act has increased over the decades; it got an especially big boost during the pandemic, now ended. The legislation was amended in 2009 to focus on Housing First, but funding remains woefully inadequate to the need. It certainly didn't help that the drastic cuts made to low-income housing programs in the early 1980s, which triggered the explosion of homelessness, were never restored. Even after Housing First became the US government's official approach, homelessness increased while affordable housing options shrank.[26] Once the pandemic ended, the extra funding dried up and housing costs began to soar again, pushing more people into homelessness or its brink.[27] Funding for the McKinney-Vento Act and other programs implementing the Housing First model remains vastly out of proportion to the need.

Adopting Housing First as an approach does nothing to end homelessness if you don't *fund* it to scale.

Among advocates and experts, there's widespread consensus on the effectiveness of Housing First, supported by a mountain of evidence.[28] For years, there'd also been bipartisan political consensus—the approach had actually first been proposed for federal adoption by the George W. Bush administration. One key reason is cost. Numerous studies have shown that Housing First not only helps people exit homelessness, stabilizes their health, and improves their lives, it also *saves government money*. As in Finland, the savings come from reduced spending on police, health care, and shelter.

These savings can be enormous. Cities around the country invest resources in sweeps, for example, the misguided, harmful, and sometimes illegal effort to move people and their belongings out of sight.[29] In 2019 alone, LA spent some $30 million on sweeps. Another big expense is emergency room and other hospital visits. Homelessness not only worsens health overall, but it can also directly lead to health emergencies and their resulting high expenses. Belle Ren wrote about this in *Street Sense*, a "street newspaper" in Washington, D.C., describing her own experience.[30]

A former substitute teacher, Belle lost her job during the pandemic. After her unemployment benefits ran out, she lost her apartment, too. Finding herself homeless in the nation's capital on a summer night in 2022 when the shelters were full, she put her blanket down on the street near Dupont Circle, close to the center of the city. Within minutes she was covered in blotches, her severe cockroach allergy triggered by a nearby infestation that she hadn't noticed when she'd staked out her spot. Knowing the cost—she'd also worked as an EMT—Belle hesitated to call 911. But she knew she had to get emergency medical care, and so she did. Reflecting on the experience, Belle put it plainly: "The public resources that aren't being spent to house me are being spent elsewhere."[31] An ambulance ride and emergency room visit can top $3,000.[32]

Belle's point—that housing her would save money—is one key argument for Housing First. Providing a safe place to sleep and live often prevents health risks and crises associated with being homeless. Since Housing First includes access to services like health care, health problems that do occur can be treated before they progress to the point of requiring hospitalization. The benefits to people's lives are beyond financial calculation, of course, but on all counts it's an investment that pays off.

Yet it's an investment that's not being made.

Houston: "A Sufficient Supply of Social Housing Is Just Crucial"

Despite the severe lack of funding, Housing First *is* being implemented in the United States—and it's getting attention. Houston made national headlines in 2022 for its success with the model: Over a ten-year period, the city moved some 25,000 homeless people directly from the streets into housing. Hailed by the *New York Times*, among others, the city became an object lesson that others sought to understand and replicate.[33] But for all its success, Houston also illustrates Finnish advocate Juha Kaakinen's point: For Housing First to succeed, "a sufficient supply of social housing is just crucial."

Houston launched its initiative soon after Housing First was officially adopted as federal policy. Congress amended the McKinney-Vento Act in 2009 to require communities to use the approach as a condition for receiving federal housing and shelter funds and required local service providers and governments to coordinate their efforts. In 2012, as the Obama administration was implementing the amended law, it identified Houston as one of ten "priority communities" to receive extra federal expertise—"technical assistance"—to put the model into practice, as part of a new administration initiative. The city's selection and the added federal counsel gave it an extra boost, but Houston received *no new federal funds*.[34]

The requirement for local government to coordinate with service providers made a difference. Key stakeholders in the city came together to collaborate, getting behind the Housing First approach. The group included service providers, advocates, city leaders, and businesses. Importantly, the city's housing authority, charged with administering federal low-income housing vouchers, also joined the collaborative effort—and that agency brought resources to the table, agreeing to let 250 homeless applicants jump to the front of the waiting list for vouchers each year.[35] Also critical was the strong leadership and support of then-mayor Annise Parker, who brought a personal connection to the issue. She and her wife had adopted a son who'd been homeless, and through him, Mayor Parker said, "I had an up close and personal look at what life was like for somebody on the streets who was treated as disposable."[36]

Following federal directives, the group—which named itself "The Way Home"—focused on two specific types of people.

If you were "literally" homeless—that is, living outside or in a shelter—you were eligible for "rapid rehousing." This meant twelve months of rental assistance, plus a case manager to help navigate the transition from street to housing. Case managers also helped eligible candidates connect to other kinds of help, such as food stamps and Medicaid. At the end of the year, you would have to find—and pay for—housing on your own.

The other category consisted of people who were "chronically" homeless. This was defined as living outside or in a shelter for a least a year *and* mentally and/or physically disabled. In that case, you would be eligible for permanent supportive housing—housing with supportive services like health and mental healthcare—without a built-in cutoff period. Focusing on these two groups, over several years The Way Home collaborative was able to house thousands of people.

In 2016, the city became particularly concerned about people living in encampments downtown. While small encampments had been scattered throughout the city for years, three large encampments located under highway overpasses had now "emerged," as a federal report put it.[37] Encampments had been increasing across the country ever since the foreclosure crisis and the Great Recession, but those in downtown Houston may have just become more visible, as the area was developed and people were jammed together into smaller spaces.[38] A new mayor was in office, and as the camps attracted more attention, downtown businesses, developers, and some housed city residents ratcheted up their pressure on City Hall to take action.[39]

The city developed a plan to "decommission" the encampments, a term it coined to describe its tactics—and, perhaps, to distinguish it from the inhumane sweeps prevalent around the country. There would supposedly be a specific plan in place to house every encampment resident *before* removing their tents and other belongings and fencing off the area to prevent people from returning. The Way Home would conduct outreach to encampment residents to establish trust and rapport—especially important for people who may have had bad experiences with shelters and social service providers. The group would also reach out to landlords, searching for placements that would accept tenants with housing vouchers. Many do not—and in Houston, as of 2024, in most cases this discrimination is still perfectly legal.[40]

Over six or so months in 2018, The Way Home implemented its strategy, placing most residents of one of Houston's large downtown encampments into housing while the city cordoned off the area. An infusion of new federal funds during the pandemic allowed the group to house over a hundred encampment residents, the majority of whom remained housed three years later.[41] In 2022, the mayor announced a grant of an additional $100 million—with city, county, state, and federal funds—to cut the number of people experiencing homelessness in half by 2025.[42] Meanwhile, private foundations also pumped millions of dollars into the effort.[43]

The Way Home's work in Houston is touted as a success story. And in many ways, it is. People *were* housed, ending their homelessness. Multiple individuals, organizations, and agencies worked hard and worked together, showing that this, too, is possible. But zoom out and evaluate homelessness overall in Houston and the success looks much more limited. For one thing, consider the numbers.

Houston reported a 53 percent drop in the city's homeless population from 2011 to 2021—on its face an impressive statistic. The data that statistic is based on, however, are questionable. The numbers come from the annual HUD "point-in-time count," carried out by volunteers who fan out across the city to physically tally people they judge to be homeless. Aside from this built-in subjectivity, they are instructed not to venture into abandoned buildings, alleys, or other places that might be dangerous—in other words, exactly the places where unhoused people are likely to seek shelter. The need to hide is made more acute by the risk of arrest under the city and state's anti-camping ordinances.[44]

The optimistic numbers also only include those deemed homeless according to HUD's narrow definition. Excluded are people who have lost their own housing and are living doubled or tripled up, sleeping on the couches or floors of friends or relatives, typically moving from place to place, as Dominique Walker and her fellow Moms 4 Housing did in 2019 or as Florence Koster, Deborah Dean, and their families and others had done decades earlier. If "ending homelessness" is defined in such a way as to leave out those who still *technically* have a roof over their heads, it won't work. Any minor problem threatens to tip those who are not officially homeless—per HUD—over the edge.[45]

For Housing First to work, there must be enough affordable housing to meet the need—period. When Houston initiated its attempt in the early 2000s, affordable housing was still plentiful. With hindsight, then-mayor Parker observed "back then we still had slack in our housing market and reasonably priced land."[46]

This critical factor changed quickly. Since at least 2015, rents dramatically increased in Houston, outpacing incomes—especially in downtown and other rapidly gentrifying areas.[47] New residential construction focused on luxury housing. In 2021, there were just nineteen affordable and available units for every one hundred extremely low-income people.[48] By 2022, pandemic funds were largely spent, protections against evictions had lapsed, and evictions had topped pre-pandemic levels.[49]

Housing assistance is still in extremely short supply in Houston, as in the rest of the country. In 2018, the *waiting list* to receive housing vouchers was closed. It didn't reopen until January 2023, and then only for a few weeks.[50] Announcing the temporary reopening, the head of the city's housing authority noted that "Houston is experiencing one of the nation's worst affordable housing shortages right now."[51]

Yet despite this extreme shortage, to further the city's program to place homeless people into housing—and close encampments—the housing authority let 250 homeless applicants jump the line for vouchers each year. This was part of the commitment the agency made when they joined The Way Home. But while this certainly helped those who qualified for the fast track, it meant all the other poor families on the list had to wait even longer.[52]

The change in the market from abundant affordable housing to scarce affordable housing also made landlords less willing to rent to those who beat the odds and secured a housing voucher. Even though the vouchers guaranteed payment of rent by the government, in a tight housing market many private landlords would rather avoid the bureaucracy—and potential limits on profit—that come with a government program. The increasing difficulty of finding affordable housing soon threatened the ability of the city and its nonprofit partners to implement Housing First. Some help arrived when a local foundation made a $15 million grant to The Way Home in July 2023, adding to the millions of dollars in donations the organization had already received. Private support can be a substantial boon, but over the longer term, philanthropy cannot possibly make up for the lack of public funding. Nor should it.[53]

Finding affordable housing is likely to get harder still. Locally, nationally, and around the world, private equity is buying more and more housing for investment, driving up rents—and evictions.[54] In 2021, 28 percent of single-family homes in Texas were bought by institutional investors. Within Harris County—where Houston is located—the share was *38 percent*.[55] All indications are that the increasing presence of private equity in the housing market is raising the cost of renting as well as buying homes.[56]

These challenges don't even account for the built-in limitations of the Housing First model as it's currently implemented in the United States. When a housing placement *is* made, it's often only for a year. After that, the tenant is expected to come up with the rent or find another place on their own.

Terri Harris, a once-homeless mother whose story was highlighted in the *New York Times* article hailing Houston's approach, had moved from her encampment to a one-bedroom apartment thanks to the Housing First initiative. Terri had finally been able to reunite with her then three-year-old daughter, Blesit, whom she'd entrusted to her sister while she was on the street. But finding a job, childcare, and transportation within a year to meet the monthly $886 monthly rent on her own was a tall order. It kept Terri up at night with worry. In the end, local officials helped her set up a GoFundMe page to raise resources.[57]

Another sign of the looming challenges is the shift in the Houston's encampment policy. By 2023, encampments were still being "decommissioned," but residents were no longer placed into housing. Instead, they were taken to a new "housing navigation center," a low-barrier shelter with social services where they could stay while case managers attempted to find them housing. With laws against "camping" in public in place, business groups continued their pressure to sweep the remaining encampments out of sight. The mayor claimed that removing them was essential to building support for Housing First. Otherwise, his office explained, "the public didn't believe with their own eyes that homelessness was actually decreasing in the city."[58]

In a way, the mayor had a point. The visible presence of people living on the street contradicted any claim that homelessness was decreasing. The problem wasn't the encampments themselves, however, but the lack of affordable housing that both created them and prevented people from leaving. Finland implements Housing First in a context that funds social housing and many other supports for those who need them, which promotes social solidarity. In the United States, Housing First is on its own, with none of this supplemental support. This limited approach can still help individuals, but it's unlikely to solve the broader problem of homelessness. Opponents of Housing First can then shake their heads and claim that homelessness is an "intractable" problem. Citing gospel, they can say "the poor you will have with you always." They can claim that homelessness is not the result of deliberate policy choices made by elected officials about their fellow human beings.

Even with widespread support for Houston's Housing First approach, in 2023 the city remained far from building the kind of community consensus embraced in Finland. Dozens of organizations and city residents offered food and other donations to encampment residents, but the mayor urged them to stop, claiming they were interfering with the city's efforts to house people—and violating a municipal ordinance against offering food to needy people in public places. The activist group Food Not Bombs successfully challenged the city law in court, some seven years after they and other advocates had shot down a nearly identical policy in Fort Lauderdale, Florida.[59]

Houston has presented itself as championing Housing First—and in some ways, it has. But for the program to succeed, a major increase in public funding for affordable housing is essential. That requires building broad public support rooted in a sense of solidarity with people in need, much like those offering food to encampment residents showed. The mayor's message discouraging Houstonians from making even that offering undermined that solidarity. It demonstrated the exact opposite of the understanding of "human dignity" that Finnish advocate Juha emphasized politicians needed to effectively end homelessness.

Public Housing in the United States: Opportunity Gone Wrong

Finland didn't leave housing to the vagaries of the private market—it made sure this basic human need was met for all. The United States also embraced this goal, but it failed to adopt the policies to meet it.

During the Great Depression, millions of Americans lost their homes and there was much discussion about the need for government to step in. European cities, most notably Vienna, were building housing without the goal of making a profit, a model that became known as social housing. Kept off the speculative market to ensure it would remain affordable, much of this housing was directly constructed by the government or trade unions and other nonprofits. Social housing was available to all in Vienna, not just poor people, with subsidies for those who needed them, and integration became part of the model as implemented there.[60]

As the New Deal came together, American advocates promoted the social housing model, calling for government to build and subsidize housing focused on its intended use, rather than its potential value as a commodity.[61] But compromises made to overcome political opposition resulted in legislation that fell far from that goal. At the insistence of the real estate industry, eligibility for public housing was limited to those too poor to afford housing on the open market, thus protecting private owners from having to compete with the federal government's lower costs and prices. What had started as a broad vision for universal housing became a much narrower reality as industry interests won out.[62]

Racial discrimination was explicitly baked in, with "redlining" written into the law. Redlining allowed lenders to refuse loans if an applicant lived in a neighborhood deemed to be "a high financial risk," which effectively prevented many Black people from obtaining long-term mortgages to finance home purchases. Racist restrictive covenants kept Black buyers out of the private homeownership market, while discrimination prevented many from renting on the private market. Public housing, intended to serve middle-class workers generally, was segregated by race at its inception, with separate housing for Black and White residents—beginning with the New Deal and continuing for decades after. Eventually, White residents began to leave public housing for private market housing, often in the suburbs, helped by the favorable incentives that allowed them to buy homes. Black residents, shut out of homeownership, stayed behind, exacerbating segregation, and further impoverishing urban communities.[63]

Far from providing housing for all, American public housing followed a path of segregation, stigma, and division based on race as well as income. While it offered a home and sometimes community for many of its residents, it's never met more than a tiny fraction of the need. Demonized in public and political perceptions as a hotbed of crime, drugs, and all manner of social ills, public housing looms large as a symbol, but as of 2018 it constituted less than 1 percent of the country's housing stock.[64] This paltry percentage can only continue its downward trajectory, given the 1998 federal prohibition on replenishing lost public housing units.[65] Federal housing policy developed on two separate tracks, one for poor people and another for everyone else, and with public housing choked off, both now rely on the private market.

Federal vouchers are supposed to help pay the cost of housing on the private market, while allowing those poor enough to be eligible for them to choose where to live. But many landlords refuse to accept vouchers.[66] Some cities and states prohibit this practice—called source-of-income discrimination—but, to date, there is no federal prohibition.[67] And even in places that have such protections, enforcement of the law is often lax.[68]

The need for the vouchers is also much greater than the supply: Availability depends on funding allocated each year by Congress at its discretion. As of 2024, only one in four of those poor enough to be eligible for a voucher received one.[69] The rest are directed to waiting lists that are often so long it takes years for an applicant's name to come up, if ever. Some have hit a length where they've closed to new applicants entirely, as Houston's did.

Homeowners are much less likely to be impoverished than renters—but they receive a housing *entitlement*. Starting in the New Deal era, federal policy created incentives for homeownership through the tax code. Homeowners are automatically able—entitled—to deduct interest paid on their mortgage from their taxes. Embedding the policy in the tax code rather than as a direct government grant made this federal assistance virtually invisible, setting the stage for the narrative, still in place today, that public housing and other federal funding for low-income housing are "handouts" for lazy, undeserving poor people. According to this storyline, homeownership is something that the hardworking middle and upper classes earn with "their own" money. Never mind the tax incentives and benefits that make it possible.

It's not pocket change. The federal government subsidizes home-owners to the tune of billions of dollars each year. In 2023, the amount was over $150 billion, far overshadowing the $30 billion spent on low-income housing that same year.[70] It's a regressive policy that deepens economic and racial inequality: Those who benefit are disproportionately White and have a high income.[71]

VIENNA AND SOCIAL HOUSING

Vienna's social housing program takes a very different approach. First launched after World War I, when a terrible housing crisis left some 35,000 people homeless, the policy was pushed by a coalition of women, labor unions, and immigrants during the period sometimes called "Red Vienna."[72] Initiated by the then-ruling Social Democratic Party, social housing was part of an overall push to reshape the city as a livable com-munity. The construction of social housing was—and remains—subsidized by the city to meet a broad public need. It still works: Roughly half of the city's residents live in social housing.[73]

Inhabited by people with a range of incomes, Vienna's social hous-ing enjoys broad support, meaning it's not stigmatized and has a wide political constituency. In sharp contrast to US policy, where public hous-ing was developed so as *not* to compete with private landlords, Vienna's social housing competes directly with the private market, which helps keep private housing costs down, benefiting everyone. Vienna owns over 60 percent of land in the city—a huge advantage.[74] First built by the city in 1923, over time social housing expanded to include housing built by "limited profit" and nonprofit associations.[75] In 2023, 43 percent of all housing was protected from the market.[76]

The robust supply of housing, coupled with the city's zoning and rent control regulations, make renting more affordable. As many as 80 percent of households in the city *choose* to rent. On average, they spend 22 percent of their posttax income on rent. Even considering the taxes levied to support such social investments, Viennese residents shoul-der a much lighter financial burden than American renters.

In the United States, almost half of all renters pay over 30 percent of their pretax income on rent. Over one in four—26 percent—pay *more than 50 percent* of their income on rent, leaving less than half their money to meet all their other basic needs. As rents have risen while incomes have stagnated, the gap has widened. In 2022, low-income people—those making $30,000 a year or less—took home just $300 after paying their rent each month. Those who were cost burdened—paying 30 percent or more for rent—were left with as little as $170 a month for food, transportation, clothes, health care, childcare and everything else.[77]

With America's deepening housing and homelessness crises, Vienna's approach attracted the interest of US advocates and policymakers. Delegations of activists and government officials toured the city's social housing. Several US localities—including Seattle and the states of Rhode Island and New York—began developing their own proposals for social housing. Montgomery County, Maryland, which had a long-standing social housing program, increased its investment.[78]

While the Viennese approach has been effective in creating housing affordable to many people—much more so than the United States—as of 2019 more than 22,000 people were homeless across Austria—with over half (57 percent) in Vienna.[79] One contributing factor is that supply simply did not keep up with demand as the city's population rapidly grew from the early 2000s onward. By 2023, there was a two-year wait to get into social housing.[80] Housing costs also rose significantly, including for social housing, where rent is tied to inflation.[81] With diminishing supply relative to need, myriad eligibility requirements began keeping some people out.[82]

In 2023, to qualify for social housing, you had to show that you had had a fixed address in the city for at least two years—an insurmountable barrier for people who are already homeless or unstably housed. If you're not a citizen of Austria, another EU country, or a "recognized refugee," then you must prove you have been a legal resident for at least five years.[83] Depending on the housing, you may also need to put down a security deposit or show some form of special need.[84]

Herbert V. was one of those shut out. A Vienna resident, he became homeless after the death of his longtime girlfriend, with whom he'd been living. Because he hadn't had an apartment in his own name, he wasn't eligible for municipal housing. Herbert ended up at a shelter—something he said he "could never have imagined." Eventually, he was able to get permanent housing through Neunerhaus, the leading organization working to implement Housing First in the city.[85] But the need is much greater than Neunerhaus can meet. The production of social housing is going down while demand is going up, and only a small amount of new social housing is allocated to Housing First programs each year.[86]

Vienna's social housing model works well for those who can get it, but many are shut out and must struggle to find housing on the increasingly unaffordable private market. Those who can't and become homeless face a fragmented system with a complicated maze of requirements that may also exclude them.[87] How can this be happening in a city celebrated for its progressive approach to housing? Part of the disconnect may be that while Austria signed on to the UN's International Covenant on Economic, Social and Cultural Rights in 1978, the country hasn't implemented it.

Austria doesn't include a right to housing in its constitution. It hasn't adopted a national housing strategy, nor has it enacted national homelessness legislation or a national plan to address it. Without a legal basis for housing homeless people, advocates lack a key tool to hold government accountable.[88] Without a national strategy, policy and systems aren't cohesive, and homelessness is seen as a matter of social welfare, not social housing.[89]

Nonprofits such as Neunerhaus try to bridge the gaps while advocating, with others, for systemic reform that would ensure housing for all.[90] During the pandemic, the country funded a pilot project called "Arriving Home" to add 1,100 more homeless people to their Housing First program. Arriving Home ended in April 2023. Asserting that with an additional 25,000 housing units Austria could end homelessness in the country by 2025, advocates pushed to revive and expand the program.[91] The government responded—in part—agreeing to fund Housing First for about 1,000 homeless people by September 2024.

While imperfect, Vienna's model shows what can come from treating housing as a social good rather than as a commodity. It also demonstrates that the lack of the legal anchor of the human right to housing leaves a gaping hole. The United Nations has repeatedly criticized Austria's failure to codify and implement the human right to housing.[92] Filling that breach requires embedding the human right to housing in the country's laws—and fostering a national consensus that embraces them.[93]

Community Land Trusts: A US Model of Social Housing

Severely underfunded and stigmatized, American public housing as currently operated is far different from social housing in Vienna and Finland. But there are other domestic examples of housing developed for people, not profit. Scattered in communities across the country and operated by nonprofits, these are primarily small, local initiatives—like American Housing First programs, they're not nearly on the scale needed to solve homelessness or the housing crisis.[94] One example is the community land trust in Oakland, California, where Dominique Walker and her fellow Moms 4 Housing made their stand.

Community land trusts (CLTs) are nonprofit organizations that acquire land which they then hold forever—"in trust," for the benefit of the community. A trust then uses the land to develop affordable housing for low-income community members to buy.[95] The CLT retains ownership of the land, with a long-term lease to the homeowner. CLTs help prospective buyers get a mortgage, and the new owners agree that if they later sell their home, it will be at an affordable price to another low-income community member. This gives them the opportunity to build wealth while also preserving the affordability of the housing.

The CLT model can also be used to develop rental properties, with limitations on rent increases to ensure housing remains affordable for low-income people. A defining feature in both approaches is community control. CLTs are governed by a board of residents, low-income community members, public officials, and other stakeholders.

Creating either type of CLT requires an initial investment of funds. This can come from a public source, like government grants, or from a private donor, such as a foundation. In Oakland, the opportunity came when the federal government responded to the 2008 foreclosure crisis by giving states and cities funding to acquire and redevelop vacant foreclosed properties.[96]

Oakland's housing costs had risen rapidly after the city's economy boomed in the first five years of the twenty-first century. Following a familiar pattern, the incomes of moderate and low-income residents hadn't kept up, displacing tens of thousands of households. Black residents—including Dominique's own family and friends—were hit especially hard.[97] Predatory lenders targeted these communities, and by 2006 foreclosures were sharply escalating.[98] Local activists sounded the alarm, urging the city to fund a CLT to help address the increasingly urgent housing situation. A city agency agreed in 2007, putting forth its own recommendation for a land trust.[99]

When the new federal funding was announced in 2008, Oakland was ready. The city allocated some of its share of the funds to the launch the Oakland Community Land Trust. Formally incorporated in 2009,[100] the trust affirmed its commitment to the human right to housing in its founding documents.[101] It's gone on to acquire, rehabilitate, and sell some two dozen vacant foreclosed homes, apartment buildings, and vacant lots.[102]

As housing costs surged, the trust also focused on preventing displacement by acquiring homes that were already occupied. Moving them out of the private market protected the residents. When the Moms 4 Housing were evicted from the house on Magnolia Street they'd occupied in an act of desperation and defiance, the Trust stepped in and brokered a deal to buy it. In yet another variation on the CLT model, the Magnolia Street house became transitional housing—operated by the Moms—that offered a temporary home to other mothers facing homelessness.[103]

Community land trusts keep property off the speculative market for the benefit of a community, specifically its low-income members, who also have a strong decision-making voice. Inspired by models of community landownership in India and Israel, the American CLT approach sprang from the Civil Rights Movement. The first US land trust was established in Georgia in 1969 to fight segregation and economic disenfranchisement.[104] Thanks primarily to the work of grassroots activists, as of 2024 there were over 450 CLTs across the country, and interest was growing.[105]

Oakland and similar CLT success stories—including public housing successes—show that another way is possible in the United States: Housing *can* be developed and maintained to meet community needs, it doesn't *have* to be a vehicle for profit. Social housing *can* work in America.[106] But because the funds allocated to affordable housing are so low, the number of land trusts is minuscule compared to the demand. Unless that investment gets much, much bigger, the role of CLTs in addressing the affordable housing crisis will remain very limited. For this or any model of nonmarket housing to make a real difference, vastly more affordable housing is needed.[107]

Hundreds of thousands of people in this country desperately need homes, and the only way they'll get them is if policymakers start treating housing as a human right instead of as a commodity. We need a fundamental shift in priorities and funding. As of 2024, over a dozen campaigns pushing for just such a sea change were underway in communities across the country.[108]

ORGANIZING FOR SOCIAL HOUSING— HAPPENING NOW IN US CITIES

A liberal city in a rural, conservative state, Kansas City is home to a particularly active social housing campaign. In 2019, a group of local tenants came together as "KC Tenants" to advocate for themselves and others. Since then, the organization has grown rapidly—and it's gaining traction.

Kansas City has lower housing costs than many larger cities, but rising rents have been outpacing incomes there, too.[109] Tiana Caldwell, a nurse, felt the impact personally after she was diagnosed with cancer and fell behind on rent. Evicted from their apartment, Tiana, her husband, and their young son spent six months homeless. The experience led her to join forces with Tara Raghuveer and another woman to cofound KC Tenants.[110]

Proclaiming housing to be a human right, KC Tenants began organizing tenants and other allies to push for social housing, which they defined as housing that's outside the private market—"not available for profit or speculation," as Tara put it. By 2023, the group already had over 450 tenant leaders and almost 10,000 members. They view Vienna as a general model, but also set a specific agenda focused on the needs of their own community.

KC Tenants has already scored important victories, starting with the enactment of a tenants' bill of rights in December 2019. This provided concrete protections to tenants, including the right to organize, which gave the group a foundation for building support. Since then, they've organized tenants in buildings and neighborhoods across the city, helping to bring them together to address their immediate needs in their buildings as well as to advocate for new government policies.[111] Two years later, they won the right to free legal representation for tenants facing eviction. It's a big win that helps level a very unequal playing field, where over 90 percent of landlords have lawyers.

Securing free legal representation for low-income tenants is part of a trend that began in 2017, when New York City enacted the first right-to-counsel law, and it's been gaining ground around the country ever since. While the right to counsel doesn't create affordable housing, tenants represented by a lawyer have a much better chance of avoiding eviction—and the homelessness that often results—compared to unrepresented tenants. They are also in a much stronger position to negotiate an agreement that avoids an eviction record, giving them a better shot at finding housing in the future.[112] The right to counsel increases protection from arbitrary eviction, a key element of the human right to housing, and helps keep people in their homes.[113]

Like much of America, Kansas City has a severe shortage of affordable housing. In 2022, for every one hundred extremely poor households, the city had just thirty-nine rental homes affordable to them. This was still better than some of the worst large metropolitan areas—like Las Vegas, with only fourteen affordable rental homes for every one hundred extremely low-income households. But it was still far from enough.[114] In 2022, tenant organizers went door-to-door garnering public support for a ballot initiative KC Tenants spearheaded—and won $50 million to fund afford-able housing for extremely low-income people (those making 30 percent or below the area median income). This definition of extreme poverty came out to about $23,000 for a two-person household in 2022.[115]

The following year, KC Tenants' sibling organization, KC Tenants Power, also canvassed to effect change. This door-to-door campaign was on behalf of city council candidates who supported its core priorities—chief among them municipal social housing and a commitment to work collaboratively with constituents on policy solutions. Four of the group's candidates won seats on the city council, including one of its own tenant leaders, Jonathan Duncan.[116]

A Black Army combat veteran who grew up poor and working class, Jonathan had enlisted to pay for college. When he returned home from Iraq with PTSD, he discovered that the mental health services he'd been promised were not actually available. Instead, Jonathan said, his commu-nity of fellow veterans helped save his life. As a city council candidate, he promoted a vision of community "where your neighbors and your chosen leaders have your back."[117]

Hailing the election results, the new councilman-elect exulted that voters had chosen "people over profits."

In January 2024, KC Tenants won another important victory: a city law banning source-of-income discrimination.[118] Crafted and passed with strong leadership from the group, and support from Jonathan Duncan, other allies on the city council, and the mayor, the measure prohibits landlords from rejecting prospective tenants simply because they hold a housing voucher. This common practice is still a major barrier for poor people—especially poor people of color—trying to rent in many parts of the country.[119]

Mere months after the triumphant city council election, however, the challenge ahead sharpened: News reports announced that the Kansas City metro area had seen the highest rent increases in the nation.[120]

"Compassionate Seattle": Sweeps or Social Housing?
In Seattle, the campaign for social housing grew out of a fight against a proposal that would have enshrined sweeps in the city's charter. Billing

itself as a "community driven" effort to respond to the city's growing homelessness crisis, "Compassionate Seattle" may have sounded like it was coming from a good place. In reality, it was created by business groups, real estate interests, and wealthy city residents who funneled some $1 million into what the group called a "new approach" to homelessness.[121] Launched in April 2021, the campaign proposed amending the Seattle charter through a ballot initiative to "address homelessness and keep areas clear of encampments." The poorly drafted initiative required the city to provide two thousand housing units in one year, along with mental health and substance disorder services to homeless people—with no funding to do any of this. It also mandated that the city "balance keeping public spaces clear of encampments with avoiding harm to individuals."[122]

The campaign went to great lengths to appear reasonable—what could be wrong with "balancing" interests, especially when proposed by a group with "compassion" in its name? Plenty. For one thing, that last part could be read as sanctioning city sweeps. To many advocates, it sounded like a dog whistle for doing just that. Real Change, a Seattle nonprofit that publishes a weekly street newspaper and advocates for racial equity and social and economic justice, called it a way to codify sweeps as *the* response to homelessness in the city's foundational document.

Real Change created the House Our Neighbors! campaign to counter the pro-sweep amendment and its misleading claim to be a "compassionate" response that would help solve homelessness. Bringing together a large coalition that included mutual aid groups, labor and faith organizations, and people who had experienced homelessness, they mobilized to defeat the ballot initiative. Early polls showed strong support for the initiative among likely voters—some 61 percent in favor—so the advocates focused on education and outreach to dispel misinformation and build resistance.[123] Working with the local chapter of the ACLU and others, they also filed a court challenge, which successfully got the proposed amendment removed from the November 2021 ballot on technical legal grounds.[124]

Real Change didn't stop there, either. Having claimed this victory, the group decided to fight for proactive solutions, pivoting from a defensive position to a positive vision for change. The group's advocacy director, Tiffani McCoy, and another staff member had been part of a delegation of activists and policymakers that visited Vienna in 2022 to learn about its social housing program. They shared what they had learned with their coalition, and the group decided to push for the creation of a social housing development authority for Seattle. The group's proposal defined social housing as open to people earning a range of incomes up to 120 percent of area median income. Rental income would help pay for maintenance, and the estimated value of future rents would support bond issues to fund construction, along with some city funding. Social housing would function as a social good serving a human need, instead of as a commodity to generate profit.

The group explicitly linked the homelessness crisis to the critical lack of affordable housing, framing their proposal as "halting the pipeline into houselessness." Real Change committed Tiffani and one other staff member to lead the campaign.[125] The two organizers shifted the committees and other structures they'd assembled to fight the pro-sweep initiative to promote the new House Our Neighbors! campaign for social housing. Lacking local governmental support, the coalition decided to push for a ballot initiative. This meant an all-out organizing effort to get the public behind it.[126]

House Our Neighbors! faced early opposition from established nonprofit housing developers, who feared that a new social housing developer would siphon off some of what little funding the city supplied. The campaign pushed back against what it called a "scarcity mindset," noting that the social housing program would complement existing efforts rather than competing with them, and that it would be largely self-sustaining.

The organizing paid off, and they built a coalition that was even bigger than the one they'd formed to take down the Compassionate Seattle amendment. Several elected officials backed the campaign, and over time even some nonprofit housing developers came around. Having an agenda that reached a wider range of income levels helped.[127]

The campaign's proposal to develop a city social housing authority was placed on the ballot, and in February 2023 Initiative 135 was approved by 57 percent of voters. As enacted, it included a host of progressive policies protecting tenants. It also provided for oversight by a thirteen-member governing board that includes residents and unhoused people, who would be paid for their work—thereby making their participation feasible. The initiative only included municipal funding to support the new social housing authority for eighteen months, though. Later that year, House Our Neighbors! launched a new initiative to create a dedicated funding stream to provide the necessary long-term support. Calling on its existing coalition and expanding it further, the campaign began planning a ballot initiative, to levy a fee on local businesses that have employees earning $1 million or more.[128]

Talking with Tiffani McCoy about this plan, I thought back to Seattle's short-lived "head tax" on large businesses. Passed by the city council in 2018 to raise funds for housing homeless and other very poor people, Amazon led a pressure campaign that forced Seattle to repeal it just two months later.[129] But despite this discouraging precedent, Tiffani was optimistic that the campaign could mobilize enough public support to succeed. She was right: On February 12, the ballot initiative passed with over 68% of the vote.

I know from personal experience that optimism is an occupational hazard for advocates. You must believe that a better world is possible to do advocacy work effectively. It's a moral imperative: The belief in a more just world is what drives advocacy. And acting on that belief, the education campaigns of Tiffani's group—and those of many other organizations, over years and decades—may be building public understanding and support for housing as the only true solution to homelessness.

After all, when we first started advocating for a federal response to homelessness in the mid-1980s, we were dismissed as politically unrealistic. Two years later, the McKinney-Vento Homeless Assistance Act was enacted, launching homelessness as an issue for national policy. When we began pushing for the human right to housing in the mid-1990s, we were called hopelessly naive. But in 2020, four major presidential candidates embraced it, including President Biden.

No longer laughable, our proposed solutions had entered mainstream policy discussions.

"Decade of Doom": Laying a Foundation for a Right to Housing Campaign?

The proliferation of laws punishing homelessness—and the advocacy to stop them—may be spurring more social housing campaigns. Like their Seattle counterparts, Denver activists are building on their fight against criminalization to campaign for housing.

Denver's camping ban turned ten years old in 2022, and activists marked the occasion with a march highlighting what they dubbed the "decade of doom." The following June, a new mayor came into office. Term limits had required Mayor Michael B. Hancock to step down after a twelve-year tenure. Advocates weren't sorry to see him go—Hancock, a Democrat, had initiated and championed the camping ban. His successor, Mike Johnston, had campaigned on a promise to end homelessness. Once in office, Mayor Johnston prioritized "decommissioning" encampments downtown, embracing Houston's euphemistic term for sweeps. In theory, this meant moving people into housing, but in practice the premise turned out to be a bit elastic. Some homeless people were moved into former hotels renovated into housing for this purpose, with services also provided. But others were moved to crowded congregate shelters— with dozens of residents in a single space—or to a spot on the floor of a family member or friend.[130]

Activists continued to protest the city's ongoing sweeps, but some started focusing more attention on the fight for housing. They were led by a new organization, Housekeys Action Network Denver (HAND). Founded in 2022 by activists including Terese Howard, the organizer who spent years leading the fight against the camping ban, HAND believes "housing should be a human right for all, not a commodity for the rich."[131] HAND began working toward that vision by asking unhoused Denverites what they wanted.

In the spring of 2022, the organization surveyed over eight hundred people who were or had recently been houseless, almost 20 percent of the city's total unhoused population. HAND asked about their housing needs and desires, including whether they wanted housing. Working with data professionals, HAND analyzed the responses and published their findings the following March. Of those surveyed, between

93 percent and 99 percent said they wanted housing.[132] The top barrier they cited? Affordability.[133]

Taking the survey results as their mandate, HAND worked to formulate their policy proposals. They began investigating models for social housing, inspired by Vienna's model and the success of Seattle's Real Change.[134]

TRUMP AND FRIENDS: ATTACK ON HOUSING FIRST

Momentum for the human right to housing has been building since at least the mid-1990s, when advocates first confronted the Clinton administration. And support for Housing First has been growing since the early 2000s, when the George W. Bush administration embraced it.

But while the overwhelming consensus remains that Housing First is the best way forward, some of its bipartisan support has eroded, abetted by a frontal attack from the Trump administration during its first reign.

In the spring of 2019, Fox News ramped up its coverage of homelessness, claiming that the Democratic mayors of large cities were to blame—and that a win by Democrats in the 2020 elections would portend the end of "civilization."[135] After paying virtually no attention to homelessness for the bulk of his term, then-president Trump suddenly expressed an interest. He claimed during an interview with Tucker Carlson in July 2019 that his administration was looking at how to "get the whole thing cleaned up"[136] On a trip to California that September, a little over a year before the presidential election, Trump elaborated, focusing on property values: "We have people living in our . . . best highways, our best streets, our best entrances to buildings . . . where people in those buildings pay tremendous taxes, where they went to those locations because of the prestige."[137]

Later that month, the Trump administration issued a report proposing increased use of law enforcement to get people off the streets—and to force them into remote federal properties.[138]

A critical moment came toward the end of the year, when the administration ousted the then-head of the US Interagency Council on Homelessness, Obama-appointee Matthew Doherty. Replacing Doherty was Robert Marbut, a former San Antonio city council member turned homelessness consultant. Instead of Housing First, Marbut advocated an approach he called "housing fourth." That's how he put it in the press interviews that followed the announcement of his appointment.[139] That's also what he said when he shuffled into the Law Center offices to meet with us. He seemed to think it was clever.

Marbut was making the rounds himself, visiting organizations working on homelessness soon after his appointment was announced. We were on his list. A gregarious man, Marbut had a friendly, agreeable demeanor. When we expressed our concerns about his widely known support for criminalizing homelessness, he assured us he no longer took that position. This promise proved false almost immediately, surprising nobody. During our talk, he defended his view that housing should only be offered as a "reward" for meeting treatment goals.

Before Trump appointed him to his federal role, Marbut was best known as the founding president of a shelter in San Antonio, Texas, where hundreds of homeless people slept outdoors on a concrete lot. Calling his approach a "velvet hammer," he advocated making indoor shelter contingent on following rules ranging from passing a drug test to being "respectful."[140] Those violating the rules would have to sleep outside. New arrivals had to stay there too, until they "earned" an indoor spot. At a facility Marbut ran in St. Petersburg, Florida, after leaving San Antonio, one homeless man described sleeping on bare pavement under metal tents in the rain: "Those things have no sides on 'em. The water's still hitting you. You're soaking wet."[141]

Requiring someone to sleep outside until they "earn" a spot inside a shelter—and then wait there still longer to "move up" to housing—is the opposite of Housing First. Viewed most charitably, it's an especially rickety version of the old "staircase" model, which the evidence shows is less effective than Housing First. More realistically, it's a punitive, paternalistic approach akin to incarceration. Marbut's facility in St. Petersburg was even *housed* in a former jail. According to local advocate G. W. Rolle, not much had changed—the shelter was "still a jail."[142]

Within a year of his appointment as executive director of the US Interagency Council on Homelessness (USICH), Marbut was pushing to dismantle the federal government's Housing First policy. Marbut and the Trump administration pointed to increases in homelessness while federal funding to address it was also rising as proof that Housing First wasn't working and a new approach was needed.[143] The administration used this same "evidence" to substantially cut housing assistance for low-income Americans in its 2021 budget proposal, including eliminating funding for 160,000 subsidized units.[144]

Only one aspect of the Trump administration's claim contained an element of truth: While Housing First was ending homelessness for hundreds of thousands of people across the country each year, it wasn't solving the crisis. But that was not because the approach was wrong, it was because funding was wildly insufficient to meet the need. And it was also because, unlike Finland and Vienna, the United States has neither adequate social housing nor social supports in place. Nor has our country cultivated a sense of social solidarity that says, as Finland's Juha Kaakinen put it, "This is a national problem that *we should solve together*."[145]

The pandemic stalled Marbut and Trump's effort to undermine Housing First, and the advent of the Biden administration ended it.[146] As Biden came into office, he said explicitly that "housing should be a right, not a privilege." HUD secretary Marcia Fudge also embraced that view, USICH, with Jeff Olivet as its new head, affirmed that housing should be treated as a human right.[147] The administration followed up with specific policy proposals in its Build Back Better proposal, ultimately shot down by a narrow margin in the Senate.[148]

To the disappointment of advocates, the Biden administration took a big step backward in 2023 by coordinating with the District of Columbia police to carry out a high-profile sweep of an encampment near the White House.[149] Apparently succumbing to pressure from downtown businesses, the administration unapologetically and blatantly contradicted its own policies and guidance, which urged against closing encampments—unless they were carried out in a "coordinated, humane, and solutions-oriented way that makes housing and supports adequately available."[150] None of these conditions were met. Given Trump's re-election, we'll never know whether this was an inadvertent blip in an otherwise forward-thinking administration.[151]

HANDCUFFS, *NOT* HOUSING: THE CICERO INSTITUTE

The right-wing attack on Housing First hasn't let up in the meantime, with an organization calling itself the "Cicero Institute" taking up the charge. The group simultaneously works to undermine Housing First and encourage criminalizing homelessness. They don't call it that, but their campaign is essentially Handcuffs, Not Housing—a reversal of what we and other advocates have been promoting for decades. Ominously, the group brings a lot of money to the table.

Founded by a tech billionaire and venture capitalist whose investments include private prisons, Cicero says it aims to "fix broken systems" with "innovative public policies." In 2019, after the city of Austin *slightly* loosened its anti-camping law—requiring police to determine that an encampment in fact presented a health or safety risk before enforcing the ban—Cicero developed and lobbied for a new state law to make camping in public a crime. Their proposed amendment further mandated that all cities in Texas enforce it and similar punitive measures, on pain of losing state funding.[152] Two years later, Texas enacted the law. Emboldened by this success, Cicero established its headquarters in Austin, turned the Texas law into a model state bill—a template for others to follow—and began promoting it nationally.

As of late 2024, Georgia, Tennessee, Utah, Oklahoma, and Florida have adopted some version of the Texas template, and new bills had been introduced and were pending in about half a dozen states. Even more alarmingly, in April 2024, Kentucky enacted a draconian measure to add "unauthorized camping" to the state's "stand your ground" law, with the Republican supermajority overriding Democratic governor Beshear's veto. Effective as of July 2024, the Safer Kentucky Act allows property owners and renters to order homeless people camping on the property to leave and, if they feel "threatened," to use force, including deadly force, to remove them.[153]

On top of calling for the statewide criminalization of sleeping in public, the Cicero playbook calls for directing funding away from permanent housing and to mental health treatment, shelters, and short-term housing. It's another take on Trump appointee Robert Marbut's "housing fourth" approach. What makes it so dangerous is that it simply doesn't work—and it diverts already grossly inadequate funding away from Housing First, which does. And beyond the immediate harm Cicero causes, it promotes the false narrative that homelessness is driven by personal, not systemic, failures. Unhoused people are supposedly dangerous, "other," not true members of the community. They are less than human.

This noxious portrayal is the opposite of solidarity—and some of its champions are not shy about saying so.

An Arizona state senator was one such proponent. The state had been considering the Cicero model bill, but it faced vigorous opposition by advocates and failed to gather enough support. Joining activists to speak out against the bill was a Republican lawmaker who'd experienced homelessness himself—an echo of the "strange bedfellows" that had propelled the enactment of the McKinney-Vento Act decades earlier, and an example of solidarity crossing party lines.[154] But anti-homeless advocates tried again with a bill similar to the Cicero model, this one drafted by the Goldwater Institute (another right-wing activist group) and sponsored by State Senator Justine Wadsack.[155]

Arguing for her bill, Wadsack claimed that "unhoused people are not our neighbors."[156] The proposal spurred an outcry by advocates and concerned citizens, who cited increasing homelessness, decreasing affordable housing, and rising rents in mobilizing opposition. They also noted that Wadsack's proposal offered no solutions—and that she had voted against funding for affordable housing, rental assistance, and eviction prevention.[157] Nevertheless, the bill passed. Fortunately, Governor Katie Hobbs vetoed it, inviting the state legislature to join her in seeking "more productive solutions that respect constitutional and human rights."[158]

But Wadsack's proposal, and her unrepentant assertion that homeless people aren't our neighbors, reflect an attack on the very idea of social solidarity, and this attitude is increasingly popular in some quarters. In late 2023, then-former and now President Trump, released a plan to force homeless people into remote "tent cities" on pain of arrest.[159] And in March of 2024, Governor Ron DeSantis effectively did just that, banning unhoused people from sleeping outside and ordering every town in Florida to create and oversee a sanctioned, large-scale encampment.[160]

Finland's success with Housing First turned in large part on broad political consensus backing the goal and the program, as well as a societal commitment to "treating homeless people like everybody else." Viewing housing as a fundamental human right has been crucial. But as of 2021, the national Finnish government stepped back from its leadership role, and nonprofit leaders expressed concern about future funding.[161] And in June 2023, after a very tight election, a new right-wing government pressing for a more market-based approach to housing came into office—sparking concern among Housing First proponents like Juha Kaakinen.

When we spoke, though, Juha reasoned that if the new government pursues detrimental policies, voters will see the impact—including on themselves—and no longer back it. Ultimately, he believed Finns would not support this alternate view of their society. His confidence reminded me of the comments offered by Tom, the American man who became homeless in Helsinki and was helped into housing: "Finns would never let this happen to their own."

Many Americans do let this happen to their own. But the growing domestic movement for the human right to housing offers hope. It also poses one of the most important questions we can ask ourselves: What kind of society do we want to live in?

Chapter Nine

"Am I a Citizen?"

Decades ago, I sat behind a card table with other volunteer lawyers at a makeshift law office in the massive shelter in downtown Washington, D.C. We'd set up in a hallway since there was no other free space. A far cry from the refined settings of corporate law, we had only a few metal folding chairs for our clients and ourselves, and a handwritten "legal clinic" sign taped to the wall behind us. Just minutes from the US Capitol, the run-down building held over a thousand people.[1]

One evening in 1986 or 1987, I can't remember exactly, an older Black resident with an unassuming demeanor approached me with a simple question: "Am I a citizen?"

I inquired about his birthplace, assuming from his uncertainty that he'd been born elsewhere. No, he'd been born in the United States. Yet despite his unambiguously being American, he'd posed the question softly and tentatively, as if being a citizen might be too much to ask. Some details have faded, yet the man's query remains crystal clear in my memory. I'd been astonished, but I shouldn't have been. Given how his country was treating him, his question was perfectly reasonable.

A home is essential to carrying out just about every aspect of human life, from the basics like sleeping, eating, washing, doing laundry, or using the bathroom to activities like playing, doing homework, reading, listening to music, watching TV, raising a family, socializing with friends, dressing for work, and relaxing after it. The home also provides an address, that fundamental entryway to civic life and a requirement for just about every kind of participation in society, access to virtually any opportunity. It's part of citizenship in its broadest sense: membership in society.

The radical cuts to housing and other social programs in the early 1980s that triggered the modern-day crisis of mass homelessness moved US policy further away from ensuring that place to *be* for everyone: a home. Coupled with narratives that put the blame on unhoused and low-income people themselves—claiming they "chose" to live on the street or exploited aid as "welfare queens"—Reagan's policies and verbal attacks on the poor also did something less obvious: They further eroded the sense of belonging that underlies citizenship or membership in a greater whole. The message that poor and homeless people had chosen their plight made them different from "regular" Americans. They were "other," and the visibility of their suffering only served to magnify this message of difference to the broader public.

Newly homeless in 1982, eight-year-old Edward Koster felt the sense of alienation keenly. He and his large family were sleeping in a dilapidated pickup truck, scrimping on food, and peeing in old coffee cans for lack of a bathroom.[2] As the family drove around and around, his parents vainly looking for a place they could afford to rent, what Edward noticed most was everyone around them. "We lived on peanut butter and jelly sandwiches, and people drove around in their silly Cadillacs. They had a house and they didn't care about anyone else."[3]

Inequality has only grown since then, reaching record highs. Young Edward's observation was his own, but the feeling of marginalization he expressed certainly wasn't unique. As homelessness continues to grow—and punitive responses to it accelerate—the language of ostracization is sharpening. During his first administration and his failed 2020 presidential campaign, Trump and his allies referred to homeless people as "filth" that needed to be cleaned up.[4] Some Democratic city officials use the same language, arguing that public health and safety require "cleaning up" public city areas, as if the people living there are no more than human garbage.[5] The commonly used term "sweep" could not be clearer.

In 2022, Louis Lopez recalled his years living on Boston's streets and in its shelters as being worse than being in jail. Searching for jobs or trying in any way to "better" himself while he was homeless was incredibly stressful because "people know that you're homeless." Potential employers could "sense" that something was "not right." After several years, Louis finally got his own studio apartment with the help of a government subsidy. He described it as one of the best days of his life.[6]

A year after Louis finally moved into his own place, Danny felt "forgotten, brushed aside," as he literally froze under a tarp on the winter streets of his native Denver. That neglect cost him part of a leg and the toes on his remaining foot. Amy, the Mutual Aid volunteer who helped him, considered his loss the then-current price of moving up the waiting list for city housing. Danny characterized what happened to him as being *forgotten*, but I think that may have been a charitable way to put it. What he endured was deliberate exclusion, punishment, and dehumanization—being treated as less than human.

Danny's experience is part of a trend has been building for decades, and it cannot be described simply as a problem of individuals not caring. Our fundamental structures, institutions, and laws protect property for those who have it but offer few protections or rights for those who do not. The consequences of being without a basic form of property—a home—in a system built around it are far-reaching. People who lack it are not just being forgotten; they are being explicitly cut out of American society.

The lack of housing is fundamental, but a constellation of other factors also contribute to homelessness and the exclusion it entails: inadequate wages, lack of health care, food, childcare, education, and transportation. The absence of a societal commitment to a basic level of material well-being drives and allows the extreme inequality that exists today, with homelessness as one of its most visible signs.

Unhoused and other poor people obviously feel the impact most severely. But the failure to ensure—as fundamental human rights—the economic baseline that all human beings need to survive and to participate equally in society affects everyone.

Voting While Homeless: "These Laws Are Undemocratic and Un-American"

One key marker of membership in a democratic society is participation in voting. More often than not, unhoused individuals are shut out.

Peter Dyer was among those excluded. A Native American from Oklahoma, he'd moved to New York City in 1970. He found work at the American Indian Community House, a nonprofit organization. Peter had been there for ten years when the group's funding was cut and he was laid off. Before long, he could no longer afford to rent the apartment that had been his home for six years. Peter moved out and began living in a park during the summer and in the train station during the winter. When he tried to register to vote in February 1984, he was turned away. The same thing happened when he tried again that June. Peter met all the eligibility requirements to vote except for one: He didn't have an address.[7]

Peter was one of thousands (at least) being denied this basic right of citizenship. He joined a class-action lawsuit advocates had filed in federal court. Later that year, the court agreed that depriving homeless persons of the right to vote over the lack of a permanent address violated the US Constitution. If the individual had a place to which they regularly returned, even if it was a park bench, and a place to receive mail, such as a shelter, other program, or a friend's house, they could register and they could vote.[8] Subsequent cases brought by advocates in other cities—including Philadelphia and Santa Barbara—yielded similar victories, with courts ruling that people couldn't be denied their constitutional right to vote simply because they were homeless.[9]

In the decades to come, however, restrictions on voting rights tightened, especially in the wake of 9/11. New photo identification requirements stymied a broad range of voters, not just those lacking housing. Litigation proliferated.[10] In 2011, the Law Center and a coalition of other organizations challenged a restrictive Wisconsin law that affected people who couldn't practicably meet its requirements, including veterans, students, and unhoused people. One of the plaintiffs in the case was Carl Ellis, a fifty-two-year-old US Army veteran living in a homeless shelter in Milwaukee. Carl's only identification was a veteran ID card with his photograph, which was not accepted under the law.[11]

To get a legally acceptable form of ID, Carl needed a certified copy of his birth certificate, which he didn't have. It's a common problem: Such documents are often lost during evictions, sweeps, or the general turmoil of precarious, temporary living situations. Getting a certified birth certificate would have set Carl back $20, not including transportation to the relevant government office. Given his dire financial situation, doing so would mean foregoing other necessities. "If I can serve my country, I should be able to vote for who runs it," Carl said at the time. "Veterans and others who do not have a certain type of photo ID should not be kept from voting. These laws are undemocratic and un-American."[12]

Thanks to persistent advocacy, as of 2020 every state in the country had *some* process in place to allow unhoused people to vote. On paper, anyway—in practice, many eligible people don't know these processes exist. Even if they do, they still often have trouble complying with requirements such as filling out a formal document attesting to having a usual place of residence, if only a park bench, or providing a mailing address, or bringing someone with them who can attest to their identity. Voter registration campaigns, typically run by under-resourced advocacy groups, manage to reach some but leave many more out. A 2020 study reported that only about 10 percent of the homeless population voted.[13] This is consistent with studies showing that voter participation decreases as income decreases.[14] As the poorest of the poor, homeless people are at the very bottom.

Onerous requirements aside, voting is often impossible for unhoused people to prioritize. Living on the street, in a shelter, or an unstable doubled-up arrangement fraught with uncertainty and frequent moves all make it hard to pay attention to politics, much less engage in the political process. Eugene, an unhoused man in Washington, D.C., overcame these obstacles and tried to mobilize his peers. But, as Eugene explained: "Politics, laws, and guidance, and rulemaking, all that stuff is about tomorrow. . . . And if you're in a today-I-need-this-that survival mode thing, you don't even care about anyone that mentions the word tomorrow. . . . They want to know, how is it gonna get me out of this shelter or off the street today?"[15]

Without access to basic economic rights—including a home—exercising civil rights like voting can be nearly impossible. Voting may seem like the least urgent of the dire problems faced by people who are unhoused, as Eugene noted. But it's one also that clearly calls into question ideals on which American democracy purports to be founded. Being shut out of voting means being denied the opportunity to affect laws and policies—including those that drive and perpetuate homelessness. It's a perfect example of the vicious nature of exclusion. You're not only shut out, but that very fact makes it that much harder to change the systems that keep you out.

With the increasing influence of money in politics, more people are seeing the power of their votes—and their ability to influence policy—diluted.[16] People who are poor are more likely to be excluded from voting at all, not just having their voice weakened at the ballot box. And as always, the unhoused are the least likely to be able to take part—which is to say, have any impact on the policies that affect them.

The systemic exclusion extends beyond the ability to influence politics. Laws and policies raise money through taxes and create rules to allocate funding. Complex legal systems determine access to the rights and resources created by these laws and policies, often requiring specialized legal help (usually lawyers) for a layperson to navigate. It's another way that people who can't pay for that help are excluded even from rights they already have.

For unhoused people, the result is that critical needs like access to education or disability benefits often go unmet. For those so poor they're at risk of losing their homes, the result can be homelessness.

A NATION OF LAWS—FOR SOME

Randy Dillard was a single father of five living in the Bronx in the early 2000s when he received an eviction notice from his landlord.

Years later, he described the feeling: "Once the landlord sends you papers—you don't even know how to begin to read them, how to understand."

Randy's daughter, terrified that the family would have to go to a shelter, struggled in school, her grades plummeting. Fortunately, Randy heard about "Know Your Rights" workshops organized by community activists and, with their help, was able to get a lawyer, win his case, and prevent his family's eviction.[17]

Landlord-tenant laws signaled some degree of progress. They replaced an earlier "self-help" system that allowed landlords to forcibly remove tenants with a legal remedy mediated through the courts.[18] Landlords now had to use legal skill and the court process instead of brute force—and tenants had to defend their rights on the same battlefield. But few people can navigate that process alone. For most, lawyers are essential to understand the process and assert any rights the law gives you. Anyone who can't afford to hire a lawyer simply doesn't have access to the full protection of the law.

For Randy and his family, having a lawyer meant the difference between staying housed and becoming homeless. They were very lucky: Almost all landlords had lawyers at that time, while only 1 percent of low-income people facing eviction in housing court were represented by counsel. Predictably, given the complexity of the law, some 90 percent of unrepresented tenants lost their cases.[19] Many never even made it before a judge: Unscrupulous lawyers for landlords pressured many tenants to sign unfair agreements and leave their homes. This typically left them with an eviction record that would compromise future efforts to find other housing.

Reflecting on his experience, Randy said it'd been "a living hell, a living nightmare, when you know that you can't protect your children." Not wanting other families "to go through what [he] went through," in 2014 Randy joined the group that had helped him find his lawyer. The Right to Counsel NYC Coalition was—and is—a citywide group of tenants and other advocates working to ensure that low-income tenants fighting eviction in housing court had a lawyer. Randy soon became a leader in the group's campaign to enact a legal right to counsel.

In 2017, after twenty years of work by the coalition and other supporters, New York City became the first jurisdiction in the country to enact a right to legal counsel for low-income tenants facing eviction in housing court. This success inspired a nationwide movement: By December 2024, a total of eighteen cities, five states, and two counties had enacted a right to counsel in housing court.[20] The need remains great: Nationally, according to data last updated in November 2024, only 4 percent of tenants facing eviction court had a lawyer, as opposed to 83 percent of landlords.[21]

This power imbalance can only be corrected by evening the scales. As Randy Dillard put it, the right to counsel gives tenants "the power to organize and not be afraid of their landlord because they know they have an attorney."[22]

In the words of another tenant activist, recognizing this right means "living in dignity and being treated as a human being."[23] Retaining counsel is critical to tenants' ability to even enter a complicated legal system, let alone successfully navigate it. And gaining the right to counsel is also essential to tenants' assertion of their own agency.

But the fight, in New York City and elsewhere, is not over. Lawyers representing tenants are largely drawn from legal aid organizations, which partially rely on public funding—and that funding is not remotely adequate. The same system that declines to sufficiently fund the lawyers needed to make the right a reality doesn't hesitate to propel the machinery of eviction forward—counsel or no counsel. Denied representation in the legal system that theoretically could and should protect them, impoverished people are pushed into homelessness.

Despite the name, the right to counsel is not yet truly a right. Contingent on discretionary funding, it's dependent on the political choice to provide that funding. Exclusion from the right to vote—both legal and practical—means that the influence of unhoused people on that choice is extremely limited. With a broad coalition of tenants and allies, Randy and the Right to Counsel NYC Coalition are pushing to overcome the obstacles and expand—and fund—this necessary right.[24]

Legal representation is critical, but it's also just one step in leveling a very uneven playing field where poor people are at a severe disadvantage. While access to existing rights is undeniably important, creating new rights—new *economic* rights—is even more fundamental.

"LIBERTY AND JUSTICE FOR ALL"—AND HOUSING FOR SOME

Our society and social structures place private property at their center. The home—a form of "real property"—is arguably the most essential. Yet those same structures allow some people to have none at all.

The "American dream" may be homeownership, but many people rent and, of course, that's home, too. What's key is that you have your own place, somewhere where you have a legal right to be as long as you pay the mortgage or rent. You have a measure of control and agency over the space and your use of it. You can go out, maybe drive around in your car, whether it's a "silly Cadillac" or something humbler, knowing you have a place to go back to.[25]

Being homeless means having nowhere that you have a legal right to be, whether by ownership or lease. People in a shelter or transitional housing program are subject to its rules, including the possibility of ejection at any time. Those living doubled up with friends or family depend on their hosts' generosity and ability to keep housing them.[26] Individuals and families who are staying outside in a public place likely have no rights over that space at all. Worse still, as punitive anti-homeless laws spread, people living in public may be subject to arrest and criminal prosecution just for being there. Lacking a legal claim to a place of one's own means being shut out of a cornerstone of American society.[27]

Some have argued that without some form of real property, a person cannot truly be free.[28] The reasoning is that without property, a person lacks any place they have control over. And because anything that anyone does has to be done *somewhere*, that means they depend on others for the ability to carry out their lives. Without any place of their own, people who are homeless are subordinated to those who do have property rights. It's that lack of control—of agency and autonomy—that many unhoused people describe as so demeaning about shelters. When we were investigating access to school for homeless students in Washington, D.C., Shirley Riley, mother of eleven-year-old Antwaun, characterized it this way: "Living in a shelter is a living hell, with feeding schedules and other people telling you what to do with your children."

That phrase—"a living hell"—was also how Randy Dillard described his fight against eviction in New York City. Whether it's the experience of having lost one's home or just the threat of it, in our society being deprived of *your place* can feel like a fate worse than death.

Without their own place, people who are homeless must carry out their lives on the terms of others. Property rights are intentionally structured that way: They do more than define who has control and power over a space; they limit who has access to it. Laying out this analysis, one legal philosopher calls homelessness a form of "structural subordination."[29] That's obviously a problem for the people experiencing it—and for anyone committed to living in a society where all human beings have equal rights.

Homelessness cultivates the feeling that you are not "part of society," as Louis Lopez put it. It's why Dominique Walker said with perfect clarity that her children could not really be free without a home. What's so obvious to Louis and Dominique and others with direct experience of homelessness calls into question the underlying basis of American society. The country's founding document, the Declaration of Independence, proclaimed equality a "self-evident" truth.[30] A system of property that undermines that truth also undermines our society's proclaimed values.[31]

Of course, many things do, and inequality is at its highest point since the 1920s.[32] And while equality was extolled in the Declaration of Independence, at the time of the country's founding, this "self-evident" truth applied only to White male property owners.[33] Others were relegated to subhuman status, treated as property, bought, sold, and enslaved. Since that time, a civil war ended official slavery. Thanks to powerful movements for civil rights, women's rights, and others, the foundational "truths" of the Declaration of Independence have expanded to include more of us—in theory, though often not in practice.[34] However poorly protected it frequently is, the basic equality of human beings is a fundamental American value.

Treating unhoused people as subhuman clearly undermines that value. It may also be one sign of a growing threat of authoritarianism. When he was president the first time, Donald Trump publicly referred to people experiencing homelessness in dehumanizing terms and considered proposals to relocate them to remote federal facilities.[35] Following his reelection in 2024, he vowed to "create tent cities" on "large parcels of inexpensive land" where homeless people can be "relocated," presumably, as he said during his campaign, at the "outer reaches" of cities."[36] Trump was building on and making explicit trends that have been underway for decades, promoted by Democrats and Republicans alike. It's not too much of a leap from dehumanizing unhoused people to dehumanizing anyone else deemed by those in power to be "other." By late 2023, the former president had made his plans for asserting dictatorial powers explicit.[37]

One counter to these trends is growing recognition of the importance of belonging. According to medical experts, social belonging is essential to our physical and mental health.[38] On an individual level, nearly every aspect of our identities and lives revolves around belonging to something—a family, a group, a place. More globally, it informs how society organizes itself into communities, associations, governments. Business experts have also recognized a sense of workplace belonging as critical: It's good for business and the bottom line.[39] Even politicians are promoting it.[40] Increasingly, belonging is recognized as a basic human need.

A human rights framework offers specific ways to meet that need.[41] It's a framework that draws us all in by centering our common humanity. There are rights we all have simply by virtue of being human—the focus is on our commonality. This isn't to say that everyone doesn't also have responsibilities, just that the key values of human dignity and equality must be respected.[42] Among other things, it means recognizing that everyone needs a place to be—and that housing is a human right.

During the pandemic, the importance of housing took center stage. Americans—and people around the world—were instructed to stay at home, wash our hands, and isolate if we got sick. Yet for those without homes, or those in overcrowded, unsafe living situations, these basic precautions were impossible. As people lost their jobs, housing insecurity expanded, and many feared losing their own home and ending up on the streets. Polls taken at the time reflect this elevated concern. They also reflect increased public support to provide housing for those who were already homeless.[43]

Current laws and policies leave many people with precarious property rights, such as those tenants paying more than half of their income to hang on to their homes. And many are left out altogether—those who are homeless. But there is nothing innate or necessary about the system of property we have put in place. By itself, land is "just a piece of dirt," an undifferentiated part of Earth.[44] Laws and legal systems organize it and turn it into property, give it value, determine how it is acquired and used, who has rights to it—and who doesn't.[45] For people who are poor or homeless, navigating the system of laws that determine rights and allocate resources can be impossible. Dispossession begets more dispossession.

No matter how complex, these laws are simply a set of rules by which our society governs itself. They are a choice. This is crucial because it means that people can collectively choose differently. We can choose to honor the human rights of all people. We can recognize that ensuring everyone has a home is essential—not just for the sake of those who are unhoused, but for all of us. We can come to see that it's in everyone's collective self-interest.

Shifting to a framework that recognizes housing as a human right will require a fundamental shift in priorities. It will take the support of a big coalition. The makings of one are already here.

"I LIVED IN MY CAR AND NOW I'M IN CONGRESS"

After cofounding Moms 4 Housing, Dominique Walker moved across the Bay, rented an apartment, and enrolled in premed classes at Berkeley City College. In Berkeley, Dominque saw the same housing challenges that Oakland faced, and she continued her work as an organizer. Dominque's own experience with homelessness had made her "jump into the fight headfirst and want to be part of the change."[46] She ran for commissioner of the city's rent stabilization board, part of a human right to housing slate, because she believed that "everyone should have a right to affordable and accessible housing." Dominique won in December 2020.[47] Since then, she's continued to be a leader for housing reform in her community, helping to push for an amendment to the state constitution to add housing as a right.

Dominique wasn't alone. She ran as part of the "Housing Is a Human Right Slate for Rent Board" assembled by community organizers, winning together with its four other members.[48] Among them was Leah Simon-Weisberg, the lawyer who had represented Moms 4 Housing, who became chair of the rent board.

Beyond the rent board, Carroll Fife, the formerly homeless community organizer who cofounded Moms 4 Housing, won election to the Oakland city council.[49] The human right to housing was one of Carroll's stated top three priorities, along with economic justice and addressing the harms of racial injustice through a Black New Deal.[50] Two years later, in November 2022, another formerly homeless Oakland City Council member, Sheng Thao, was elected mayor—also becoming the first Hmong mayor of a major US city.[51]

Around the same time, Cori Bush was elected to the US House of Representatives, assuming office in January 2021.[52] Born and raised in St. Louis, Bush would go on to become a registered nurse, but she started out as a childcare worker, living paycheck to paycheck on minimum wage. She became unhoused with two young children, living with them and her partner in their car for months, mixing their formula in fast-food restaurants.[53]

In Congress, Bush drafted the "Unhoused Persons Bill of Rights," promoting her resolution in an opinion piece for *Time* magazine titled "I Lived in My Car and Now I'm in Congress. We Need to Solve America's Housing Crisis."[54] First introduced by Bush in July 2021, and again in July 2023, the resolution calls for recognition of the human right to housing, along with other economic and social rights: a livable wage, health care, education, and access to employment opportunities. The "Unhoused Persons Bill of Rights" also includes civil rights, such as freedom of movement in public spaces.[55]

Bush made headlines again a few weeks later, when she camped out for five days and four nights in front of the Capitol. She slept in the rain and the heat to protest her House colleagues departing for the summer without taking action to extend the federal eviction moratorium mid-pandemic. Holding a "housing is a human right" sign, Bush was joined by several colleagues. As the group grew to dozens of supporters, pressure mounted on the Biden administration to act. The CDC ultimately issued another, somewhat narrower moratorium—a major win for Bush and her supporters that provided extra time for tenants to apply for the already available federal aid.[56]

The US Supreme Court soon struck down the new moratorium, again putting millions of poor, disproportionately Black, households at risk of homelessness.[57] But in addition to buying tenants some time, Bush's bold action helped spawn increased activism for renters' rights—leading to the enactment of hundreds of new protections in dozens of communities around the country.[58] She also inspired more direct action by tenant activists, including takeovers of vacant properties similar to what Moms 4 Housing had done in Oakland. In Bush's home state, KC Tenants weren't fazed by the Supreme Court decision: "A faulty eviction moratorium wasn't ever going to save us. We take care of us."[59]

Reflecting on her activism as a member of Congress, Bush observed, "We have a lot of work to do . . . until we have more people seated in Congress who understand some of the struggles and burdens that everyday people in our communities face. Until [politicians] are able to really understand, empathize and speak . . . about all of the nuances to poverty."[60]

Just a year earlier, Juha Kaakinen, a leader of Finland's successful (though still ongoing) effort to end homelessness, had made a very similar comment while looking back on that work. Emphasizing that "the main thing is treating homeless people like everybody else—people who have the same rights and [to] see housing as a human right," Juha concluded that "I think that it demands politicians who have an understanding of human dignity."[61]

Not all formerly homeless politicians share the perspective of Cori Bush.[62] But many do, and having more elected leaders with personal experience of being unhoused will almost certainly help promote solutions to homelessness. Over the past two decades, their numbers have been growing. Dennis Kucinich, a 2004 and 2008 presidential candidate—and former Cleveland councilmember and mayor, Ohio state legislator, and US representative—experienced homelessness as a child, living with his parents in their car when his father was unemployed. As a politician, he considers housing a basic human right.[63] The elections of Dominique Walker, Carroll Fife, Cori Bush, and others suggest a building trend. Still, Bush's primary loss to a well-funded challenger makes clear the path forward will be neither easy nor linear.

Outside pressure on political leaders and private sector players is also on the rise, spurred by the pandemic's housing crisis. Rent strikes, takeovers of vacant properties, and eviction defense actions—where activists physically block law enforcement from removing tenants—are all increasing.[64] Indeed, once Bush became a member of Congress, where change is generally effected through official legislative channels, her accomplishments were in part due to activism she directed at her colleagues and the Biden administration.

Getting—and keeping—more politicians with firsthand experience in Congress and other decision-making bodies remains a challenge, though, especially in the United States, where the influence of money in politics is pervasive. The same obstacles that prevent many homeless people from voting also make electing unhoused candidates extremely challenging—almost impossible. But as more people experience homelessness, there's an expanding pool of now-housed people who once lived on the streets, in shelters, in cars, or doubled up. While such candidates also face high hurdles, they're better equipped than currently homeless individuals to run, galvanize the support of activists and others, and win.

Crucially, more people who have experienced homelessness are becoming organizers and advocates, mobilizing others—including those who are or have been unhoused, as well as allies without direct experience—to exert political pressure.[65] And as advocacy continues and access to education cracks slightly open, more formerly unhoused people are making their way into college, graduate school, and law school—including the most elite institutions—creating a potential pipeline of future leaders who can influence policy.[66]

The pool of people with relevant direct experience is expanding. The most severely affected are the over eleven million extremely poor renters who pay over 50 percent of their income for rent; any unexpected expense can plunge them over the edge into homelessness. But the numbers of renters who are cost burdened, albeit less severely, are also growing. And the traditional "dream" of homeownership is increasingly out of reach for many Americans.[67] As more people feel the impact of unaffordable housing, the constituency of supporters for solutions has the potential to grow.

Housing is the overriding issue for people who become unhoused, but it's not the only one. Low wages are the flip side of unaffordable housing: Higher wages—livable wages—help make housing affordable. Other essential needs come into play as well. Finland's successful effort to address homelessness relies on the county's constitutional guarantee of the right to housing, and laws and funding to implement it, but also on the guarantee of help for those unable to support themselves, along with health care, childcare, education, and a panoply of other social supports.[68]

Low-wage workers are increasingly advocating for a living wage and forming unions to demand it. Tenants are organizing for expanded protections, including the right to counsel and social housing. As housing precarity intensifies, these efforts are likely to strengthen. They point to the potential for an expanded coalition of activists and political leaders who support the call for the human right to housing—and for economic rights for all.

"PART OF SOCIETY AGAIN"

The numbers of people who have experienced homelessness are growing, as are the numbers of people who are on the brink of it. More people have firsthand experience of what it means to be without housing, or at risk of losing it. There is a growing potential constituency of those who understand the need to recognize housing as a human right—and have the will to act on it.

But the potential is there for a much larger constituency. Direct experience may be the clearest path to this understanding, but it's hardly the only one.

Many belief systems prioritize economic justice, including many faiths. Think of the Christian directive to feed, clothe, and invite in the stranger.[69] Similar teachings can be found in Jewish, Muslim, and Hindu texts, among other major world religions. In the United States, many shelters, food pantries, and soup kitchens are faith-based.[70] Religious conviction can also extend beyond service provision to advocacy for social change. The Catholic worker movement has been doing so for almost a century.[71]

The relationship between religion and human rights is complicated, but some core values—like the call to economic justice—are shared.[72] Secular belief systems can also embed a moral obligation to care for others and take action to fight oppression.[73] Some philosophers explicitly call out the obligation as reciprocal: The freedom of an individual can only be achieved when others are free.[74] Activists have made a similar argument. In a 1971 speech, Fannie Lou Hamer famously declared that "nobody's free until everybody's free."[75]

A sense of patriotism—a commitment to fundamental American values and ideals—can also give impetus not only care but also to act. In addition to the "self-evident" truth of equality, the Declaration of Independence recognized "certain inalienable Rights, that among these are Life, Liberty and the pursuit of Happiness."[76] The pledge of allegiance, recited daily in countless public schools, affirms the nation's commitment to "liberty and justice for all."

Human rights law offers the framework for putting such convictions into place—that's what it was designed to do. It's a framework that honors the rights and dignity of all of us as human beings.

And even people who don't care about the spiritual, moral, social justice, or patriotic dimensions of the problem may still care about wasting money. Dozens of studies show that it's overall more expensive to let people remain homeless than it is to provide housing and all necessary social services. Ending homelessness is financially prudent and cost-effective. There's an economic case for ensuring everyone has a home.

No matter what it is, everyone has—or can have—their own reason to care about ending homelessness. And it *is* their own reason. This isn't just a matter of feeling sorry that our fellow human beings are living—and often dying—in terrible, preventable distress. It's also a matter of everyone's own financial, moral, and spiritual self-interest. It's not an issue of charity. It's a matter of who *we* collectively are. And that is a choice we make.[77]

When Lewis Lopez finally landed in his apartment after years spent homeless, he said he "felt so free . . . like part of society again." Maybe his sense of relief was akin to what I saw long ago on the face of the older gentleman at our makeshift legal clinic when I assured him that he was, indeed, a citizen. The importance of a sense of belonging cannot be overstated.

But the question is far bigger than an individual person's sense of being part of society. It also encompasses what it means to be a member of a community—to be a citizen in the largest sense. Ultimately, the question is what kind of a society we collectively choose to be.

It's up to each of us to make it one that affirms everyone's humanity—including our own.

Acknowledgments

This book has been years in the making, and I have many people and organizations to thank for helping to make it a reality.

The idea began percolating over a decade ago, but it was not until 2016 that I was able to set aside some time to begin sketching out what a book might look like. That year I was honored to receive the Katharine and George Alexander Law prize from the Santa Clara University School of Law. The prize included funds that I donated to the Law Center; in exchange, I spent a few hours every week outlining a possible book. I am grateful for this early opportunity.

Work on the book would not truly progress until I stepped down from leading the Law Center in 2021, freeing up time and energy for what would become a long process. I am grateful to the Rockefeller Foundation for granting me a residency at its Bellagio Center, an amazing place and experience. Pilar Palaciá and her staff created a welcoming and energizing environment, and my fellow residents offered insights and inspiration that continue to this day.

Early on, colleagues and friends helped with encouragement and advice, and I especially appreciate the support I received from Jason DeParle, Peter Edelman, Dan McMillan, and Kim Hopper. Lisa Adams was more than generous as well as extremely helpful as I worked on the proposal for the book, as was Mary-Claire Blakeman. Kyle Gordon, and Xylo Lee, my Columbia Law School student research assistants during the (pandemic) summer of 2021, contributed excellent early research. Lauren Kranzlin followed as a top-notch volunteer research assistant. Much later, Jesse Bullington helped enormously with editorial comments and suggestions on the manuscript, and I very much appreciate his careful eye and unfailing enthusiasm.

Students in my Homelessness Law and Policy Seminar at Columbia Law School, which I co-taught with Kim Hopper from 2018 to 2023 (and as of 2024 have taught solo), regularly inspired me with their passion, insights, and questions. Some of their papers led me to additional, fruitful research, as noted in the text, and I thank them for that. Collaborating with Kim on the class was a joy, and I benefited greatly from it, as did the book.

Much of the advocacy at the core of the book derives from the work of the National Homelessness Law Center, the organization I founded in June 1989 and led until March 2021. (Before August 2020 it was known as the National Law Center on Homelessness & Poverty.)

I am grateful to all the Law Center's staff, fellows, and interns over all those decades for their energy, intelligence, and commitment—and for the efforts that underlie this book.

Special thanks to just a few whose work informs the book: Diane Aten, Tristia Bauman, Catherine Bendor, Greg Christianson, Kelly Cunningham-Bowers, Greg Ernst, Antonia Fasanelli, Janelle Fernandez, Lorraine Friedman, Chrysanthe Gussis, Teresa Hinze, Janet Hostettler, Patricia Julianelle, Sally McCarthy, LaTissia Mitchell, Joy Moses, Tulin Ozdeger, Pallavi Rai, Jeremy Rosen, Michael Santos, Justine Stamen, Darrell Stanley, Eric Tars, Sara Simon Tompkins, Rebecca Troth, and Laurel Weir.

I am especially grateful that the Law Center is continuing its vigorous advocacy—unfortunately still urgently needed—and I appreciate the current staff for their hard work and dedication. I am doubly grateful to my successor, Antonia Fasanelli: first, for her work at the Law Center as a VISTA volunteer from 1996 to 1998, and again, starting in April 2021, as its executive director.

I began my advocacy at the National Coalition for the Homeless, and I also thank the staff there, especially Colleen Harrington and Julie Akins, who joined the office I established and headed in Washington, D.C. That office became the organization's sole office after I left and the New York office split off; I appreciate the help of the group's current executive director, Donald Whitehead, and DeBorah Gilbert White, its director of public education.

Pro bono work by law firms and corporate legal departments has been critical to the advocacy featured in the book, and I am grateful for the contributions of many pro bono partners to that work. They include Baker & McKenzie, Bank of America, Carlyle, Covington & Burling, Dechert, Fried Frank, Goodwin Procter, Jenner & Block, King & Spalding, Kirkland & Ellis, Latham & Watkins, Microsoft, Simpson Thacher & Bartlett, Sullivan & Cromwell, WilmerHale, and many others. A special thank-you to Jessica Klein, pro bono director at Sullivan & Cromwell, for her help with tracking down old files related to the *Koster v. Perales* case. Thank you also to Beth Polner, Vicki Lens, Ettie Taichman, and Doug Ruff for helping me with details on that case.

Partnerships with allied groups are likewise critical to advocacy, and I am grateful to key partners for their work as well as for their willingness to take the time to talk with me as I worked on the book. Special thanks to Paul Boden, Amy Beck, Brian Carome, Barbara Duffield, Terese Howard, Tiffani McCoy, Nan Roman, Julie Turner, Jodi Peterson-Stigers, and Virya Kelsing. Thank you to Juha Kaakinen and Barbara Unterlerchner for offering an important international perspective.

I am grateful to Mark Horvath for his work and for the website he has created, Invisible People, which served as an important source of stories and inspiration and helped keep me grounded in reality. I am profoundly thankful to all the unhoused people who shared their experiences on the site, some of whom also figure in my book. Their courage and eloquence in the face of suffering cannot be overstated. Special thanks also to *Street Sense, Street Spirit, Real Change*, and other street newspapers for their important work in covering the lives and experiences of unhoused people and the issues they face; they are an invaluable resource.

I am immensely grateful to those who took the time to share their lived experiences of homelessness with me for the book. I admire all they have accomplished, and their willingness to speak openly about their own experience and, in many cases, turn it into advocacy. Special thanks and much appreciation to Danny Maestas, Craig Champ, Xyzlo Lee, Khadijah Williams, Karim Walker, and Paul Boden. My gratitude also to the many others I have met and worked with over the past decades, some of whose stories appear in the book, but with whom I've now lost touch.

It turned out that much more than research and writing is involved in having a book published. Big thanks to my agent, Andy Ross, for showing the way and helping to make it happen. Thank you also to my publisher, Prometheus Books, and especially to Jonathan Kurtz for his enthusiasm and support.

My parents, Nicolas and Rosa, spurred me to care about the world and the people in it; and to take action against injustice. They are long gone, but their values live on with me and inspire me. My uncle Nikos, whom I never met, left behind in his letters a call to action that echoes in my mind and heart. I am grateful to my family for giving me a clear sense of justice and hope.

My husband, Nathan Stoltzfus, has been a constant source of love and encouragement. Always willing to read and comment on drafts with insight and care, he steadfastly supported my work on this book, despite the constraints my often inflexible writing schedule imposed on both of us. Beyond four walls and a roof—the necessary elements so many lack—home is where the heart is. I am grateful beyond measure to have found mine with Nathan.

NOTES

INTRODUCTION

1. "Dullanni," *Invisible People*, April 18, 2023, https://invisiblepeople.tv/videos/homeless-man-arrested-20-times-san-diego/.

2. Danny Maestas, interviewed by the author, September 29, 2023; Amy Beck, interviewed by the author, July 2, 2023; Amy Beck, email to the author July 4, 2023.

3. Paige Oamek and Rohan Montgomery, "Kentucky Is About to Pass the Cruelest Criminal-Justice Bill in America," *Nation*, March 15, 2024, https://www.thenation.com/article/society/kentucky-crime-bill/; Gilbert McClanahan, "Safer Kentucky Act may have unintended consequences," WCHS ABC 8, April 17, 2024, https://wchstv.com/news/local/safer-kentucky-act-may-have-unintended-consequences.

4. *Congressional Record* (daily edition, March 23, 1987), H.

5. City of Grants Pass v. Johnson, 603 U.S. 520 (2024).

6. Many were evicted; in 1932 alone, 250,000 families lost their homes. Michelle Wakin, *Homelessness in America: A Reference Handbook* (ABC-CLIO, 2022), 8–9; 15–16.

7. E. J. Montini, "Bill Pushed by Republican Lawmakers Attacks the Homeless for Being Houseless," *Arizona Central*, February 22, 2023, https://www.azcentral.com/story/opinion/op-ed/ej-montini/2023/02/22/arizona-legislature-bill-attacks-homeless-for-being-houseless/69929974007/.

8. Between 300,000 and 400,000 people died of starvation in a single year in Athens. "German Occupation," Memories of the Occupation in Greece, https://www.occupation-memories.org/en/deutsche-okkupation/ergebnisse-des-terrors/index.html.

9. His execution was in reprisal for the killings of Nazis by Greek Resistance fighters, one of tens of thousands. For every Nazi officer killed, one hundred Greeks were executed; for every Nazi soldier killed, fifty Greeks were executed. The differential value of life has a long history. Wireless to the *New York Times*, "Many Greeks Die in Nazi Reprisals," *New York Times*, January 24, 1944.

10. On file with the author. Translation from the original Greek by the author.

11. Throughout the book, I use first names for advocates, service providers and people experiencing homelessness, and last names for government officials.

Sometimes these categories overlap, in which case I maintain my first use. I use *people experiencing homelessness*, *homeless people*, and *unhoused people* interchangeably.

CHAPTER ONE

1. Ronald Reagan Presidential Library and Museum, "The Reagan Presidency," National Archives, https://www.reaganlibrary.gov/reagans/reagan-administration/reagan-presidency; Ronald Reagan, "Nomination Acceptance Speech," Republican National Convention, Detroit, Michigan, July 17, 1980, https://www.4president.org/speeches/1980/reagan1980acceptance.htm; Vartanig V. Vartan, "Wall St. Winners and Losers," *New York Times*, December 31, 1982, https://www.nytimes.com/1982/12/31/business/wall-st-winners-and-losers.html.

2. Sister Mary Jane Hicks of St. Brigid's Parish wrote to the Department of Social Services itemizing the money the parish paid to motels to shelter families, including one found huddled in their doorway. Sister Mary explained that they had depleted their resources and had to turn people away, ending with a plea: "Emergency housing is desperately needed in Nassau County."

3. John Cummings, "Nassau Family's Challenge," *Newsday*, September 25, 1984.

4. Kathy Kafur, "Homelessness: A Hidden Problem," *New York Times*, November 21, 1982. *Newsday* also featured the Kosters, including a photo of the family with their truck, as part of a series the paper published on the rise of homelessness on Long Island; John Cummings, "Nassau Family's Challenge," *Newsday*, September 25, 1984.

5. As with lower-income people in general, most homeless people lack a social network with resources to help. This is especially true for members of minoritized communities. It undoubtedly helped that the Kosters were White. Their participation in a relatively high-profile lawsuit also broadened their connections to resources.

6. Jeff Leibowitz, "Growing Number of Homeless Perplexes L.I.," *New York Times*, February 7, 1988, https://www.nytimes.com/1988/02/07/nyregion/growing-number-of-homeless-perplexes-li.html. This was according to Nassau County officials, who used a narrower definition of homelessness than the Hofstra professor, and thus estimated a lower total number. Hyman Enzer, chair, Department of Sociology, Hofstra University, "Memorandum to Nassau Action Coalition," April 12, 1984, reproduced in US House of Representatives, *HUD Report on Homelessness*, Joint Hearing before the Subcommittee on Housing and Community Development of the Committee on Banking, Finance and Urban Affairs and the Subcommittee on Manpower and Housing of the Committee on Government Operations, May 24, 1984, 191–99.

7. In a class action, "named" plaintiffs, like the Kosters, "represent" the interests of a "class" of plaintiffs who are "similarly situated"—that is, face the same problem—but are not individually identified. The class may also have subclasses reflecting different aspects of a problem. In our case, we had two: families whose request for

emergency shelter were outright denied, like the Kosters, and those who were placed in grossly substandard and dangerous temporary accommodations, represented by another family—later identified as the Deans, after the family we had originally identified to represent this subclass found housing and was no longer homeless. An important advantage of class actions is that the case can continue if the complaints of individual members are resolved—often a deliberate tactic by defendants to "moot" a case—yet the challenged policies and practices continue.

8. The legal profession has a tradition of pro bono service, now codified as a professional responsibility of all members of the bar. Big firms like mine, and many smaller ones, already had formal programs to help its lawyers fulfill this by representing indigent clients at no charge. Some firms have more generous pro bono policies than others, meaning that they treat pro bono work like paying work. Others limit the time their lawyers may devote to this free work or even deduct time spent on pro bono from lawyers' compensation.

9. Enzer, "Memorandum to Nassau Action Coalition."

10. Description of the Myers family based on memory, with identifying details altered to protect privacy.

11. Koster v. Perales, Amended Complaint, 82 Civ. 2892 (ILG), filed September 25, 1984; Deposition of Deborah Dean, October 9, 1984; Michael Alexander, "Nassau's Homeless Become Its Hopeless," *Newsday*, September 24, 1984; Vicki Lens, *Poor Justice, How the Poor Fare in the Courts* (Oxford University Press, 2016).

12. Michael Alexander, "Nassau's Homeless Become Its Hopeless," *Newsday*, September 24, 1984; Deposition of Deborah Dean, October 9, 1984.

13. Between 300,000 and 400,000 people died of starvation in a single year in Athens. "German Occupation," Memories of the Occupation in Greece, https://www.occupation-memories.org/en/deutsche-okkupation/ergebnisse-des-terrors/index.html.

14. Lyle Moran, "Largest Law Firms Charge Nearly $1,000 an Hour, Report Finds," *Legal Dive*, December 11, 2023, https://www.legaldive.com/news/am-law-100-hourly-rates-largest-law-firms-brightflag-analysis/702164/. This was the *average* for the top one hundred US law firms.

15. Courts must appoint lawyers to represent indigent defendants in criminal cases, but not in most civil cases—including denial of public benefits or eviction. Recent initiatives are beginning to change this in a few cities, providing legal representation where very important interests are at stake, such as in eviction court.

16. Sophisticated legal work is critical to creating and maintaining wealth. Katharina Pistor, *The Code of Capital: How the Law Creates Wealth and Inequality* (Princeton University Press, 2019).

17. National Coalition for a Civil Right to Counsel (NCCRC), "The Right to Counsel for Tenants: Enacted Legislation," NCCRC, last modified December 2024, https://civilrighttocounsel.org/resources/organizing_around_right_to_counsel/#rtclaws. The movement is part of a broader effort to secure a right to

counsel in civil cases involving critical issues beyond housing, including child custody and health care. Currently, as interpreted by the US Supreme Court, the Constitution ensures a right to a lawyer only in criminal cases, not civil ones.

18. This meant that there were so many families facing the same problem that it made more sense to define a "class" rather than join them all together in one giant group of plaintiffs.

19. Koster v. Perales, Amended Complaint, 82 Civ. 2892 (ILG), September 25, 1984.

20. Koster v. Perales, 108 F.R.D. 46 (1985).

21. It also obligated the county to provide prompt and written notice of any decision that a family was not eligible for emergency housing, and it obligated the state to supervise the county's compliance with each of its provisions. Koster v. Perales, 903 F.2d 131 (2d Cir. 1990); Matthew Chayes, "How 2 Families Sparked Nassau's Shelter Mandate," *Newsday*, October 1, 2023.

22. The county's recognition that homelessness even existed, and its stated commitment to act, were a step forward. But the new shelters—which would house only one hundred people—were just a drop in the bucket.

23. Our case, filed against Nassau County and the State of New York, was novel in that we were making our claim under federal law, in federal court. At the time, the Aid to Families with Dependent Children (AFDC) program provided federal funds to states for modest cash aid to poor families with children. To get federal funds, states had to submit a plan stating what forms of assistance they would provide; they had the option to provide emergency shelter to eligible families, and New York State had taken that option. Our case argued that New York was thus committed, as a matter of federal law, to actually do so, and because of how the federal law worked, Nassau County was required to carry out this mandate by providing emergency shelter to homeless families such as the Kosters. The county and state had disputed this reading of the law and asked the judge to throw the case out. But the judge denied their request. To win, we still had to show that our version of the facts—that our plaintiffs had been denied the emergency shelter for which they were eligible—was correct. I came into the case just after the judge made that ruling; my first task was to identify additional plaintiffs and build the case for class certification. It bears noting that in 1996 President Bill Clinton signed into law Congress's repeal of the AFDC program as part of "welfare reform" and his own commitment to "end welfare as we know it."

24. Chayes, "How 2 Families Sparked Nassau's Shelter Mandate."

25. US House of Representatives, *HUD Report on Homelessness*, 218.

26. US House of Representatives, *HUD Report on Homelessness*, 214.

27. National Low Income Housing Coalition, *The Gap: A Shortage of Affordable Homes* (2023), https://nlihc.org/gap. This includes the shortage for those who are "extremely low-income," a term defined by the federal government to mean people living at the poverty level or below 30 percent of their area's median income,

whichever is higher, plus those who are "very low-income," with incomes at or below 50 percent of their area's median.

28. Kim Hopper, "Homelessness Old and New: The Matter of Definition," in *Understanding Homelessness: New Policy and Research Perspectives*, ed. Dennis P. Culhane and Steven P. Hornburg (Fannie Mae Foundation, 1991, 1997), 20.

29. US General Accounting Office, *Homelessness: A Complex Problem and the Federal Response* (April 1985), 11. The report measured increases by increased demand in requests for emergency shelter, with 28 percent of big-city mayors reporting "major" increases.

30. Julie Kosterlitz, "They're Everywhere," *National Journal*, February 28, 1987; "The Homeless Become an Issue," *New York Times*, February 7, 1987.

31. Many were evicted—in 1932 alone, a quarter of a million families lost their homes. Michele Wakin, *Homelessness in America: A Reference Handbook* (ABC-CLIO, 2022), 8–9; 15–16.

32. Wakin, *Homelessness in America*; Hopper, "Homelessness Old and New."

33. Richard Rothstein, *The Color of Law: A Forgotten History of How Our Government Segregated America* (Liveright, 2017); Stanford Center on Poverty and Inequality, "State of the Union," *Pathways: A Magazine on Poverty, Inequality, and Social Policy*, Special Issue 2017.

34. Many moved between the streets and temporary lodging in single-room occupancies (SROs) and cheap roominghouses as funds from welfare checks or day labor jobs ran out. Kim Hopper, *Reckoning with Homelessness* (Cornell University Press, 2003), 55.

35. US General Accounting Office, *Homelessness: A Complex Problem and the Federal Response* (April 1985); US Conference of Mayors, *Status Report: Emergency Food, Shelter, and Energy Programs in 20 Cities* (1984).

36. Kim Hopper and Norweeta G. Milburn, "Homelessness among African Americans: A Historical and Contemporary Perspective," in *Homelessness in America*, ed. Jim Baumohl (Oryx Press, 1996), 123–31; US General Accounting Office, *Homelessness*.

37. Cuts actually began at the end of the Carter administration, but these were across-the-board cuts, not cuts aimed specifically at social programs, and tied to deficit reduction. Michele Wakin, *Otherwise Homeless: Vehicle Living and the Culture of Homelessness* (FirstForum Press, 2013), 34.

38. Cushing N. Dolbeare and Sheila Crowley, "The Federal Budget and Housing Assistance," 1976–2007, National Low Income Housing Coalition (August 2002), Appendix B, Table 6, https://nlihc.org/sites/default/files/Changing-Priorities-Report_August-2002.pdf. Both fell short of the annual goal of 600,000 new units set by Congress in the 1968 Housing Act. Oksana Mironova and Thomas J. Waters, "Social Housing in the U.S," Community Service Society (February 18, 2020), https://www.cssny.org/news/entry/social-housing-in-the-us.

39. Will Fischer, "Housing Investments in Build Back Better Would Address Pressing Unmet Needs," Center on Budget and Policy Priorities (February 10, 2022), https://www.cbpp.org/research/housing/housing-investments-in-build-back-better-would-address-pressing-unmet-needs.

40. Kim Hopper, Ezra Susser, and Sarah Conover, "Economies of Makeshift: Deindustrialization and Homelessness in New York City," *Urban Anthropology and Studies of Cultural Systems and World Economic Development* 14, nos. 1–3 (Spring-Summer-Fall, 1985).

41. US General Accounting Office, *Homelessness*, 19.

42. In December 1982, unemployment reached a monthly high of 10.8 percent. In a 1985 New York City study, up to 90 percent of men entering shelters for the first time had been in "unskilled or low-skilled jobs offering neither decent pay nor job security." Hopper et al., "Economies of Makeshift, 207. Temporary and part-time jobs grew much faster than total employment, reaching an estimated 30 percent by 1986, signaling what the *New York Times* called a "fundamental change" in the workplace. "News Summary," *New York Times*, Wednesday, July 9, 1986, https://www.nytimes.com/1986/07/09/nyregion/news-summary-wednesday-july-9-1986.html?searchResultPosition=3.

43. Joel Blau, *The Visible Poor: Homelessness in the United States* (Oxford University Press, 1992), 41; "History of Federal Minimum Wage Rates under the Fair Labor Standards Act, 1938–2009," US Department of Labor, https://www.dol.gov/agencies/whd/minimum-wage/history/chart.

44. These included AFDC, the main cash support program for needy families, and SSI and SSDI, the Social Security disability programs that provided income support to poor disabled individuals. US General Accounting Office, *Homelessness*, 23–24. Reexaminations of eligibility of persons receiving these benefits resulted in their loss for an estimated 491,000 people; more than 200,000 of these were reinstated on appeal. These changes were litigated at length in court, with further legislative reform addressing some of the impact. These benefits are still very hard to get, however, due to an extremely onerous process. The latest data show that only some 14 percent of homeless people receive SSI, although some 40 percent are likely eligible.

45. John L. Palmer and Isabel V. Sawhill, "Perspectives on the Reagan Experiment," in *The Reagan Experiment*, ed. John L. Palmer and Isabel V. Sawhill (Urban Institute Press, 1982), 17, https://www.google.com/books/edition/The_Reagan_Experiment/clik4pH4vGQC?hl=en&gbpv=1.

46. US General Accounting Office, *Homelessness*, 24.

47. Deinstitutionalization is often cited as a cause of homelessness, but the real cause was the failure to follow through on the promise of residential community care to replace institutional facilities. Beginning in the 1960s, advances in the understanding and treatment of psychiatric disorders, coupled with public exposés of horrendous conditions in mental institutions, led to a movement to stop

institutionalizing people and instead treat them in community settings. In 1963, plans were for 2,000 federally supported community mental health centers, but only 800 were actually funded. Many of those who had previously resided in institutions in fact ended up in SROs. As gentrification accelerated, those were destroyed, and their former residents became homeless. See chapter 3, infra.

48. Stewart Taylor Jr., "Reagan Moves to End Program that Pays for Legal Aid for the Poor," *New York Times*, March 6, 1981; Stuart Taylor Jr., "Legal Aid for the Poor: Reagan's Longest Brawl," *New York Times*, June 8, 1984.

49. US General Accounting Office, *Homelessness*, 32; Wakin, *Homelessness in America*, 44; Maria Foscarinis, "Beyond Homelessness: Ethics, Advocacy, and Strategy," *Saint Louis University Public Law Review* 12, no. 1 (1993).

50. "The First Court Decision in *Callahan v. Carey* Requiring the Provision of Shelter for Homeless Men in New York City," Coalition for the Homeless, https://www.coalitionforthehomeless.org/wp-content/uploads/2014/07/CallahanvCareyFirstDecision1979.pdf.

51. Because the case was settled, no final ruling was issued by the court.

52. Eldredge v. Koch, 118 Misc.2d 163, 459 N YS.2d 960 (Sup.Ct.N.Y.Co.), rev'd on other grounds, 98 A.D.2d 675, 469 N.Y.S.2d 744 (1983) (women); McCain v. Koch, 117 A.D.2d 198 (1st Dept. 1986) (families). Callahan was brought on behalf of homeless men because of the gendered nature of shelter provision.

53. It also defined the process by which applications for shelter would be made and addressed. "The *Callahan* Consent Decree: Establishing a Legal Right to Shelter for Homeless Individuals in New York City," Coalition for the Homeless, https://www.coalitionforthehomeless.org/wp-content/uploads/2014/08/CallahanConsentDecree.pdf.

54. Callahan v. Carey, final judgment by consent, Index No. 42582/79; "The *Callahan* Consent Decree."

55. "Creating Affordable Housing: How Koch Did It," *Gotham Gazette*, https://www.gothamgazette.com/624-creating-affordable-housing-how-koch-did-; Andre Shashaty, "U.S. Cuts Back and Shifts Course on Housing Aid," *New York Times*, October 18, 1981, https://www.nytimes.com/1981/10/18/realestate/us-cuts-back-and-shifts-course-on-housing-aid.html.

56. "Number of People Currently Sleeping in NYC Shelters Each Night," Coalition for the Homeless, https://www.coalitionforthehomeless.org/facts-about-homelessness/.

57. Luis Ferré-Sadurní and Wesley Parnell, "New York Begins Evicting Migrant Families Who Hit a Shelter Time Limit," *New York Times*, January 9, 2024, https://www.nytimes.com/2024/01/09/nyregion/migrant-families-homeless-shelter-evictions.html.

58. Andy Newman and Dana Rubinstein, "Chaos, Fury, Mistakes: 600 Days inside New York's Migrant Crisis," *New York Times*, December 26, 2023, https://www.nytimes.com/2023/12/26/nyregion/migrant-crisis-mayor-eric-adams.html.

59. Philip Buck, Paul Toro, and Melanie Ramos, "Media and Professional Interest in Homelessness over 30 Years (1974–2003)," *Analyses of Social Issues and Public Policy* 4, no. 1 (2004), 151–71.

60. By Bob Hayes, Kim Hopper, and Ellen Baxter.

61. These included New Jersey, West Virginia, and California. In Washington, D.C., a right to shelter was enacted by referendum in 1984—and repealed, also by referendum, in 1990. See Maria Foscarinis, "Homelessness, Litigation, and Law Reform Strategies: A United States Perspective," *Australian Journal of Human Rights* (2004), 109.

62. The offer included a salary at a fraction of my law firm earnings and operating expenses for an office with no staff. Unlike the law firm, we would have no paying clients—all our clients would be homeless, with no ability to pay. For more details, see Crystal Nix, "The New Social Reformers," *New York Times*, October 26, 1986.

63. Hopper, *Reckoning with Homelessness*, 172.

64. Steven V. Roberts, "Reagan on Homelessness: Many Choose to Live in the Streets," *New York Times*, December 23, 1988, http://www.nytimes.com/1988/12/23/us/reagan-on-homelessness-many-choose-to-live-in-the-streets.html. Ed Meese, Reagan's attorney general, commented that people were going to soup kitchens not because they were hungry but "because the food is free and that that's easier than paying for it." Robert D. McFadden, "Comments by Meese on Hunger Produce a Storm of Controversy," *New York Times*, December 10, 1983. https://www.nytimes.com/1983/12/10/us/comments-by-meese-on-hunger-produce-a-storm-of-controversy.html.

65. In 1983, the secretary of the Department of Health and Human Services (HHS), Margaret Heckler, created the Federal Task Force on the Homeless, which consisted of representatives of fifteen federal agencies, chaired by HHS. Its role was to "cut red tape and to act as a 'broker' between the federal government and the private sector when . . . available federal facility resources [were] identified." US General Accounting Office, *Homelessness*. The Federal Task Force on the Homeless was terminated in 1987 with the creation by the McKinney Act of the Interagency Council on the Homeless. "INACTIVE—ALL ITEMS SUPERSEDED OR OBSOLETE," National Archives, https://www.archives.gov/records-mgmt/rcs/schedules/departments/department-of-health-and-human-services/rg-0292/n1-292-88-001_sf115.pdf.

66. Maria Foscarinis, "Beyond Homelessness: Ethics, Advocacy, and Strategy," *Saint Louis University Public Law Review* 12, no. 1 (1993).

67. The language of blame was hardly invented by Reagan—it has a long history going back at least to Elizabethan poor laws (see, e.g., Hopper). But its use by Reagan and his allies at the dawn of the modern-day crisis of homelessness shaped the modern discourse as the issue evolved.

Chapter Two

1. In November 1986, renovations began on the building, the payoff of a risky weeks-long fast by Mitch Snyder and other CCNV members that brought Mitch to the brink of death. The publicity CCNV was able to garner coupled with political pressure on the eve of the election forced the Reagan administration to agree to CCNV's demand to fund the renovation. Victoria Rader, *Signal through the Flames: Mitch Snyder and America's Homeless* (Sheed & Ward, 1986), 222–29.

2. Descriptions taken from notes I took at the time, with names changed.

3. It was then the Veterans Administration; it changed its name after becoming a cabinet-level agency in 1989. "United States Department of Veterans Affairs," Wikipedia, https://en.wikipedia.org/wiki/United_States_Department_of_Veterans _Affairs.

4. From SSA's Supplemental Security Income (SSI) program, which provides modest benefits to low-income people who are also disabled and/or elderly. "Supplemental Security Income (SSI)," Social Security Administration, https:// www.ssa.gov/ssi?gad_source=1&gclid=CjwKCAiAopuvBhBCEiwAm8jaMRx lE6AAONdDXSEVZ7NBRH36um6QT6nnkx9SarZpoeFrdnv_brtngRoC9TE-QAvD_BwE.

5. "History of Federal Minimum Wage Rates under the Fair Labor Standards Act, 1938–2009," US Department of Labor, https://www.dol.gov/agencies/whd/ minimum-wage/history/chart. In 1990 the federal minimum wage went up to $3.80, and crept higher until it reached $7.25 in 2009, where it has remained. "Federal Minimum Wage for 2023, 2024," Minimum-Wage.org, https://www.minimum -wage.org/federal. Some states and the District of Columbia have higher minimums; as of 2023, in D.C. it was $16.50.

6. Others wanted help finding a job that paid enough to cover rent, and there was even less we could do to help with that. Public works programs launched by FDR as part of the "New Deal" were long since gone.

7. Homeless Persons' Survival Act of 1986, H. R. 5140, 99th Cong. (1986), https://www.congress.gov/bill/99th-congress/house-bill/5140; Homeless Persons' Survival Act of 1986, S. 2608, 99th Cong. (1986), https://www.govtrack.us/congress /bills/99/s2608.

8. We debated whether to pare the list down and focus on politically "realistic" proposals or maintain our ambitious list that reflected the reality of the need. In the end, we combined the two approaches, keeping the ambitious proposal as our goal but also focusing on pieces that could be pushed separately.

9. School eligibility is address-based, and homeless children would be denied enrollment because they had none or forced to switch schools based on where they were living at the moment. See chapter 6 for a detailed discussion.

10. The $4 billion was based on section-by-section estimates derived mainly from the original coalition that had assembled the proposal. The $11 billion number

is based on the "CPI Inflation Calculator," US Bureau of Labor Statistics, https:// data.bls.gov/cgi-bin/cpicalc.pl?cost1=4000000&year1=198601&year2=202311.

11. Frank Newport, Jeffrey M. Jones, and Lydia Saad, "Ronald Reagan from the People's Perspective: A Gallup Poll Review," Gallup, https://news.gallup.com/poll /11887/ronald-reagan-from-peoples-perspective-gallup-poll-review.aspx.

12. Hedrick Smith, "Reagan's Effort to Change Course of Government," *New York Times*, October 23, 1984, https://www.nytimes.com/1984/10/23/us/reagan-s -effort-to-change-course-of-government.html.

13. The Supreme Court's 1976 ruling in *Buckley v. Valeo* was one early key development. Smith, "Reagan's Effort to Change Course of Government." It was followed much later by Citizens United v. Federal Election Commission, 558 U.S. 310 (2010), which significantly expanded that influence.

14. I outlined the problem and our proposed solution in a memo that I called "Homelessness in America: The Need for a Federal Response," which NCH later published as a report. Drawing on the research that was already accumulating, I argued that the broad demographic and geographic scope of the problem meant it was a national issue that the federal government had an obligation to address. The political powerlessness of the homeless population, and general inability to affect local politics, added to the need for a federal response. I could have added, citing my law school casebooks, that it affected a "discrete and insular minority" and that the federal government thus had a special obligation to protect them.

15. A key contact was Marc Smolensky, staffer for Ted Weiss, a liberal Democratic congressman from New York City representing Manhattan's Upper West Side. He was helpful and supportive but ultimately unable to take the lead.

16. Early on, I made most of these visits alone. Later, I was typically joined by others: pro bono lawyers, interns, and allies with other organizations.

17. Leland died tragically in a plane crash in Ethiopia in 1989 at age forty-four while on a humanitarian mission. "Mickey Leland," Congressional Hunger Center, https://www.hungercenter.org/who-we-are/leland/.

18. I had also been meeting with the relevant committees to build support for the separate pieces of the proposal. After Leland agreed to sign on, I went back to them to ask for their support of all or part of the bill.

19. Of these, thirty-six were "original" cosponsors, meaning they put their name on the bill at the time of introduction; others added their names after that time. "Cosponsors: H.R.5140—99th Congress (1985–1986)," Congress.gov, https:// www.congress.gov/bill/99th-congress/house-bill/5140/cosponsors.

20. Helen Peterson, "Gore's Tipper: All-American Cheerleader," *New York Daily News*, August 13, 2000. Tipper also helped arrange a meeting with Al Gore's chief of staff.

21. Al Gore's staff had expressed concern about the proposal's potential cost and feared that if enacted, there would be pressure to restore other benefits that had been cut, further adding to the expense. For example, regarding a proposal to restore

aid to students aged eighteen to twenty-one to prevent youth homelessness, a staffer noted that though it had been a couple of years since Social Security benefits were eliminated for students after high school, their office still heard from constituents trying to get their benefits back. He was concerned that such requests would increase if AFDC student benefits were restored. (Internal memo on file with the author.) Homelessness for young people is a pressing issue that is getting renewed attention today. See https://www.usich.gov/news-events/news/usich-announces-creation -national-youth-homelessness-partnership. But its causes go back at least to these original cuts, and the reluctance to address them.

22. Senator Daniel Patrick Moynihan of New York became the second. He had a long-standing interest in poverty and a constituency that was increasingly concerned about homelessness.

23. We had endorsements from almost one hundred national, state, and local organizations, and a total of sixty-two congressional sponsors. I had been working with other national advocates to get their support and endorsement of the proposal and convening weekly strategy meetings. Barry Zigas, then head of the National Low Income Housing Coalition, an allied group, had advised me to do this. He suggested holding the meetings right after his own weekly housing strategy sessions, in the same location, since there would undoubtedly be overlap among our groups. I was also getting the word out to groups across the country. My organization, the National Coalition for the Homeless, had a network of statewide coalitions with local members, and they were instrumental in publicizing the legislative effort within their communities.

24. Both the House and Senate have lawyers—legislative counsel, or "leg counsel" for short—who specialize in turning proposals into legislative language and who could work with Leland's staff and me. To bolster my newly acquired knowledge, I turned to the group of legal services lawyers who had authored individual pieces of the proposal for help.

25. Crafting the definition would be complex and highly consequential, and I called on one of the few experts who could help: Kim Hopper. An anthropologist, Kim had conducted a groundbreaking study of homelessness in New York City, along with Ellen Baxter. Published in 1981, it had been instrumental in bringing attention to the issue. He had cofounded the Coalition for the Homeless in New York and the National Coalition for the Homeless that grew out of it. He also bore a striking resemblance to the singer Kris Kristofferson and was quite often mistaken for him. Kim came down to D.C. from New York to accompany me to a meeting with leg counsel.

26. US Department of Housing and Urban Development (HUD), *A Report to the Secretary on the Homeless and Emergency Shelters* (HUD, 1984).

27. Bruce G. Link, Ezra Susser, Ann Stueve, Jo Phelan, Robert E. Moore, and Elmer Struening, "Lifetime and Five-Year Prevalence of Homelessness in

the United States," *American Journal of Public Health* 84, no. 12 (December 1994), https://ajph.aphapublications.org/doi/pdf/10.2105/AJPH.84.12.1907.

28. According to HUD, these could take the form of "armories, schools, church basements, government buildings, former firehouses and, where temporary vouchers are provided by private or public agencies, even hotels, apartments, or boarding homes."

29. In addition to streets, HUD specified "parks, subways, bus terminals, railroad stations, airports, under bridges or aqueducts, abandoned buildings without utilities, cars, trucks, or any other public or private space that is not designed for shelter." HUD also included people temporarily in jails or hospitals whose usual residence was in shelters or streets and other public places. HUD, *A Report to the Secretary.*

30. McKinney Act (P.L. 100-77, sec 103(2)(1), 101 stat. 485 (1987).

31. Advocacy organizations take positions, often vehemently, for or against particular definitions. Some believe the narrower HUD definition better "targets" limited resources. Others view the ED definition as better reflecting the reality of homelessness. "Homelessness: The Wrong Way/Two Bills Opposed by the Alliance," National Alliance to End Homelessness, https://endhomelessness.org/legislation/the-alliances-general-legislative-agenda/ (opposing bill to expand definition); "Bipartisan Legislation to Help Homeless Children and Youth Reintroduced," SchoolHouse Connection, August 15, 2023, https://schoolhouseconnection.org/hcya/ (supporting bill to expand definition).

32. Eventually, these interpretations were codified in legislation.

33. The most egregious problems are with the count required by HUD, which has two parts: the shelter count and the unsheltered (or "street") count. The shelter count is relatively straightforward—shelter operators report the number of people in their facilities at a designated point in time. (As of 2022, they also report the number of different people who stayed there at any point during the year, for an annual count.) The unsheltered count includes streets, parks, and open rural areas, among others. Gathering accurate numbers here is a virtually impossible task, largely left to minimally trained volunteers who are expected to carry it out over a few hours on a single night. There's little guidance, and often conflicting instructions, for this critical work. The Department of Education, using the broader definition, is required to count the number of homeless students in K–12 public schools during a given school year. States report these numbers which they collect from local school districts, which get them from the schools. It is also likely an undercount: It depends on the schools accurately identifying all homeless children in their classrooms. Teachers may not be adequately trained to do this, families and children may hide their homelessness due to real or perceived stigma, or both. The understandable fear of having children taken away by child protective services due to the family's homelessness may also impact disclosure by the teacher, the student, or the family. For a detailed discussion, see National Law Center on Homelessness & Poverty (NLCHP), *Don't*

Count On It: How the HUD Point-in-Time Count Underestimates the Homelessness Crisis in America (NLCHP, 2018), https://homelesslaw.org/wp-content/uploads/2018/10/HUD-PIT-report2017.pdf.

34. Tim Davis, a lobbyist at Akin Gump Strauss Hauer & Feld, a big corporate law firm known for its political connections, especially to Democrats, helped me early on with the basics of developing a strategy and introductions to key people on the Hill. Now I needed reinforcements and more hands-on help.

35. As of 2023, Covington & Burling was ranked at the top among major US firms for its pro bono work. "Covington Ranks First in American Lawyer's Pro Bono Scorecard," Covington, https://www.cov.com/en/news-and-insights/news/2023/07/covington-ranks-first-in-american-lawyers-pro-bono-scorecard.

36. The firm still offers the program. "Tom Williamson Endowment Fund," Neighborhood Legal Services Program, https://www.nlsp.org/donate/tom-williamson-endowment-fund.

37. In 1989, Rod would again take leave to serve as Deputy Secretary of Labor in the administration of President George H. W. Bush, under Secretary Elizabeth Dole.

38. Over the course of a year, about 25 percent are people living with mental disorders. Also important was that we had an active local partner organization in New Mexico, which was able to engage key local officials to help lobby our case. Domenici's wife, Nancy, was also part of the Congressional Wives for the Homeless group. Marian Moser Jones, "Creating a Science of Homelessness during the Reagan Era," *Milbank Quarterly* 93, no. 1 (March 2015), 139–78; Keith Schneider, "Pete Domenici, Long a Powerful Senate Voice on Fiscal Policy, Dies at 85," *New York Times*, September 13, 2017, https://www.nytimes.com/2017/09/13/us/politics/pete-domenici-dead.html.

39. Joe Trujillo, the senator's staffer on this issue and our main contact, was at the meeting with us. Domenici was very personable and warm. He asked whether I had a been a "good lawyer" before moving to advocacy on homelessness. When I cheekily replied that I had been at Sullivan & Cromwell and that they usually try to hire good lawyers, Domenici graciously commented that they would never have hired him. After the meeting, Joe called to say the senator had been very impressed.

40. On June 26, when Gore and Moynihan introduced the HPSA, Domenici was not a sponsor. But on that same day, he introduced his own bill, the National Clearinghouse for the Homeless Act of 1986, with one cosponsor—Al Gore.

41. The "Domenici package" required the federal agencies to develop a way to get benefits and payments to people without an address for AFDC, Medicaid, SSI, and VA benefits, and specifically removed permanent address requirements to apply for VA benefits. It also included homeless people in the JTPA. It allowed (but did not require) homeless people to use food stamps for shelter meals—a way to support shelters.

42. Another possibility we considered was a bill relating to insecticides. But we would be better off with something "germane," or related to our issues. Contemporaneous notes, on file with author.

43. Two other important bills became law at about the same time. The Homeless Housing Act created the Emergency Shelter Grant Program, funded at $10 million, which was designed to allocate money to state and local governments to cover operating and rehabilitation costs of shelters. The Transitional Housing Program authorized $5 million in grants for which state and local governments, as well as private nonprofits, could apply. P.L. 99-500, 100 Stat. 1783 (1986). See Maria Foscarinis, "Federal Legislative and Litigative Strategies: An Overview," *Maryland Journal of Contemporary Legal Issues* 1 (1990).

44. At the first congressional hearing on modern homelessness, held in 1982 by the House Subcommittee on Housing and Community Development, chaired by Representative Henry Gonzalez, advocate Mitch Snyder called on Congress to "at a minimum—make space available." *Homelessness in America: Hearing before the Subcomm. on Housing and Community Development of the Comm. on Banking, Finance and Urban Affairs*, 97th Cong. (1982), 26. At a hearing just over a year later, Harvey Vieth, director of the newly created Federal Interagency Task Force on Food and Shelter, assured the committee that federal agencies, including the defense department, were hard at work doing just that. US House of Representatives, *Homelessness in America II: Hearing before the Subcomm. on Housing and Community Development of the Comm. on Banking, Finance and Urban Affairs*, 98th Cong. (1984), 290–92.

45. The law required the Department of Defense to issue regulations to implement the program, but the agency had failed to do so.

46. Bruce v. DoD, Complaint; Bruce v. United States Dep't of Defense, 1987 U.S. Dist. LEXIS 14944 (DDC, June 16, 1987), Lexis, https://plus.lexis.com/api/document/collection/cases/id/3S4N-CFR0-003B-62NM-00000-00?cite=1987%20U.S.%20Dist.%20LEXIS%2014944&context=1530671.

47. Bruce v. DoD, memorandum in Support of Motion for Preliminary Injunction, Affidavit of Mitchell Snyder, February 15, 1987, on file with author.

48. Bruce v. DoD, affidavit of Barry Russell Bruce, memorandum in Support of Motion for Preliminary Injunction, February 16, 1987, on file with author.

49. Memorandum from Maria Foscarinis, to DoD Team, Re: Factual investigation, October 22, 1986, on file with author.

50. We published a report on January 14, 1987, documenting the failure; it was covered in the *New York Times*. Suzanne Daley, "Homeless Report Accuses Pentagon," *New York Times*, January 15, 1987, https://www.nytimes.com/1987/01/15/us/homeless-report-accuses-pentagon.html?searchResultPosition=59.

51. The Court granted plaintiffs' motion for summary judgment and ordered that if the DoD did not have final regulations ready before its self-imposed deadline of November 18, 1987, then the proposed rules would become interim regulations until the DoD published final regulations. Bruce v. United States Dep't of Defense,

1987 U.S. Dist. LEXIS 14944 (DDC, June 16, 1987), Ben A. Franklin, "Pentagon Lag on Homeless Assailed," *New York Times*, June 18, 1987, https://www.nytimes .com/1987/06/18/us/pentagon-lag-on-homeless-assailed.html.

52. CCNV operated as a kind of collective: All members lived together at the downtown shelter, or at one of the two CCNV "houses," located further out in the northwest quadrant of the city. Certain homeless residents served as staff, helping to run the shelter, including cooking meals for the residents—an enormous undertaking.

53. The focus on homelessness dated to the mid-1970s. In 1980, CCNV published a national report on homelessness, instigating the first congressional hearing on the issue. See Victoria Rader, *Signal through the Flames: Mitch Snyder and America's Homeless* (Sheed & Ward, 1986.

54. Rader, *Signal through the Flames*. Among other actions, CCNV organized a demonstration in Lafayette Park, outside the White House, setting up tents to publicize the plight of people without housing. After they were denied a permit from the National Park Service, CCNV filed suit in federal court, losing in the district court before filing a successful appeal, winning on first amendment grounds. CCNV v. Watt, 703 F.2d 586 (1983) (en banc). The Supreme Court reversed this decision, based on the fact that homeless demonstrators were actually sleeping in the tents, not simply using them as symbols; thus, they were violating the Park Service's ban on camping—which, the Court said, was a reasonable regulation that did not did not run afoul of the First Amendment. Clark v. CCNV, 468 US 188 (1984). This case came at the dawn of the crisis of modern homelessness, as the word itself was entering public discourse. Email from Arlene Kanter (counsel for plaintiffs) to the author, January 31, 2024.

55. In 1984, Mitch staged a hunger strike to pressure Reagan to agree to renovate the shelter, an abandoned federal building that had been turned over to CCNV the previous year (following an earlier campaign). In November, days before the presidential election—Reagan was running for a second term—with Snyder's health rapidly deteriorating, and just before a positive *60 Minutes* feature on him was to air, the administration had agreed to renovate the building. It would take more activism in 1985, including another fast by Mitch, to extract the funds for the renovations. Rader, *Signal through the Flames*.

56. The lore was that Mitch had worked in advertising on Madison Avenue in New York City and been arrested and imprisoned for some minor crime. In reality, he'd worked for a job counseling program located on Madison Avenue. In prison, he'd met Daniel and Philip Berrigan, Catholic brothers who were serving time for civil disobedience committed as part of their activism against the Vietnam War. Through them, Mitch became committed to faith-based activism and the use of nonviolent civil disobedience. After his release, he moved to Washington, D.C., and joined CCNV, a "radical-Catholic" organization founded in 1970 by Ed Guinan, a

Paulist priest. CCNV was serving and advocating for poor and homeless people, and Mitch eventually emerged as the de facto leader of the community.

57. Because of his media exposure, Mitch was widely recognizable. He was regularly approached on the street, and generally avoided being in public—aside from his protests. He rarely ate out; there was only one restaurant, El Tamarindo, a dive serving Salvadoran food north of the city's center, where he would go. He claimed that was the only place that would respect his privacy. (Personal recollection of the author.)

58. Mitch proposed this joint work on a call in which he first asked who I thought I was, coming to Washington out of nowhere, going up to the Hill, working on legislation. He had been doing this for fifteen years, and here I was acting as if I was his equal! I was shocked, of course, and offended. But once I calmed down, I appreciated his honesty—and also realized he had a point. I was new to this and probably could stand to learn from those with greater experience. From then on, I made sure to show respect for his experience and some degree of deference, and I was able to work with him effectively.

59. How exactly the money would be used was less important than the amount to Mitch. He'd followed our work on the Homeless Eligibility Clarification Act and seemed offended that Congress had passed it as a "no cost" bill.

60. This approach was consistent with CCNV's emphasis on emergency shelter. See for example, Mary Ellen Hombs and Mitch Snyder, *Homelessness in America: A Forced March to Nowhere* (Community for Creative Non-Violence, 1983), which includes a proposal for emergency shelters as the solution to homelessness, with no mention of housing or other more permanent measures.

61. For a more detailed account, see Maria Foscarinis, "Strategies to Address Homelessness in the Trump Era: Lessons from the Reagan Years," *Journal of Affordable Housing & Community Development Law* 27, no. 1 (2018), 161–81, https://www.americanbar.org/content/dam/aba/publications/journal_of_affordable _housing/volume_27_number_1/ah_27-1_12foscarinis.pdf

62. There was an "explosion of coverage" during the period from 1981 to 1987. David Levinson, ed., *Encyclopedia of Homelessness* (Sage, 2004), 304.

63. *Samaritan: The Mitch Snyder Story*, CBS, May 19, 1986.

64. The proceeds were distributed through the Robert Wood Johnson Foundation to fund health care services for homeless people across the country.

65. It was controversial—both CCNV and NCH dismissed it as a publicity stunt and questioned how the funds would be used. President Reagan initially resisted calls to participate but eventually was persuaded to do so after discussions with his wife, Nancy, and his daughter, Maureen, and her husband. Ben Weintraub, "Reagan Decides to Join Hands Across America," *New York Times*, May 24, 1986, https://www.nytimes.com/1986/05/24/us/reagan-decides-to-join-hands-across -america.html; UPI, "Hands Across America Head Says Project was Successful,"

New York Times, May 27, 1986, https://www.nytimes.com/1986/05/27/us/hands
-across-america-head-says-project-was-successful.html.

66. The mayors' convening focused on affordable housing, not emergency shelter; the group of homeless people echoed that demand. William K. Stevens, "U.S.
Advocacy Group for Homeless Is Born," *New York Times*, February 16, 1986. http://
www.nytimes.com/1986/02/16/us/us-advocacy-group-for-homeless-is-born.html.
Unfortunately, the Union of the Homeless went into decline a few years later, perhaps not surprisingly given the difficulty of organizing people who are struggling to
survive. It was reestablished in 2020. "National Union of the Homeless," National
Union of the Homeless, https://nationalunionofthehomeless.org/.

67. Foscarinis, "Strategies to Address Homelessness," 171.

68. To build more support, Mitch invited activists from around the country to
join him in his vigil, typically for a week at a time. Michael Stoops, an activist from
Portland, Oregon, who would later become part of my staff in the Washington,
D.C., office of the National Coalition for the Homeless, joined Mitch for most of
the winter. He and others sometimes came with us on lobbying visits to the Hill.
Foscarinis, "Strategies to Address Homelessness," 161.

69. Wright, a Democrat, had replaced Tip O'Neill, also a Democrat, as
Speaker. Tom Foley was Majority Leader and Tony Coelho was Majority Whip.
"Advocates for Homeless Will Stop Protest at Capitol," *Los Angeles Times*, January
11, 1987, http://articles.latimes.com/1987-01-11/news/mn-4090_1_homeless-cou-
ple. The November elections shifted control of the Senate from the Republicans
to the Democrats, a potentially helpful change. Robert Byrd took over as Majority
Leader from Bob Dole, who became Minority Leader.

70. H.R. 558, the Foley-McKinney Urgent Relief for the Homeless Act.

71. One major omission was the national right to shelter. Our allies on the Hill
felt it was too controversial and would torpedo the bill. Instead, funding shelter
and transitional housing—without creating a right—through two small programs,
enacted at the same time as the Homeless Eligibility Clarification Act, was added.

72. January was when the official action started in Congress. On January 6,
1987, Leland reintroduced the Homeless Persons' Survival Act, joined by fifty-one
cosponsors, including Tony Coelho, a Democratic Representative from California,
the Majority Whip, another sign that we had leadership support. Leland appealed
to his colleagues to support his bill by specifically noting that "as we approach
the harshest days of winter, millions of Americans face the cold and windy nights
without the comfort of basic shelter." Dear Colleague of 1.5.87, on file with author.
Simultaneously, and in line with our agreed upon strategy, he called the Homeless
Persons' Survival Act "definitive legislation expressing a long-term federal commitment to end this national disgrace," noting that permanent affordable housing was
exponentially cheaper than emergency shelter. News release on January 7, 1987, on
file with author.

73. According to his staffer, Domenici was "charged up" and wanted to spend money. He had involved his wife, Nancy, who was also a member of the Congressional Wives for the Homeless group and was considering options from $200 to $500 million. At our urging, other members were adding parts of the Homeless Persons' Survival Act, as well as their own favored initiatives, to the bill. Moynihan was interested in taking the lead on the sections relating to access to health and welfare benefits for homeless families. In the House, Rangel was interested in the parts of the bill that concerned disability benefits. Waxman wanted to push the health pieces, but Domenici was uneasy with this—he wanted it to be "his" bill. Congressman Leon Panetta, who chaired the House Sub-Committee on Nutrition, had agreed to add food provisions from the Homeless Persons' Survival Act to the new bill; Congressman Chuck Schumer of New York added something on welfare hotels, an issue then getting a lot of attention in New York City. Congressman Dave Obey of Wisconsin had noted a "political" question of how funds would be distributed to rural areas. Author's contemporaneous notes, on file with the author.

74. January 31, 1987.

75. Working with Mitch and CCNV presented various challenges, including logistical ones in the pre-cell-phone era. Sometimes I would seek him out on his favorite heat grate. There was no way to reach him except by going in person, but I knew he would usually be there. Sometimes I would bring ouzo and kalamata olives, Greek offerings that he especially liked. I had found that they helped smooth our relationship.

76. It was held by the Subcommittee on Housing and Community Development, the House subcommittee taking the lead on the bill. The bill had also been referred to the Committee on Energy and Commerce, and its subcommittee on health. The House Committee on Education and Labor took up portions of the bill, but separately from the Urgent Relief Act. "Oversight Hearing on Jobs and Education for the Homeless," Joint Hearing before the Committee on Education and Labor and the Select Committee on Aging, House of Representatives, 100th Congress, 1st Sess., held in Los Angeles, CA, March 20, 1987. https://www.congress.gov/bill/100th-congress/senate-bill/811/summary/00; https://www.congress.gov/bill/100th-congress/senate-bill/811/summary/00.

77. New York City and State were also key lobbying forces, representing an influential part of the country that had also been publicly identified as hard hit by the crisis.

78. The Conference of Mayors represented big cities and had recently created a special task force to address the growing crisis of hunger and homelessness. Starting in 1984, the Task Force had conducted an annual survey of its members to assess the status of hunger and homelessness in their cities.

79. Mike Lowry, then a Democratic congressman from Washington State (who would later go on to become governor) and his staffer David Bley were playing a

critical, if largely behind-the-scenes, role in the House. We had heard that Lowry was trying to "depoliticize" the bill to broaden support, while the leadership was trying to politicize it. Wright had given the Democratic response to Reagan's State of the Union address and included homelessness as one of his top three priorities. Mitch and I did not testify at the hearing. The point was to show that established power players—which we most definitely were not—were behind the bill.

80. "Washington Talk; The Homeless Become an Issue," *New York Times*, February 7, 1987, https://www.nytimes.com/1987/02/07/us/washington-talk-the -homeless-become-an-issue.html; Julie Kosterlitz, "They're Everywhere," *National Journal*, February 28, 1987.

81. The previous day, the House Rules Committee issued an open rule that waived all "points of order," fast-tracking the bill. Amendments would be allowed but technical objections—such as those based on budget constraints—would not. The vote was 264 to 121, with 43 Republicans voting in favor along with 231 Democrats. The latter figure includes five members of the Democratic Farm Labor (DFL) party. *Congressional Record* (daily edition, March 5, 1987), H.

82. Kirsten Goldberg and William Montague "Shelter Kids," *Education Week*, April 24, 1987, https://www.edweek.org/education/shelter-kids/1987/04.

83. He would brief his boss, Congressman Augustus Hawkins of Los Angeles and the Democratic chairman of the Education Committee, who would then talk to his state's "power brokers" to try to get their support. See also Goldberg and Montague, "Shelter Kids."

84. More so than housed children living in poverty.

85. Kirsten Goldberg, "Many Homeless Children Reported out of School," *Education Week*, March 25, 1987. https://www.edweek.org/education/many -homeless-children-reported-out-of-school/1987/03; Fred M. Hechinger, "About Education; The Plight of the Homeless," *New York Times*, May 5, 1987.

86. The matter ended up in court, thanks to the local legal services lawyers who came to the aid of the family. The judge ruled that the children had a right to be educated, but he decided that since they were then living in Roosevelt, they should go to school there. He ordered that town's schools to enroll them. The mother's preference for her children to continue attending their original school in Freeport to minimize the disruption to their lives, the judge said, was "not at all governing." Delgado v. Freeport Public School District, 499 N.Y.S. 2d 606 (1986*)*.

87. Goldberg and Montague "Shelter Kids."

88. Our bill mandated that schools enroll the kids; they preferred an incentive. Our bill imposed sanctions on school districts that did not comply; they opposed this. It created a right to sue for violations; some opposed this, though not as much as the sanctions. It said parents could choose between the school of origin—the school the child attended before becoming homeless—and the school in the district the family was now living in, if these were different; they opposed parental choice. They also opposed any language that said there is a right to education.

89. On parental choice, we ultimately agreed that the decision would be made based on the best interests of the child. I had taken a class in family law in law school and remembered that this was a standard used in child custody cases, so it was a known term in legislation. And, I thought, who could object to the best interests of the child? On other issues we ended up having to cede more ground. Rather than a clearly stated right to education for these kids, we had to accept a more muted statement that it was "the policy of Congress" that homeless children have a right to education. We agreed to a requirement that state education agencies develop a plan to ensure access to school for homeless kids. There was no explicit right to sue, and no sanctions for noncompliance. Nonetheless, we were able to establish clear rights, including through later amendments and litigation. See chapter 6.

90. Most critical were calls and visits from concerned citizens in California, Vermont, and Michigan to Augustus Hawkins (D-CA), chair of House Education and Labor Committee; Jim Jeffords (R-VT), the top Republican on the Committee; and William Ford (D-MI), a member of the committee who would later succeed Hawkins as chair. As such, they were key decision-makers. Senator Edward Kennedy (D-MA) had included the provisions in the Senate version. This meant that negotiations could continue in the "conference committee" that would be constituted to resolve the differences. There the House leadership and Lowry leaned heavily on the committee to adopt strong language protecting the education rights of homeless children. Some other key allies were the Junior League, the Child Welfare League of America, the American Federation of Teachers, National Network for Runaway and Homeless Youth. the Center on Law and Education, and the National Parent Teachers Association

91. Goldberg and Montague, "Shelter Kids."

92. These included very specific requirements about ensuring transportation, records transfers, and the removal of other barriers for homeless children. We paid careful attention to the language, ensuring we got in as many "shalls" as possible.

93. I also drafted report language, explaining congressional authority to enact the provision apart from its funding power—rooted in the equal protection clause of the Fourteenth Amendment to the US Constitution—in case this was ever challenged. Senator Edward Kennedy's staffer had agreed to get the senator to put this in for us, creating some helpful legislative history.

94. To get to $500 million, we'd either have to find funds within the existing budget, which would mean cutting something else, or, we would have to go outside it, which would require a budget waiver. That would take more than a simple majority, and we would need bipartisan support. Unlike the House, the Senate did not have a process for a general budget waiver. Instead, each senator would have to vote for it. Debate 100-77, Part 3, 2. Earlier in the year, Congress had approved a $50 million "supplemental" appropriation for emergency shelter and transitional housing; this was essentially an emergency funding measure outside the regular process. My pro bono team at Covington & Burling reviewed the *Congressional Record* to see

who had voted for it; we would argue that they had already effectively voted for a budget waiver. Personal contemporaneous notes, days before April 6, 1987, on file with author.

95. The bill, S.809, was introduced by Robert Byrd, the Senate Majority Leader. Of the twenty-seven original cosponsors, ten were Republicans, including Bob Dole, the Minority Leader, and Pete Domenici, the top Republican on (and former chair of) the budget committee.

96. We had had to overcome a challenge posed by Gordon Humphrey, a Republican senator from New Hampshire, who wanted to repeal a congressional pay raise that had automatically gone into effect without any member of Congress having to vote on it. A fiscal conservative, Humphrey was outraged by Reagan's maneuver, and he wanted to attach an amendment to our bill repealing the pay raise. It had nothing to do with homelessness; it was a strategy to force senators go on record for or against their pay raise. Senate Majority Leader Robert Byrd wanted to avoid such a vote: He didn't want to force his colleagues to have to choose between forgoing a pay raise—which they wanted—and publicly going on record to vote for it, which would make them look bad politically. Byrd wanted to invoke "cloture," a move that would preclude any amendments, including Humphrey's, that were not relevant to the bill. This would require sixty votes as well as "unanimous consent." Meanwhile, winter was slipping away, and we feared losing our window for urgent action. Mitch wanted to stage a sit-in in Humphrey's office. Bob Dole's staff, possibly having caught wind of this plan or simply fearing Mitch's known propensity for such tactics, warned us against attacking Republicans, and advised keeping a low profile. We eventually found allies in New Hampshire who could lobby Humphrey to withdraw his amendment. We also put out a press release, not attacking anyone in particular, but calling on the Senate to act quickly to help homeless Americans. The motion for cloture passed sixty-eight to twenty-nine. Was it because of Mitch's threatened sit-in? Rod's connection to Dole? Our constituent pressure and focused press outreach? It may have been a combination of all these factors.

97. The final conference committee report, filed June 19, included authorization for two years, with $443 million for 1987 and $616 million for 1988.

98. Vans hired by day labor companies often make regular stops outside shelters to pick up workers, or at street sites where homeless people congregate. Day labor does not necessary take place during the day. It just means that the labor is temporary, by the "day," without a long-term commitment and certainly without benefits. The jobs themselves include construction, maintenance work, delivery, loading, and moving—manual labor of all kinds, where needs may fluctuate, and employers are always looking to cut costs.

99. Usually, Congress first *authorizes* legislation then *appropriates* funding for it. In this case, because it took so long to work out the compromise language authorizing the bill, the appropriations came first, as part of a larger package in early June. Authorization was approved at the end of June. See also Robert Pear, "President

Signs $1 Million [*sic*] to Aid Homeless," *New York Times*, July 24, 1987 (the *New York Times* incorrectly substituted "million" for "billion" in its headline).

100. The Senate passed it on June 27 and the House passed it on June 30. Stewart B. McKinney Homeless Assistance Act, H.R.558, 100th Cong. (1987), https://www.congress.gov/bill/100th-congress/house-bill/558/actions.

101. It was enacted as the Stewart B. McKinney Homeless Assistance Act of 1987.

102. US Constitution, art. 1, sec. 7. It would become law automatically provided Congress remained in session.

103. Pear, "President Signs $1 Million [*sic*] to Aid Homeless.".

104. It quoted me with this assessment: "The new law will provide material aid that is badly needed. It also represents an important recognition of the Federal responsibility to deal with homelessness. But it is only a first step. There must be longer-term efforts to address the causes of the problem, as well as the symptoms."

105. Congress authorized $443 million in 1987 and $616 million in 1988. It appropriated $355 million for 1987, and $365 million for 1988.

106. The council superseded a Federal Task Force on the Homeless created in 1983 through administrative action. We could point to the council as a single agency responsible for responding to the crisis; Mitch in particular thought this was critical for holding the federal government accountable.

107. National Coalition for the Homeless, *Saving Lives: Emergency Federal Aid Reaches the Streets* (National Coalition for the Homeless, 1987); National Coalition for the Homeless, *Necessary Relief: The Stewart B. McKinney Homeless Assistance Act* (National Coalition for the Homeless, 1988).

108. *Congressional Record* (daily edition, March 23, 1987), S3683.

109. Hodgkins lymphoma particularly affects young people; I was thirty at the time. The salary bump was at the initiative of the national coalition's then-director. The additional lawyer was Julie Akins, who had already been helping us pro bono while working at a private firm. The cancer would recur three years later.

110. Link et al., "Lifetime and Five-Year Prevalence."

111. In November 1986, renovation began on the building, the result of a risky weeklong fast by Snyder and other CCNV members that brought Mitch to the brink of death. The publicity CCNV was able to garner coupled with political pressure on the eve of the election forced the administration to agree to CCNV's demand to fund the renovation. Rader, *Signal through the Flames*, 222–29.

112. Recent national studies estimate that over the course of a year 53 percent of sheltered homeless people and 40 percent of unsheltered homeless people work in the formal labor market. This does not include income-generating activities such as childcare, recycling, and panhandling. But they do not earn enough to afford housing. Bruce D. Meyer, Angela Wyse, Alexa Grunwaldt, Carla Medalia, and Derek Wu, "Learning about Homelessness Using Linked Survey and Administrative Data," National Bureau of Economic Research Working Paper No. 28861, May

2021, https://www.nber.org/papers/w28861; Andrew Hall, "Rising Rents and Inflation Are Likely Increasing Low-Income Families' Risk of Homelessness," National Alliance to End Homelessness, June 17, 2022, https://endhomelessness .org/blog/rising-rents-and-inflation-are-likely-increasing-low-income-families-risk -of-homelessness/.

113. Reginald Black and Eric Falquero, "CCNV Residents Say They Need Case Management and Accountability More Than Anything," Street Sense Media, May 5, 2016, https://www.streetsensemedia.org/article/ccnv-shelter-covenant-sparks -conversation/#.Y1wIeezMJZ2.

114. Two of the three were missions that would only let Lawrence stay more than seventeen days if he enrolled in their religious program, which he really didn't want to do. The third, Interfaith Sanctuary, had no religious requirements, but it was almost always full, and he'd been turned away many times.

115. https://www.usich.gov/sites/default/files/document/All_In.pdf.

116. Dennis Culhane, Dan Treglia, Ken Steif, Randall Kuhn, and Thomas Byrne, "Estimated Emergency and Observational/Quarantine Capacity Need for the US Homeless Population Related to COVID-19 Exposure by County; Projected Hospitalizations, Intensive Care Units and Mortality," University of Pennsylvania, University of California Los Angeles, Boston University, unpublished paper, March 27, 2020, https://works.bepress.com/dennis_culhane/237/.

117. Matthew Gerken and Abby Boshart, "The CARES Act Supports Key Programs, but More Is Needed Soon," Urban Institute, April 2020, https:// www.urban.org/sites/default/files/publication/102078/the-cares-act-supports-key- programs-but-more-is-needed-soon_0.pdf; "COVID-19 Federal Resource Guideline Series: CARES Act Emergency Solution Grants (ESG)," National Alliance to End Homelessness, https://endhomelessness.org/wp-content/uploads /2020/05/ESG-one-pager.pdf.

118. Brian Holmes, "Homeless Population in Ada County Has Doubled in the Last Three Years, According to CATCH," KTVB, April 25, 2022, updated May 2, 2022, https://www.ktvb.com/article/news/local/208/number-homeless-ada-county -doubled-last-three-years-catch/277-4ef838ba-e340-4873-962f-4fbc0feae9d0.

119. US Department of Housing and Urban Development (HUD), *The 2023 Annual Homelessness Assessment Report (AHAR) to Congress: Part 1: Point-in-Time Estimates of Homelessness in the US* (HUD, 2023), https://www.huduser.gov/portal/ sites/default/files/pdf/2023-AHAR-Part-1.pdf.

120. HUD, *2023 AHAR Part 1*.

121. NLCHP, *Tent City, USA: The Growth of America's Homeless Encampments and How Communities are Responding* (National Homelessness Law Center, 2017), https://homelesslaw.org/wp-content/uploads/2018/10/Tent_City_USA_2017.pdf.

CHAPTER THREE

1. Martha Cast, "Star: On the Loneliness of Living Unsheltered," Street Spirit, May 5, 2022, https://thestreetspirit.org/2022/05/05/star-on-the-loneliness-of-living-unsheltered/.

2. Homeless Loki, "Homeless, Disabled, Elderly, and Waiting for Death," Invisible People, September 24, 2022, https://invisiblepeople.tv/homeless-disabled -elderly-and-waiting-for-death/.

3. "Jim," Invisible People, April 22, 2018, https://invisiblepeople.tv/videos/jim -homeless-traverse-city/.

4. A 2021 "meta study" that reviewed studies of homelessness in high-income countries internationally concluded that one in eight homeless people suffered from "treatable" mental disorders, specifically schizophrenia or major depression. The studies focused on people living in shelters or public places, largely excluding those living doubled up. The meta review also found that about 37 percent suffered from alcohol disorders and 22 percent from other substance dependencies, both about ten times more than the general population; however, it noted that some of this may have been a way of coping with homelessness. Some of these numbers overlap. Stefan Gutwinski, Stefanie Schreiter, Karl Deutscher, and Seena Fazel, "The Prevalence of Mental Disorders among Homeless People in High-Income Countries: An Updated Systematic Review and Meta-Regression Analysis," *PLOS Medicine* 18, no. 8, August 2021, https://journals.plos.org/plosmedicine/article?id =10.1371/journal.pmed.1003750.

5. Albert Q. Maisel, "Bedlam 1946: Most US Mental Hospitals Are a Shame and a Disgrace," *Life Magazine*, May 6, 1946, reprinted in *American Experience*, PBS, https://www.pbs.org/wgbh/americanexperience/features/lobotomist-bedlam -1946; Albert Deutsch, *The Shame of the States* (Harcourt, Brace, 1948).

6. Chris Koyanagi, "Learning from History: Deinstitutionalization of People with Mental Illness as Precursor to Long-Term Care Reform," Kaiser Commission on Medicaid and the Uninsured, August 2007, https://www.kff.org/wp-content/ uploads/2013/01/7684.pdf.

7. Martha R. Burt, *Over the Edge: The Growth of Homelessness in the 1980s* (Russell Sage Foundation, 1993), 121.

8. Carol L. Caton, *The Open Door: Homelessness and Severe Mental Illness in the Era of Community Treatment* (Oxford University Press, 2017), 6; Burt, *Over the Edge*, 121; Koyanagi, "Learning from History," 10–12.

9. For a time in the 1970s, some went or were put into nursing homes, where their stays were paid for by Medicaid, which had been created in 1965—hardly consistent with the goal of living in the community. Caton, *The Open Door*, 6.

10. First initiated as part of President Roosevelt's New Deal in 1935, it provided benefits to retired workers as well as to needy people who were elderly or visually impaired. Much later, it included elderly people who could no longer work. During the Nixon administration, needy disabled people in general were added with

enactment of the SSI program in 1972. "Historical Background and Development of Social Security," Social Security Administration, https://www.ssa.gov/history/briefhistory3.html; Koyanagi, "Learning from History," 6.

11. Some were able also to earn a little money through odd jobs and to receive small state welfare payments then available. US General Accounting Office (GAO), *Homelessness: A Complex Problem and the Federal Response*, HRD-85-40 (GAO, 1985), https://www.gao.gov/assets/hrd-85-40.pdf.

12. GAO, *Homelessness*.

13. Ellen Baxter and Kim Hopper, *Private Lives/Public Spaces: Homeless Adults on the Streets of New York City* (Community Service Society, 1981), 34–35, 37–38.

14. A variety of government incentives, including federal funds for "urban renewal" and slum clearance and local tax breaks helped support this. GAO, *Homelessness*, 24–26.

15. Baxter and Hopper, *Private Lives/Public Spaces*, 34.

16. GAO, *Homelessness*, 20–21, 23.

17. Mental Health Systems Act, S. 1177, 96th Cong. (1980), https://www.govtrack.us/congress/bills/96/s1177. In 1981, with the Reagan administration's emphasis on shrinking the federal government, the Act was repealed. Koyanagi, "Learning from History." Funds remaining for community mental health centers were diverted by the new Reagan administration into block grants to the states. Caton, *The Open Door*.

18. Robert Pear, "Fairness of Reagan's Cutoffs of Disability Aid Questioned," *New York Times*, May 9, 1982, https://www.nytimes.com/1982/05/09/us/fairness-of-reagan-s-cutoffs-of-disability-aid-questioned.html.

19. National Law Center on Homelessness & Poverty (NLCHP), *Social Security: Broken Promises to America's Homeless* (NLCHP, 1990).

20. "Frequently Asked Questions (FAQs) for Representative Payees," Social Security Administration, https://www.ssa.gov/payee/faqrep.htm?tl=5.

21. Some states had and still have a "state supplement"—an additional, albeit very modest, amount funded by the state government—that adds to each of the federal benefits. Many of these state supplements specifically included funds for specialized housing for recipients with mental disabilities, in group homes, or other supervised living arrangements. These could be significant (as high as $678 per month in Maryland, for example). NLCHP, *Social Security: Broken Promises*, 11.

22. If a recipient reaches full retirement age while receiving SSDI, they convert to retirement benefits at the same amount. "Frequently Asked Questions," Social Security Administration, last modified October 7, 2022, https://faq.ssa.gov/en-us/Topic/article/KA-01861. In 1989, average SSDI payments were just over $600 a month for men, and just over $450 a month for women. Joseph Bondar, "Effects of Social Security Benefit Increase," *Social Security Bulletin* 53, no. 4 (April 1990), https://www.ssa.gov/policy/docs/ssb/v53n4/v53n4p14.pdf.

23. The reviews were formally begun under a 1980 law signed by President Carter. The Reagan administration accelerated them and made them much more onerous, including by putting the burden on the applicant to show continued eligibility and initiating the "nonacquiescence" policy.

24. Angela M. Johnson, "The Social Security Administration's Policy of Nonacquiescence," *Indiana Law Journal* vol. 62, no. 4 (Fall 1987), http://www.repository.law.indiana.edu/cgi/viewcontent.cgi?article=2094&context=ilj.

25. GAO, *Homelessness*.

26. Pear, "Fairness of Reagan's Cutoffs."

27. GAO, *Homelessness*, 23, citing US Conference of Mayors, "Homeless in America's Cities," 6–7, 26, 30, 36.

28. It would do so within the same federal circuit—whose precedents should have been binding. See, for example, Johnson, "The SSA's Policy of Nonacquiescence."

29. While the SSA agreed to modify its policy of nonacquiescence in 1985, it did not concede that the policy was illegal, and it did not agree to review terminations until 1992. Dan Rodricks, "Shameful Legacy: Reagan's Policy toward Disabled," *Sun Sentinel*, April 26, 1992, updated September 25, 2021, https://www.sunsentinel.com/news/fl-xpm-1992-04-26-9202050025-story.html; Johnson, "The SSA's Policy of Nonacquiescence;" Robert Pear, "U.S. to Reconsider Denial of Benefits to Many Disabled," *New York Times*, April 19, 1992, https://www.nytimes.com/1992/04/19/us/us-to-reconsider-denial-of-benefits-to-many-disabled.html?searchResultPosition=4.

30. Robert Pear, "New Reagan Policy to Cut Benefits for the Aged, Blind and Disabled," *New York Times*, October 16, 1987, https://www.nytimes.com/1987/10/16/us/new-reagan-policy-to-cut-benefits-for-the-aged-blind-and-disabled.html. This was put in place in October 1987.

31. Operated by the Coalition on Temporary Shelter (COTS), a private nonprofit still active in Detroit.

32. By 2022 it had gone up to $841, reflecting inflation: "$368 in 1989 is worth $920.97 today," CPI Inflation Calculator, accessed March 30, 2024, https://www.in2013dollars.com/us/inflation/1989?amount=368.

33. Declaration of Yvonne Bacon, NLCHP v. HHS, reprinted in NLCHP, *Social Security: Broken Promises*, Appendix A.

34. Declaration of Timothy Godfrey, NLCHP v. HHS, reprinted in NLCHP, *Social Security: Broken Promises*, Appendix A.

35. See Declarations of Wayne Pippin; Patrick Babcock, NLCHP v. HHS, reprinted in NLCHP, *Social Security: Broken Promises*, Appendix A.

36. For recent discussions of how the prominence of homeless people with mental disorders in media reports, coupled with stigma, negatively affect public perceptions of homelessness, see Kaitlyn Ranney quoting Deborah Padgett, "FAQs about Mental Health and Homelessness," Community Solutions, May 10, 2023, https://community.solutions/

faqs-about-mental-health-and-homelessness/?gad_source=1&gclid=Cj0KCQ-
iA2KitBhCIARIsAPPMEhJdUFbB5O0Nk0Y0We2ZE5NFrNjSvFobgFGsfv4V4
SvYlXXNJ78wLdsaAoqcEALw_wcB; Nicole Wetsman, "Why Experts Say Some
Unhoused People Are Unfairly Assumed to Be Dangerous," ABC News, October
17, 2023, https://abcnews.go.com/Health/unhoused-people-perceived-dangerous/
story?id=103751928.

37. *Outreach in the Supplemental Security Income Program: Are the Needy Being
Informed? Joint Hearing before the Select Comm. on Aging and the Subcomm. on
Retirement Income and Employment of the Select Comm. on Aging*, 101st Cong. (1990)
(statement of Frank M. Pruden).

38. NLCHP, *Social Security: Broken Promises.*

39. Complaint, NLCHP et al. v. HHS, et al., Civil Action No. 89-3331,
filed U.S.D.C. Dist. D.C. (Dec. 13, 1989). We obtained the memos through the
Freedom of Information Act. (On file with author.)

40. Deena Shanker, "New Data Shows US Food Waste Is Getting Worse,"
Bloomberg, April 20, 2023, https://www.bloomberg.com/news/articles/2023-04
-20/the-us-has-a-food-waste-problem-and-it-s-getting-worse; Josh Bivens and
Jori Kandra, "CEO Pay Declined Slightly in 2022," Economic Policy Institute,
September 21, 2023, https://www.epi.org/publication/ceo-pay-in-2022/.

41. At the time, the District of Columbia and thirty-seven states offered
extremely modest cash grants to poor individuals—the only such help a poor, childless individual could receive. Since that time, these state-level "general assistance"
programs have been eliminated or, in most states where they still exist, limited
to those deemed "unemployable," meaning too sick, old, or disabled to work. In
2020, benefits ranged from as high as $797 in New Hampshire, to as low as $79 in
Delaware. Liz Schott, "State General Assistance Programs Very Limited in Half
the States and Nonexistent in Others, Despite Need," Center on Budget and Policy
Priorities, updated July 2, 2020, https://www.cbpp.org/research/family-income-
support/state-general-assistance-programs-very-limited-in-half-the-states.

42. Over time, the influence of the office I'd established in Washington, D.C.,
had increased, but so had visits from the New York City–based head of the organization, who had a habit of referring to women as "broads," "tomatoes," and "skirts"—
among other sources of strife.

43. The original name was the National Law Center on Homelessness & Poverty,
or just "the Law Center" for short. I'd chosen the name to make clear the connection between homelessness and poverty at a time when this was still being disputed.
But the name was unwieldly and over time the connection between homelessness
and poverty was more widely accepted—we had made our point—and the organization shortened its name in 2020. "Message of the Executive Director," *In Just Times*,
August 2020. https://homelesslaw.org/ijt-august-2020/

44. NLCHP v. HHS, Civ. Action No. 89-3331, D.D.C., filed Dec. 13, 1989.
The organization was then called the National Law Center on Homelessness &

Poverty; we changed the name in August 2020. Hogan Lovells, the global law firm that was then called Hogan & Hartson, worked with us pro bono.

45. National Law Center on Homelessness & Poverty v. Department of Health & Human Services, 1990 U.S. Dist. LEXIS 1160, https://plus.lexis.com/api /document/collection/cases/id/3S4N-9FB0-0054-42C9-00000-00?cite=1990%20U .S.%20Dist.%20LEXIS%201160&context=1530671.

46. NLCHP, *Social Security: Broken Promises.*

47. As reported by his staffer.

48. Along with Pete Stark, Robert Matsui (D-CA) was also an "original cosponsor," meaning he put his name on the bill when it was first introduced. A companion bill was introduced in the Senate by Donald Riegle (D-MI), Al Gore (D-TN), John Kerry (D-MA), Mark Hatfield (R-OR), and Ted Kennedy (D-MA).

49. This would be $1,055 in 2024 dollars. CPI Inflation Calculator, accessed April 2, 2024, https://data.bls.gov/cgi-bin/cpicalc.pl?cost1=412.00&year1=198901 &year2=202402.

50. Shawn Pogatchnik, "Up to 4.6 Million Are Losing Out on Special Benefits: Social Security: Unwieldy Application Process Is Confusing Elderly Poor Who Qualify for Supplemental Income," *Los Angeles Times*, April 6, 1990, http://articles .latimes.com/1990-04-06/news/mn-661_1_social-security.

51. "Social Security Fails to Deliver," *In Just Times: A Newsletter of the National Law Center on Homelessness and Poverty* (April 1992). *Outreach Efforts in the Supplemental Security Income and Qualified Medicare Beneficiary Programs: Hearing before the Subcomm. on Social Security, the Subcomm. on Health, and the Subcomm. on Human Resources of the Comm. on Ways and Means*, 102ⁿᵈ Cong. (1992), https:// books.google.com/books/about/Outreach_Efforts_in_the_Supplemental_Sec.html ?id=ewAtAAAAMAAJ. SSA announced that it had put an agency-wide plan into place to reach homeless people who might be eligible. This primarily consisted of distributing pamphlets and posters to local offices and giving staff at these offices the option of assisting homeless people if they chose—and if they had time in their already overburdened schedules. See *Outreach Efforts in the SSI*, 102ⁿᵈ Cong. (testimony of Joseph Manes of the Mental Health Law Project).

52. A law we and allies got passed in 1987 required SSI to continue benefits for up to three months for people in medical facilities so they could retain their housing while in the hospital. *Outreach Efforts in the SSI*, 102nd Cong. (testimony of Joseph Manes), 115, citing §1611(e)(l)(E) (42 U.S.C. §1382(e)(1)(E)) modified by Pub. L. No. 100-203, Omnibus Budget Reconciliation Act of 1987, §9115.

53. In May 1992, we released a report focusing on SSA's failure to implement this law, enacted in 1986 as part of our first successful legislative campaign, for the Homeless Eligibility Clarification Act. It was meant to ensure that people in mental institutions, hospitals, correctional facilities, and the like could apply for SSI benefits before their release—so that they could have a source of income upon release. The law required suspension of benefits during institutionalization, so that

even if they had previously managed to get them, they would subsequently lose them. Without these benefits, they would simply be abandoned to the streets, and this was the title of our report. NLCHP, *Abandoned to the Streets*, May 1992, summarized in NLCHP testimony submitted for the record to *Old, Poor, and Forgotten: Elderly Americans Living in Poverty: Hearing before the Select Committee on Aging, House of Representatives*, 102nd Cong. (1992), and in "Center Faults Pre-Release Program Implementation," *In Just Times: A Newsletter of the National Law Center on Homelessness and Poverty* 3, no. 6 (June 1992).

54. Chris Spolar and Marcia Slacum Greene, "Mitch Snyder Found Hanged in CCNV Shelter," *Washington Post*, July 6, 1990.

55. From the Congressional Budget Office, charged with estimating costs of legislation. NLCHP, *Social Security Fails to Deliver*.

56. *Outreach Efforts in the SSI*, 102nd Cong. (testimony of Joseph Manes).

57. *Outreach Efforts in the SSI*, 102nd Cong.

58. *Outreach Efforts in the SSI*, 102nd Cong. (testimony of William Lawrence Melton). Larry accompanied me at the hearing, at which I testified on behalf of the Law Center.

59. This change was made by welfare reform and the Contract with America Advancement Act of 1996. Paul Davies, Howard Iams, and Kalman Rupp, "The Effect of Welfare Reform on SSA's Disability Programs: Design of Policy Evaluation and Early Evidence," Social Security Administration, https://www.ssa .gov/policy/docs/ssb/v63n1/v63n1p3.pdf. Before this change, drug addicts or alcoholics had to receive payments through a representative payee and participate in a treatment program.

60. In October 1993, the Homeless Outreach Act was introduced again. "Homeless Outreach Act Introduced," *In Just Times: A Newsletter of the National Law Center on Homelessness and Poverty* 4, no. 10 October 1993). Senator Donald Riegle took the lead in the Senate with Representatives Pete Stark and Robert Matsui in the House.

61. The work would be funded by a federal grant to the other group, and we would get a small subgrant for our contribution. Federal funding of any kind—even indirectly, through a subgrant—was new for us. It was something we had shied away from, not wanting to be in a position where we were financially dependent on an agency we were advocating with—or undermine our ability to sue the agency in court if we needed to. But this indirect funding of a small amount—just over $20,000—seemed innocuous enough.

62. NLCHP, *Photo Identification Barriers Faced by Homeless Persons: The Impact of September* 11 (NLCHP, 2004), https://homelesslaw.org/wp-content/uploads/2019 /03/Photo-ID-Barriers-Faced-by-Homeless-Persons-2004.pdf.

63. We initially tried to interest the Social Security Administration in adopting some of the lessons of its own successful demonstration programs. But even though

the whole point of such programs is to "demonstrate" policies and implement successful ones broadly, we got nowhere.

64. The grants were to be awarded to local government agencies and nonprofit groups.

65. SOAR stands for "SSI/SSDI Outreach, Advocacy and Recovery." Jeremy Rosen and Yvonne Perret, *Stepping Stones to Recovery: A Case Manager's Manual for Assisting Adults Who Are Homeless, with Social Security Disability and Supplemental Security Income Applications* (Center for Mental Health Services, Substance Abuse and Mental Health Services Administration, 2005). The lead author, Jeremy Rosen, was a lawyer with just a few years' experience whom we'd been able to hire initially through a two-year fellowship program designed to promote public interest law, now known as Equal Justice Works. Yvonne Perret, the coauthor, had established and led a successful "demonstration" program in Baltimore.

66. Jacqueline F. Kauff, Elizabeth Clary, Kristin Sue Lupfer, and Pamela J. Fischer, "An Evaluation of SOAR: Implementation and Outcomes of an Effort to Improve Access to SSI and SSDI," Psychiatric Services, May 2, 2016, https://ps .psychiatryonline.org/doi/10.1176/appi.ps.201500247.

67. Substance Abuse and Mental Health Services Administration (SAMHSA), "2021 National SOAR Outcomes," SOAR WORKS, https://soarworks.samhsa.gov /article/2021-national-soar-outcomes.

68. SAMHSA, "OAT and Outcomes," SOAR WORKS, 2023. https:// soarworks.samhsa.gov/about-the-model/oat-and-outcomes. The exact number reported was 65,372.

69. In 2023, SOAR helped 2,604 (on initial application) + 324 (on appeal = 2,928) eligible homeless or at-risk people receive disability benefits. SAMHSA, "2023 National Outcomes," SAMHSA, https://soarworks.samhsa.gov/sites/default /files/media/documents/2023-10/2023%20Outcomes%20Infog-TextAlt.pdf. This is significantly down from 4,265 in 2020. SAMHSA, "2020 National Outcomes," SOAR WORKS, 2020, https://soarworks.samhsa.gov/article/2020-national-soar -outcomes. According to what is likely a very significant undercount, at least 143,105 were eligible for these benefits that year. US Department of Housing and Urban Development (HUD), *The 2023 Annual Homelessness Assessment Report (AHAR) to Congress: Part 1: Point-in-Time Estimates of Homelessness in the US* (HUD, 2023), 77, https://www.huduser.gov/portal/sites/default/files/pdf/2023-AHAR-Part-1.pdf. This estimate of the homeless population, sponsored by HUD, is widely viewed to be an undercount. See, for example, NLCHP, *Don't Count on It: How the HUD Point-in-Time Count Underestimates the Homelessness Crisis in America* (NLCHP, 2018), https://homelesslaw.org/wp-content/uploads/2018/10/HUD-PIT-report2017.pdf. In addition, by its own terms the HUD estimate of chronically homeless individuals leaves out youth, children, and members of homeless families.

70. "Disabled Americans Are Conservatives' New 'Welfare Queens,'" National Committee to Preserve Social Security and Medicare, July 10, 2014, https://www

.ncpssm.org/entitledtoknow/disabled-americans-are-conservatives-new-welfare
-queens/; Tom Harkin and Max Richtman, "Two More Parting Shots from Trump
Aimed Squarely at Disabled Workers," *The Hill*, November 24, 2020, https://thehill
.com/opinion/white-house/527277-two-more-parting-shots-from-trump-aimed
-squarely-at-disabled-workers/.

71. Andy Jones, "Biden Undoes Key Trump Rules Affecting Disability
Community," Academy of Special Needs Planners, https://attorney.elderlaw
answers.com/biden-administration-undoes-key-trump-regulations-affecting-people
-with-disabilities-18163.

72. In 2021, Senator Sherrod Brown held the first congressional hearings on SSI
since 1998, and proposed reforms to address some of the inequities. *Policy Options
for Improving SSI: Hearing before the Subcomm. on Social Security, Pensions, and Family
Policy of the Comm. on Finance*, 107th Cong. (2021).

73. It was $1,371 per month for an eligible couple—where each person is eligi-
ble—or $16,452 per year. "SSI Federal Payment Amounts for 2024," Social Security
Administration, https://www.ssa.gov/oact/cola/SSI.html.

74. "Average monthly apartment rent in the United States from January 2017
to November 2023, by apartment size," Statista, https://www.statista.com/statistics
/1063502/average-monthly-apartment-rent-usa/. Most—but not all—states offer a
"supplement" to the federal payment. Average monthly amounts of these supplements vary widely, from $37.28 (NJ) to $483.61 (HI) in 2023. Jackie Jakab, "SSI
Supplemental Payments by State," *Atticus*, June 30, 2023, https://www.atticus.com
/advice/disability-help-by-state/ssi-supplemental-payments-by-state. These state
supplements remain woefully inadequate, given the rising cost of living and especially housing. Taking the supplements into account yields an average monthly
benefit of just $983 in 2023. "Priced Out: The Housing Crisis for People with
Disabilities," Technical Assistance Collaborative, https://www.tacinc.org/resources/
priced-out/.

75. The latest federal data—certainly a severe undercount—state that on a single
night in January 2023 more than 152,000 people were "chronically" homeless—
defined as people with a disability who have been "continuously homeless for one
year or more or ha[ve] experienced at least four episodes of homelessness in the last
three years where the combined length of time homeless on those occasions is at
least 12 months." HUD, *2024 Annual Homelessness Assessment Report*, vi.

76. Only 4 percent of apartments rented for $1,000 or less. "Charlotte, NC
Rental Market Trends," RentCafe, https://www.rentcafe.com/average-rent-market
-trends/us/nc/charlotte/.

77. "Brown during Finance Subcommittee Hearing: It's Time to Bring SSI into
the 21st Century," Sherrod Brown U.S. Senator for Ohio, September 21, 2021,
https://www.brown.senate.gov/newsroom/press/release/brown-finance-subcommit
-tee-ssi-21st-century. Brown also proposed raising the asset limits, which as of
2023 were set at $2,000 for individuals and $3,000 for couples, unchanged since

1989. Brown also proposed updating the income rules to allow recipients to receive benefits from other safety-net programs, as well as some limited income through work, without reducing their SSI benefits. As of late 2023, part of his proposal—to reform asset and income limits—was gaining bipartisan, bicameral support. "In Latest Sign of Momentum, Eight Bank Executives Endorse Brown's Bipartisan Push to Fix the Supplemental Security Income Program," Sherrod Brown U.S. Senator for Ohio, December 6, 2023, https://www.brown.senate.gov/newsroom/press/release/in-latest-sign-of-momentum-eight-bank-executives-endorse-browns-bipartisan-push-to-fix-the-supplemental-security-income-program.

78. Burt, *Over the Edge*, 109. Caton, *The Open Door*, vii.

79. In 2020, nearly 20 percent of American adults lived with a mental disorder, and over 5 percent lived with a serious mental disorder. "Mental Illness," National Institute of Mental Health, https://www.nimh.nih.gov/health/statistics/mental-illness.

80. Jacquelyn Simone, "Coalition for the Homeless' Statement on Mayor Adams' Mental Health Address and Legislative Agenda," Coalition for the Homeless, November 29, 2022, https://www.coalitionforthehomeless.org/press/coalition-for-the-homeless-statement-on-mayor-adams-mental-health-address-and-legislative-agenda/; Deborah K, Padgett, "Homelessness, Housing Instability and Mental Health: Making the Connections," *BJPsych Bulletin* 44, no. 5 (October 2020), 197–201.

81. See, for example, Senwin Pareja, "The Impact of Homelessness on People with Disabilities (PWD)," Homemore, September 7, 2022, https://thehomemoreproject.org/the-impact-of-homelessness-on-people-with-disabilities-pwd/#.

82. Alice S. Baum and Donald W. Burnes, *A Nation in Denial: The Truth about Homelessness* (Westview Press, 1993). The book attracted unexpected attention, perhaps because of its use of "denial," a pop-psychology concept then gaining currency among the public.

83. Josh Levin, interviewed by Megan Thompson, "The True Story behind the 'Welfare Queen' Stereotype," *PBS News Weekend*, June 1, 2019, https://www.pbs.org/newshour/show/the-true-story-behind-the-welfare-queen-stereotype.

84. Elisabeth Bumiller, "In Wake of Attack, Giuliani Cracks Down on Homeless," *New York Times*, November 20, 1999, https://www.nytimes.com/1999/11/20/nyregion/in-wake-of-attack-giuliani-cracks-down-on-homeless.html.

85. Michael D. Shear, "Trump Expresses Shock at Homelessness, 'a Phenomenon That Started Two Years Ago,'" *New York Times*, July 2, 2019, https://www.nytimes.com/2019/07/02/us/politics/trump-homeless.html; Alissa Walker, "Trump's Grotesque Plan to 'End Homelessness' Is Already Mainstream Policy," *Curbed*, July 28, 2022, https://www.curbed.com/2022/07/donald-trump-homelessness-rick-caruso.html.

86. Janaki Chadha and Amanda Eisenberg, "'Back to the Giuliani era': Adams' Order to Clear Homeless Camps Ignites Fury in New York," *Politico*, April 2, 2022, https://www.politico.com/news/2022/04/02/adams-nypd-homeless-camps-00022473.

87. Kim Hopper, writing with colleagues in 1985, noted that "the growth [of homelessness] is commonly attributed to defects or disabilities that lie within the homeless themselves. We argue, instead, that the roots of homelessness are found in the economic restructuring of the city." Kim Hopper, Ezra Susser, and Sarah Conover, "Economies of Makeshift: Deindustrialization and Homelessness in New York City," *Urban Anthropology and Studies of Cultural Systems and World Economic Development* 14, nos. 1–3 (Spring-Summer-Fall, 1985), 183–236.

88. Megan Brenan, "Record-High Worry in U.S. about Hunger, Race Relations," Gallup, March 26, 2021, https://news.gallup.com/poll/341954/record-high-worry -hunger-race-relations.aspx.

CHAPTER FOUR

1. HUD, *The 2022 Annual Homelessness Assessment Report (AHAR) to Congress: Part 1: Point-in-Time Estimates of Homelessness in the US* (HUD, 2022), https://www .huduser.gov/portal/sites/default/files/pdf/2022-AHAR-Part-1.pdf.

2. Cynthia Griffith, "Tennessee Moves to Make Camping on Public Land a Felony," Invisible People, June 14, 2022. https://invisiblepeople.tv/tennessee-moves -to-make-camping-on-public-land-a-felony/; Jonathan Mattise, "Homeless Camps on Public Land Risk Felony in Tennessee Bill," AP News, April 14, 2022, https:// apnews.com/article/nashville-tennessee-homelessness-poverty-1b79a1ac05d2a8b 38597a1646004553b; Associated Press, "Tennessee Is about to Become the First State to Make Camping on Public Land a Felony," NPR, May 26, 2022, https:// www.npr.org/2022/05/26/1101434831/public-camping-felony-tennessee-homeless -seek-refuge/.

3. "Housing Needs by State: Tennessee," National Low Income Housing Coalition, https://www.nlihc.org/housing-needs-by-state/tennessee.

4. Gregory Raucoules, "East TN Senator Invokes Hitler during Debate on Bill Penalizing Homeless," WREG.com, April 15, 2022, https://wreg.com/news/your -voice-your-vote/east-tn-senator-invokes-hitler-during-debate-on-bill-penalizing -homeless/; Timothy Bella, "GOP Lawmaker Says Homeless People Should Look to Hitler for Inspiration," *Washington Post*, April 14, 2022; Tzvi Joffre, TN Senator Uses Hitler as Example of Homeless Person Who 'Made History,' *Jerusalem Post*, April 14, 2022.

5. Mattise, "Homeless Camps on Public Land."

6. HUD, *The 2023 Annual Homelessness Assessment Report (AHAR) to Congress: Part 1: Point-in-Time Estimates of Homelessness in the US* (HUD, 2023), 89. This includes *both* emergency shelter and "transitional housing" beds. https://www .huduser.gov/portal/sites/default/files/pdf/2023-AHAR-Part-1.pdf. The number of emergency shelter beds was only 358,435.

7. NCH et al. v. VA et al., Complaint for Injunctive and Declaratory Relief, filed Sept. 6, 1988, D.D.C.

8. National Law Center on Homelessness & Poverty (NLCHP), *Tent City, USA: The Growth of America's Homeless Encampments and How Communities Are*

Responding (National Homelessness Law Center, 2017), https://homelesslaw.org/wp-content/uploads/2018/10/Tent_City_USA_2017.pdf; HUD, Understanding Encampments of People Experiencing Homelessness and Community Responses: Emerging Evidence a of Late 2018 (HUD, 2018)

9. NLCHP, *Tent City, USA.*

10. Lyall v. City of Denver, Civil Action No. 16-cv-02155, D. Colo., filed August 25, 2016. https://denverhomelessoutloud.wordpress.com/wp-content/uploads/2016/08/denver-homeless-class-action.pdf.

11. Peter Charalambous, "Across the US, Friends and Advocates Remember Homeless Americans Who Died This Year," ABC News, December 22, 2023, https://abcnews.go.com/US/us-friends-advocates-remember-homeless-americans-died-year/story?id=105870201. Homeless people die young, at a mean age of fifty. They are sixteen times more likely to die suddenly than their housed peers. Elizabeth Fernandez, "Homeless People Are 16 Times More Likely to Die Suddenly," University of California San Francisco, October 23, 2023, https://www.ucsf.edu/news/2023/10/426426/homeless-people-are-16-times-more-likely-die-suddenly; Cara Murez, "Homeless Americans Face 16 Times the Odds for Sudden Death," *U.S. News and World Report*, October 24, 2023, https://www.usnews.com/news/health-news/articles/2023-10-24/homeless-americans-face-16-times-the-odds-for-sudden-death.

12. November 19, 2016.

13. Catherine Bennett, "Police Take Blankets from Denver Homeless after Urban Camping Ban," *France 24*, updated December 29, 2016, https://observers.france24.com/en/20161228-denver-urban-camping-ban-police-take-blankets-homeless.

14. The ordinance defines "to camp" as "to reside or dwell temporarily in a place, with shelter." It further defines "shelter" to include not only tents, tarps, and lean-tos, but also sleeping bags, blankets, and any form of cover or protection from the elements other than clothing. Eating falls under the definition of "reside or dwell." Meredith Sell, "What You Need to Know about Denver's Urban Camping Ban," *5280*, February 18, 2020, https://www.5280.com/2020/02/what-you-need-to-know-about-denvers-urban-camping-ban/; Denver Unauthorized Camping Ban, May 14, 2012, Denver Municipal Code, 38.86.2, which defines *camping* as using "without limitation, any tent, tarpaulin, lean-to, sleeping bag, bedroll, blankets, or any form of cover or protection from the elements other than clothing."

15. Declaration of Jerry Roderick Burton, Lyall v. Denver, Civil Action No. 16-cv-02155, D. Colo., September 7, 2016, https://denverhomelessoutloud.files.wordpress.com/2016/08/declaration-of-jerry-roderick-burton.pdf.

16. Bennett, "Police Take Blankets."

17. Jack Healy, "Rights Battles Emerge in Cities Where Homelessness Can Be a Crime," *New York Times*, January 9, 2017, https://www.nytimes.com/2017/01/09/us/rights-battles-emerge-in-cities-where-homelessness-can-be-a-crime.html.

18. Interfaith Alliance of Colorado, Courtney Brown, and Alye Sharp, "Move Along to Where? A Public Dialogue & Call to Action (Public forum, EXDO Event Center, December 15, 2016)," Facebook Events, https://www.facebook.com/events/1615478012081603/?active_tab=discussion.

19. Interfaith Alliance of Colorado, Brown, and Sharp, "Move Along to Where?"

20. "Move Along to Where Public Forum," Denver Homeless Out Loud, December 8, 2016, https://denverhomelessoutloud.org/2016/12/08/move-along-to-where-public-forum-1215/.

21. Stephanie Snyder, "Albus Brooks: Getting Rid of Denver's Camping Ban Wouldn't Help the Homeless," *Denverite*, December 16, 2016, https://denverite.com/2016/12/16/albus-brooks-getting-rid-denvers-camping-ban-wouldnt-help-homeless/.

22. Joe Rubino, "Denver Mayor Vetoes City Council's Ban on Homeless Sweeps in Sub-freezing Temperatures," *Denver Post*, February 2, 2024, https://www.denverpost.com/2024/02/02/denver-mike-johnston-veto-ban-homeless-sweeps-freezing-weather-city-council/; the city council failed to muster the votes to override it, Joe Rubino, Veto of Measure to Limit Denver Homeless Sweeps in Sub-freezing Weather Stands as City Council Override Veto Fails, *Denver Post*, February 12, 2004, https://www.denverpost.com/2024/02/12/denver-city-counci-homeless-sweeps-freezing-weather-mike-johnston-veto-override/.

23. "Anti-Okie" laws targeted poor farmers displaced by the Dust Boal and the Great Depression. "Ugly laws" targeted poor disabled people. For an overview of this history, see Harry Simon, "Towns without Pity: A Constitutional and Historical Analysis of Official Efforts to Drive Homeless Persons from American Cities," *Tulane Law Review* 66, no. 44 (March 1992), https://www.tulanelawreview.org/vol-66-issue-4; Javier Ortiz, Matthew Dick, and Sara Rankin, *The Wrong Side of History: A Comparison of Modern and Historical Criminalization* (Seattle University School of Law, 2015), https://digitalcommons.law.seattleu.edu/cgi/viewcontent.cgi?article=1003&context=hrap.

24. Risa Lauren Goluboff, *Vagrant Nation: Police Power, Constitutional Change, and the Making of the 1960s* (Oxford University Press, 2016).

25. Papachristou v. City of Jacksonville, 405 U.S. 156 (1972).

26. Ortiz, et al., *The Wrong Side of History.*

27. Maria Foscarinis, "Downward Spiral: Homelessness and Its Criminalization," *Yale Law & Policy Review* 14, no. 1 (1996); NLCHP, *Go Directly to Jail: A Report Analyzing Local Anti-homeless Ordinances* (NLCHP, 1991).

28. NLCHP, *Go Directly to Jail.*

29. Nancy Lewis, "Cities Accused of Hiding the Homeless," *Washington Post*, December 17, 1991. https://www.washingtonpost.com/archive/politics/1991/12/18/cities-accused-of-hiding-the-homeless/1d1922e9-f78f-4024-84d1-7ab721a0767d/.

30. A major law enforcement organization, the Police Executive Research Forum, also conducted a national survey of police chiefs and published a report on

its findings. The group found that homeless people were not regularly involved in property crimes, but that their presence increased the fear of crime among others. The group noted a need for better coordination of police with social service agencies and invited us to address their annual conference later that year. NLCHP, "Police Attitudes toward 'Street People' Examined," *In Just Times: A Newsletter of the National Law Center on Homelessness and Poverty* (August 1992).

31. NLCHP, *Housing Not Handcuffs 2019: Ending the Criminalization of Homelessness in US Cities* (NLCHP, 2019), https://homelesslaw.org/housing-not -handcuffs-2019/.

32. Christopher Giamarino, Evelyn Blumenberg and Madeline Brozen, "Who Lives in Vehicles and Why? Understanding Vehicular Homelessness in Los Angeles," *Housing Policy Debate* 34, no. 1 (2024), https://www.tandfonline.com /doi/full/10.1080/10511482.2022.2117990; Tyrone Ray Ivey, Jodleyn Gilleland, and Sara Rankin, *Hidden in Plain Sight: Finding Safe Parking for Vehicle Residents* (Seattle University School of Law, 2018), https://digitalcommons.law.seattleu.edu/ cgi/viewcontent.cgi?article=1012&context=hrap; Graham Pruss and Karen Cheng, "The 'Punitive Push' on Mobile Homes," *Cityscape: A Journal of Policy Development and Research* 22, no. 2 (HUD, 2020), 87–94; Michele Wakin, *Otherwise Homeless: Vehicle Living and the Culture of Homelessness* (FirstForum Press, 2013).

33. National Low Income Housing Coalition, *The Gap: A Shortage of Affordable Homes 2024* (NLIHC, 2024).

34. National Low Income Housing Coalition, Out of Reach 2023: The High Cost of Housing (NLIHC, 2023)

35. The lower appeals court decision, later reversed, quoted the city memoranda describing these policies, calling them "astonishing." Tobe v. City of Santa Ana, 32 Cal. App. 4th 941, 945–46 (1994); Foscarinis, "Downward Spiral," 23.

36. Tobe v. Santa Ana, 9 Cal. 4th 1069 (1995), https://plus.lexis.com/api /document/collection/cases/id/3RX4-1570-003D-J3D9-00000-00?cite=9%20Cal .%204th%201069&context=1530671.

37. Tobe v. Santa Ana, 9 Cal. 4th 1069 (1995). The US Department of Justice submitted an amicus brief supporting the homeless appellees, as did NLCHP, which had urged the federal agency to do so.

38. Paul Walters, "Orange County Voices: Fixing Public's 'Broken Windows': Santa Ana Civic Center Disorder Is a 'Broken Window' That Invites More Antisocial Behavior If Not Fixed by Police," *Los Angeles Times*, August 28, 1990https://www.latimes.com/archives/la-xpm-1990-08-28-me-79-story.html.

39. George L. Kelling and James Q. Wilson, "Broken Windows: The Police and Neighborhood Safety," *Atlantic*, March 1982, https://www.theatlantic.com/ magazine/archive/1982/03/broken-windows/304465/.

40. Harry Simon, "Towns without Pity," Tul. L. Rev. 66 (1992), 631, 646, fn96.

41. See Katie Glueck and Ashley Southall, "As Adams Toughens on Crime, Some Fear a Return to 90s Era Policing," *New York Times*, March 26, 2022.

42. See, for example, Bernard E. Harcourt, *Illusion of Order: The False Promise of Broken Windows Policing* (Harvard University Press, 2001)

43. Dorothy Roberts, "Foreword: Race, Vagueness, and the Social Meaning of Order-Maintenance Policing," *Journal of Criminal Law & Criminology* 89, no. 3 (1999), https://scholarship.law.upenn.edu/cgi/viewcontent.cgi?article=1588 &context=faculty_scholarship; Robert J. Sampson and Stephen W. Raudenbush, "Seeing Disorder: Neighborhood Stigma and the Social Construction of 'Broken Windows,'" *Social Psychology Quarterly* 67, no. 4 (2004), https://scholar.harvard.edu /sites/scholar.harvard.edu/files/sampson/files/2004_spq_raudenbush.pdf.

44. Nicole Wetsman, "Why Experts Say Some Unhoused People Are Unfairly Assumed to Be Dangerous," ABC News, October 17, 2023, https://abcnews.go.com /Health/unhoused-people-perceived-dangerous/story?id=103751928; Amy Melissa Donley, "The Perception of Homeless People: Important Factors in Determining Perceptions of the Homeless as Dangerous" (PhD diss., University of Central Florida, 2008), https://stars.library.ucf.edu/cgi/viewcontent.cgi?article=4789& context=etd; David A. Snow, Susan G. Baker, and Leon Anderson, "Criminality and Homeless Men: An Empirical Assessment," *Social Problems* 36, no. 5 (December 1989).

45. Molly Meinbresse, Lauren Brinkley-Rubinstein, Amy Grassette, Joseph Benson, Carol Hall, Reginald Hamilton, Marianne Malott, and Darlene Jenkins, "Exploring the Experiences of Violence among Individuals Who Are Homeless Using a Consumer-Led Approach," *Violence and Victims* 29, no. 1 (2014), https:// nhchc.org/wp-content/uploads/2019/08/vv-29-1_ptr_a8_122-136.pdf.

46. Thacher Schmid, "Homeless People in the US Are Being Murdered at a Horrific Rate," *Jacobin*, May 17, 2022, https://jacobin.com/2022/05/homeless -homicides-data-surge-victims-suspects.

47. *Guardian* staff and agency, "Man Pleads Not Guilty to Manslaughter over Chokehold Death of Jordan Neely," *Guardian*, June 28, 2023, https://www .theguardian.com/us-news/2023/jun/28/jordan-neely-daniel-penny-court-plea.

48. John Tharp and Maria Foscarinis, "Homelessness Can't be Solved with Fines and Arrests," *HuffPost*, May 31, 2018, https://www.huffpost.com/entry /opinion-tharp-homeless-law-enforcment_n_5b0d8c7be4b0802d69ceebe8.

49. This followed a 19 percent reduction in housing affordable to extremely low income people during the 1990s. HUD, *Trends in Worst Case Needs for Housing, 1978–1999: A Report to Congress on Worst Case Housing Needs Plus Update on Worst Case Needs in 2001* (HUD, 2003), xv, https://www.huduser.gov/portal/Publications/ PDF/trends.pdf. By 2004, that number had shrunk to thirty-four. NLIHC, *The Gap: A Shortage of Affordable Homes* (NLIHC, 2024), https://nlihc.org/gap.

50. NLCHP, *Out of Sight—Out of Mind? A Report on Anti-homeless Laws, Litigation and Alternatives in 50 U.S. Cities* (NLCHP, 1999). For example, of forty-nine cities surveyed, 18 percent had enacted or amended ordinances to restrict homeless persons' use of public space, including for begging, in the previous two years.

51. See, for example, NLCHP, *Photo Identification Barriers Faced by Homeless Persons: The Impact of September* 11 (NLCHP, 2004), https://homelesslaw.org /wp-content/uploads/2019/03/Photo-ID-Barriers-Faced-by-Homeless-Persons -2004.pdf.

52. Center on Budget and Policy Priorities, "During Bush Administration, Unbalanced Priorities Weakened Housing Programs" (Center on Budget and Policy Priorities, February 24, 2009. https://www.cbpp.org/sites/default/files/atoms/files/2 -24-09hous-sec3.pdf.

53. Jo Becker, Sheryl Gay Stolberg, and Stephen Labaton, "Bush Drive for Home Ownership Fueled Housing Bubble," *New York Times*, December 21, 2008, https://www.nytimes.com/2008/12/21/business/worldbusiness/21iht-admin .4.18853088.html.

54. National Coalition for the Homeless and NLCHP, *Illegal to be Homeless* (NCH and NLCHP, 2003); NLCHP, Punishing Poverty (NLCHP, 2003).

55. See Bruce G. Link, Sharon Schwartz, Robert Moore, Jo Phelan, Elmer Struening, Ann Stueve, and Mary Ellen Colten, "Public Knowledge, Attitudes, and Beliefs about Homeless People: Evidence for Compassion Fatigue?," *American Journal of Community Psychology*, 23 no. 4 (1995); Gary Blasi, "And We Are Not Seen: Ideological and Political Barriers to Understanding Homelessness." *American Behavioral Scientist* 37, no. 4 (February 1994).

56. "Fact Sheet: Public Opinion Polling on Housing Instability during the COVID-19 Pandemic," Opportunity Starts at Home, June 1, 2020, https://www .opportunityhome.org/wp-content/uploads/2020/05/FINAL-COVID19-Poll-Fact -Sheet-002.pdf.

57. Megan Brenan, "Record-High Worry in U.S. about Hunger, Race Relations," Gallup, March 26, 2021, https://news.gallup.com/poll/341954/record -high-worry-hunger-race-relations.aspx?utm_source=alert&utm_medium =email&utm_content=morelink&utm_campaign=syndication.

58. Fred Backus, "Over a Quarter of Americans Have Worried about Homelessness," CBS News, May 20, 2021, https://www.cbsnews.com/news /homelessness-worries-opinion-poll/.

59. Jack Tsai, Crystal Y. S. Lee, Jianxun Shen, Steven M. Southwick, and Robert H. Pietrzak, "Public Exposure and Attitudes about Homelessness," *Journal of Community Psychology* 47 no. 1 (2019).

60. Jack Tsai, Crystal Yun See Lee, Thomas Byrne, Robert H. Pietrzak, and Steven M. Southwick, "Changes in Public Attitudes and Perceptions about Homelessness between 1990 and 2016," *American Journal of Community Psychology* 60, nos. 3–4 (2017).

61. Link et al., "Public Knowledge, Attitudes, and Beliefs."

62. Tsai, et al., "Changes in Public Attitudes"; see also *2020 USC Price-USC Schwarzenegger Institute Poll on Homelessness* (USC Price, 2020), https://priceschool .usc.edu/wp-content/uploads/2020/02/USC-Price-USC-Schwarzenegger-Institute

-Homeless-Poll-Results.pdf. California voters named homelessness or housing the number one issue facing the state. The poll also includes findings that 65 percent support providing interim housing and simultaneously removing people off the streets; only 28 percent favor an "enforcement first" policy to "enforce removal of homeless encampments on the street before establishing more interim housing shelters for homeless people."

63. Carl Bialik and Taylor Orth, "Who Do Americans Blame for Homelessness?" YouGov, May 17, 2022, https://today.yougov.com/politics/articles/42548-american-attitudes-on-homelessness-poll?

64. Bialik and Orth, "Who Do Americans Blame"; see also Tsai, et al, "Public Exposure and Attitudes."

65. NHLC, Housing Not Handcuffs 2021: State Law Supplement (NHLC, 2021); "Emergent Threats: State Level Homelessness Criminalization," Housing Not Handcuffs, accessed January 25, 2024, https://housingnothandcuffs.org/emergent-threats-homelessness-criminalization/.

66. "About," Cicero Institute, https://ciceroinstitute.org/about/; "Joe Lonsdale: Chairman of the Board," Cicero Institute, https://ciceroinstitute.org/authors/joe-lonsdale/.

67. Cicero Institute, Model Bill: Reducing Street Homelessness Act (based on Missouri HB 1606 (2022) (Cicero Institute, 2022), https://ciceroinstitute.org/wp-content/uploads/2023/02/Homelessness-Policy-Model-Language-.pdf.

68. The Tennessee law included some but not all of Cicero's template language. But the group endorsed the bill, helping it become law. "Emergent Threats," Housing Not Handcuffs.

69. Bialik and Orth, "Who Do Americans Blame."

70. Tristan Baurick, "150 More Homeless People Given Hotel Rooms in New Orleans to Slow Spread of Coronavirus," NOLA.com, May 7, 2020. By the end of that spring, over six hundred homeless people had been housed in vacant hotel rooms. Unity of Greater New Orleans, A Gathering Storm: Homelessness during the Pandemic (Unity, 2020). https://unitygno.org/wp-content/uploads/2020/11/A-Gathering-Storm-October-2020-Report-on-Homelessness-During-the-Pandemic.pdf.

71. Denver Homeless Out Loud v. Denver, 32 F.4th 1259 (10th Cir. 2022).

72. Kirk Siegler, "Why Some Cities Are Operating Legal Homeless Camps Even in the Dead of Winter," NPR, January 7, 2022, https://www.npr.org/2022/01/07/1070966346/why-some-cities-are-operating-legal-homeless-camps-even-in-the-dead-of-winter.

73. Cynthia Griffith, "Government-Sanctioned Homeless Encampments Are an Ominous Solution," Invisible People, August 17, 2023, https://invisiblepeople.tv/government-sanctioned-homeless-encampments-are-an-ominous-solution/.

74. "Policing Doesn't End Homelessness. Supportive Housing Does," Housing Matters, October 25, 2022, https://apps.urban.org/features/ending-homelessness-through-supportive-housing-not-policing/.

75. Karen Kroll, "Homeless Encampment Sweeps Costly and of Limited Long-Term Effectiveness, According to Federal Research," *Smart Cities Dive*, February 21, 2023, https://www.smartcitiesdive.com/news/homeless-encampment-sweeps-costly-limited-effectiveness/643091/.

76. "WATCH the Horrible Reality of Los Angeles's Homeless Sweeps," Invisible People, July 28, 2022, https://invisiblepeople.tv/watch-the-horrible-reality-of-los-angeless-homeless-sweeps/.

77. HUD, *Houston, Texas: Community Encampment Report* (HUD, 2020), https://www.huduser.gov/portal/sites/default/files/pdf/Houston-Encampment-Report.pdf.

78. Marisa Kendall, "State Program to Clear Homeless Encampments Show [sic] Signs of Success, but Housing Remains Elusive," *CalMatters*, updated January 18, 2024, https://calmatters.org/housing/homelessness/2024/01/california-homeless-encampments-2/.

79. NLCHP, *Housing Not Handcuffs: A Litigation Manual* (NLCHP, 2018), https://homelesslaw.org/wp-content/uploads/2018/10/Housing-Not-Handcuffs-Litigation-Manual.pdf; NHLC, Housing Not Handcuffs 2021: State Law Supplement (NHLC, 2021).

80. Pottinger v. Miami, 810 F. Supp. 1551 (S.D. Fla.1992). In 2019 the park was renamed Maurice A. Ferre park. "Museum Park (Miami)," Wikipedia, https://en.wikipedia.org/wiki/Museum_Park_(Miami).

81. Pottinger v. Miami, 810 F. Supp. 1551 (S.D. Fla. 1992).

82. Pottinger v. Miami, 810 F. Supp. 1551 (1992). For a more comprehensive review of this and other early challenges, See Foscarinis, "Downward Spiral."

83. Originally filed in December 1988, the case first sought a court order to stop anticipated "sweeps" by the city ahead of the Orange Bowl. The court denied that request because he was unable to fashion an injunction with the requisite specificity. 810 F. Supp. 1551 (S.D. Fla. 1992).

84. Anatole France, *The Red Lily* (Calmann-Lévy, 1894).

85. The Law Center was involved as informal advisors and also as amicus on appeal.

86. Joyce v. City & County of San Francisco, 846 F. Supp. 843 (N.D. Cal.1994) (denying homeless plaintiffs' motion for preliminary injunction); Joyce v. City & County of San Francisco, 1996 U.S. App. LEXIS 16519 (9th Cir. Cal. June 14, 1996) (appeal dismissed as moot after city official ended its "Matrix" program). We filed an amicus brief on appeal.

87. NLCHP, *The Right to Remain Nowhere: A Report on Anti-homeless Laws and Litigation in 16 U.S. Cities* (NLCHP, 1993), 37.

88. The Supreme Court precedent says that punishing someone for their necessary, involuntary otherwise innocent conduct implicates the Eighth Amendment. A law or municipal policy that bans sleeping at all times, everywhere in the city, is clearly problematic. But a city can argue that sleeping in a particular location

or at a particular time is not necessary. Similarly, other successful arguments have invoked the constitutional right to travel, sometimes thought to reside in the Equal Protection Clause of the Fourteenth Amendment. Again, the argument turns on the breadth of the prohibition. Citywide bans that apply at all times make it impossible for homeless persons to travel to—or remain—in the city. Other arguments, such as those based on a more general freedom of movement under the Due Process Clause, are less dependent on these specific fact patterns but also harder to make successfully.

89. Roulette v. City of Seattle, 850 F. Supp. 1442 (W.D. Wa. 1994); aff'd, 78 F.3d 1425, 3125 (9th Cir.1996) The lower court had interpreted the law narrowly, and as such upheld it. In a two-to-one decision, the appeals court agreed. See Foscarinis, "Downward Spiral."

90. NLCHP, *Right to Remain Nowhere*, vi, 23.

91. Compare, for example, NLCHP, *No Homeless People Allowed: A Report on Anti-homeless Laws, Litigation and Alternatives in 49 U.S. Cities* (NLCHP, 1994), finding 26 percent of forty-nine cities surveyed had enacted or enforced public place restrictions, and 24 percent had conducted sweeps, with NLCHP, *Out of Sight* finding 73 percent of forty-nine cities surveyed had laws restricting sleeping or camping in public, and 48 percent had engaged in sweeps in the previous two years. Unlike those we conducted beginning in 2006, these surveys did not compare the identical group of cities over time. They do, however, indicate the overall trend.

92. For a comprehensive overview, see NLCHP, *Housing Not Handcuffs: A Litigation Manual*.

93. Martin v. Boise, 920 F.3d 584 (9th Cir. 2019), cert. denied, 140 S. Ct. 674 (2019).

94. The third shelter, Interfaith Sanctuary, accepted both men and women as well as a few families and did not have religious messaging or requirements. But it, and the others, were often full.

95. The nine states are Alaska, Arizona, California, Hawaii, Idaho, Montana, Nevada, Oregon, and Washington. Also included are Guam and the Northern Mariana Islands.

96. Manning v. Caldwell for City of Roanoke, 930 F.3d 264 (4th Cir. 2019) (en banc).

97. Abbie VanSickle, "Supreme Court to Hear Case over Homelessness Rules in Oregon," *New York Times*, January 12, 2024, https://www.nytimes.com/2024/01/12/us/politics/supreme-court-homeless-camps-oregon.html; Shawn Hubler, "In Rare Alliance, Democrats and Republicans Seek Legal Power to Clear Homeless Camps," *New York Times*, September 28, 2023, https://www.nytimes.com/2023/09/27/us/in-rare-alliance-democrats-and-republicans-seek-legal-power-to-clear-homeless-camps.html.

98. "The tragedy is that these decisions are actually harming the very people they purport to protect." VanSickle, "Supreme Court to Hear Case."

99. France, *The Red Lily*.

100. *City of Grants Pass v. Johnson*, No. 23-175, 2024 U.S. LEXIS 2881 (June 28, 2024). Chief Justice John Roberts and Justices Clarence Thomas, Samuel Alito, Brett Kavanaugh, and Amy Coney Barrett joined Justice Gorsuch's opinion; Justice Thomas also wrote a separate concurrence to say that he would have overruled, not simply failed to apply, earlier precedent, and that in his view the Eighth Amendment to the US Constitution was not implicated at all. *City of Grants Pass*, Thomas, J., concurring. Justice Sonia Sotomayor filed a powerful dissent, joined by Justices Elena Kagan and Ketanji Brown Jackson. *City of Grants Pass*, Sotomayor, J., dissenting.

101. Under earlier Supreme Court precedent, the distinction between status and conduct is arguably not decisive; what matters is whether the conduct being punished is "volitional" or not. In *Grants Pass*, sleeping outside was clearly not "volitional" given the extreme lack of shelter. But the majority concluded that counting the number of homeless people and beds in order to determine whether or not there was in fact a choice was just too complicated—and expensive.

102. In a sign of the strength of her disagreement with the majority, Justice Sotomayor read her dissent from the bench. Abbie VanSickle, "Supreme Court Upholds Ban on Sleeping Outdoors in Homelessness Case," *New York Times*, June 28, 2024.

103. Complaint, Singleton v. Montgomery (M.D.Ala., filed February 12, 2020) https://www.splcenter.org/sites/default/files/documents/filed_complaint.pdf.

104. NLCHP, *Housing Not Handcuffs 2019*.

105. Tanya Manus, "Rapid City Debuts Giving Meters to Help Those in Need," *Rapid City Journal*, August 21, 2023, https://rapidcityjournal.com/news/local/rapid -city-debuts-giving-meters-to-help-those-in-need/article_c7df2d7e-3d25-11ee -bc29-7b28cf3778a5.html.

106. Scott Keyes, "Everything You Think You Know about Panhandlers Is Wrong," ThinkProgress, October 30, 2013, https://thinkprogress.org/everything -you-think-you-know-about-panhandlers-is-wrong-36b41487730d/; Rohit Bose and Stephen W. Hwang, "Income and Spending Patterns among Panhandlers," *Canadian Medical Association Journal* 167, no. 5 (2002), https://www.cmaj.ca/ content/167/5/477.short; Kayla Robbins, "How Much Do Panhandlers Actually Make?," Invisible People, October 4, 2019, https://invisiblepeople.tv/how-much-do -panhandlers-actually-make/.

107. In 2020 dollars. Daniel Reinhard, D, "How Much Do They Make? A Systematic Review of Income Generated from Begging," *International Criminal Justice Review* 33, no. 1 (2021), https://doi-org.ezproxy.cul.columbia.edu/10.1177 /10575677211036498.

108. One prominent program was in Albuquerque, New Mexico. Despite its success, it was replaced by a ban in 2017. J. B. Wogan, "Once a National Model for Helping Panhandlers, Albuquerque's New Law Could Land Them in Jail," *Governing*, December 14, 2017, https://www.governing.com/archive/gov-albuquerque -panhandling-pedestrian-aclu.html.

109. Judy F. Minkove, "New Research and Insights into Substance Use Disorder," *Brainwise* Spring/Summer 2022 (Johns Hopkins Medicine, 2022), https://www.hopkinsmedicine.org/news/articles/new-research-and-insights-into-substance-use-disorder.

110. "Andrew," Invisible People, October 14, 2019, https://invisiblepeople.tv/videos/harrisburg-homeless-man/.

111. See, for example, Loper v. New York City Police Department, 999 F.2d 699 (2d Cir. 1993). Some courts have called it "much more conduct than speech." See also, Young v. NYC Transit Authority, 903 F.2d 146 (2d Cir. 1990). However, this increasingly seems to be the minority view.

112. The 2015 US Supreme Court ruling in Reed v. Town of Gilbert, 576 U.S. 155 (2015), made clear that any restrictions on speech based on its content would have to meet a very high bar to be constitutional. Citing the new Supreme Court decision, the court in our case invalidated the law. Norton v. Springfield, 806 F. 3d 411 (7th Cir. 2015).

113. Singleton v. Taylor, 2023 U.S. Dist. LEXIS 40560, Lexis, https://plus.lexis.com/api/document/collection/cases/id/67RN-DY81-DYFH-X1NY-00000-00?cite=2023%20U.S.%20Dist.%20LEXIS%2040560&context=1530671.

114. "Homeless Feeding Ban Prompts ACLU Suit," *News & Notes*, NPR, August 14, 2006, https://www.npr.org/templates/story/story.php?storyId=5643494; Sacco v. City of Las Vegas, Docket No. 2:06-CV-0714-RCJ-LRL (D. Nev. June 12, 2006).

115. The National Coalition for the Homeless (NCH) and NLCHP, *Feeding Intolerance: Prohibitions on Sharing Food with People Experiencing Homelessness* (NCH and NLCHP, 2007); NCH and NLCHP, *A Place at the Table: Prohibitions on Sharing Food with People Experiencing Homelessness* (NCH and NLCHP, 2010); NLCHP, *Criminalizing Crisis: Advocacy Manual* (NLCHP, 2011), 138–39.

116. Associated Press, "90-Year-Old Florida Man Faces Jail for Giving Food to the Homeless," Jacksonville.com, November 5, 2014. https://www.jacksonville.com/story/news/2014/11/05/90-year-old-florida-man-faces-jail-giving-food-homeless/15642578007/.

117. Food Not Bombs is a worldwide, all-volunteer organization dedicated to nonviolent social change, consisting of a network of autonomous local groups Each group recovers food that would otherwise be thrown out and makes fresh hot vegan and vegetarian meals that are served outside in public spaces to anyone without restriction. "Our Story," Food Not Bombs, https://foodnotbombs.net/new_site/story.php.

118. Fort Lauderdale Food Not Bombs v. City of Fort Lauderdale, 11 F.4th 1266 (11th Cir. 2021); see NLCHP, *Housing Not Handcuffs: A Litigation Manual*, 71; "Ft. Lauderdale Food Not Bombs, et al. v. City of Ft. Lauderdale," Southern Legal Counsel, https://www.southernlegal.org/case-work/food-sharing-is-not-a-crime.

119. The United States has created some entitlements to food statutorily, including through a food stamp program, now known as the Supplemental Nutrition Assistance Program (SNAP) and school meals programs. These are far from a universal right to food. But a movement is growing to make food a right in the United States: In 2021, Maine voters approved an amendment to the state's constitution recognizing the "natural, inherent and unalienable right" to food, the first in the nation. Patrick Whittle, "Maine Passes Nation's 1st 'Right to Food' Amendment," AP News, November 3, 202, 1, https://apnews.com/article/election-2021-maine -right-to-food-605019e60df5b3e32bc70c86dcf957b3. While limited—for example it didn't provide for funding—it was nonetheless an important step toward recognizing the right to food. Tess Brennan, "Maine becomes the first US state to recognize the Right to Food in a Constitutional amendment," Universal Rights Group, January 19, 2022, https://www.universal-rights.org/maine-becomes-the-first-us -state-to-recognise-the-right-to-food-in-a-constitutional-amendment/.

120. See, for example, Housekeys Action Network Denver (HAND), *Pipe Dreams and Picket Fences: Direction from Denver's Houseless People on Housing Needs & Priorities in the Context of Today's Public Housing* (HAND, 2023), https://houseke ysactionnetwork.com/pipe-dreams-and-picket-fences/.

121. In addition to "cruel and unusual punishments," the Eighth Amendment also prohibits "excessive fines," and the district court in *Grants Pass v. Johnson* had upheld a challenge to the city's ordinance on those grounds. That was not challenged by the city in its appeal to the Ninth Circuit, which did not consider it, and thus that part of the ruling was not before the Supreme Court. *Grants Pass v. Johnson*, Sotomayor, J., dissenting. In addition, the Fourth and First Amendments to the Constitution offer protections as do the Due Process and Equal Protection Clauses under the Fifth and Fourteenth Amendments. Federal laws such as the Americans with Disabilities Act and the Religious Freedom Restoration Act. State laws and constitutions may as well. See NHLC, *Litigation Manual Supplement: Criminalization of Homelessness Case Summaries* (2022). And state and local governments can also *enact* laws to protect unhoused people. Some have: Grants Pass itself enacted a law in 2021 codifying the protections of Martin v. Boise. Congress could of course also act to protect homeless people.

122. "National Parking Program List," National Vehicle Residency Collective, https://vehicleresidency.org/resources/safe-parking-programs/.

CHAPTER FIVE

1. Ko Lyn Cheang, "It Hurts So Much: Evicted Family Sleeps in Car as Housing Crisis Looms," *Indianapolis Star*, September 1, 2022.

2. Eric Steiner and Polis Center, "Follow the Money: Indianapolis Evictions in 2022," SAVI, August 5, 2022, https://www.savi.org/follow-the-money-india-napolis-evictions-in-2022/.

3. "Lilian," Invisible People, April 6, 2023, https://invisiblepeople.tv/videos/elderly-homeless-woman-oakland/.

4. Annemarie Cuccia, "There Are 40,000 People on DC's Housing Waitlist," *Street Sense Media*, June 15, 2022, https://www.streetsensemedia.org/article/40000-people-d-c-s-housing-waitlist/#.ZELTa-zMKfU.

5. Arthur D. Gayer, *Public Works in Prosperity and Depression* (National Bureau of Economic Research, 1935), https://www.nber.org/system/files/chapters/c5613/c5613.pdf; see also Jill Watts, "As Coronavirus Magnifies America's Housing Crisis, FDR's New Deal Could Offer a Roadmap Forward," *Time*, April 24, 2020. https://time.com/5826392/coronavirus-housing-history/.

6. As the country was emerging from the depths of the Great Depression, Roosevelt emphasized in his second inaugural address that many Americans were still suffering, with "one-third of a nation ill-housed, ill-clad, and ill-nourished." Franklin D. Roosevelt, "Second Inaugural Address" (speech, Washington, D.C., January 20, 1937), The Avalon Project, https://avalon.law.yale.edu/20th_century/froos2.asp.

7. Roosevelt, "Second Inaugural Address."

8. The 1934 Housing Act created home financing mechanisms that explicitly denied mortgages in or near African American neighborhoods, and supported developments that expressly prohibited sales of properties to African Americans. The public housing program built in segregation, with separate projects for White and Black citizens. As the new mortgage insurance program encouraged homeownership for White people, demand for public housing skewed toward Black people kept out of homeownership, and segregation intensified.

9. Terry Gross, "A 'Forgotten History' of How the U.S. Government Segregated America," *Fresh Air*, NPR, May 3, 2017, https://www.npr.org/2017/05/03/526655831/a-forgotten-history-of-how-the-u-s-government-segregated-america; Richard Rothstein, *The Color of Law: A Forgotten History of How Our Government Segregated America* (Liveright, 2017).

10. The National Housing Act of 1934, enacted as bank foreclosures pushed people from their homes, created the Federal Housing Administration, through which the federal government insured mortgages, protected the private lenders that made them, made homeownership more affordable, and encouraged construction. Public housing programs were first created through the Public Works Administration in 1934 and then through the US Housing Act of 1937, Public Law 75–896; September 1, 1937.

11. The goal was included in "precatory" language, meaning it lacked the force of law.

12. "Housing Choice Vouchers Fact Sheet," US Department of Housing and Urban Development (HUD), https://www.hud.gov/topics/housing_choice_voucher_program_section_8.

13. Cushing N. Dolbeare and Sheila Crowley, *Changing Priorities: The Federal Budget and Housing Assistance 1976–2007* (National Low Income Housing Coalition [NLIHC]/LIHIS, 2002), https://nlihc.org/sites/default/files/Changing-Priorities -Report_August-2002.pdf. Beginning in 1959, new federal legislation enacted in 1959 has already begun to encourage private developers to build affordable housing, and created the first, limited, rental subsidy program. See Maggie McCarty, Libby Perl, and Katie Jones, *Overview of Federal Assistance Programs and Policy* (Congressional Research Service, 2019).

14. Steven V. Roberts, "Reagan on Homelessness: Many Choose to Live in the Streets," *New York Times*, December 23, 1988, http://www.nytimes.com/1988/12 /23/us/reagan-on-homelessness-many-choose-to-live-in-the-streets.html, Ronald Reagan, "Inaugural Address" (speech, Washington, D.C., January 20, 1981), Ronald Reagan Presidential Foundation & Institute, https://www.reaganfoundation .org/ronald-reagan/reagan-quotes-speeches/inaugural-address-2/: "Government is not the solution to our problem, government is the problem." "'Welfare Queen' Becomes Issue in Reagan Campaign," *New York Times*, February 15, 1976, https:// www.nytimes.com/1976/02/15/archives/welfare-queen-becomes-issue-in-reagan -campaign-hitting-a-nerve-now.html.

15. "Presidential Candidates Debate," C-Span, September 25, 1988, https:// www.c-span.org/video/?4309-1/presidential-candidates-debate. The McKinney-Vento Act was far from widely known, and the promise was undoubtedly unintelligible to 99.99 percent of viewers, who had almost certainly never heard of it. But it elated advocates. It wasn't that we thought the McKinney-Vento Act was by any stretch enough—but the promise marked a big shift from Reagan's rhetoric. It could be something to build on.

16. They proposed to spend $728 million over three years for housing for homeless people specifically. Using the administration's own low estimates of the homeless population, this would reach just 3 percent. But their estimates of the homeless population were almost certainly too low. *Homelessness in the 1990's: Hearing before the Task Force on Urgent Fiscal Issues of the Comm. on the Budget*, 101st Cong. (1989) (testimony of Anna Kondratas, assistant secretary of HUD); *Homelessness in the 1990's*, 101st Cong. (testimony of Maria Foscarinis).

17. George Bush, Address Accepting the Nomination at the Republican National Convention in New Orleans, The American Presidency Project, August 8, 1988, https://www.presidency.ucsb.edu/documents/address-accepting-the-presidential -nomination-the-republican-national-convention-new.

18. Gwen Ifill, "Kemp Pledges Campaign to help Nation's Poor," *Washington Post*, January 28, 1989, https://www.washingtonpost.com/archive/politics/1989 /01/28/kemp-pledges-campaign-to-help-nations-poor/4e8924c2-eb25-4d47 -a82e-16bcabd8f4e3/; Morton M. Kondracke, "In Kemp, a Republican Role Model," *Roll Call*, November 21, 2012, https://rollcall.com/2012/11/21/in-kemp-a -republican-role-model/.

19. Michael Allan Wolf, "HUD and Housing in the 1990s: Crises in Affordability and Accountability," *Fordham Urban Law Journal* 18, no. 3 (1991), https://ir.lawnet.fordham.edu/ulj/vol18/iss3/3; US General Accounting Office (GAO), "Giving Priority to the Availability and Affordability of Low-Income Housing," *Housing and Urban Development Issues*, OCG-89-22TR (GAO, 1988). Much of the feared conversion would be delayed by temporary measures enacted by Congress. See "Brief History of HUD-Subsidized Mortgage Preservation Issues," National Housing Law Project, https://www.nhlp.org/wp-content/uploads/Brief -History-of-HUD-Subs-Mortgage-Pres-Issues-for-CW.pdf.

20. Congressman Vento spearheaded a bipartisan bill, the Permanent Housing for the Homeless Act, calling for $2 billion annually for low-income housing for homeless people.

21. Participants included including the Rev. Jesse Jackson, Governor Dick Celeste of Ohio, Coretta Scott King, Stevie Wonder, Tracy Chapman, and Los Lobos.

22. Allan R. Gold, "Thousands March on Washington in Protest against Homelessness," *New York Times*, October 8, 2989, https://www.nytimes.com/1989 /10/08/us/thousands-march-on-washington-in-protest-against-homelessness.html. It yielded some immediate political promises: In a meeting with the organizers, HUD Secretary Kemp gave assurances of his "desire to work full-time to win this war against poverty, homelessness and despair." Kemp also promised to set aside some five thousand vacant government-owned properties to house homeless people. It was a commonsense idea. But getting the government to turn over its vacant property for this purpose turned out to be much harder than anyone could have imagined. Decades later, it remains an ongoing battle.

23. The Democratic Congress, disinclined to support Kemp's "free market" approach, significantly cut his budget request. "Jack Kemp," Wikipedia, https://en .wikipedia.org/wiki/Jack_Kemp#Cabinet_(1989%E2%80%931993); Mark Byrnes, "How Jack Kemp Rewrote the Urban Poverty Playbook," Bloomberg, January 6, 2020, https://www.bloomberg.com/news/articles/2020-01-06/when-jack-kemp -took-on-urban-poverty-and-lost.

24. Larger properties also were transferred under the program, with some combining housing and services, like an old hotel in New York City's Times Square, an old hospital building in downtown Manhattan, and an apartment building on LA's Wilshire Boulevard. GAO, *Resolution Trust Corporation: Affordable Housing Disposition Program Achieving Mixed Results*, GAO/GGD-94-202 (GAO, 1994) https://www.gao.gov/assets/ggd-94-202.pdf. In addition to not publicizing the program, sometimes the agency moved to evict low-income tenants who were already living in the property that the agency had just acquired.

25. Because this would likely mean the loss of defense contracts and thus jobs in affected communities, there was the potential for big political fights over which bases would be targeted for closure. To avoid this, Congress established an independent

commission to select bases for closure. "Base Closure and Realignment (BRAC): Background and Issues for Congress," EveryCRSReport.com, April 25, 2019, https://www.everycrsreport.com/reports/R45705.html#_Toc7516510.

26. NLCHP, *To Protect and Defend: Converting Military Housing and Other Vacant Property to Help Homeless Americans* (NLCHP, 1994).

27. *Congressional Record* 140, no. 144 (Thursday, October 6, 1994), S., https://www.govinfo.gov/content/pkg/CREC-1994-10-06/html/CREC-1994-10-06-pt1-PgS106.htm. The legislative attack was triggered by the application of a largely unknown two-year-old organization to use the entire former Norton Air Force Base in San Bernardino, California, to provide food and housing to 2,000 people, and job training to over 15,000. It also proposed to use the airport runway to fly humanitarian missions around the world and to engage a retired Nebraska lawyer to manufacture a nutritional supplement that could alleviate AIDS symptoms. The application for the full base was not approved, but it triggered alarm among local officials who, apparently oblivious to the McKinney-Vento Act—or perhaps simply ignoring it—had begun their own plans to convert the base into an international airport, generating more money than the base ever did, through commercial flights, leases to private businesses, and multimillion government contracts. Tom Gorman, "A Bolt from the Blue: A 4-Year Effort to Turn Norton Air Force Base into a Civilian Airport May Be Grounded by an 11th-Hour Bid to Create a Huge Homeless Aid Center," *Los Angeles Times*, September 26, 1993, https://www.latimes.com/archives/la-xpm-1993-09-26-mn-39391-story.html.

28. Pryor and other members of Congress, Democrats and Republicans alike, claimed that the issue was balancing communities' need to mitigate the economic harm caused by the closure of the bases against the needs of their homeless residents. But the closures and resulting job losses also risked creating more homelessness, a prospect militating in favor of bolstering affordable housing and services.

29. Some, like Senator Feinstein, argued that while small properties were fine, large ones like military bases could not possibly have been intended to come under the program. But years later, a Denver applicant was turned down in part because he proposed to use only a portion of a property; the government claimed that to be considered, the group had to apply for all of it. Colo. Coalition for the Homeless v. GSA, 2019 U.S. Dist. LEXIS 109179, 2019 WL 2723857 (D. Colo. July 1, 2019).

30. Big law firms like Covington & Burling generally rely on lawyers specializing in "government relations" to carry out lobbying work. But nonlawyers also serve as lobbyists, monitoring legislation, meeting with legislators and their staffs, and promoting their clients' interests.

31. For decades, HHS limited uses of Title V property to shelter and transitional housing, despite nothing in the law or regulations requiring this limitation; we advocated for years for permanent housing to be included. Finally, in 2006, we won an important concession with the inclusion of permanent supportive housing. US Department of Health and Human Services Program Support Center,

"Use of Federal Real Property to Assist the Homeless," Federal Register, January 26, 2006. https://www.federalregister.gov/documents/2006/01/26/E6-1016/use-of -federal-real-property-to-assist-the-homeless. Then, in 2016, we were able to get a legislative amendment making clear properties could be used for permanent housing. NLCHP, *Public Property/Public Need: A Toolkit for Using Vacant Federal Property to End Homelessness* (NLCHP, 2018), https://homelesslaw.org/wp-content/uploads /2018/10/Public-Property-Public-Need-1.pdf.

32. Laurel Weir, the Law Center's policy director at the time, was key to our success. Having spent years helping groups around the country apply for Title V properties, she was so distraught at the prospect of its evisceration that she became literally sick to her stomach. But she channeled her distress into levelheaded, patient advocacy. Laurel Weir, author interview, July 8, 2021. Coupled with the experience, savvy, and high-level connections of Rod DeArment, our pro bono lobbyist at Covington & Burling, this made a critical difference, while my litigator's eye helped ensure strong language. Giving up a right still hurt, but the process rights we had won were specific and promised inclusion—arguably a stronger position. It had been extremely helpful that current law was very much in our favor; the burden was on our opponents to win support for a change.

33. On October 25, 1994, Congress passed the Base Closure Community Redevelopment and Homeless Assistance Act of 1994, S.2534, 103rd Cong. (1993–1994), https://www.congress.gov/bill/103rd-congress/senate-bill/2534/text.

34. *Need for Permanent Housing for the Homeless: Hearing before the Subcomm. on Housing and Community Development of the Comm. on Banking, Finance, and Urban Affairs*, 103rd Cong. (1993), https://www.google.com/books/edition/Need_for _Permanent_Housing_for_the_Homel/3CIFpZzWoUYC?hl=en&gbpv=.

35. In 1995, an amendment proposed by Congressman Ernest Istook, an Oklahoma Republican, passed the House. It would limit advocacy to just 5 percent of the budget for nonprofit organizations receiving any federal funds. While it failed in the Senate, the issue had been raised, and Istook continued to push it, making many organizations fearful and causing them to limit their advocacy. Robert J. Pekkanen, Steven Rathgeb Smith, and Yutaka Tsujinaka, eds., *Nonprofits and Advocacy: Engaging Community and Government in an Era of Retrenchment* (Johns Hopkins University Press, 2014), 289.

36. *Need for Permanent Housing*, 103rd Cong.

37. Craig Champ, author interview, May 24, 2023.

38. Minutes, "Beyond McKinney" strategy session, January 15-16, 1993.

39. The proposal called for policies and funds to ensure housing for all, and for adequate incomes—livable wages for those who were able to work and adequate levels of assistance for those unable to work. It called for sufficient services—like health and mental health care, substance abuse treatment, education, and job training—to meet the need. And it called for civil rights protections to stop the criminalization of

homelessness and ensure people could participate in the political process, including exercising their right to vote.

40. Jason Deparle, "Washington Memo; Housing Secretary Is Suddenly Assertive on Aiding Homeless," *New York Times*, January 30, 1993, https://www .nytimes.com/1993/01/30/us/washington-memo-housing-secretary-is-suddenly -assertive-on-aiding-homeless.html.

41. Assistant Secretary for Community Planning and Development.

42. Soon after its creation, USICH was criticized by the Law Center and other advocates for its inactivity. In response, the agency published a report on homelessness and mental illness, launched a newsletter, and held workshops. It also published a "Federal Plan to Help End Homelessness." See *United States Interagency Council on Homelessness Historical Overview* (USICH, 2012), https://cybercemetery.unt.edu /archive/oilspill/20120915175502/http://www.usich.gov/resources/uploads/asset _library/RPT_USICH_History_final__2012.pdf.

43. Potentially, this might have given it further clout. But the failure of the White House to support funding for USICH in Congress—especially after having made it the focus of its Executive Order—was ominous. Guy Gugliotta, "Resurrected Homeless Council Gains a Patron at White House," *Washington Post*, November 20, 1993, https://www.washingtonpost.com/archive/politics/1993/11 /20/resurrected-homeless-council-gains-a-patron-at-white-house/798f6939-6ab8 -4925-ba30-8a765d9746e8/.

44. NLCHP, "Proposed Housing Budget Offers Good, Bad Elements," *In Just Times: A Newsletter of the National Law Center on Homelessness and Poverty* (February 1994).

45. We were not opposed to reorganizing the programs, though proposals to "block grant" them raised some alarms. Block grants that simply give federal dollars to local governments risk removing federal oversight and accountability; at a time when local government was not necessarily friendly to efforts to house or help homeless people, this could be dangerous. As a result, we developed a set of criteria that we advocated for the federal government to attach to any block grant. *H.R. 3838; Housing and Community Development Act of 1994—Part II, before the Subcomm. on Housing and Community Development of the Comm. on Banking, Finance, and Urban Affairs*, 103rd Cong., 2nd Sess. (April 24, 1994) (testimony of Maria Foscarinis), https://www.google.com/books/edition/H_R_3838_Housing _and_Community_Developme/uNMaAQAAMAAJ?hl=en&gbpv=1; NLCHP, "McKinney Reorganization Bill Sent to Congress," *In Just Times: A Newsletter of the National Law Center on Homelessness and Poverty* (May 1994).

46. Victoria M. Massie, "Lillie Harden Was Bill Clinton's Welfare Reform Success Story. Welfare Reform Failed Her," *Vox*, August 23, 2016, https://www.vox .com/2016/8/22/12583376/welfare-reform-history-clinton-lillie-harden; Jordan Weissmann, "The Failure of Welfare," *Slate*, June 1, 2016, https://slate.com/news -and-politics/2016/06/how-welfare-reform-failed.html.

47. NLCHP, *No Way Out: A Report Analyzing Options Available to Homeless and Poor Families in 19 American Cities* (NLCHP, 1993).

48. Many were fearful of having their children taken from them by child welfare agencies, some of which considered homelessness a form of child abuse and thus cause for placing children into foster care. Some city shelter administrators explicitly threatened this as a way to manage their shelter overload: Families fearful of losing their children were less likely to seek shelter if any other option was possible at all. This might mean another night on someone's kitchen floor or staying in an abusive relationship—scenarios that continue to this day. See Kathryn Feltey and Laura Nichols, "Homeless Women with Children in Shelters: The Institutionalization of Family Life," in *Homelessness in America. Vol. 1*, ed. R. McNamara (Praeger Publishers, 2008); Elizabeth Rochin, "Homelessness Is Not Neglect," National Perinatal Information Center, July 26, 2022. https://npic.org/blog/2022/07/26/homelessness-is-not-neglect/.

49. NLCHP, *No Way Out: A Report Analyzing Options Available to Homeless and Poor Families in 19 American Cities* (NLCHP, 1993).

50. NLCHP, "Federal Funding for FY96 Finalized," *In Just Times: A Newsletter of the National Law Center on Homelessness and Poverty* (April 1994); NLCHP, *Smart Programs, Foolish Cuts* (NLCHP, 1995).

51. Most cuts were in the late 1980s to the late 1990s; 2011 saw a new round of cuts. GAO, *Homelessness: A Complex Problem and the Federal Response*, HRD-85-40 (GAO, 1985), https://www.gao.gov/assets/hrd-85-40.pdf]; Council of the District of Columbia, Right to Overnight Shelter [Repealed] (1991), https://code.dccouncil.gov/us/dc/council/code/titles/4/chapters/7; "Protecting the Legal Right to Shelter," Coalition for the Homeless; https://www.coalitionforthehomeless.org/our-programs/advocacy/legal-victories/protecting-the-legal-right-to-shelter; Liz Schott and Clare Cho, "General Assistance Programs: Safety Net Weakening Despite Increased Need," Center on Budget and Policy Priorities, updated December 19, 2011.

52. NLCHP, *Out of Sight—Out of Mind? A Report on Anti-homeless Laws, Litigation and Alternatives in 50 U.S. Cities* (NLCHP, 1999). For example, of forty-nine cities surveyed, 18 percent had enacted or amended ordinances to restrict homeless persons' use of public space, including for begging, in the previous two years.

53. NLCHP, *No Homeless People Allowed: A Report on Anti-Homeless Laws, Litigation And Alternatives in 49 U.S. Cities* (NLCHP, 1994); NLCHP, *Out of Sight.* In 1994, we surveyed forty-two cities around the country and found that 26 percent had enacted or enforced laws restricting homeless peoples' use of public space—like bans on sleeping, sitting, or lying in public—and 24 percent had conducted "sweeps" to force people out of specific city areas. By 1999, 73 percent of the forty-nine cities we surveyed had laws restricting sleeping or camping in public, and 48 percent had

engaged in sweeps. The surveys tracked most but not all the same cities; the numbers are not exact but are indicative of overall trends.

54. "Policy Basics: The Earned Income Tax Credit," Center on Budget and Policy Priorities, updated April 28, 2023. https://www.cbpp.org/research/policy-basics-the-earned-income-tax-credit. This is the most recent year for which this information is available.

55. NLCHP, *Due Credit: Increasing Homeless Workers' Earnings through the Earned Income Tax Credit* (NLCHP 1998), 8–9.

56. A larger anti-poverty organization, the Center on Budget and Policy Priorities, conducted a broad outreach campaign aimed at lower-income people generally; our efforts focused on those who were homeless.

57. NLCHP, *Due Credit.*

58. NLCHP, *Due Credit.*

59. NLCHP, *Due Credit.* The Earned Income Tax Credit is sometimes abbreviated as EIC instead of EITC.

60. Bruce D. Meyer, Angela Wyse, Alexa Grunwaldt, Carla Medalia, and Derek Wu, *Learning about Homelessness Using Linked Survey and Administrative Data* (Becker Friedman Institute, 2021), 37, https://bfi.uchicago.edu/wp-content/uploads/2021/06/BFI_WP_2021-65.pdf.

61. "What You Need to Know: Earned Income Tax Credit for Homeless + Foster Youth," National Network for Youth, March 10, 2022, https://nn4youth.org/2022/03/10/what-you-need-to-know-earned-income-tax-credit-for-homeless-foster-youth/.

62. See Natasha Pilkauskas and Katherine Michelmore, "The Effect of the Earned Income Tax Credit on Housing and Living Arrangements," *Demography* 56, no. 4 (August 2019), https://www.ncbi.nlm.nih.gov/pmc/articles/PMC6669080/. Working homeless families face the added expense of childcare, making employment much more challenging.

63. "Policy Basics: The Earned Income Tax Credit," Center on Budget and Policy Priorities.

64. See, for example, Teresa Ghilarducci and Aida Farmand, "What's Not to Like about the EITC? Plenty, It Turns Out," *American Prospect*, June 28, 2019, https://prospect.org/economy/like-eitc-plenty-turns-out./.

65. President's Proposed Budget of the United States, FY2003, Department of Housing and Urban Development, 179, https://www.govinfo.gov/content/pkg/BUDGET-2003-BUD/pdf/BUDGET-2003-BUD-3-7.pdf; Steve Berg, "Ten-Year Plans to End Homelessness," *National Low Income Housing Coalition Advocates Guide* (NLIHC, 2015).

66. Libby Perl and Erin Bagalman, *Chronic Homelessness: Background, Research, and Outcomes* (Congressional Research Service, 2015), https://sgp.fas.org/crs/misc/R44302.pdf; Dennis Culhane, *Chronic Homelessness* (Center for Evidence-based

Solutions on Homelessness, 2018), http://www.evidenceonhomelessness.com/wp -content/uploads/2018/04/evidence-page-chronic-homelessness-April-2018.pdf.

67. Randall Kuhn and Dennis P. Culhane, "Applying Cluster Analysis to Test a Typology of Homelessness by Pattern of Shelter Utilization: Results from the Analysis of Administrative Data," *American Journal of Community Psychology* 26, no. 2 (April 1998), 211.

68. Malcolm Gladwell, "Million-Dollar Murray," *New Yorker*, February 5, 2006, https://www.newyorker.com/magazine/2006/02/13/million-dollar-murray.

69. Tom Porter, "The Winning Slogan from Every US Presidential Campaign since 1948," *Business Insider*, May 15, 2019, https://www.businessinsider.com /every-winning-slogan-from-us-presidential-campaigns-1948-2016-2019-5#2000 -george-w-bush-compassionate-conservatism-14.

70. Emily Horton, "The Legacy of the 2001 and 2003 'Bush' Tax Cuts," Center on Budget and Policy Priorities, updated October 23, 2017, https://www .cbpp.org/research/the-legacy-of-the-2001-and-2003-bush-tax-cuts.

71. See, for example, NLCHP, *Photo Identification Barriers Faced by Homeless Persons: The Impact of September* 11 (NLCHP, 2004), https://homelesslaw.org /wp-content/uploads/2019/03/Photo-ID-Barriers-Faced-by-Homeless-Persons -2004.pdf.

72. Email from Nan Roman (former CEO of NAEH), to the author, February 22, 2024.

73. Muata Langley, "Mangano Explains Federal Plan to End Homelessness in 10 Years," Street Sense Media, February 15, 2004, https://www.streetsenseme-dia.org/article/mangano-explains-federal-plan-to-end-homelessness-in-10-years/# .ZB3SO-zMKqA.

74. Christopher Swope, "Philip Mangano," *Governing*, 2006, https://www .governing.com/poy/philip-mangano.html. Permanent supportive housing also combines permanent housing with services. Not all programs use a Housing First approach, which emphasizes respecting the autonomy and choices of the individual, but many do, and that is the federal recommendation. "Housing First in Permanent Supportive Housing," HUD, https://files.hudexchange.info/resources/documents /Housing-First-Permanent-Supportive-Housing-Brief.pdf; NLIHC, CWS, and the National Alliance to End Homelessness (NAEH), *The Case for Housing First* (NLIHC, 2023), https://nlihc.org/sites/default/files/Housing-First-Research.pdf; Perl and Bagalman, *Chronic Homelessness*; HUD, "Housing First: A Review of the Evidence," *Evidence Matters* (Spring/Summer 2023), https://www.huduser.gov/ portal/periodicals/em/spring-summer-23/highlight2.html.

75. Berg, "Ten-Year Plans."

76. Dennis P. Culhane, et al., "Accountability, Cost-Effectiveness and Program Performance: Progress Since 1998," in *Towards Understanding Homelessness: The 2007 National Symposium on Homelessness Research*, ed. Deborah Dennis, Gretchen

Locke, Jill Khadduri (HHS and HUD, 2007) https://www.huduser.gov/publications /pdf/homeless_symp_07.pdf.

77. Michael Shapcott, "U.S. Homeless Czar Mangano Preaches Local Action as U.S. Federal Government Cuts Funding," Homeless Hub, April 29, 2007, https://www.homelesshub.ca/resource/us-homeless-czar-mangano-preaches-local -action-us-federal-government-cuts-funding.

78. National Center for Homeless Education, Data Collection Summary, Education for Homeless Children and Youth Program, Table 2 (NCHE, 2010), https://nche.ed.gov/wp-content/uploads/2019/04/data_comp_06-08.pdf. Some of these figures may reflect changes in data collection and reporting processes. But they also miss many children, almost certainly understating the total numbers on which these percentage changes are based.

79. Barbara Sard and Douglas Rice, "Decade of Neglect Has Weakened Federal Low-Income Housing Programs," Center on Budget and Policy Priorities (February 25, 2009), https://www.cbpp.org/research/decade-of-neglect-has-weakened-federal -low-income-housing-programs. At the end of his presidency, after years of work by housing advocates, Bush signed legislation that created the National Housing Trust Fund to establish a designated source of funding for low-income housing—but not funding for it. The first funding allocations were made in 2016. NLIHC, National Housing Trust Fund. https://nlihc.org/explore-issues/projects-campaigns/national -housing-trust-fund.

80. Associated Press, "Bush Offers Up 'Ownership Society,'" NBC News, February 2, 2005, https://www.nbcnews.com/id/wbna6902224.

81. Suzanne Lanyi Charles, "The Financialization of Single-Family Rental Housing: An Examination of Real Estate Investment Trusts' Ownership of Single-Family Houses in the Atlanta Metropolitan Area," *Journal of Urban Affairs* 16 (November 2020); Francesca Mari, "A $60 Billion Housing Grab by Wall Street," *New York Times Magazine*, updated October 22, 2021, https://www.nytimes.com /2020/03/04/magazine/wall-street-landlords.html.

82. Manuel B. Aalbers, *The Financialization of Housing: A Political Economy Approach* (Routledge, 2016).

83. Report of the special rapporteur on adequate housing as a component of the right to an adequate standard of living (UN Human Rights Council, 2017) and on the right to non-discrimination in this context, https://documents.un.org/ doc/undoc/gen/g17/009/56/pdf/g1700956.pdf?token=AD0STeDjSSLBncjX8t&fe =true; David Madden and Peter Marcuse, *In Defense of Housing: The Politics of Crisis* (Verso, 2016); Alana Semuels, "When Wall Street Is Your Landlord," *Atlantic*, February 13, 2019, https://www.theatlantic.com/technology/archive/2019/02/single -family-landlords-wall-street/582394/; Jo Becker, Sheryl Gay Stolberg, and Stephen Labaton, "Bush Drive for Home Ownership Fueled Housing Bubble," *New York Times*, December 21, 2008, https://www.nytimes.com/2008/12/21/business /worldbusiness/21iht-admin.4.18853088.html.

84. National Coalition for the Homeless (NCH), the National Health Care for the Homeless Council, NAEH, the National Association for the Education of Homeless Children and Youth, NLCHP, the National Low Income Housing Coalition, and the National Policy and Advocacy Council on Homelessness, *Foreclosure to Homelessness 2009: The Forgotten Victims of the Subprime Crisis* (NCH, 2009).

85. NCH, et al., *Foreclosure to Homelessness 2009*.

86. NCH, et al., *Foreclosure to Homelessness 2009*; Jacob William Faber, "On the Street During the Great Recession: Exploring the Relationship between Foreclosures and Homelessness," *Housing Policy Debate* 29, no. 4 (2019); NLCHP, *Eviction (without) Notice: Renters and the Foreclosure* Crisis (NLCHP, 2012).

87. NLCHP, *Tent City, USA: The Growth of America's Homeless Encampments and How Communities Are Responding* (National Homelessness Law Center, 2017), https://homelesslaw.org/wp-content/uploads/2018/10/Tent_City_USA_2017.pdf.

88. NLCHP & NCH, *Homes Not Handcuffs: The Criminalization of Homelessness in US Cities*, at 10 (NCH & NLCHP, 2009).

89. Office of Special Needs Assistance Programs, Office of Community Planning and Development, HUD, *Homelessness Prevention and Rapid Re-Housing Program (HPRP): Year 3 & Final Program Summary* (HUD, 2016), https://files.hudexchange.info/resources/documents/HPRP-Year-3-Summary.pdf; "Factsheet: Homelessness Prevention and Rapid Re-Housing Program," Center for Evidence-Based Solutions to Homelessness, http://www.evidenceonhomelessness.com/fact-sheet/hprp/.

90. The new legislation, called the Homeless Emergency Assistance and Rapid Transition to Housing (HEARTH) Act, reauthorized the McKinney-Vento shelter and housing programs, incorporating elements of HPRP. See "Summary of HEARTH Act," NAEH, October 21, 2008, https://endhomelessness.org/resource/summary-of-hearth-act-2/.

91. Matt Bevilacqua, "With Homeless Prevention Program Expiring, Homeless Rates Remain Ominous," Next City, January 23, 2012, https://nextcity.org/urbanist-news/with-homeless-prevention-program-expiring-homeless-rates-remain-ominous.

92. Saskia Sassen, *Expulsions: Brutality and Complexity in the Global Economy* (Belknap Press, 2014), 128–29,

93. Mari, "A $60 Billion Housing Grab."

94. *Hearing on How Private Equity Landlords Are Changing the Housing Market, Testimony before the Senate Comm. on Banking, Housing, and Urban Affairs*, 117th Cong. (October 21, 2021) (statement of Desiree Fields, assistant professor of Geography and Global Metropolitan Studies, UC Berkeley), https://www.banking.senate.gov/imo/media/doc/Fields%20Testimony%2010-21-21.pdf.

95. Richard Kogan, Hannah Katch, Dottie Rosenbaum, Douglas Rice, Kathleen Romig, Ife Floyd, and Sharon Parrott, "Cuts to Low-Income Assistance Programs

in President Trump's 2020 Budget Are Wide-Ranging," Center on Budget and Policy Priorities, May 15, 2019, https://www.cbpp.org/research/federal-budget /cuts-to-low-income-assistance-programs-in-president-trumps-2020-budget-are; Elayne Weiss, "The Trump Administration's Impact on Public and Assisted Housing," *Human Rights Magazine* 44, no. 2 (May 21, 2021), https://www .americanbar.org/groups/crsj/publications/human_rights_magazine_home/vol -44--no-2--housing/the-trump-administration-s-impact-on-public-and-assisted -housing/; NLIHC, "President Trump Signs Executive Order on Deregulation and Housing," NLIHC, July 1, 2019, https://nlihc.org/resource/president-trump-signs -executive-order-deregulation-and-housing. A Trump initiative to give tax breaks for investments in poor neighborhoods ("opportunity zones") ended up being a tax break for luxury developments. Jesse Drucker and Eric Lipton, "How a Trump Tax Break to Help Poor Communities Became a Windfall for the Rich," *New York Times*, updated September 27, 2020, https://www.nytimes.com/2019/08/31/busi- ness/tax-opportunity-zones.html.

96. Semuels, "When Wall Street Is Your Landlord." It was a trend that had already been underway in some parts of the country. In New York City alone, pri- vate equity bought 100,000 rent-stabilized units from 2005 to 2009. Desiree Fields and Sabina Uffer, *The Financialization of Rental Housing Urban Studies* 53 (2016), 1486, 1493; Madden and Marcus, *In Defense of Housing*. Many thanks to Larissa Speaks, a student in my Homelessness Law and Policy seminar with Kim Hopper at Columbia Law School for her excellent research and paper on this topic, which helped inform my discussion here.

97. Lily Katz and Sheharyar Bokhari, "Investors Are Buying Roughly Half as Many Homes as They Were a Year Ago," *Redfin News*, February 15, 2023, https:// www.redfin.com/news/investor-home-purchases-q4-2022/. While investor pur- chases fell significantly in 2022 compared to 2021, as interest rates rose and prices started to cool, their overall share compared to all US home purchases held fairly steady: 18 percent in 2022 vs 19 percent in 2021.

98. Desiree Fields and Sabina Uffer, "The Financialisation of Rental Housing: A Comparative Analysis of New York City and Berlin," *Urban Studies Journal Limited* 53, no.7 (May 2016); "Landlord Tech Watch," Anti-Eviction Mapping Project, https://antievictionmappingproject.github.io/landlordtech/. Many thanks to Larissa Speaks for her excellent research and paper on this topic.

99. "Evictions Are Increasing Dramatically since the Lifting of Pandemic-Era Protections," *Morning Edition*, NPR, June 21, 2023, https://www.npr.org/2023 /06/21/1183408490/evictions-are-increasing-dramatically-since-the-lifting-of -pandemic-era-protecti; Michael Casey and R. J. Rico, "Eviction Filings Soar over 50% above Pre-pandemic Levels in Some Cities as Rents Increase," *PBS NewsHour*, June 17, 2023, https://www.pbs.org/newshour/nation/eviction-filings-soar-over-50 -above-pre-pandemic-levels-in-some-cities-as-rents-increase; "Eviction Tracking," Eviction Lab, https://evictionlab.org/eviction-tracking/.

100. NLIHC, *The Gap: A Shortage of Affordable Homes* (NLIHC, 2024), https:// nlihc.org/sites/default/files/gap/2024/Gap-Report_2024.pdf.

101. "Auction Set for Dec. 5 for Old Fed Building," *Daily Journal of Commerce*, November 7, 2014, https://www.djc.com/news/re/12071702.html; Casey Jaywork, "Homeless Advocates say They Should Get Former Fed Building," *Seattle Met*, July 9, 2014, https://www.seattlemet.com/news-and-city-life/2014/07/homeless-advocates-say-they-should-get-former-fed-building-july-2014.

102. Jeffrey Selbin, Stephanie Campos-Bui, Joshua Epstein, Laura Lim, Shelby Nacino, Paula Wilhelm, and Hannah Stommel, *Homeless Exclusion Districts: How California Business Improvement Districts Use Policy Advocacy and Policing Practices to Exclude Homeless People from Public Space* (University of California: Berkeley Law Policy Advocacy Clinic, 2018), https://www.law.berkeley.edu/wp-content/uploads /2018/09/SSRN-id3221446.pdf.

103. Selbin, et al., *Homeless Exclusion Districts*.

104. Winnie Hu, "'Hostile Architecture': How Public Spaces Keep the Public Out," *New York Times*, updated November 14, 2019, https://www.nytimes.com /2019/11/08/nyregion/hostile-architecture-nyc.html; Christopher McFadden, "15 Examples of 'Anti-Homeless' Hostile Architecture Common to Cities," *Interesting Engineering*, November 22, 2020, https://interestingengineering.com/culture/15 -examples-of-anti-homeless-hostile-architecture-that-you-probably-never-noticed -before.

105. Nat'l Law Ctr. on Homelessness and Poverty v. United States Dep't of Veterans Affairs, 931 F. Supp. 2d 167 (2013)

106. USICH, *All In: The Federal Strategic Plan to Prevent and End Homelessness* (USICH, 2022), 61.

CHAPTER SIX

1. Details taken from lawsuit filed against New York City; names of mother and children have been fictionalized. E.G. v. City of New York, S.D.N.Y., filed 11.20.20.

2. E.G. v. City of New York, S.D.N.Y., filed 11.20.20.

3. The program was originally authorized under Title VII, Part B of the McKinney-Vento Homeless Assistance Act (McKinney-Vento Act; P.L. 100-77, as amended); it was most recently reauthorized as part of the Every Student Succeeds Act of 2015 (ESSA, P.L. 114-95), signed into law in December 2015. See Adam K. Edgerton, *Education for Homeless Children and Youths: Data and Issues* (Congressional Research Service, 2023).

4. They also cited the US Constitution and our earlier case (National Law Center on Homelessness & Poverty v. State of New York, 224 FRD (EDNY 2004) establishing that it also protected homeless children's right to an education.

5. Cliff Yung-Chi Chen, Elena Byrne, and Tanya Vélez, "Impact of the 2020 Pandemic of COVID-19 on Families with School-Aged Children in the United

States: Roles of Income Level and Race," *Journal of Family Issues* 43, no. 3 (March 2022); National Law Center on Homelessness & Poverty (NLCHP), *Small Steps: An Update on the Education of Homeless Children and Youth Program* (NLCHP, 1991).

6. Daniel S. Miller and Elizabeth H. B. Lin, "Children in Sheltered Homeless Families: Reported Health Status and Use of Health Services," *Pediatrics* 81, no. 5 (May 1988); David L. Wood, R. Burciaga Valdez, Toshi Hayashi and Albert Shen, "Health of Homeless Children and Housed, Poor Children," *Pediatrics* 86, no. 6 (December 1990); Linda Weinreb, Robert Goldberg, Ellen Bassuk, and Jennifer Perloff, "Determinants of Health and Service Use Patterns in Homeless and Low-Income Housed Children," *Pediatrics* 102, no. 3 (September 1998); Patricia F. Julianelle, and Maria Foscarinis, "Responding to the School Mobility of Children and Youth Experiencing Homelessness: The McKinney-Vento Act and Beyond." *Journal of Negro Education* 72, no. 1 (2003): 39–54. https://doi.org/10.2307/3211289.

7. Cliff Yung-Chi Chen, et al., "Impact of the 2020 Pandemic"; NLCHP, *Small Steps.*

8. Children who frequently transfer to new schools are more likely to repeat a grade, have poor attendance, exhibit behavioral problems, and have worse overall academic performance than those who do not. It takes children four to six months to academically recover from each school transfer, and six to eighteen months to regain a sense of equilibrium, security, and control. See, for example, Bassuk and Rosenberg, "Psychosocial Characteristics of Homeless Children;" Julianelle and Foscarinis, "Responding to the School Mobility."

9. NLCHP, *Shut Out: Denial of Education to Homeless Children* (NLCHP, 1990).

10. NLCHP, *Stuck at the Shelter: Homeless Children and the DC School System* (NLCHP, 1990).

11. Albert's ten-year-old sister, Pamela, said she got mad when she had to miss school. "I miss learning. . . . But I have no [bus] tokens to get to school." NLCHP, *Stuck at the Shelter*, A-7.

12. NLCHP, *Stuck at the Shelter*, 3.

13. NLCHP, *Stuck at the Shelter*, 18.

14. Declaration of Brenda Lampkin, Lampkin v. DC. She was turned away on her first attempt to get help, after being told there was no room for them. Brenda returned the next day with a certified letter saying that they could no longer stay at their last residence and had nowhere else to go.

15. The provision's overarching mandate is to ensure homeless children have "access to a free appropriate public education which would be provided to a resident" and "services comparable to services offered to other children." Schools are required to remove a host of barriers in addition to transportation, including residency requirements, and to ensure school records are transferred in a timely fashion in the event a child changes schools. The law required that each state create a Coordinator

of Education of Homeless Children and Youth Education, develop a plan to remove the barriers specified, and ensure that its local education agencies comply. Additional specifics were added by amendments over the years (42 USC sec. 11431 et seq.).

16. Wallace was director of the D.C. school system's Homeless Children and Youth Technical Assistance Branch of the D.C. Public Schools, the local agency responsible for administering education services under the McKinney-Vento Act. See Keith Harriston, "Helping Homeless Students," *Washington Post*, September 5, 1990, C5.

17. These included a dictionary, pens, pencils, scissors, a book bag, and a notebook. They also placed decals with the phone number of their office in shelters for parents who had any problems. Harriston, "Helping Homeless Students."

18. NLCHP, *Small Steps.*

19. NLCHP, *Small Steps.* At the time, the Board of Education was responsible for setting the city's education policy, which was then carried out by the Office of the State Superintendent of Education (OSSE). This changed in 2007, when responsibility for the public education system came directly under the mayor's purview. District of Columbia State Board of Education, Roles and Responsibilities, History, https://sboe.dc.gov/page/roles (accessed April 30, 2024). These distinctions and changes are not relevant to this discussion.

20. Aubrey's mother later filed suit against the District of Columbia seeking damages for her son's injuries, arguing that the District knew the dangers when it placed the family there without providing a bus to take the boy to school. The case was dismissed, with the court finding no special duty on the part of the District. The judge's comments reveal the bias facing homeless people: "We are unable to agree that the District's provision of rent-free housing to a homeless family (which counsel for plaintiff infelicitously characterize as a restraint on personal liberty comparable to incarceration or institutionalization) placed the District *in loco parentis* or required it to supplant Ms. Ricks and to supervise Aubrey's activities in crossing the street." Even though the District had *placed* the family there, Aubrey's mother was solely responsible, and the District bore no resposibility. Powell ex rel. Ricks v. District of Columbia, 634 A.2d 403 (1993).

21. NLCHP, *Small Steps*, 14.

22. NLCHP, *Small Steps*, A-21.

23. NLCHP, *Small Steps*, A-22.

24. Wallace added: "We could not support a bus program with the $50,000 in federal funds we get from the McKinney money." Sari Horowitz, "District Failing Homeless Students, Suit Says," *Washington Post*, April 15, 1992, https://www.washingtonpost.com/archive/local/1992/04/16/district-failing-homeless-students-suit-says/d0157c87-be96-4569-bdeb-06d0005a0a6e/.

25. We were asking for "injunctive relief," as is typical in "law reform" cases that seek to change policy. The Law Center also joined as a plaintiff.

26. Brian Carome, Declaration in Support of Plaintiffs' Motion for Preliminary Injunction, *Lampkin v. DC*.

27. Suter v. Artist M. 503 U.S. 347 (1992). Funding statutes are enacted pursuant to the Constitution's Spending Clause, which gives Congress authority to attach conditions to federal funds. The requirements that such conditions must meet to be constitutional have been much disputed, which was the issue in this case.

28. NCH v. DOE, filed D.D.C 1987. We resolved the lawsuit after the education department agreed to a favorable settlement. For more details about the case, see Julianelle and Foscarinis, "Responding to the School Mobility."

29. 27 F.3d 605 (DC Cir. 1994). Kerrie Dent, a young associate at King & Spalding, part of the pro bono team working on the case, argued the appeal on our behalf.

30. "Best interests of the child" is a doctrine in family law used by US courts and around the world to make decisions on matters such as custody and visitation. Miriam Abaya, "Fact Sheet: The 'Best interests of the Child' Standard," First Focus on Children, August 2, 2022, https://firstfocus.org/resources/fact-sheet/fact -sheet-the-best-interests-of-the-child-standard; "Legal Information Institute: Best Interests (of the Child)," Cornell Law School, https://www.law.cornell.edu/wex/ best_interests_(of_the_child).

31. 115 S. Ct. 578 (Nov. 28, 1994). https://www.clearinghouse.net/detail.php ?id=16019.

32. Intersectionality pervades homelessness. To cite just a few examples, some 40 percent of homeless Americans are Black, compared to 28 percent of poor and 12 percent of all Americans. Some 40 percent of homeless youth are LGBTQ+. United States Interagency Council on Homelessness (USICH), *All In: The Federal Strategic Plan to Prevent and End Homelessness* (USICH, 2022), https://www.usich.gov/sites /default/files/document/All_In.pdf; M. H. Morton, G. M. Samuels, A. Dworsky, and S. Patel, *Missed Opportunities: LGBTQ Youth Homelessness in America* (Chapin Hall at the University of Chicago, 2018).

33. Lampkin v. DC, 879 F. Supp. 116 (D.D.C. 1995).

34. Lampkin v. DC, 886 F. Supp. 56 (D.D.C. 1995).

35. The District went to great lengths to avoid the injunction, calling an emergency legislative session to amend its own laws that required it to seek all available federal funding. 886 F. Supp. 56 (D.D.C., 1995).

36. Almost ten years later, another federal court accepted our argument that the Equal Protection Clause of the US Constitution requires equal access to education for homeless children. This means that even if a state doesn't accept federal funds under the Education of Homeless Children and Youth program—and thus may not be subject to its many detailed requirements—it still has to ensure equal access. National Law Center on Homelessness & Poverty v. State of New York, 224 F.R.D. 314 (EDNY 2004).

37. Salazar v. Edwards, 92 CH 5703 (1996), https://www.clearinghouse.net/detail.php?id=2. Laurene Heybach, the coalition lawyer representing the families, said that as a result tens of thousands of students and their families benefited each school year. https://www.clearinghouse.net/detail.php?id=2.

38. Despite withdrawing from the federal program, the city continued distributing tokens—in effect complying with the law without the benefit of federal money. Around this time, a series of lawsuits had been filed against the District of Columbia for failing to comply with various federal laws, resulting in multiple federal court orders; the mayor was also under congressional criticism for overspending the city's budget. Racial politics that pitted a majority Black city against the White congressional power structure were often a subtext in D.C.-federal politics.

39. Gonzaga v. Doe, 536 U.S. 273 (2002).

40. We argued that failure to ensure access to education for homeless children violated the Equal Protection Clause of the Fourteenth Amendment to the Constitution, and the court agreed. National Law Center on Homelessness & Poverty v. New York, 224 F.R.D. 314 (2004).

41. National Center for Homeless Education, Consolidated State Performance Reports, FY 2006–07; email from Lauren Krazlin, to the author, June 3, 2022. By 2005, the District government had given up almost $1.6 million in federal funds intended to help homeless children go to school—funds it could not get back. Joe Davidson, "The Funds Not Taken," *Washington Post*, July 14, 2005, https://www.washingtonpost.com/archive/local/2005/07/14/the-funds-not-taken/fbb7b4e2-a4d5-4782-b913-c6fc1b7f8238/. Not all is well, however; violations continue. "Our Advocacy," Playtime Project, https://playtimeproject.org/what-we-do/advocacy/.

42. *Job Training and Education for the Homeless: Hearing before the Subcomm. on Employment and Productivity of the Comm. on Labor and Human Resources*, 101st Cong. (1990), 51 (testimony of Kendrick Williams).

43. These included amendments to the McKinney-Vento education provisions, such as clarifying the applicability of the McKinney-Vento Act provisions to public preschool. Maria Foscarinis, "The Federal Response: The Stewart B. McKinney Homeless Assistance Act," in *Homelessness in America*, ed. Jim Baumohl (Oryx Press 1996), 169. They also included changes to larger anti-poverty programs to add provisions and resources to address the needs of homeless children, as part of a successful multiyear strategy carried out by the Law Center and our allies. These changes included amendments to the Individuals with Disabilities Education Act, which helps disabled students; Head Start, which offers early childhood education resources to poor children; and Title I—the large education program for poor schoolchildren. Homeless kids were made presumptively eligible for free school lunches, improving access. And we worked with foster care advocates to get the protections of the McKinney-Vento education program into the federal law governing foster care—freeing up more resources in McKinney-Vento for kids who were *not*

in foster care. NLCHP, *No Barriers: A Legal Advocate's Guide to Ensuring Compliance with the Education Program of the McKinney-Vento Act*, 2nd ed. (NLCHP, 2018), https://homelesslaw.org/wp-content/uploads/2018/10/NoBarriers-1.pdf.

44. NLCHP, *Separate and Unequal: A Report on Educational Barriers for Homeless Children and Youth* (NLCHP, 2000), 12, and sources cited therein; US Department of Education Office of Elementary and Secondary Education (ED), *Education for Homeless Children and Youth Program: Title VII, Subtitle B of the McKinney-Vento Homeless Assistance Act: Report to Congress Fiscal Year 2000*, ED-462-508 (ED, 2000), https://files.eric.ed.gov/fulltext/ED462508.pdf.

45. Some of this may have been due to differences in identification, enrollment, and attendance. Attendance in particular is critical, and is dependent on providing transportation, among other things. For example, according to the 2000 US Department of Education report to Congress, 87 percent of K–12 homeless children and youth were enrolled in school, but only 77 percent attended regularly. ED, *Education for Homeless Children and Youth Program.*

46. Amendments included increased deference to the judgment of the parents on their children's best interest.

47. NLCHP, *A Foot in the Schoolhouse Door: Progress and Barriers to the Education of Homeless Children* (NLCHP, 1995).

48. There might well have been others that we weren't aware of. In at least some instances, homeless parents protested placement of their children in these schools, forcing change. NLCHP, *Separate and Unequal*, 70.

49. See, for example, Michael Janofsky, "Debate Weighs Merits of Schools for Homeless," *New York Times*, September 19, 2001, https://www.nytimes.com/2001/09/19/us/debate-weighs-merits-of-schools-for-homeless.html; Andrea B. Berkowitz, "Homeless Children Dream of College Too: The Struggle to Provide America's Homeless Youth with a Viable Education," *Hofstra Law Review* 31, no. 2 (2002), http://scholarlycommons.law.hofstra.edu/hlr/vol31/iss2/6.

50. ED, *Report on the Status of Separate Schools for Homeless Children and Youths in Counties Exempted from the Prohibition of Separate Schools* (ED, 2020), https://oese.ed.gov/files/2020/10/Report-to-Congress-re-Separate-Schools_August-2020.pdf; Daniel Mollenkamp, "Homeless Students Are Missing School. Does Having a Separate School for Them Help or Hurt?," *EdSurge*, December 14, 2023, https://www.edsurge.com/news/2023-12-14-homeless-students-are-missing-school-does-having-a-separate-school-for-them-help-or-hurt.

51. Paul Vitello, "Katrina," *New York Times*, December 28, 2005, https://www.nytimes.com/2005/12/28/archives/katrina.html.

52. As noted by the judge in *McWaters v. FEMA*, "More than 90,000 people in the affected areas had incomes of less than $10,000 per year." Moreover, "about one of every three people who lived in areas hit hardest by Katrina were African American; in contrast, one of every eight people in the nation is African American." 408 F.Supp.2d 221 (E.D.La. 2005).

53. Intentional racial discrimination has long segregated housing, as powerfully documented by Richard Rothstein, *The Color of Law: A Forgotten History of How Our Government Segregated America* (Liveright, 2017). One result is the disproportionate racial impact of homelessness, see, for example, Jeffrey Olivet and Marc Dones, "Time for Change: Findings from the SPARC Study on Race and Homelessness, National Alliance to End Homelessness," National Alliance to End Homelessness, April 11, 2018, https://endhomelessness.org/blog/time-change-findings-sparc -study-race-homelessness/.

54. Over half of all poor residents and 65 percent of poor elderly households did not have a vehicle. McWaters v. FEMA, 408 F.Supp.2d 221 (E.D.La, 2005).

55. McWaters v. FEMA, 408 F. Supp. 2d 221, 225 (E.D.La, 2005) (evacuees were dispersed to forty-five states); Laura Bliss, "10 Years Later, There's So Much We Don't Know about Where Katrina Survivors Ended Up," Bloomberg, August 25, 2015, https://www.bloomberg.com/news/articles/2015-08-25/8-maps-of -displacement-and-return-in-new-orleans-after-katrina?embedded-checkout=true.

56. In a 2007 report to the UN Committee on Human Rights, advocates called out the United States for racially discriminatory policies before Katrina that left victims highly vulnerable and characterized federal actions after the storm as a form of ethnic cleansing. See Monique Harden, Nathalie Walker, and Kali Akuno, *Hurricane Katrina: Racial Discrimination and Ethnic Cleansing in the United States in the Aftermath of Hurricane Katrina: A Response to the 2007 Periodic Report of the United States of America* (Office of the United Nations High Commissioner for Human Rights [OHCHR], 2007), https://www2.ohchr.org/english/bodies/cerd/docs/ngos/ usa/USHRN23.doc; Thomas Craemer, "Evaluating Racial Disparities in Hurricane Katrina Relief Using Direct Trailer Counts in New Orleans and FEMA Records." *Public Administration Review* 70, no. 3 (May/June 2010).

57. As the judge also noted, by law FEMA is required to provide assistance "without discrimination on the grounds of race, color, religion, nationality, sex, age, or economic status." 42 U.S.C. § 5151(a) (emphasis added).

McWaters v. FEMA, 408 F.Supp. at 233. We had recruited Schulte Roth & Zabel, a New York City–based law firm, to help us develop litigation, and partnered with the Lawyers' Committee for Civil Rights Under Law, as well as other national allies and local groups. Howie Godnick, a sharp, funny, talented, and compassionate litigation partner who had been an actor and comedian before going to law school, led the pro bono team.

58. Led by Michael Brown ("Heck-of-a job, Brownie," per President George W. Bush, then in office), FEMA complained that "citizens have come to think of every problem in the United States as a federal problem and that the federal government is responsible for them." This did not sit well with the judge, who noted that regardless of whether that view was true or not as a general matter, "certainly in this instance, by *law and mandate*, the federal government *is* responsible." McWaters v. Brown, 408 F.Supp.2d at 235.

59. The state had asked the Church of Jesus Christ of Latter-Day Saints to pro-vide food, and church leaders were preparing for the possibility of hosting evacuees in their homes. Kirsten Stewart, Jessica Ravitz, and Brooke Adams, "Katrina: Utah Military, Others Gear Up to Help Refugees," *Salt Lake Tribune*, September 2, 2005, https://archive.sltrib.com/story.php?ref=/ci_2994851; *Deseret Morning News* editorial, "Utah takes in the homeless, tempest tossed," *Deseret News*, September 4, 2005, https://www.deseret.com/2005/9/4/19910257/utah-takes-in-the-homeless-tempest -tossed.

60. Daniel Golden, "Separate but Equal? Schooling of Evacuees Provokes Debate," *Wall Street Journal*, September 14, 2005, https://www.wsj.com/articles/ SB112666498176540100.

61. Secretary Spellings's request was in fact later included in the plan the administration presented to Congress. *Katrina's Displaced Schoolchildren: Hearing before the Subcomm. on Education and Early Childhood Development of the Comm. on Health, Education, Labor, and Pensions*, 109th Cong. (2005), https://www .govinfo.gov/content/pkg/CHRG-109shrg23696/html/CHRG-109shrg23696 .htm. (Statement of Henry L. Johnson, assistant secretary for elementary and sec-ondary education. US Department of Education).

62. Golden, "Separate but Equal?"; Lois Romano and Shankar Vedantam, "'No Child' Rules to Be Eased for a Year," *Washington Post*, September 30, 2005, https:// www.washingtonpost.com/wp-dyn/content/article/2005/09/29/AR2005092902156 .html.

63. *Katrina's Displaced Schoolchildren: Hearing*, 109th Cong.

64. See, for example, *Katrina's Displaced Schoolchildren: Hearing*, 109th Cong. (statements by Senators Alexander [R-TN], Lott [R-MS], and Enzi [R-WY]).

65. According to the *Wall Street Journal*, the state brought in two Black educa-tors to advise local teachers on "cultural sensitivity." Golden, "Separate but Equal?"

66. UN reports likened the response to apartheid. NLCHP, *"Simply Unacceptable": Homelessness and the Human Right to Housing In the United States 2011* (NLCHP, 2011). The impact is long-lasting and continuing, see, for example, Gary Rivlin, "White New Orleans Has Recovered from Hurricane Katrina. Black New Orleans Has Not," Talk Poverty, August 29, 2016, https://talkpoverty.org/2016/08 /29/white-new-orleans-recovered-hurricane-katrina-black-new-orleans-not/. Some groups likened the response to "ethnic cleansing." Luft, Rachel E. "Beyond Disaster Exceptionalism: Social Movement Developments in New Orleans after Hurricane Katrina." *American Quarterly* 61, no. 3 (2009): 499–527.

67. Greenville Associated Press, "Tech college Administrator Loses Job after Using Slur in Reference to Evacuees," WIS 10, updated September 17, 2005, https://www.wistv.com/story/3850144/tech-college-administrator-loses-job-after -using-slur-in-reference-to-evacuees/; Staff, "Survivors of New Orleans Say: 'They Treated Us Like Dogs,'" Fight Back News Service, September 10, 2005, https://

lists.h-net.org/cgi-bin/logbrowse.pl?trx=vx&list=h-afro-am&month=0509&week
=b&msg=04GSWmoUP3Lv4Jh24UGp4w&user=&pw=.

68. Jason Dearen and Kelli Kennedy, "Yellow Wristbands, Segregation for Florida Homeless in Irma," *Salt Lake Tribune*, September 29, 2017, https://www.sltrib.com/news/nation-world/2017/09/29/yellow-wristbands-segregation-for-florida-homeless-in-irma/. This is just one example of the many ways issues of class and race intersect, often inseparably, in homelessness.

69. Litigation in the wake of Katrina helped address racial inequities in helping homeowners: Michael A. Fletcher, "HUD to Pay $62 million to La. Homeowners to Settle Road Home Lawsuit," *Washington Post*, July 6, 2011, https://www.washingtonpost.com/business/economy/hud-to-pay-62-million-to-la-homeowners-to-settle-road-home-lawsuit/2011/07/06/gIQAtsFN1H_story.html.

70. Christopher Flavelle, "As Climate Shocks Worsen, FEMA Tries a New Approach to Aid," *New York Times*, January 19, 2024, https://www.nytimes.com/2024/01/19/climate/fema-disaster-aid-climate.html; Chris Clow, "HUD to Invest $174 Million for Climate Resiliency in Multifamily," *HousingWire*, December 21, 2023, https://www.housingwire.com/articles/hud-to-invest-174-million-for-climate-resiliency-in-multifamily/; Timothy A. Schuler, "Who Will Manage the US Climate Retreat?," Bloomberg, December 12, 2023, https://www.bloomberg.com/news/features/2023-12-12/climate-migration-s-billion-dollar-question-who-manages-the-retreat/.

71. Guest Blog, "Our Names Are Destiny, Lorinda, and Jose: Navigating Homelessness during COVID-19," SchoolHouse Connection, May 26, 2020, https://schoolhouseconnection.org/our-names-are-destiny-lorinda-and-jose-navigating-homelessness-during-covid-19/.

72. That's according to a 2021 national survey of over two hundred colleges, including both two-year community colleges and four-year institutions. See Jessie Hernandez-Reyes and Brittani Williams, "How to End the Hunger and Homelessness Crisis among College Students," The Education Trust, November 18, 2021, https://edtrust.org/resource/how-to-end-the-hunger-and-homelessness-crisis-among-college-students/.

73. *The Hope Center Survey 2021: Basic Needs Insecurity during the Ongoing Pandemic* (Temple University: The Hope Center, March 2021), https://hope.temple.edu/sites/hope/files/media/document/HopeSurveyReport2021.pdf.

74. Vanessa Romo, "Hunger and Homelessness Are Widespread among College Students, Study Finds," *The Two-Way*, NPR, April 3, 2018, https://www.npr.org/sections/thetwo-way/2018/04/03/599197919/hunger-and-homelessness-are-widespread-among-college-students-study-finds.

75. The Student Government Resource Center and the College and University Food Bank Alliance (CUFBA), *Running a Campus Food Pantry: Student Government Toolkit*, Studentsagainsthunger.org, http://studentsagainsthunger.org/wp-content/uploads/2017/10/NSCAHH_Food_Pantry_Toolkit.pdf.

76. Sara Goldrick-Rab, Christine Baker-Smith, Vanessa Coca, and Elizabeth Looker, *California Community Colleges #RealCollege Survey* (Temple University: The Hope Center and California Community Colleges, March 2019), https://www.cccco.edu/-/media/CCCCO-Website/docs/report/real-college-cccco-report.pdf?la=en&hash=52940277F947C5B5F986DC6A8FC6A6AEFD610927.

77. Lois Beckett, "'My Car Is My Home': The California Students with Nowhere to Live," *Guardian*, April 2, 2022, https://www.theguardian.com/us-news/2022/apr/02/college-students-unhoused-school-help; Alicia Robinson, "Long Beach City College to Join Trend of Community Colleges Offering Student Housing," *Long Beach Post*, June 25, 2023, https://lbpost.com/news/long-beach-city-college-to-join-trend-of-community-colleges-offering-student-housing/?__cf_chl_tk=XgwGzjnnWO1XpYaLHOrTo6aFoqrJEqHuINCseF_tqlg-1708004254-0.0-4114.

78. Beckett, "'My Car Is My Home.'"

79. Robinson, "Long Beach City College."

80. Beckett, "'My Car Is My Home.'"

81. Stefanos Chen, "A New Lifeline for the Unseen: Homeless College Students," *New York Times*, December 18, 2022, https://www.nytimes.com/2022/12/18/realestate/college-housing-homeless-students.html.

82. Ann Shalof, "Some College Students Face an Extra Challenge: Homelessness," *Times Union*, September 24, 2023, https://www.timesunion.com/opinion/article/college-students-face-extra-challenge-18383491.php.

83. Chen, "A New Lifeline."

84. Anthony P. Carnevale, Tamara Jayasundera, and Artem Gulish, *America's Divided Recovery: College Haves and Have-Nots* (Georgetown University Center on Education and the Workforce, 2016), https://cew.georgetown.edu/wp-content/uploads/Americas-Divided-Recovery-web.pdf.

85. *The Hope Center Survey 2021.*

86. "State Laws Supporting College Students Experiencing Homelessness," SchoolHouse Connection, June 12, 2022, https://schoolhouseconnection.org/state-laws-supporting-college-students-experiencing-homelessness/; "Appropriations for Housing Unhoused Post-Secondary Students," State Index on Youth Homelessness, https://youthstateindex.com/maps/appropriations-for-housing-unhoused-post-secondary-students/.

87. Earl J. Edwards, "Advice from a Formerly Homeless Youth," *Education Week*, April 18, 2017; "Earl J. Edwards: Assistant Professor," Boston College Carolyn A. and Peter S. Lynch School of Education and Human Development Faculty Directory, https://www.bc.edu/bc-web/schools/lynch-school/faculty-research/faculty-directory/Earl-Edwards.html.

88. Jason DeParle, "A One-Woman Rescue Squad for Homeless Students," *New York Times*, updated June 22, 2023, https://www.nytimes.com/2022/04/11/us/politics/homeless-students-texas.html.

89. Penelope L. Maza and Judy A. Hall, *Homeless Children and Their Families: A Preliminary Study* (Child Welfare League of America, 1988), 2. The same year, a different survey reported that 34 percent of homeless children were shut out of school by barriers stemming from their homelessness. Center for Law and Education (CLE), *Education Problems of Homeless Children* (CLE, 1987), 2 (from a survey of 104 shelters across the country).

90. ED, *Education for Homeless Children and Youth Program.*

91. Nation Center for Homeless Education (NCHE), *Student Homelessness in America: School Years 2019–20 to 2021–22* (NCHE, 2023), https://nche.ed.gov /wp-content/uploads/2023/12/SY-21-22-EHCY-Data-Summary_FINAL.pdf; NCHE, *Chronic Absenteeism among Homeless Students in America: School Years 2016– 17 to 2020–21* (NCHE, 2022), https://nche.ed.gov/wp-content/uploads/2022/11/ Homeless-Student-Absenteeism-in-America-2022.pdf.

92. This was an increase of 79 percent since the 2004–2005 school year. NCHE, *Student Homelessness in America.* These numbers are less meaningful than they might first appear. Increases could be—and most likely are—partially the result of greater awareness of the law and of the presence of homeless students, leading to more students identified as homeless by schools.

93. A nonprofit advocacy organization, SchoolHouse Connection, and the University of Michigan estimated that approximately 420,000 homeless schoolchildren had not been identified by the fall of 2020. They also noted that the true numbers were likely much larger. SchoolHouse Connection and Poverty Solutions at the University of Michigan, *Lost in the Masked Shuffle and Virtual Void: Children and Youth Experiencing Homelessness Amidst the Pandemic* (SchoolHouse Connection and Poverty Solutions at the University of Michigan, 2020), https://schoolhouseconn ection.org/wp-content/uploads/2020/11/Lost-in-the-Masked-Shuffle-and-Virtual -Void.pdf.

94. Cheyanne Mumphrey, "Schools Lost Track of Homeless Kids during the Pandemic. Many Face a Steep Path to Recovery," AP News, updated July 28, 2023; SchoolHouse Connection and Poverty Solutions at the University of Michigan, *Lost in the Masked Shuffle.*

95. SchoolHouse Connection and Poverty Solutions at the University of Michigan, *Lost in the Masked Shuffle.*

96. SchoolHouse Connection, 2025 Fact Sheet: Educating Children and Youth Experiencing Homelessness, https://schoolhouseconnection.org/article/2025-fact-sheet-educating-children-and-youth-experiencing-homelessness.

97. NCHE, *Chronic Absenteeism among Homeless Students.*

98. SchoolHouse Connection, 2025 Fact Sheet.

99. "Overview of U.S. Department of Education Guidance on American Rescue Plan Act Homeless Children and Youth Funding," SchoolHouse Connection, July 6, 2021, https://schoolhouseconnection.org/overview-of-used-guidance-on-arp/.

100. NCHE, *Student Homelessness in America*, SchoolHouse Connection, *The Education of Children and Youth Experiencing Homelessness: Current Trends, Challenges, and Needs* (SchoolHouse Connection, March 2024), https://schoolhouseconnection .org/wp-content/uploads/2024/03/FY25-EHCY-Fact-Sheet.pdf.

101. NCHE, *Federal Data Summary: School Years 2016–17 through 2018–19: Education for Homeless Children and Youth* (NCHE, April 2021), https://nche .ed.gov/wp-content/uploads/2021/04/Federal-Data-Summary-SY-16.17-to-18.19 -Final.pdf.

102. Since 1998, the Department of Education has funded a private outside group to provide "technical assistance" to parents, students, teachers, schools, and state and local education agencies seeking help with education issues related to homelessness. And state coordinators have banded together, creating an association to press the federal government for increased support. A nonprofit national advocacy organization focusing specifically on the education of homeless children, SchoolHouse Connection, has emerged. The Law Center also offers guidance, with the added ability to file suit to enforce compliance, if need be, which is sometimes privately welcomed by education agency staff—many of whom are genuinely committed to the kids they are charged with serving and frustrated when the larger bureaucracy stymies their efforts.

103. See, for example, NLCHP and Columbia Legal Services, *Beds and Buses: How Affordable Housing Can Help Reduce School Transportation Costs* (NLCHP, 2011), https://homelesslaw.org/wp-content/uploads/2018/10/Beds_and_Buses.pdf.

104. SchoolHouse Connection, *Current Trends, Challenges, and Needs*. See also Paul Koegel, Elan Melamid and M. Audrey Bumam, "Childhood Risk Factors for Homelessness among Homeless Adults," *American Journal of Public Health* 85, no. 12 (December 1995), https://ajph.aphapublications.org/doi/pdf/10.2105/AJPH.85 .12.1642.

105. SchoolHouse Connection, "The Issue: Child and Youth Homelessness Is Widespread and Devastating—but Hidden. Education Can Help Break the Cycle," SchoolHouse Connection, https://schoolhouseconnection.org/the-issue/.

106. See, for example, S.C. v. Riverview Gardens Sch. Dist., No. 2:18-cv-04162-NKL, 2019 U.S. Dist. LEXIS 29282 (W.D. Mo. Feb. 25, 2019)

107. NLCH, *No Barriers*.

108. Rep. Bush experienced homelessness as a single mother of young children and brought that experience to bear to advocate successfully for an extension of the eviction moratorium during the pandemic. Poppy Noor, "Interview: 'It was just unconscionable': Cori Bush on Her Fight to Extend the Eviction Moratorium," *Guardian*, August 8, 2021, https://www.theguardian.com/society/2021/aug/08/cori -bush-interview-eviction-moratorium.

CHAPTER SEVEN

1. Vivian Ho, "'This Movement Is Just Beginning': Homeless Moms Evicted after Taking Over Vacant House," *Guardian*, January 15, 2020. https://www.theguardian.com/us-news/2020/jan/15/moms-4-housing-oakland-homelessness-eviction; Rachel Hahn, "These Moms Fought for a Home—and Started a Movement," *Vogue*, May 12, 2020, https://www.vogue.com/article/moms-4-housing.

2. The Alliance of Californians for Community Empowerment was instrumental in bringing them together and supporting their efforts, along with progressive lawyers. Andrew Cohen, "On the Front Lines: Moms 4 Housing Leaders Discuss Movement Lawyering," *Berkeley Law*, March 2, 2020, https://www.law.berkeley.edu/article/on-the-front-lines-moms-4-housing-leaders-discuss-movement-lawyering/; "Moms 4 Housing: Meet the Oakland Mothers Facing Eviction after Two Months Occupying Vacant House," *Democracy Now!*, January 14, 2020, https://www.democracynow.org/2020/1/14/oakland_california_moms_4_housing.

3. Ho, "'This Movement Is Just Beginning.'"

4. Marisa Endicott, "The Rent in the Bay Area Is Too Damn High. So These Moms Occupied a Vacant House," *Mother Jones*, December 23, 2019. https://www.motherjones.com/politics/2019/12/bay-area-moms-homeless-squatters/.

5. Ho, "'This Movement Is Just Beginning.'"

6. Endicott, "The Rent in the Bay Area Is Too Damn High."

7. "Homeless Mothers Reclaim Vacant Oakland Home," Moms 4 Housing, November 18, 2019, https://moms4housing.org/news/moms-move-in.

8. Jeffery Martin, "Activist Group 'Moms for Housing' Occupies Vacant Home in Oakland to Protest City's Homeless Crisis," *Newsweek*, November 18, 2019. https://www.newsweek.com/activist-group-moms-housing-occupies-vacant-home-oakland-protest-citys-homeless-crisis-1472535.

9. Franklin D. Roosevelt, "State of the Union Address" (speech, Washington, D.C., January 6, 1941), University of Virginia Miller Center, https://millercenter.org/the-presidency/presidential-speeches/january-6-1941-state-union-four-freedoms.

10. Roosevelt, "State of the Union Address" (speech, Washington, D.C., January 11, 1944), FDR Presidential Library and Museum, https://www.fdrlibrary.org/address-text. In fact, FDR said that the country had already accepted it.

11. United Nations, "Preparatory Years: UN Charter History," https://www.un.org/en/about-us/history-of-the-un/preparatory-years.

12. United Nations, *The Charter of the United Nations*, Chapter 1, Purposes and Principles, art. I (UN, October 24, 1945). The Charter was signed in June 1945.

13. United Nations, "History of the Declaration," https://www.un.org/en/about-us/udhr/history-of-the-declaration.

14. For brevity, I refer to them in the text as civil rights and economic rights. In 1993, the UN would explicitly confirm that they are in fact indivisible and interdependent. United Nations, *Universal Declaration of Human Rights* (*UDHR*) (UN,

December 10, 1948), https://www.un.org/en/about-us/universal-declaration-of -human-rights; United Nations, "Preparatory Years."

15. United Nations, *UDHR*, art. 25.1: "Everyone has the right to a standard of living adequate for the health and well-being of himself and of his family, including food, clothing, housing and medical care and necessary social services, and the right to security in the event of unemployment, sickness, disability, widowhood, old age or other lack of livelihood in circumstances beyond his control." Work shifted to crafting two separate treaties by 1952.

16. Mónica Pinto, "International Covenant on Economic, Social and Cultural Rights: New York, 16 December 1966," Audiovisual Library of International Law, November 2020, https://legal.un.org/avl/ha/icescr/icescr.html; Human Rights Advocacy and the History of International Human Rights Standards, "Interdependence and Indivisibility of Economic and Political Rights," https:// humanrightshistory.umich.edu/problems/indivisibility/; Maya Hertig Randall, "The History of the Covenants: Looking Back Half a Century and Beyond," in *The Human Rights Covenants at 50: Their Past, Present, and Future*, ed. Daniel Moeckli, Helen Keller, and Corina Heri (Oxford University Press, 2018), https://doi.org/10 .1093/oso/9780198825890.003.0002.

17. The ICESCR's recognition of the right to housing tracks its recognition in the Universal Declaration of Human Rights as part of the right to an adequate standard of living. United Nations, *International Covenant on Economic, Social and Cultural Rights* (*ICESCR*) (UN, December 16, 1966), https://www.ohchr.org/en/ instruments-mechanisms/instruments/international-covenant-economic-social-and -cultural-rights.

18. Office of the High Commissioner on Human Rights, *International Covenant on Civil and Political Rights* (*ICCPR*) (UN, December 16, 1966), https:// www.ohchr.org/en/instruments-mechanisms/instruments/international-covenant -civil-and-political-rights.

19. UN Committee on Economic, Social and Cultural Rights, "Background to the Covenant" (UN), https://www.ohchr.org/en/treaty-bodies/cescr/background -covenant.

20. Jimmy Carter, "United Nations Remarks on Signing International Covenants on Human Rights" (speech, New York City, October 5, 1977), The American Presidency Project, https://www.presidency.ucsb.edu/documents/united -nations-remarks-signing-international-covenants-human-rights. In his post-presidency, Carter explicitly advocated for treating housing as a right. See, for example, Richard Florida, "Jimmy Carter Believes Housing Is a Basic Human Right," Bloomberg, July 27, 2017, https://www.bloomberg.com/news/articles/2017-07-27 /jimmy-carter-housing-is-a-basic-human-right; Jimmy Carter, "Decent Housing Is Not Just a Wish, It Is a Human Right," *Guardian*, June 20, 2011, https://www .theguardian.com/housing-network/2011/jun/20/decent-housing-not-just-wish.

21. In a statement at the time, Carter criticized the United States for "sanctimoniously picking and choosing" which provisions it will accept. Jimmy Carter, "U.S. Finally Ratifies Human Rights Covenant," *Christian Science Monitor*, June 29, 1992.

22. In 1993, it would be explicitly spelled out by the UN and agreed to by all member countries. United Nations, Vienna Declaration and Programme of Action (UN, June 25, 1993), https://www.ohchr.org/en/instruments-mechanisms/instruments/vienna-declaration-and-programme-action.

23. With this phrase he was quoting from an old English property law court case, which said "necessitous men are not, truly speaking, free men," *Vernon v Bethell* (1762) 28 ER 838, www.commonlii.org/int/cases/EngR/1762/18.html.

24. Otis Rolley, "Dr. Martin Luther King, Jr. and His Push for Economic Justice," Rockefeller Foundation, January 15, 2021, https://www.rockefellerfoundation.org/blog/martin-luther-king-jr-and-his-push-for-economic-justice/; Dr. Martin Luther King Jr. (MLK), "The Last Steep Ascent," reprinted as "MLK's Forgotten Call for Economic Justice," *Nation*, March 14, 1966, https://www.thenation.com/article/economy/last-steep-ascent/; Douglas E. Thompson, "Economic Equality: Martin Luther King Jr.'s Other Dream," *Washington Post*, January 21, 2019, https://www.washingtonpost.com/outlook/2019/01/21/economic-equality-martin-luther-king-jrs-other-dream/.

25. "Quotations from Rev. Dr. Martin Luther King, Jr." (The Kairos Center for Religions, Rights, and Social Justice, 2014), https://kairoscenter.org/wp-content/uploads/2014/11/King-quotes-2-page.pdf. Other early leaders of the Civil Rights Movement later sparred over this point, before ultimately giving way to pressure from Eleanor Roosevelt to focus on civil and political rights exclusively. See Carol Anderson, *Eyes Off the Prize: The United Nations and the African American Struggle for Human Rights, 1944–1955* (Cambridge University Press, 2003).

26. Martin Luther King Jr., "The Other America" (speech, Grosse Pointe, MI, March 14, 1968), Grosse Pointe Historical Society, http://www.gphistorical.org/mlk/mlkspeech/mlk-gp-speech.pdf.

27. See, for example, *Guide to the Issues: Understanding the Difference between Positive and Negative Rights*, Alabama Policy Institute, https://alabamapolicy.org/wp-content/uploads/2020/11/GTI-Brief-Positive-Negative-Rights-1-1.pdf. When viewed through the lens of individual rights, as opposed to government obligations, the distinction is sometimes framed as "freedom *to*" versus "freedom *from*." For a discussion of the latter framing, see Sandro Galea, "Freedom 'to' vs. Freedom 'from,'" Boston University School of Public Health, March 19, 2017, https://www.bu.edu/sph/news/articles/2017/freedom-to-vs-freedom-from/.

28. Endicott, "The Rent in the Bay Area Is Too Damn High."

29. Julian Brave NoiseCat, "The House on Magnolia Street: How a Group of Homeless Mothers Took On a Housing Crisis," *California Sunday Magazine*, March 19, 2020, https://story.californiasunday.com/moms-4-housing-oakland/.

30. "Interdependence and Indivisibility of Economic and Political Rights," Human Rights Advocacy and the History of International Human Rights Standards, https://humanrightshistory.umich.edu/problems/indivisibility/; UN, Vienna Declaration and Programme of Action.

31. Cass R. Sunstein, "Sunstein on FDR's Second Bill of Rights," University of Chicago Law School, October 1, 2004, https://www.law.uchicago.edu/news/sunstein-fdrs-second-bill-rights; Jill Priluck, "The Second Bill of Rights: How Franklin D. Roosevelt Envisioned Economic and Social Rights as Human Rights," *Lapham's Quarterly*, June 11, 2018, https://www.laphamsquarterly.org/roundtable/second-bill-rights; Sophie Vaughan, "How Bernie Sanders Is Reviving the Promise of FDR's Economic Bill of Rights," *Progressive*, February 25, 2020, https://progressive.org/latest/sanders-reviving-fdr-economic-rights-vaughan-200225/.

32. United Nations, *Report of Habitat: United Nations Conference on Human Settlements* (aka the "Vancouver Declaration on Human Settlements") (UN, 1976). Jonathan Andrews, "What Did We Learn from Habitat I and II?" *Cities Today*, October 7, 2016, https://cities-today.com/learn-habitat-i-ii/. The Vancouver Declaration called attention to a broad range of concerns, including wide inequalities in wealth, discrimination, and social segregation.

33. Invitations went out to a group of US advocates to join the official US delegation to the conference in Istanbul, to be headed by HUD Secretary Henry Cisneros. The invitation included a requirement to make no public statements critical of the US position. I had to decline on principle: I was going to the conference to advocate for the human right to housing and didn't feel I could commit to supporting the US position, which was then opposed to it. I went to Istanbul on behalf of the Law Center—not as part of the US delegation. I was the only one to decline; many US advocates joined the delegation, and during the conference I worked with some of them as part of an "inside-outside" strategy.

34. The press release announcing the event was titled: "NGOs Confront the United States Attack on the Right to Housing at Habitat II," on file with author.

35. United Nations, *CESCR General Comment No. 4: The Right to Adequate Housing (Art. 11 (1) of the Covenant)* (OHCHR, December 1991), https://www.refworld.org/legal/general/cescr/1991/en/53157.

36. Also included are secure tenancy (a right not to be arbitrarily evicted); habitability; availability of services (like water, sanitation, and heating); location near work, school, childcare, health care, and other social services; accessibility, and cultural adequacy. UN, *CESCR Committee General Comment No. 4*.

37. "Worst Case Needs—Housing Trends Data," HUD Office of Policy Development and Research (PD&R), https://www.huduser.gov/portal/worstcase.html.

38. According to the most recent data available as of January 2024, Joint Center for Housing Studies of Harvard University (JCHS), *America's Rental Housing*

2024 (JCHS, 2024), 3, https://www.jchs.harvard.edu/sites/default/files/reports/files/Harvard_JCHS_Americas_Rental_Housing_2024.pdf.

39. As recounted by the Earth Negotiations Bulletin, which provided a daily account of meeting leading up to the conference as well as the conference itself. Earth Negotiations Bulletin, "Summary Report, 24 April–5 May 1995: 2nd Session of the Habitat II Preparatory Committee," International Institute for Sustainable Development, https://enb.iisd.org/events/2nd-session-habitat-ii-preparatory-committee/summary-report-24-april-5-may-1995.

40. A coalition of NGOs, including the Law Center, was urging changes to the US draft. A UN process produced a report directly challenging the United States. See Peter Adriance and Jeff Barber, Memo, US Network for Habitat II (September 11, 1995), on file with author; Phillip Alston, "The US and the Right to Housing: A Funny Thing Happened on the Way to the Forum," *European Human Rights Law Review* (1996).

41. "U.S. Position on Adequate Shelter for All," February 2, 1996, on file with author; Alston, "A Funny Thing Happened on the Way to the Forum"; Earth Negotiations Bulletin, "Summary Report, 24 April–5 May 1995."

42. Compiled from news services and staff reports, "US Drops Opposition to UN Declaration That Housing Is a Right," *Washington Post*, June 8, 1996.

43. The US explained the contrasting views this way: "The EU believes that the Habitat Agenda must refer to 'the right to adequate housing.' In contrast, the US and other countries believe that housing is an important component of the right to an adequate standard of living." Habitat II, "Right to Adequate Housing, U.S. Position," May 15, 1996, on file with author.

44. The US position included references to security of tenure, increasing the supply of affordable housing, providing rental subsidies, and supporting nonprofit housing. Habitat II, "Right to Adequate Housing, U.S. Position," May 15, 1996

45. The agenda called on countries to "take appropriate action in order to promote, protect and ensure the full and progressive realization" of the right. United Nations, *Report of the United Nations Conference on Human Settlements (Habitat II)* (hereafter *Habitat Agenda*) (UN, 1996), paras. 53–241, para. 61. See generally National Law Center on Homelessness & Poverty (NLCHP), *Homelessness in the United States and the Human Right to Housing* (NLCHP, 2004).

46. Nan Roman, of the National Alliance to End Homelessness, and I worked on that together, using an "inside-outside" strategy. Nan was on the official delegation and worked to persuade its members. Having declined to sign on to the required agreement not to criticize the US position, I was not, and thus could exert pressure from the outside.

47. See NLCHP, *Homelessness in the United States*; Maria Foscarinis, "Homelessness and Human Rights: Towards an Integrated Strategy," *Saint Louis University Public Law Review* 19, no. 2 (2000).

48. NLCHP, *Mean Sweeps: A Report on Anti-homeless Laws, Litigation and Alternatives in 50 U.S.* Cities (NLCHP, 1996).

49. Meeting America's Housing Needs (MAHN) was launched by the AFL-CIO Housing Trust Fund, the National Alliance to End Homelessness, the National Homelessness Law Center (NHLC), and the National Low Income Housing Coalition (NLIHC); the groups hired Cushing Dolbeare, founder and former director of NLIHC, to serve as director of the project. MAHN held a series of events around the country that brought together a range of stakeholders with a goal of finding common ground and developing pragmatic strategies on key issues related to housing and homelessness. Cushing Dolbeare, *Final Project Report, Meeting America's Housing Needs: A Domestic Follow Up to the UN Habitat II Conference, January 1997 to June 1999*, on file with author.

50. Ben Austen, "The Towers Came Down, and with Them the Promise of Public Housing," *New York Times Magazine*, February 6, 2018, https://www.nytimes.com/2018/02/06/magazine/the-towers-came-down-and-with-them-the-promise-of-public-housing.html; Rachel G. Bratt, *Housing for Very Low-Income Households: The Record of President Clinton, 1993–2000* (JCHS, 2002); "Faircloth Limit Unit Counts," Office of Indian and Public Housing, *HUD* (December 31, 2023), https://www.hud.gov/program_offices/public_indian_housing/programs/ph/capfund.

51. In 1999, a national survey of fifty major cities found that 73 percent had laws restricting sleeping or camping in public; 48 percent had engaged in sweeps in the previous two years. NLCHP, *Out of Sight, Out of Mind? A Report on Anti-homeless Laws, Litigation and Alternatives in 50 U.S. Cities* (NLCHP, 1999).

52. National Coalition for the Homeless (NCH) and NLCHP, *Illegal to Be Homeless: The Criminalization of Homelessness in the U.S.* (NLCHP, 2002).

53. NLCHP, *Photo Identification Barriers Faced by Homeless Persons: The Impact of September 11* (NLCHP, 2004), https://homelesslaw.org/wp-content/uploads/2019/03/Photo-ID-Barriers-Faced-by-Homeless-Persons-2004.pdf.

54. HUD, *United States–Habitat II Progress Report* (HUD, 2001), https://www.huduser.gov/Publications/pdf/habitat.pdf. The event, known as Istanbul + 5, was held in the summer of 2001.

55. NCH and NLCHP, *Illegal to Be Homeless*, 40.

56. Kothari had been codirector, with Scott Leckie, of the Centre on Housing Rights and Evictions, then based in Geneva.

57. NLCHP, Homelessness in the United States and the Human Right to Housing, *NLCHP*, January 15, 2004, citing Roman Rollnick, "Does America Alone Have the Monopoly to Define What Is Right for the World?" *Earth Times*, May 20, 2001.

58. The Law Center worked with the Geneva-based Centre on Housing Rights and Evictions (COHRE), then a prominent organization promoting the human right to housing globally. The meeting was the first of what would become a regular

event: the National Forum on the Human Right to Housing. After COHRE ceased operations, the Law Center continued to organize the event.

59. It was playing out on a parallel track in gatherings of advocates working on other social justice issues, including workers' rights, prisoners' rights, and immigrants' rights. Separately and together, we were looking to established international human rights principles to help support our claims for economic justice here at home. In 2004, the US Human Rights Network was founded to support the new movement. Several funders, including the Ford Foundation, created a new funding collaborative, the US Human Rights Fund, to support groups working on human rights in the United States.

60. *City of Chicago 2019 Homeless Point-in-Time Count & Survey Report* (Chicago Department of Family & Support Services and Nathalie P. Voorhees Center for Neighborhood & Community Improvement, University of Illinois at Chicago, 2019), 2005–2019 data, https://www.chicago.gov/content/dam/city/depts /fss/supp_info/Homeless/2019PITReportFinal110819.pdf; Chicago Coalition for the Homeless (CCH), *How Many People Are Homeless in Chicago? An FY 2006 Analysis* (CCH, 2006), https://chicagohomeless.issuelab.org/resource/how-many -people-are-homeless-in-chicago-an-fy-2006-analysis.html. Part of the difference is due to the city's use of the "narrow" definition.

61. They were "extremely low-income," a technical term defined as earning 30 percent or less of "area median income"—the median income for a region area. In Cook County at the time, an extremely low-income family of four had an income at or below $22,500. Julie Dworkin, "How a Bill Becomes a Law: The Story of One Campaign's Struggle," *DePaul Journal for Social Justice* 1, no. 1 (Fall 2007), https:// via.library.depaul.edu/cgi/viewcontent.cgi?referer=&httpsredir=1&article=1087 &context=jsj; Cook County Clerk, Resolution 04-R-105, March 23, 2004, https:// cookctyclerk.com/html/032304resdoc.htm.

62. Steele read this passage from Kothari's statement at the hearing: "What we are witnessing in Chicago today is occurring all across the United States, and in fact, across the world. Governments are dismantling social housing, housing subsidies and affirmative actions for low-income people in the name of liberalization and are placing primacy in the market and privatization as panacea to solve the global crisis of millions living in inadequate and insecure housing." *Hearing on the Human Right to Adequate Housing, Inter-American Commission for Human Rights, Organization of American States*, March 4, 2005 (testimony of Carol Steele, president, Coalition to Protect Public Housing), on file with author.

63. Cook County Clerk, Resolution 04-R-105; Maria Foscarinis, "The Growth of a Movement for a Human Right to Housing in the United States," *Harvard Human Rights Journal* 20 (2007), 35, 38–39.

64. *Hearing on the Human Right to Adequate Housing* (testimony of Carol Steele).

65. Maria Foscarinis, "Advocating for the Human Right to Housing: Notes from the United States," *NYU Review of Law and Social Change* (2006).

66. *Hearing on the Human Right to Adequate Housing* (testimony of Carol Steele).

67. *Hearing on the Human Right to Adequate Housing* (testimony of Carol Steele).

68. Hearing on the Human Right to Adequate Housing (testimony of Carol Steele). Social housing is a term encompassing a "range of housing ownership, subsidy, and regulation models," typically used in Europe and other countries around the world. Key common elements of social housing are that it defines housing as a public good, ensuring it is insulated from market forces and permanently affordable; it promotes social equality, reducing segregation based on race and income; and it is democratically controlled by residents. Oksana Mironova and Thomas J. Waters, "Social Housing in the U.S.," Community Service Society, February 18, 2020, https://www.cssny.org/news/entry/social-housing-in-the-us; "What Is Social Housing?" Alliance for Housing Justice, https://www.allianceforhousingjustice.org/us-social-housing-principles (accessed May 7, 2024).

69. Alejandra Cancino, "Cabrini-Green: A History of Broken Promises," *Block Club Chicago*, December 15, 2021, https://blockclubchicago.org/2021/12/15/cabrini-green-a-history-of-broken-promises/.

70. At the time, allegations of human rights abuse by the United States in Iraq and Guantanamo were in the news, and the US Supreme Court had looked to international comparisons in deciding high-profile cases, giving further impetus to the growing movement by grassroots groups and their allies. See, for example, Noah Leavitt, "International Human Rights Law Violations Here in the US," *FindLaw*, May 6, 2004, https://supreme.findlaw.com/legal-commentary/international-human-rights-violations-here-in-the-us-1.html; Foscarinis, "The Growth of a Movement."

71. The Associated Press, "Homeless in Vegas: Going Bust in a Boomtown," NBC News, December 18, 2006, https://www.nbcnews.com/id/wbna16270138.

72. *LIED Institute 2005 Real Estate Roundtable: Developing Attainable Housing: How Do We Do It?* (The Lied Institute for Real Estate Studies, 2005), https://www.leg.state.nv.us/App/InterimCommittee/REL/Document/22913.

73. Randal C. Archibold, "Las Vegas Makes It Illegal to Feed Homeless in Parks," *New York Times*, July 28, 2006, https://www.nytimes.com/2006/07/28/us/28homeless.html. The law defined "indigent" as anyone whom "a reasonable ordinary person would believe to be entitled to apply for or receive" public assistance. The language was not only offensive and absurd, but it was also unconstitutionally vague. A federal court struck the law down after the Nevada ACLU brought a challenge on behalf of a volunteer who had offered food; the Law Center filed an amicus brief in support. Sacco v. City of Las Vegas, Nos. 2:06-CV-0714-RCJ-LRL, 2:06-CV-0941-RCJ-LRL, 2007 U.S. Dist. LEXIS 62397 (D. Nev. Aug. 20, 2007).

74. Human Rights Committee, Consideration of Reports Submitted by States Parties under Section 40 of the Covenant, United States of America, United Nations, November 2005.

75. UN, *ICCPR*, art. 6.

76. Kim's full remarks were not included in the official summary of the hearing, Human Rights Committee, 87th Session, Summary Record of 2380th meeting, 27 July 2006. But they were heard and noted by the Law Center staff member at the hearing, Eric Tars, and we quoted them in our press release. NLCHP, "U.N. Says Racial Impact of Homelessness Is Human Rights Abuse," July 28, 2006. On file with author. I also quoted Kim's remarks in a July 24, 2006, letter to David Hubb, a lawyer at DLA Piper, who had worked with the Law Center pro bono to help prepare our shadow report. Letter on file with author.

77. Maria Foscarinis and Eric Tars, "Housing Rights and Wrongs: The U.S. and the Right to Housing," in *Bringing Human Rights Home Volume 3*, ed. Cynthia Soohoo, Catherine Albisa, and Martha Davis (Praeger, 2008), 168.

78. As of 2024, New York City is the only city in the country with a right to shelter, established by consent decree under the state constitution. Massachusetts is often described as recognizing a right to shelter for families, but the obligation is subject to appropriations and is thus not a "right." Jenna Russell, "Amid Migrant Influx, Massachusetts Will No Longer Guarantee Shelter," *New York Times*, October 16, 2023, https://www.nytimes.com/2023/10/16/us/amid-migrant-influx -massachusetts-will-no-longer-guarantee-shelter.html.

79. UN, *Concluding Observations of the Human Rights Committee: United States of America*, UN Human Rights Committee (87th sess., 2006), https://digitallibrary .un.org/record/589849?ln=en&v=pdf. Current estimates are that Black people make up 37 percent of the homeless population, compared to 13 percent of the general population. The National Alliance to End Homelessness (NAEH), "Homelessness and Racial Disparities," NAEH, updated December 2023, https://endhomelessness .org/homelessness-in-america/what-causes-homelessness/inequality/. The most recent review of the United States by the Human Rights Committee for compliance with the ICCPR was in 2023, and the results were similar to the earlier reports. The committee noted the increase in state and local laws criminalizing homelessness, the increase in violence toward homeless people, and the higher rates of premature death. It noted the disproportionate impact of homelessness on marginalized communities. The Committee called for the abolition of laws criminalizing people for their homelessness and the adoption of laws protecting their human rights; financial and legal incentives for decriminalization; intensification of efforts to end homelessness, including redirecting resources away from criminal justice responses and toward housing and shelter; and reviewing "criminal records policies and practices" that can lead to homelessness. UN, *Concluding Observations of the Human Rights Committee: United States of America* (2023), https://documents.un.org/doc/undoc/ gen/g23/232/66/pdf/g2323266.pdf?token=KPfu7xCe5Lfz3Ms2rh&fe=true.

80. "Declarations and Reservations," UN Treaty Collection, Status of Treaties, *International Convention on the Elimination of All Forms of Racial Discrimination* (UN, March 7, 1966), https://treaties.un.org/pages/ViewDetails.aspx?src=TREATY &mtdsg_no=IV-2&chapter=4&clang=_en#EndDec.

81. UN, *Sixth Periodic Report of the United States of America on the Comm. on the Elimination of Racial Discrimination* (UN, May 2007), 79–90, para. 248.

82. US Conference of Mayors, *Hunger and Homelessness Survey: A Status Report on Hunger and Homelessness in America's Cities, a 24-City Survey, December 2005* (Sodexho, December 2005), https://www.novoco.com/public-media/documents/usmayors_survey.pdf.

83. Beyond Shelter, et al., *A Report to the Committee on the Elimination of Racial Discrimination on Racial Discrimination in Homelessness and Affordable Housing in the United States* (NLCHP 2007) ("CERD Shadow Report"), 6, para. 17. The report was officially submitted by a coalition of nine US organizations and endorsed by dozens of additional organizations and experts.

84. CERD Shadow report, para 19. The citations were part of L.A.'s "Safer Cities Initiative," launched in 2006, which brought fifty new police officers to downtown's Skid Row, a rapidly gentrifying, fifty-two-block area where some four thousand homeless individuals and families lived. At an annual cost of more than $6 million—more than the city spent on shelter and social services in the entire rest of the city—the new officers targeted homeless people, who were overwhelmingly Black, for minor offenses such as littering and jaywalking. In the first year, the police department confiscated only three handguns—but issued an average of one thousand citations a month, primarily for jaywalking violations to African Americans. Gary Blasi, *Policing Our Way out of Homelessness: The First Year of the Safer Cities Initiative on Skid Row* (USC Center for Sustainable Cities, 2007).

85. CERD Shadow Report, paras. 30–35.

86. NLCHP and NLIHC, *Without Just Cause: A 50-State Review of the (Lack of) Rights of Tenants in Foreclosure* (NLCHP, 2009).

87. NCH, the National Health Care for the Homeless Council, NAEH, the National Association for the Education of Homeless Children and Youth, NLCHP, NLIHC, and the National Policy and Advocacy Council on Homelessness, *Foreclosure to Homelessness 2009: The Forgotten Victims of the Subprime Crisis* (NCH, 2009), https://nationalhomeless.org/wp-content/uploads/ForeclosuretoHomelessness2009.pdf.

88. Two-thirds of this growth came after the Great Recession was officially declared over. NLCHP, *Tent City, USA: The Growth of America's Homeless Encampments and How Communities Are Responding* (NHLC, 2017), https://homelesslaw.org/wp-content/uploads/2018/10/Tent_City_USA_2017.pdf.

89. NLCHP, *Housing Not Handcuffs: Ending the Criminalization of Homelessness in U.S. Cities* (NLCHP, 2019), https://homelesslaw.org/wp-content/uploads/2019/12/HOUSING-NOT-HANDCUFFS-2019-FINAL.pdf; NHLC, *Housing Not*

Handcuffs 2021: State Law Supplement (NHLC, 2021), https://homelesslaw.org/wp
-content/uploads/2021/11/2021-HNH-State-Crim-Supplement.pdf.

90. Terry Carter, "Battle of Atlanta: Fight over a Downtown Homeless Shelter
Strains Some Down-Home Ties," *ABA Journal* 97, no. 5 (May 2011), https://
www.bakerdonelson.com/files/Battle%20of%20Atlanta%20-%20Fight%20over
%20a%20downtown%20homeless%20shelter%20strains%20some%20down-home
%20.pdf.

91. Zahid Arab, "Homeless Voters Inspired by Obama," *Hawaii News Now*,
November 6, 2008, https://www.hawaiinewsnow.com/story/9302162/homeless
-voters-inspired-by-obama/.

92. HUD, "Secretaries Shinseki and Donovan host first meeting of the US
Interagency Council on Homelessness under the Obama Administration," *HUD
Archive: News Releases*, June 18, 2009, https://archives.hud.gov/news/2009/pr09
-092.cfm.

93. Human Rights Project at the Urban Justice Center (HRP), *A Practical Guide
to the United Nations' Universal Periodic Review (UPR)* (HRP, 2010), https://cwgl
.rutgers.edu/docman/universal-periodic-review-upr/344-upr-toolkit-1/file; Eric S.
Tars and Déodonné P. Bhattarai, "Opening the Door to the Human Right to
Housing: The Universal Periodic Review and Strategic Federal Advocacy for a
Rights-Based Approach to Housing," *Clearinghouse Review Journal of Poverty Law
and Policy* 45, nos. 5–6 (September–October 2011), 197, 200, https://homelesslaw
.org/wp-content/uploads/2018/10/Clearinghouse_Opening_the_Door_2011.pdf.

94. The Law Center and other advocates had by then conducted dozens of trainings on using international human rights mechanisms to advocate for the human
right to housing, producing reports, manuals, and other materials to support advocates. See, for example, Martha Davis, "Law, Issue Frames and Social Movements:
Three Case Studies," *University of Pennsylvania Journal of Law and Social Change* 14
(2011), https://scholarship.law.upenn.edu/cgi/viewcontent.cgi?article=1141&con-
text=jlasc; Foscarinis, "The Growth of a Movement."

95. David Sullivan, Office of the Legal Adviser, Department of State (DOS),
at an event called "Human Rights on the Hill," held in Washington, D.C., on May
25, 2010, cited in Tars and Bhattarai, "Opening the Door."

96. UN Human Rights Council, National report submitted [by the United
States] in accordance with paragraph 15 (a) of the annex to Human Rights Council
resolution 5/1 (August 23, 2010) ("US Report, UPR") para. 76 (2010).

97. Quoted in Tars and Bhattarai, "Opening the Door." Michael H. Posner,
"The Four Freedoms Turns 70" (speech, Washington, D.C., March 24, 2011),
DOS, https://2009-2017.state.gov/j/drl/rls/rm/2011/159195.htm. Elaborating, he
added: "We will push back against the fallacy that countries may substitute human
rights they like for human rights they dislike, by granting either economic or political rights. To assert that a population is not 'ready' for universal human rights is

to misunderstand the inherent nature of these rights and the basic obligations of governments."

98. Alana Semuels, "When Wall Street Is Your Landlord," *Atlantic*, February 13, 2019, https://www.theatlantic.com/technology/archive/2019/02/single-family -landlords-wall-street/582394/.

99. Francesca Mari, "A $60 Billion Housing Grab by Wall Street," *New York Times Magazine*, updated October 22, 2021, https://www.nytimes.com/2020/03/04 /magazine/wall-street-landlords.html.

100. David Mader, "A National Strategy for Reducing the Federal Government's Real Estate Footprint," *White House Blog*, March 25, 2015. https://obamawhitehouse .archives.gov/blog/2015/03/25/national-strategy-reducing-Federal-government-s -real-estate-footprint. Previously, such sales were permitted; now they were being promoted and required.

101. Title V of the McKinney-Vento Homeless Assistance Act, Public Law 101-645 (42 U.S.C. 11411).

102. US Human Rights Network, "Housing Rights in the Housing Crisis, Part 2.mp4," YouTube, November 4, 2010, https://www.youtube.com/watch? v=aQi6bk8naHQ.

103. US Human Rights Network, "Housing Rights in the Housing Crisis, Part 2.mp4."

104. In 2010, the UN had explicitly recognized the human right to water and sanitation; in 2015, the international human rights body recognized it as a separate and distinct right. UN General Assembly, Resolution Adopted by the General Assembly on 28 July 2010, 64/292, The Human Right to Water and Sanitation (UN, 2010), https://documents.un.org/doc/undoc/gen/n09/479/35/pdf/n0947935 .pdf?token=tg07Luefsk2Mv8LfUz&fe=true; UN General Assembly, Resolution 70/169, Adopted 17 December 2015 (UN, 2015).

105. UN, *Report of the Special Rapporteur on the Human Right to Safe Drinking Water and Sanitation, Catarina de Albuquerque* (UN General Assembly, August 2011), https://www2.ohchr.org/english/bodies/hrcouncil/docs/18session/A-HRC -18-33-Add4_en.pdf.

106. Brett Walton, "Disturbing US WASH Report: Water and Sanitation Lacking for Poorest Americans," *Circle of Blue*, September 21, 2011, https:// www.circleofblue.org/2011/world/disturbing-u-s-wash-report-water-and-sanita- tion-lacking-for-poorest-americans/; Whitney Gent, "UN Expert Condemns Cruel Treatment of Homeless in US," *Street Sprit*, September 1, 2011, https:// thestreetspirit.org/2011/09/01/un-expert-condemns-cruel-treatment-of-homeless -in-u-s-2/.

107. UN, *Report of the Special Rapporteur*, 14.

108. Picture the Homeless, Wikipedia, https://en.wikipedia.org/wiki/Picture _the_Homeless (accessed May 7, 2024); Picture the Homeless, Housing Justice Oral

History Project, Columbia University Oral History Project, https://housingjusticeo ralhistory.org/projects/picture-the-homeless-1 (accessed May 7, 2024).

109. Picture the Homeless (PTH), *Banking on Vacancy: Homelessness and Real Estate Speculation* (PTH, 2012), https://www.issuelab.org/resources/14899 /14899.pdf.

110. PTH, *Banking on Vacancy.*

111. PTH, *Banking on Vacancy.*

112. Rent stabilization laws limited rent increases to keep housing affordable, but they made an exception known as the "vacancy bonus" that, after a vacancy, allowed landlords to raise the rent above and beyond the increases already permitted. And once the rent reached a certain level—$2,774 as of late 2022—rent stabilization limits no longer applied. By keeping properties vacant, landlords could, in time, not only raise rent but remove properties from rent regulation. The 2019 law tried to curb this practice by eliminating the "vacancy bonus" and the ability to remove units from rent regulation. Sam Rabiyah, "More Than 60,000 Rent-Stabilized Apartments Are Now Vacant—and Tenant Advocates Say Landlords Are Holding Them for 'Ransom,'" *City*, October 19, 2022, https://www.thecity.nyc/housing /2022/10/19/23411956/60000-rent-stabilized-apartments-vacant-warehousing-nyc -landlords-housing.

113. Landlords with one hundred or more units owned 88 percent of them. Rabiyah, "More Than 60,000 Rent-Stabilized Apartments."

114. By some estimates, the number was up to ninety thousand in 2022. Sam Rabiyah, "NYC Had 88,830 Vacant Rent-Stabilized Apartments Last Year, City Housing Agency Estimates," *City*, October 20, 2022, https://www.thecity.nyc /2022/10/20/vacant-rent-stabilized-apartments-nyc/. The actual number has been a point of controversy. According to an August 2023 report by New York City's independent budget office, the total number as of February 2024 was nearly 13,400. "NYC Comptroller Report Cites Warehousing as Big Problem," The Coalition to End Apartment Warehousing, February 13, 2024, https://endapartmentwarehous-ing.blogspot.com/. According to one group representing small and medium-sized landlords, as of early 2024 at least 26,000 rent-stabilized units were estimated to be vacant. Greg David, "Tens of Thousands of Rent-Stabilized Apartments Remain Off the Market during Record Housing Shortage," *City*, February 14, 2024, https:// www.thecity.nyc/2024/02/14/rent-stabilized-apartments-vacant/.

115. Kathryn Brenzel and Georgia Kromrei, "RSA, CHIP File Lawsuit Challenging New York's New Rent Law," The Real Deal, July 16, 2019, https:// therealdeal.com/new-york/2019/07/16/rsa-chip-file-lawsuit-challenging-new-yorks -new-rent-law/; Kim Velsey, "Landlords Want the Supreme Court to Kill Rent Stabilization," *Curbed*, May 9, 2023, https://www.curbed.com/2023/05/landlords -supreme-court-rent-stabilization-challenge.html. Both the lower court and the federal appeals courts threw the case out, and the US Supreme Court denied review.

Cmty. Hous. Improvement Program v. City of New York, 59 F.4th 540, *cert. denied*, 144 S. Ct. 264 (2023).

116. Underlying their assertion may be the common adage that "possession is nine-tenths of the law." Possession is one way to establish ownership, but ultimately recognizing it as such in law is not foreordained—it is a choice. For interesting discussions of this point, see Michael A. Heller and James Salzman, *Mine! How the Hidden Rules of Ownership Control Our Lives* (Doubleday, 2021), 58, 79; Katharina Pistor, *The Code of Capital: How the Law Creates Inequality and Wealth* (Princeton University Press, 2019), ch. 2.

117. Rabiyah, "More Than 60,000 Rent-Stabilized Apartments."

118. Cmty. Hous. Improvement Program v. City of New York, 59 F.4th 540, *cert. denied*, 144 S. Ct. 264 (2023).

119. In some countries, for example, laws restrict warehousing when there is a housing crisis. Fondation Abbé Pierre and the European Federation of National Organisations working with the Homeless (FEANTSA), *Filling Vacancies: Vacant Real Estate: Seizing the Opportunity to Find Affordable Housing Solutions in Europe* (Fondation Abbé Pierre and FEANTSA, updated 2016), https://ec.europa.eu/futurium/sites/futurium/files/long_version_en.pdf.pdf.

120. Danny Maestas, author interview, September 29, 2023.

121. Russell Haythorn, "Activists, City of Denver, Spar over Homeless Encampment Clean-Up Policies," Denver7 News, updated March 31, 2023, https://www.denver7.com/news/front-range/denver/activists-city-of-denver-spar -over-homeless-encampment-clean-up-policies.

122. Maestas interview.

123. Amy Beck, author interview, July 2, 2023; Amy Beck, email to the author, July 4, 2023.

124. Haythorn, "Activists, City of Denver, Spar."

125. Haythorn, "Activists, City of Denver, Spar."

126. Some cities have "sanctioned encampments," which are not subject to sweeps and provide some basic city services, like the one Frankie lived in in snowy Missoula, Montana. While in no way comparable to true, housing-based solutions, they can be preferrable to sweeps, property destruction, and other forms of criminal punishment. See NLCHP, Tent City USA.

127. Virya Kelsang, email to the author, July 8, 2023, video attachment, https://photos.google.com/share/AF1QipNWsSVJ0L8kVGNRQ81C0S6oMbryKbWJuwl7bkbQLvHKtecAir_vCsQgV3ErUfDKSw?key=MzNBNXNGWnpSTEVDNm1kaWNyWDRmQnVGbUE3b0JR.

128. Kelsang email, video attachment.

129. ICCPR, Human Rights Committee, General Comment 36, para. 26 (2019). https://documents.un.org/doc/undoc/gen/g19/261/15/pdf/g1926115.pdf ?token=mHfZK8dCcxeV4qBfZ7&fe=true,

130. Housekeys Action Network Denver (HAND), Mutual Aid Money, and Friends of South Denver, "Immediate Actions for Incoming Denver Mayor Re: Houselessness—No Money Needed," HAND, July 5, 2023, https://housekeysac tionnetwork.com/2023/07/05/immediate-actions-for-incoming-denver-mayor-re -houselessness-no-money-needed/.

131. UN, Vienna Declaration and Programme of Action.

132. US Office of Treaty Affairs, "Treaties Pending in the Senate," DOS, June 22, 2023, https://www.state.gov/treaties-pending-in-the-senate/.

133. Martin v. City of Boise, 920 F.3d 584 (9th Cir.), cert. denied (2019); Mike Baker, "Punished for Sleeping on the Streets, They Prevailed in Court," *New York Times*, December 16, 2019, https://www.nytimes.com/2019/12/16/us/boise-idaho -homeless-supreme-court.html; Johnson v. Grants Pass, 50 F. 4th 787 (9th Cir. 2022), cert. granted, 2024 US LEXIS 422 (Jan. 12, 2024).

134. Rob Robinson and Erin McElroy, "Picturing the Homeless, Building International Solidarities," *Radical Housing Journal* 4, no. 1 (July 2022), https:// radicalhousingjournal.org/wp-content/uploads/2022/07/RHJ_Issue-4.1_09 _Conversation_RobinsonandMcElroy_141-150.pdf.

135. Joe Biden (@POTUS) "Housing should be a right—not a privilege. But far too many people are struggling to keep a roof over their head. I look forward to working with @SecFudge to help renters and homeowners get through this crisis and ensure every American has access to quality, affordable housing," Twitter, March 10, 2021, 9:16 p.m., https://twitter.com/POTUS/status/1369834567411109891; Joe Biden, "Housing should be a right—not a privilege. But far too many Americans lack access to affordable, quality, and safe housing. Today, I'm releasing my $640 billion plan to change that," Facebook, February 24, 2020, https://www.face-book.com/joebiden/posts/housing-should-be-a-right-not-a-privilege-but-far-too -many-americans-lack-access/10156672346401104/; Human Rights Clinic of the University of Miami School of Law (HRC), NHLC, National Coalition for a Civil Right to Counsel, and RESULTS, *Human Right to Housing Report Card 2023: Grading the United States Response to Housing and Homelessness* (HRC and NHLC, 2023), https://homelesslaw.org/wp-content/uploads/2023/09/ReportCard2023.pdf; *In Just Times: A Publication of the National Homelessness Law Center* (October 2020), https://homelesslaw.org/ijt-october-2020/.

136. Camille Squires, "The US's Top Housing Authority Just Declared Housing a Human Right," *Quartz*, March 23, 2022, https://qz.com/2145610/us-hud-sec-retary-marcia-fudge-just-declared-housing-a-human-right; Kriston Capps, "Can an 'Activist HUD' Make Housing a Human Right?" Bloomberg, January 29, 2021, https://www.bloomberg.com/news/articles/2021-01-29/marcia-fudge-wants -to-transform-u-s-housing-rights.

137. United States Interagency Council on Homelessness (USICH), *All In: The Federal Strategic Plan to Prevent and End Homelessness* (USICH, 2022), https://www .usich.gov/sites/default/files/document/All_In.pdf.

138. "Federal Budget & Spending," NLIHC, https://nlihc.org/federal-budget -and-spending.

139. Biden/Harris 2020 Presidential Campaign, "The Biden Plan for Investing in Our Communities through Housing," Wayback Machine, August 17, 2020, https:// web.archive.org/web/20200817155308/https://joebiden.com/housing/#.

140. John Cassidy, "Joe Manchin Kills the Build Back Better Bill," *New Yorker*, December 19, 2021, https://www.newyorker.com/news/our-columnists/joe- manchin-kills-the-build-back-better-bill; Hans Nichols, "Scoop: Sinema Throws Cold Water on Build Back Better Revival," *Axios*, April 5, 2022, https://www.axios .com/2022/04/06/sinema-gives-last-rites-to-bbb.

141. HRC, NHLC et al., *Human Right to Housing Report Card 2023*, 7.

142. Erin Baldassari and Molly Solomon, "How Moms 4 Housing Changed Laws and Inspired a Movement," KQED, October 19, 2020, https://www.kqed.org /news/11842392/how-moms-4-housing-changed-laws-and-inspired-a-movement.

143. Alastair Boone, "Housing Activist Dominique Walker Runs for Berkeley Rent Board," *Street Spirit*, October 1, 2020, https://thestreetspirit.org/2020/10/01 /housing-activist-dominique-walker-runs-for-berkeley-rent-board/; "Dominique Walker," Berkeley Rent Board, https://rentboard.berkeleyca.gov/elected-rent-board /meet-contact-board/dominique-walker.

144. "Carroll Fife," City of Oakland: City Officials, https://www.oaklandca.gov /officials/district-3-councilmember; "Carroll Fife," Ballotpedia, https://ballotpedia .org/Carroll_Fife.

145. ACLU California Action, Alliance of Californians for Community Empowerment (ACCE) Institute, NHLC, Western Center on Law & Poverty, *Recognizing the Right to Housing: Why We Need a Human Right to Housing in California* (ACLU California Action, et al., 2023), https://assets.nationbuilder.com /acceinstitute/pages/1369/attachments/original/1684966069/ACLU_Journal_Final -min.pdf?1684966069.

CHAPTER EIGHT

1. Some identifying details (such as name and location) have been fictional- ized, but the impact of the foreclosure crisis generally, and in Minnesota, home to many Finnish Americans, is factual. See, for example, *The Impact of the Foreclosure Crisis on Public and Affordable Housing in the Twin Cities: Field Hearing before the Subcomm. on Housing and Community Opportunity of the Comm. on Financial Services*, 111th Cong. (January 23, 2010), https://www.govinfo.gov/content/pkg/CHRG -111hhrg56242/html/CHRG-111hhrg56242.htm.

2. Y-Foundation, *A Home of Your Own: Housing First and Ending Homelessness in Finland* (Otava Book Printing Ltd, 2017), 63, https://www.feantsaresearch.org/ download/a_home_of_your_own_lowres_spreads6069661816957790483.pdf. The Y-Foundation document did not include a name; "Tom" is my pseudonym for ease of reference.

3. Social housing is a term that describes a range of models for providing affordable housing that treat it as a public good, rather than a commodity, protecting it from market forces and ensuring it remains permanently affordable. Many models also aim to promote social equality, reduce segregation based on race and income; and ensure resident participation. See Oksana Mironova and Thomas J. Waters, "Social Housing in the U.S.," Community Service Society, February 18, 2020. https://www.cssny.org/news/entry/social-housing-in-the-us.

4. The Constitution of Finland, June 11, 1999 (731/1999, amendments up to 817/2018 included), Sec. 19, https://finlex.fi/en/laki/kaannokset/1999/en19990731 .pdf ("The public authorities shall promote the right of everyone to housing and the opportunity to arrange their own housing"); "State of Housing Rights," Housing Rights Watch, January 25, 2017, https://www.housingrightswatch.org/page/state -housing-rights-4.

5. Jon Henley, "'It's a Miracle': Helsinki's Radical Solution to Homelessness," *Guardian*, June 3, 2019, https://www.theguardian.com/cities/2019/jun/03/its-a -miracle-helsinkis-radical-solution-to-homelessness.

6. Jill Khadduri and Marybeth Shinn, "How Finland Ended Homelessness," *Cityscape* 22, no. 2 (2020), https://www.huduser.gov/portal/periodicals/cityscpe/ vol22num2/ch4.pdf.

7. The report was commissioned by the then-Minister of Housing; its four authors were a local government leader, a nonprofit leader, a former politician who was also a specialist in homeless men, and a church leader. Juha Kaakinen served as secretary of the group. For an account of the evolution of Finland's approach, see Kirsi Juhila, Suvi Raitakari, and Johanna Ranta, "Housing First: Combatting Long-Term Homelessness in Finland," in *Successful Public Policy in the Nordic Countries: Cases, Lessons, Challenges*, ed. Caroline de la Porte, Guðný Björk Eydal, Jaakko Kauko, Daniel Nohrstedt, Paul 't Hart, and Bent Sofus Tranøy (Oxford University Press, 2022).

8. Kontrast.at, "Finland Ends Homelessness and Provides Shelter for All in Need," The Better.news, November 10, 2020, https://thebetter.news/housing-first -finland-homelessness/.

9. Y-Foundation, *A Home of Your Own*, 63.

10. "Social Policy and Welfare," Nordic Co-operation, https://www.norden.org /en/information/social-policy-and-welfare; "Finnish System for Affordable Social Housing Supports Social Mixing and Brings Down Homelessness," MuniFin, November 18, 2022, https://www.munifin.fi/whats-new/finnish-system-for-affordable-social-housing-supports-social-mixing-and-brings-down-homelessness; Tahiat Mahboob, "Housing Is a Human Right: How Finland Is Eradicating Homelessness," CBC, January 24, 2020, https://www.cbc.ca/radio/sunday/the -sunday-edition-for-january-26-2020-1.5429251/housing-is-a-human-right-how -finland-is-eradicating-homelessness-1.5437402.

11. Mahboob, "Housing Is A Human Right"; Juha Kaakinen, interview with the author, October 11, 2023.

12. Mika Hyötyläinen, "'Not for Normal People': The Specialization of Social Rental Housing in Finland," *ACME: An International Journal for Critical Geographies* 19, no. 2 (2020).

13. "Finnish System for Affordable Social Housing," MuniFin.

14. The constitution also includes "the right to receive indispensable subsistence and care." Finnish Constitution, Section 19; Juhila, et al., "Housing First: Combatting Long-Term Homelessness."

15. Kaakinen interview; "Juha Kaakinen, Professor of Practice, Faculty of Social Sciences, Tampere University," LinkedIn profile, https://www.linkedin.com/in/juha -kaakinen-14368417/?originalSubdomain=fi.

16. Patrice Bergeron, "Finland's Successful Approach to Ending Homelessness Catches Eye of Quebec City," *Global News*, updated January 28, 2024, https:// globalnews.ca/news/10198145/quebec-finland-successful-approach-homelessness -model/; see also Laurence Boone, Boris Cournède, and Marissa Plouin, "Finland's Zero Homeless Strategy: Lessons from a Success Story," *Ecoscope*, December 13, 2021, https://oecdecoscope.blog/2021/12/13/finlands-zero-homeless-strategy -lessons-from-a-success-story.

17. National Low Income Housing Coalition (NLIHC), Church World Services (CWS), and National Alliance to End Homelessness (NAEH), *The Case for Housing First* (NLIHC, 2023), https://nlihc.org/sites/default/files/Housing-First -Research.pdf.

18. Mahboob, "Housing Is a Human Right"; "Public Land Ownership and Leasing in Helsinki, Finland," Housing2030, https://www.housing2030.org/project /public-land-ownership-and-leasing-in-helsinki-finland/.

19. Kaakinen interview.

20. Kaakinen interview.

21. U.S. Department of Housing and Urban Development (HUD), "Housing First: A Review of the Evidence," *Evidence Matters* (Spring/Summer 2023), https:// www.huduser.gov/portal/periodicals/em/spring-summer-23/highlight2.html.

22. HUD, "Housing First: A Review."

23. Sam Tsemberis and Ronda F. Eisenberg, "Pathways to Housing: Supported Housing for Street-Dwelling Homeless Individuals with Psychiatric Disabilities," *Psychiatric Services* 51, no. 4 (April 2000), https://ps.psychiatryonline.org/doi/10 .1176/appi.ps.51.4.487; NLIHC, et al., *The Case for Housing First.*

24. United States Interagency Council on Homelessness (USICH), *All In: The Federal Strategic Plan to Prevent and End Homelessness* (USICH, 2022), https://www .usich.gov/sites/default/files/document/All_In.pdf.

25. HUD, *Rapid Re-housing*, HUD, https://files.hudexchange.info/resources/ documents/Rapid-Re-Housing-Brief.pdf.

26. Increased federal funding during the pandemic allowed communities to place vulnerable homeless people in hotel rooms, provide rent support to prevent others from losing their homes, and even buy vacant motels and hotels, converting them into housing for homeless people. Federal estimates were that by the end of 2022, this additional funding had put some 100,000 homeless people back into housing. Jason Lalljee, "Biden's Big Pandemic Stimulus Bill Is Helping Get More Than 100,000 Homeless People into Housing by the End of the Year," *Business Insider*, December 20, 2022, https://www.businessinsider.com/biden-pandemic -stimulus-homelessness-american-rescue-plan-inflation-rent-medicaid-2022-12.

27. "It's Been 1 Year Since the Launch of 'House America.' What's Changed?" USICH, September 21, 2022, https://www.usich.gov/news/one-year-anniversary-of -huds-house-america-initiative-to-address-homelessness.

28. For a summary of some of the research, see NLIHC, et al., *The Case for Housing First*; Tim Aubry, Gary Bloch, Vanessa Brcic, Ammar Saad, Olivia Magwood, Tasnim Abdalla, Qasem Alkhateeb, Edward Xie, Christine Mathew, Terry Hannigan, Chris Costello, Kednapa Thavorn, Vicky Stergiopoulos, Peter Tugwell, and Kevin Pottie, "Effectiveness of Permanent Supportive Housing and Income Assistance Interventions for Homeless Individuals in High-Income Countries: A Systematic Review," *Lancet Public Health* 5, no. 6 (June 2020), https://www.thelancet.com/pdfs/journals/lanpub/PIIS2468-2667(20)30055-4.pdf; Brendan O'Flaherty, "Homelessness Research: A Guide for Economists (and Friends)," *Journal of Housing Economics* 44 (June 2019), https://www.sciencedirect .com/science/article/abs/pii/S1051137718302109.

29. Matt Tinoco, "LA Will Spend $30M This Year on Homeless Sweeps. Do They Even Work?" *LAist*, April 10, 2019, https://laist.com/news/homeless-sweeps -los-angeles-public-health.

30. Street newspapers are typically sold by homeless vendors, who often also write some of the content, serving as a source of income. The nonprofit organizations running them—such as Steet Sense Media, in Washington, D.C., which produces *Street Sense*—often offer other programs for vendors. Many street newspapers, and their vendors, were hard hit by the pandemic, when diminished foot traffic reduced sales, worsening a trend that had begun as people started carrying less cash. Street Sense Media developed an app to allow credit card payments, which helped, but did not solve the problem. Brian Carome, executive director, Street Sense Media, author interview, January 23, 2023.

31. Belle Ren, "Ending Homelessness Would Cost Far Less Than Treating It," Street Sense Media, August 10, 2022, https://streetsensemedia.org/article/ending -homelessness-would-cost-far-less-than-treating-it.

32. Jessica Learish, "The Most Expensive States for ER Visits, Ranked," CBS News, December 4, 2020, https://www.cbsnews.com/pictures/emergency-room -visit-cost-most-expensive-states/37/; Adrienne Santos-Longhurst, "How Much Is an Ambulance Ride? Costs and Financing Options," CareCredit, March 6, 2023,

https://www.carecredit.com/well-u/health-wellness/ambulance-ride-cost/; "The Cost of Homelessness Facts," Green Doors, https://greendoors.org/facts/cost.php.

33. Michael Kimmelman and Lucy Tompkins, "How Houston Moved 25,000 People from the Streets into Homes of Their Own," *New York Times,* updated June 15, 2023, https://www.nytimes.com/2022/06/14/headway/houston-homeless -people.html.

34. Rose Philips, "The Dedicating Opportunities to End Homelessness Initiative," *Housing News Network* 29, no. 2 (Florida Housing Coalition, June 2013), https://flhousing.org/wp-content/uploads/2013/06/The-Dedicating-Opportunities -Vol-29-No-2-June13-5.pdf. The "technical assistance" included helping the city make better use of existing federal funds, including some unspent disaster relief money. Barbara Poppe, email communication to the author, October 2, 2023; "Mayor Parker Announces New Partnership with HUD" (press release), City of Houston Housing and Community Development Department, November 29, 2011, https://houstontx.gov/housing/communication/2011/20111129.html.

35. Kimmelman and Tompkins, "How Houston Moved 25,000 People"; Michelle Homer, Public Housing Waitlist Reopening for First Time in 5 years, HHA Says, WKHOU1 11, January 13, 2023, https://www.khou.com/article/news/ local/public-housing-waitlist/285-bb339a7f-e322-42c6-a30e-4841c5c8d3bc.

36. Kimmelman and Tompkins, "How Houston Moved 25,000 People"; HUD, *Houston, Texas, Community Encampment Report* (HUD, 2021), https://www .huduser.gov/portal/publications/Houston-Encampment-Report.html.

37. HUD, *Houston, Texas, Community Encampment Report.*

38. Kimmelman and Tompkins, "How Houston Moved 25,000 People" HUD, *Houston, Texas Community Encampment Report.*

39. Sylvester Turner became mayor January 2, 2016, and remained in that office until January 1, 2024.

40. Texas law protects veterans from source-of-income discrimination, meaning they cannot be denied housing because they use a voucher to pay for it. And a state law passed in June 2023 prohibits homeowners' associations from discriminating against tenants holding vouchers. Sarah Holder and Kriston Capps, "How Texas HOAs Are Keeping Low-Income Renters Out," Bloomberg, August 31, 2023, https://www.bloomberg.com/graphics/2023-hoa-texas-homes-dallas-renters/; Diana Ionescu, "Texas Law Bars Source of Income Discrimination," Planetizen, September 8, 2023, https://www.planetizen.com/news/2023/09/125447-texas-law -bars-source-income-discrimination.

41. Aubry Vonck, "Homeless Encampment Response Strategy Released," Coalition for the Homeless, October 28, 2021, https://www.homelesshouston.org /homeless-encampment-response-strategy-released; Matt White, *City of Houston/ Harris County Homeless Encampment Response Strategy* (Coalition for the Homeless of Houston/Harris County, 2021), https://irp.cdn-website.com/2d521d2c/files/ uploaded/Encampment%20Response%20Strategy%20FINAL.pdf.

42. Kimmelman and Tompkins, "How Houston Moved 25,000 People."

43. Communications Admin, "Houston Endowment Makes $12.5 Million Investment in The Way Home," The Way Home, February 23, 2015, https://www.thewayhomehouston.org/houston-endowment-makes-12-5-million-investment-in-the-way-home; Communications Admin, "JPMorgan Chase Commits $1 million to The Way Home to Fight Homelessness in Houston," The Way Home, November 2, 2016, https://www.thewayhomehouston.org/jpmorgan-chase-commits-1-million-to-the-way-home-to-fight-homelessness-in-houston.

44. National Homelessness Law Center (NHLC), *Housing Not Handcuffs 2021: State Law Supplement* (NHLC, 2021), https://homelesslaw.org/wp-content/uploads/2021/11/2021-HNH-State-Crim-Supplement.pdf.

45. That stingy definition is also contrary to human rights.

46. Kimmelman and Tompkins, "How Houston Moved 25,000 People."

47. Stephen Averill Sherman, Daniel Potter, Andrew Kim, and Alec Tobin, *The 2023 State of Housing in Harris County and Houston* (Rice University Kinder Institute of Urban Research, 2023), https://rice.app.box.com/s/kpzz1a5toi4sycxw1e1bpt1xk86fvggq.

48. NLIHC, *The Gap: A Shortage of Affordable Homes* (NLIHC, 2023), 10, https://nlihc.org/gap/state/tx (based on US Census Bureau and HUD data).

49. David McClendon, "A Scary New Era for Evictions in Harris County," January Advisors, March 7, 2023, https://www.januaryadvisors.com/a-scary-new-era-for-evictions-in-harris-county/.

50. Ninfa Saavedra, "Houston Housing Authority Waitlist Now Open; How to Apply and What to Expect," *Click2Houston*, updated January 15, 2023, https://www.click2houston.com/news/local/2023/01/10/houston-houston-authority-waitlist-when-it-will-open-how-to-apply.

51. Homer, "Public Housing Waitlist Reopening."

52. Kimmelman and Tompkins, "How Houston Moved 25,000 People; Homer, Public Housing Waitlist Reopening."

53. Catherine Villarreal "Houston Endowment Grants $10 Million to Coalition for the Homeless of Houston/Harris County" (press release), Coalition for the Homeless, July 25, 2023, https://www.homelesshouston.org/press-release-houston-endowment-grants-10-million-to-coalition-for-the-homeless-of-houston-harris-county.

54. Kimmelman and Tompkins, "How Houston Moved 25,000 People; Sherman, et al., *The 2023 State of Housing*.

55. Rachel Carlton and Jishnu Nair, "Increasing Investor Purchases of Single-Family Homes Contributing to Rise in Rentals across Houston," *Community Impact*, July 8, 2022, https://communityimpact.com/houston/bay-area/city-county/2022/07/08/increasing-investor-purchases-of-single-family-homes-contributing-to-rise-in-rentals-across-houston/; Glenn Hunter, "Buying a Home in Texas Often Requires Outbidding Big-Money Investors," *Texas Monthly*, April 14, 2023,

https://www.texasmonthly.com/news-politics/home-buying-investors-legislature
-bills/; Alexander Hermann, "8 Facts about Investor Activity in the Single-Family
Rental Market," Joint Center for Housing Studies of Harvard University (JCHS),
July 18, 2023, https://www.jchs.harvard.edu/blog/8-facts-about-investor-activity
-single-family-rental-market.

56. Carlton and Nair, "Increasing Investor Purchases of Single-Family Homes."

57. "Support for Terri and Blesit," GoFundMe, June 15th, 2022, https://www
.gofundme.com/f/support-for-terri-and-blesit; Michael Kimmelman (@kimmelman)
"To respond to those generous readers who continue to ask me if there is a way to
help Terri and Blesit, here again is the GoFundMe page that local officials helped
Terri set up:," Twitter, July 5, 2022, 8:04 a.m., https://twitter.com/kimmelman/
status/1544291243622113281.

58. Rachel M. Cohen, "Homeless Encampments—and the Debate over What
to Do about Them—Explained," Vox, March 8, 2023, https://www.vox.com/policy
/2023/3/8/23618237/homelessness-tent-encampments-housing-affordable.

59. Michael Murney, "Tickets for Feeding Houston's Unhoused Thrown
Out after Police No-Shows," Chron, August 4, 2023, https://www.chron.com
/news/houston-texas/article/houston-food-not-bombs-texas-18279213.php;
Ashley Brown, "Food Not Bombs Volunteer Found Not Guilty after Citation
for Feeding Homeless," Houston Public Media, updated August 1, 2023,
https://www.houstonpublicmedia.org/articles/news/city-of-houston/2023/07/31
/458267/food-not-bombs-volunteer-found-not-guilty-after-citation-for-feeding
-homeless/.

60. See Gail Radford, Modern Housing (University of Chicago Press, 1996),
77–78. As mentioned earlier, varying definitions of social housing are in use. See
Mironova and Waters, "Social Housing in the US."

61. See Radford, Modern Housing.

62. Dennis Keating and Peter Marcuse, "The Failures of Conservativism and
the Limitations of Liberalism," in A Right to Housing: Foundation for a New Social
Agenda, ed. Rachel Bratt, Michael Stone, and Chester Hartman (Temple University
Press, 2006).

63. Keating and Marcuse, "The Failures of Conservativism"; Richard Rothstein,
The Color of Law: A Forgotten History of How Our Government Segregated America
(Liveright, 2017).

64. Peter Dreier, "Why America Needs More Social Housing," American
Prospect, April 16, 2018, https://prospect.org/infrastructure/america-needs-social
-housing/.

65. JCHS, The State of the Nation's Housing 2023 (JCHS, 2023), https://www
.jchs.harvard.edu/sites/default/files/reports/files/Harvard_JCHS_The_State_of_the
_Nations_Housing_2023.pdf; Drier, "Why America Needs More Social Housing";
Keating and Marcuse, "The Failures of Conservativism;" NLIHC, "Myths and

Realities about Public Housing," NLIHC, October 17, 2019, https://nlihc.org/resource/myths-and-realities-about-public-housing.

66. NLIHC, "14-1 Advancing Tenant Protections: Source-of-Income Protections," NLIHC, February 7, 2023, https://nlihc.org/resource/14-1-advancing -tenant-protections-source-income-protections.

67. Brian Knudsen, "Expanded Protections for Families with Housing Choice Vouchers," Poverty & Race Research Action Council, https://www.prrac.org/pdf/soi-voucher-data-brief.pdf.

68. Robbie Sequeira, "Some States Protect Section 8 Renters, but Enforcement Is Elusive," *Stateline*, July 21, 2023. https://stateline.org/2023/07/21/some-states -protect-section-8-renters-but-enforcement-is-elusive/.

69. National Low Income Housing Coalition, "Out of Reach" (NLICH 2023), 7; Peggy Bailey, "Addressing the Affordable Housing Crisis Requires Expanding Rental Assistance and Adding Housing Units," Center on Budget and Policy Priorities (CBPP), October 27, 2022, https://www.cbpp.org/research/housing/addressing-the-affordable-housing-crisis-requires-expanding-rental-assistance-and.

70. Federal tax breaks for homeowners include the mortgage interest deduction, deduction of state and local property taxes, and the capital gains exclusion. As of 2023, the homeowners' mortgage deduction is projected to more than triple by 2026. Emma Waters, Owen Minott, and Andrew Lautz, "Is It Time for Congress to Reconsider the Mortgage Interest Deduction?" Bipartisan Policy Center, November 2, 2023, https://bipartisanpolicy.org/explainer/is-it-time-for-congress-to -reconsider-the-mortgage-interest-deduction/.

71. Will Fischer and Barbara Sard, "Chart Book: Federal Housing Spending Is Poorly Matched to Need," CBPP, updated March 8, 2017, https://www .cbpp.org/research/chart-book-federal-housing-spending-is-poorly-matched-to -need; Andrew Aurand, "The Mortgage Interest Deduction," in *2022 Advocate's Guide* (NLIHC, 2022), https://nlihc.org/sites/default/files/2022-03/2022AG_6-09 _Mortgage-Interest-Deduction.pdf.

72. Roger Rudick, "SPUR Talk: Housing Lessons from Vienna," *Streetsblog San Francisco*, January 11, 2023, https://sf.streetsblog.org/2023/01/11/spur-talk -housing-lessons-from-vienna; Francesca Mari, "Imagine a Renters' Utopia. It Might Look Like Vienna." *New York Times Magazine*, May 23, 2023, https://www .nytimes.com/2023/05/23/magazine/vienna-social-housing.html.

73. "The 'Vienna Model': For a more equitable society," City of Vienna, https://socialhousing.wien/policy/the-vienna-model; Jake Blumgart, "Most Livable City: How Vienna Earned Its Place in Housing History," *City Monitor*, June 22, 2023, quoting Eve Blau, https://citymonitor.ai/environment/housing/red-vienna -how-austrias-capital-earned-its-place-in-housing-history; Alicia Prager, "Vienna Battles Rising Housing Costs—Can a New Policy Fix It?" *Euronews*, November 2, 2018, https://www.euronews.com/2018/10/30/vienna-battles-rising-housing-costs -can-a-new-policy-fix-it. In 2023, income limits ranged from 53,340 euros for a

single individual to 100,410 euros for four persons. "Flat Allocation Criteria: Broad Access to Subsidised Housing," City of Vienna, https://socialhousing.wien/tools/flat-allocation-criteria. Some 75 percent of the city population qualified.

74. Blumgart, "Most Livable City; Mari, "Imagine a Renters' Utopia"; Barbara Unterlerchner, policy analyst at Neunerhaus, interview with the author November 2, 2023.

75. As of 2023, these make up about half of the city's social housing supply. Built with the help of low-interest construction loans funded by the city, their rent must be limited to the associations' cost—anything more must be paid back to fund the construction of additional social housing. Mari, "Imagine a Renters' Utopia."

76. Mari, "Imagine a Renters' Utopia." Some financial analysts have called Vienna the "epicenter" of Europe's housing "woes," noting that its active rental market is dragging down prices to purchase property. Jack Sidders, Ainhoa Goyeneche and Marton Eder, "Vienna Becomes Epicenter of Europe's Housing Woes," BNN Bloomberg, May 18, 2023, https://www.bnnbloomberg.ca/vienna-becomes-epicenter-of-europe-s-housing-woes-1.1921739.

77. Mari, "Imagine a Renters' Utopia;" JCHS, *America's Rental Housing 2024* (JCHS, 2024), 41, https://www.jchs.harvard.edu/sites/default/files/reports/files/Harvard_JCHS_Americas_Rental_Housing_2024.pdf.

78. Josh Cohen, "Seattle's Social Housing Campaign, Explained," Cascade PBS, May 26, 2022, https://crosscut.com/news/2022/05/seattles-social-housing-campaign-explained; Rachel M. Cohen, "How State Governments Are Reimagining American Public Housing," *Vox*, August, 2022, https://www.vox.com/policy-and-politics/23278643/affordable-public-housing-inflation-renters-home; Paul E Williams, "Carving Out a Path for Public Developers," *Social Housing Chronicle*, July 14, 2022, https://housingchronicle.substack.com/p/carving-out-a-path-for-public-developers; "Vienna's Unique Social Housing Program," *PD&R Edge*, https://www.huduser.gov/portal/pdredge/pdr_edge_featd_article_011314.html; "Council Approves $50 Million Construction Fund for Public-Private Housing Model" (press release), Montgomery County Council, March 24, 2021, https://www2.montgomerycountymd.gov/mcgportalapps/Press_Detail.aspx?Item_ID=33968&Dept=1; Mari, "Imagine a Renters' Utopia."

79. Amnesty International (AI), *If Housing Was a Human Right, I Wouldn't Live Like This: Barriers to Accessing Homeless Assistance Services in Austria* (AI, 2022), 34, https://www.amnesty.org/en/wp-content/uploads/2022/04/EUR1354582022ENGLISH.pdf; This is most likely a low estimate—as in the United States, many homeless people are "hidden" and not counted. BAWO, "Housing for All" (BAWO 2019), https://bawo.at/101/wp-content/uploads/2019/12/Policy-Paper-English.pdf.

80. Christopher Cheung, "Unaffordable Cities, Look to Quality Public Housing in Vienna," *Tyee*, May 17, 2017, https://thetyee.ca/News/2017/05/17/Imagine-Vancouver-Quality-Housing/.

81. Prager, "Vienna Battles Rising Housing Costs;" Cheung, "Unaffordable Cities;" Joe Copeland, "The City That Solved Homelessness," Cascade PBS, June 27, 2017, https://crosscut.com/2017/06/homelessness-housing-crisis-seattle-vienna -solution; Agenda Austria, "Housing Costs Are Rising in All Sectors," *Agenda Austria*, January 17, 2022, https://www.agenda-austria.at/grafiken/mieten-steigen -in-allen-segmenten-2/. Housing costs rose more in the private market, also driven by increasing interest from developers, including institutional investors. In August 2023, the government enacted rent caps to try to address rising rents. Marton Eder, "Austria Caps Home Rent Increases to Ease Inflation Pressure," Bloomberg, August 30, 2023, https://www.bloomberg.com/news/articles/2023-08-30/austria -caps-home-rent-increases-to-ease-inflation-pressure#xj4y7vzkg.

82. Cheung, "Unaffordable Cities."

83. "Rented FLAT Types," City of Vienna, https://www.wien.gv.at/english/ living-working/housing/renting/flat-types.html.

84. Limited profit housing typically requires prospective tenants to pay a "down payment" for entry, which is refunded save for a 1 percent administrative free if the tenant leaves. Municipal housing requires tenants to show they are living in over-crowded housing, they are over thirty years old and still living with their parents, or they are over sixty-five and have special needs. Justin Kadi and Johanna Lilius, "The Remarkable Stability of Social Housing in Vienna and Helsinki: A Multi-Dimensional Analysis," *Housing Studies* (November 6, 2022), "Rented Flat Types," City of Vienna; "Flat Allocation Criteria," City of Vienna.

85. "Zuerst ein Zuhause, dann alles weitere," Neunerhaus, August 26, 2022, https://www.neunerhaus.at/blog/zuerst-ein-zuhause-dann-alles-weitere/.

86. Unterlerchner interview.

87. AI, *If Housing Was a Human Right*.

88. Elisabeth Hammer, "Don't Look Away: How a Society without Homelessness Is Possible," *European Journal of Homelessness* 17, no. 2 (2023).

89. Unterlerchner interview.

90. BAWO, "Housing for All."

91. Emine Özkan and Gerhard Schützinger, "'Arriving Home'—How Strategic Alliances Boost Housing First in Austria," Housing First Europe Hub, https:// housingfirsteurope.eu/blog/arriving-home-how-strategic-alliances-boost-housing -first-in-austria-emine-ozkan-gerhard-schutzinger/. As of 2024, the plan was still limited to one thousand. Harry Markham, "Off the Street and into a Home: Over 1,000 Homeless in Austria Get a Flat," The Good Men Project, February 5, 2024, https://goodmenproject.com/featured-content/off-the-street-and-into-a-home -over-1000-homeless-in-austria-get-a-flat/.

92. AI, *If Housing was a Human Right*, 15. It also noted that preventing and ending homelessness is a "minimum" obligation under the treaty.

93. Lindsay B. Flynn, "How Do We Talk about Housing Equality in an Unequal Europe?" *EuropeNow*, July 12, 2023, https://www.europenowjournal.org

/2023/07/06/how-do-we-talk-about-housing-equality-in-an-increasingly-unequal -europe/.

94. Housing First is a programmatic model for using housing in a particular way, not a model for developing housing.

95. Michela Zonta, *Community Land Trusts: A Promising Tool for Expanding and Protecting Affordable Housing* (Center for American Progress, June 2016), https://cdn.americanprogress.org/wp-content/uploads/2016/06/14141430/ CommunityLandTrusts-report.pdf.

96. Through the Neighborhood Stabilization Program, established July 2008. Paul A. Joice, "Neighborhood Stabilization Program" (policy brief), *Cityscape: A Journal of Policy Development and Research* 13, no. 1 (2011), https://www.huduser.gov /periodicals/cityscpe/vol13num1/Cityscape_March2011_dept_policy_briefs.pdf.

97. "Oakland's Displacement Crisis: As Told by the Numbers," PolicyLink, https://www.policylink.org/sites/default/files/PolicyLink%20Oakland's %20Displacement%20Crisis%20by%20the%20numbers.pdf.

98. Housing and Economic Rights Advocates (HERA) and California Reinvestment Coalition (CRC), *Foreclosed: The Burden of Homeownership Loss on City of Oakland and Alameda County Residents* (HERA, 2007), https://docs.google .com/viewerng/viewer?url=https://dl.dropboxusercontent.com/s/200plmnomslxnb7 /HERA_CRC_BurdenofHomeownershipLoss_Dec2007.pdf.

99. City of Oakland, Agenda Report, Memorandum to the Office of the City Administrator, from Community and Economic Development Agency, February 27, 2007, https://docs.google.com/viewerng/viewer?url=https://dl.dropboxusercontent .com/s/uz0uiloitufjd8u/CLT_IDA_staff_report_2-27-07.pdf.

100. "OakCLT Timeline," Oakland Community Land Trust (OakCLT), https://oakclt.org/about/history/.

101. City of Oakland, Agenda Report; "OakCLT Timeline."

102. "OakCLT Timeline."

103. E. Tammy Kim, "Moms 4 Housing: Redefining the Right to a Home in Oakland," *New York Review*, March 9, 2020, https://www.nybooks.com /online/2020/03/09/moms-4-housings-redefining-the-right-to-a-home-in -oakland/; Peter Sabonis and Zachary Murray, *Creating Community Controlled, Deeply Affordable Housing: A Resource Toolkit for Community Activists and Allied Community-Based Housing Developers* (Partners for Dignity & Rights, Spring 2021), https://dignityandrights.org/wp-content/uploads/2021/05/PDR-Housing-Report -Final-R2.pdf; "OakCLT Timeline"; City of Oakland, Agenda Report. The model has also been used more broadly to develop commercial and other properties for community benefit. Zonta, *Community Land Trusts*; "What Is a Community Land Trust?" International Center for Community Land Trusts (ICCLT), https://cltweb .org/what-is-a-community-land-trust/.

104. "What Is a Community Land Trust?" ICCLT; Zonta, *Community Land Trusts.*

105. "About the Land Trust Accreditation Commission," Land Trust Accreditation Commission, https://www.landtrustaccreditation.org/about; Zonta, *Community Land Trusts*. CLTs are a form of "shared equity," a type of owner-occupied homeownership that is shared between the homeowner and a nonprofit entity that ensures its ongoing affordability.

106. There is much variation in how CLTs are implemented, leading some researchers to caution that not all equally fulfill the three main goals of social housing: permanent affordability, social equality, and democratic resident control. Mironova and Waters, "Social Housing in the U.S."

107. Similarly, public housing works well when it is adequately funded and maintained. Alana Semuels, "The Power of Public Housing," *Atlantic*, September 22, 2015, https://www.theatlantic.com/business/archive/2015/09/public-housing-success/406561/.

108. H. Jacob Carlson and Gianpaolo Baiocchi, "Social Housing: How a New Generation of Activists Is Reinventing Housing," Shelterforce, June 30, 2023, https://shelterforce.org/2023/06/30/social-housing-how-a-new-generation-of-activists-are-reinventing-housing/.

109. Savannah Hawley-Bates, "Rents in Kansas City and Missouri Are Rising Faster Than Almost Anywhere Else in the U.S.," KCUR, February 28, 2024, https://www.kcur.org/housing-development-section/2024-02-28/rents-kansas-city-missouri-housing-prices-affordable-kc-tenants.

110. KC Tenants, "Meet Tiana Caldwell, a member of our core leadership team. For five months, Tiana has been living in a Kansas City hotel with her husband Derrick and their 11-year-old son AJ. She was recently re-diagnosed with ovarian cancer, fell behind on rent, and got evicted. Tiana's in the lowest moment of her life but knows she's actually better off than some. So, a few weeks ago Tiana told her story in public for the first time and declared her commitment to organize other tenants in KC. Inspired by MLK, Tiana said: 'Let us be dissatisfied until no person ever has to choose between their health and keeping a roof over their head. Let us be dissatisfied until every person in KC lives in a safe, decent, and truly affordable home,'" Facebook, February 12, 2019, https://www.facebook.com/kctenants/posts/meet-tiana-caldwell-a-member-of-our-core-leadership-team-for-five-months-tiana-h/295165971147321/.

111. Urban Institute, "Tenant Organizing," Pursuing Housing Justice: Interventions for Impact, https://www.urban.org/apps/pursuing-housing-justice-interventions-impact/tenant-organizing.

112. Jennifer S. Prusak, "Expanding the Right to Counsel in Eviction Cases: Arguments for and Limitations of 'Civil Gideon' Laws in a Post-COVID 19 World," *Journal of Civil Rights and Economic Development* 36, no. 2 (Fall 2022), https://scholarship.law.stjohns.edu/jcred/vol36/iss2/4/; Ericka Peterson, "Building a House for Gideon: The Right to Counsel in Evictions," *Stanford Journal of Civil*

Rights & Civil Liberties 16 no. 1 (February 2020) https://law.stanford.edu/wp
-content/uploads/2020/02/Petersen_Final.pdf.

113. UN, *CESCR General Comment No. 4: The Right to Adequate Housing (Art. 11
(1) of the Covenant)* (OHCHR, December 1991), https://www.refworld.org/legal/
general/cescr/1991/en/53157.

114. NLIHC, *The Gap.*

115. Kynala Phillips, "Kansas City Votes for $50 Million for Affordable Housing.
What That Means and What's Next," *Kansas City Star*, updated November 9, 2022,
https://www.kansascity.com/news/politics-government/election/article268528747
.html.

116. "Citywide Tenant Union," KC Tenants, https://kctenants.org/member;
KC Tenants Power (@kctenantspower), "Co-governance begins TODAY. It's
Inauguration Day in Kansas City—a day to celebrate our winning candidates as well
as begin co-governing with all city councilmembers, endorsed and otherwise. City
Hall is the people's house. Over the next four years, KC Tenants Power will continue to organize the people of our city across the lines that are usually used to divide
us to ensure the people closest to the problem are creating the solutions. We are the
ones we've been waiting for," Instagram, August 1, 2023, https://www.instagram
.com/p/CvajNb3JeXS/; Betsy Webster, "KC Tenants Leader Wins Council Seat,"
KCTV 5, June 2023, https://www.kctv5.com/2023/06/21/kc-tenants-political-arm
-celebrates-wins-election-night/; Celisa Calacal, "This Election, KC Tenants Power
Gets Its First Shot at Shifting the Balance of Power in Kansas City," KCUR,
June 19, 2023, https://www.kcur.org/politics-elections-and-government/2023-06
-19/this-election-kc-tenants-power-gets-its-first-shot-at-shifting-the-balance-of
-power-in-kansas-city.

117. "Why I'm Running," Jonathan Duncan for City Council 6th District:
In-District, https://www.duncanforkc.com/about.

118. Tara Raghuveer (@taraghuveer), "Today @KCTenants won a STRONG
ban on source of income discrimination. The best part of my day was meeting Jackie
who made this shirt and got herself to City Hall for her first ever anything with us.
After, she said, 'I'm hooked, what's next?' I love the tenant union," Twitter, January
25, 2024, 8:14 p.m., https://twitter.com/taraghuveer/status/1750688509457748009;
Celisa Calacal, "Kansas City Renters Who Use Housing Vouchers Now Have
More Protection against Discrimination," KCUR, January 26, 2024, https://www
.kcur.org/housing-development-section/2024-01-26/kansas-city-renters-who-use
-housing-vouchers-now-have-more-protection-against-discrimination.

119. Elisabeth Elustin, "A New Kansas City Ordinance Outlaws Sources
of Income Discrimination and Allows Vouchers for Housing," *Kansas City
Defender*, February 6, 2024, https://kansascitydefender.com/housing/a-new-kansas
-city-ordinance-outlaws-sources-of-income-discrimination-and-allows-vouchers
-for-housing/; Daniel Teles and Yipeng Su, *Source of Income Protections and Access
to Low-Poverty Neighborhoods* (Urban Institute, 2022), https://www.urban.org/sites

/default/files/2022-10/Source%20of%20Income%20Protections%20and%20Access %20to%20Low-Poverty%20Neighborhoods.pdf.

120. KC Tenants (@KCTenants), "But it doesn't have to be this way. KC Tenants is now 10,000 strong and at the top of our to-do list is taking our city back and housing the people. We're fighting for a Kansas City where everyone has a truly, permanently affordable home. Join us today": Twitter, September 7, 2023, 8:45 a.m., https://twitter.com/KCTenants/status/1699765787983048773.

121. Compassion Seattle, "Compassion Seattle" (community profile page), Facebook, https://www.facebook.com/CompassionSeattle/.

122. Petition to Appeal Ballot Title, In re: Ballot Title of Proposed Seattle Charter Title Amendment 29 (Sup. Ct. Was. King Co. 2021), https://publicola.com /wp-content/uploads/2021/05/CA-29-Ballot-Title-Petition.pdf.

123. Tiffani McCoy, interview with the author, October 6, 2023; Andrew Villeneuve, "Most voters Favor Seattle Charter Amendment 29 (concerning homelessness) out of the Gate," *Cascadia Advocate*, July 23, 2021, https:// www.nwprogressive.org/weblog/2021/07/most-voters-favor-seattle-charter -amendment-29-concerning-homelessness-out-of-the-gate.html?fbclid=IwAR0 _PCF68KY7k8rG2T7A_V8PtI48psT_qWPBz4vixNc1OJkQsYI29651X4A.

124. Natalie Bicknell Argerious, "Appeal Denied: Compassion Seattle's Charter Amendment Is Dead," *Urbanist*, September 3, 2021, https://www.theurbanist.org /2021/09/03/appeal-denied-compassion-seattles-charter-amendment-is-dead/.

125. "Social Housing. Climate Action. Connected Communities," House Our Neighbors, https://www.houseourneighbors.org/; J. Cohen, "Seattle's Social Housing Campaign; Hannah Krieg, "In a Seeming Twist, LIHI Endorses Social Housing Initiative," *The Stranger*, June 16, 2022, https://www.thestranger.com/news /2022/06/16/75144929/in-a-seeming-twist-lihi-endorses-social-housing-initiative.

126. McCoy interview.

127. McCoy interview.

128. McCoy interview. The group's goal was for the initiative to be on the November 2024 ballot, but the city council delayed it until February 2025. "Seattle City Council Pushes Social Housing Funding to 2025, Delays Vote on Initiative 137," *Seattle Medium*, August 16, 2024, https://seattlemedium.com/seattle-housing -initiative-delayed/.

129. Alana Semuels, "How Amazon Helped Kill a Seattle Tax on Business," *Atlantic*, June 13, 2018, https://www.theatlantic.com/technology/archive/2018/06/ how-amazon-helped-kill-a-seattle-tax-on-business/562736/.

130. Esteban L. Hernandez, "Denver's Latest Encampment Sweep Focuses on Providing Housing," *Axios Denver*, September 27, 2023, https://www.axios.com/ local/denver/2023/09/27/homeless-unhoused-housing-sweep-encampment; Kyle Harris, "Here's How Mike Johnston Will Measure Success Housing 1,000 Homeless People in Denver," *Denverite*, September 18, 2023, https://denverite.com/2023 /09/18/heres-how-mike-johnston-will-measure-success-housing-1000-homeless

-people-in-denver/; Ernest Gurulé, "Mayor Mike Johnston Plans to Solve Denver's Homelessness," *La Voz Colorado*, September 27, 2023, https://lavozcolorado .com/2023/09/27/mayor-mike-johnston-plans-to-solve-denvers-homelessness/. Still, they were counted as having had a "housing outcome" if they stayed for at least two weeks, even if that "housing" turned out to be untenable and the person was back on the street.

131. "Housing Is a Human Right," Housekeys Action Network Denver (HAND), https://housekeysactionnetwork.com/.

132. HAND, *Pipe Dreams and Picket Fences: Direction from Denver's Houseless People on Housing Needs and Priorities in the Context of Today's Public Housing* (HAND, 2023). Most important to those surveyed was safety, freedom, and sense of community. They named some specific features of housing they felt were critical: control over the temperature, a bathroom with shower access, and a viable location.

133. Of the group, 85 percent needed housing that cost under $1,000 a month, 65.6 percent needed it to be under $600 a month, and 17 percent needed it to be free. Most wanted financial help, 22 percent wanted mental health support, and 10 percent wanted substance abuse support. HAND, *Pipe Dreams and Picket Fences*.

134. Terese Howard, lead organizer of HAND, interview with the author, June 16, 2023.

135. Courtney Hagle, "Fox News Zeroes In on a New Target: The Homeless," Media Matters for America, June 4, 2019, https://www.mediamatters.org/fox-news /fox-news-zeroes-new-target-homeless.

136. Aaron Blake, "Trump's Incoherent Monologue on Homelessness," *Washington Post*, July 2, 2019, https://www.washingtonpost.com/politics/2019/07 /02/trumps-incoherent-monologue-homelessness/.

137. Bess Levin, "Trump Worried Unsightly Homeless Are Hurting Property Values," *Vanity Fair*, September 17, 2019, https://www.vanityfair.com/news/2019 /09/donald-trump-homeless-property-values.

138. Joanne Zuhl, "Losing Ground: How the Trump Administration Has Reversed U.S. Housing Policy," *Street Roots*, October 21, 2020, https://www .streetroots.org/news/2020/10/21/losing-ground-how-trump-administration -has-reversed-us-housing-policy; Council of Economic Advisers, "The State of Homelessness in America," September 2019, https://trumpwhitehouse.archives.gov /wp-content/uploads/2019/09/The-State-of-Homelessness-in-America.pdf.

139. Kriston Capps, "The Consultant Leading the White House Push against Homelessness," Bloomberg, December 12, 2019, https://www.bloomberg.com /news/articles/2019-12-12/trump-s-homeless-policy-gets-a-controversial-boss; Laurel Wamsley, "White House Names Controversial Pick to Head Homelessness Office," NPR, December 5, 2019, https://www.npr.org/2019/12/05/785129572/ white-house-names-controversial-pick-to-head-homelessness-office.

140. Capps, "The Consultant Leading the White House Push;" Arthur Delaney, "How a Traveling Consultant Helps America Hide the Homeless," *HuffPost*, updated December 6, 2017, https://www.huffpost.com/entry/robert-marbut_n _6738948.

141. Delaney, "How a Traveling Consultant."

142. Arthur Delaney, "Robert Marbut's Nomination Signals a Big Shift in Homeless Policy," *HuffPost*, updated December 16, 2019, https://www.huffpost .com/entry/homelessness-robert-marbut-trump_n_5de952c9e4b0913e6f8d35db.

143. USICH, *Expanding the Toolbox: The Whole-of-Government Response to Homelessness* (USICH, 2020) https://www.usich.gov/sites/default/files/document/ USICH-Expanding-the-Toolbox.pdf.

144. Zuhl, "Losing Ground."

145. Mahboob, "Housing Is a Human Right" (emphasis added).

146. Jason DeParle, "Federal Policy on Homelessness Becomes New Target of the Right," *New York Times*, June 20, 2023, https://www.nytimes.com/2023/06/20/ us/politics/federal-policy-on-homelessness-becomes-new-target-of-the-right.html.

147. Joe Biden (@POTUS) "Housing should be a right—not a privilege. But far too many people are struggling to keep a roof over their head. I look forward to working with @SecFudge to help renters and homeowners get through this crisis and ensure every American has access to quality, affordable housing," Twitter, March 10, 2021, 9:16 p.m., https://twitter.com/POTUS/status/1369834567411109891; Patrick Range, "President Joe Biden Says Housing Is a Right. It's a Game Changer," Housing Is a Human Right, January 19, 2021, https://www.housingisah umanright.org/president-joe-biden-says-housing-is-a-right-its-a-game-changer/; Camille Squires, "The US's Top Housing Authority Just Declared Housing a Human Right," *Quartz*, March 23, 2022, https://qz.com/2145610/us-hud-secretary -marcia-fudge-just-declared-housing-a-human-right; USICH, *All In*, 6.

148. John Cassidy, "Joe Manchin Kills the Build Back Better Bill," *New Yorker*, December 19, 2021, https://www.newyorker.com/news/our-columnists/joe-man- chin-kills-the-build-back-better-bill.

149. Cynthia Griffith, "The Unsurprising Aftermath of Clearing the McPherson Square Encampment," Invisible People, April 14, 2023, https://invisiblepeople.tv/ the-unsurprising-aftermath-of-clearing-the-mcpherson-square-encampment/.

150. USICH, *All In*, 20; Kriston Capps, "Biden Administration Defies Own Playbook on Homelessness," Bloomberg, February 16, 2023, https://www.bloomberg .com/news/articles/2023-02-16/dc-clears-homeless-encampment-in-defiance-of -federal-playbook.

151. The administration's budget request for fiscal year 2025, submitted to Congress on March 11, 2024, included a request for $8 billion in "mandatory fund- ing" to expand temporary and permanent housing for people experiencing home- lessness. Mandatory funding is akin to an entitlement—that is, not dependent on the discretion of Congress. That would be a step toward an entitlement-for-housing

voucher that was included in the ill-fated Build Back Better proposal. The proposed 2025 budget also included protections for renters and funding to address the broader housing crisis. Given the current makeup of Congress, no one expects these proposals to have any prospect of moving forward. But the inclusion of these items does indicate some level of continued commitment to the right to housing by the administration. "Biden Administration Releases FY25 Budget Request," NLIHC, March 15, 2024, https://nlihc.org/resource/biden-administration-releases -fy25-budget-request-0; US Office of Management and Budget, *Budget of the U.S. Government: Fiscal Year 2025* (US Government Publishing Office, 2024), https:// www.whitehouse.gov/wp-content/uploads/2024/03/budget_fy2025.pdf.

152. NHLC, *Housing Not Handcuffs 2021*, 8–9.

153. "Emergent Threats: State Level Homelessness Criminalization," Housing Not Handcuffs, accessed February 22, 2024, https://housingnothandcuffs.org/ emergent-threats-homelessness-criminalization/; Associated Press, "GOP Lawmakers Override Governor's Veto of Safer Kentucky Act," WASH11abc, April 12, 2024, https://www.whas11.com/article/news/politics/gop-lawmakers -override-governor-veto-safer-kentucky-act-law/417-05f160af-86f3-45b3-9259 -34440b5f3710.

154. Bob Christie, "Arizona Senator Cites Own Time Being Homeless as He Opposes Bill," Tuscon.com, updated Feb 27, 2024, https://tucson.com/news/state -regional/arizona-lawmaker-cites-own-time-being-homeless-as-he-opposes-bill/ article_7328db82-990a-11ed-8573-f3ec24f7ee3e.html.

155. That bill would have made camping in public a crime and required local governments in the state to remove encampments.

156. E. J. Montini, "Bill Pushed by Republican Lawmakers Attacks the Homeless for Being Houseless," *Arizona Republic*, February 22, 2023, https://www .azcentral.com/story/opinion/op-ed/ej-montini/2023/02/22/arizona-legislature-bill -attacks-homeless-for-being-houseless/69929974007/.

157. "SB1413," Sack Wadsack, https://sackwadsack.com/why-recall/sb1413/.

158. Gloria Rebecca Gomez, "Katie Hobbs Vetoes GOP Bills Criminalizing Homelessness, Ranked-Choice Voting," *Arizona Mirror*, June 5, 2023, https://azmirror .com/2023/06/05/katie-hobbs-vetoes-gop-bills-criminalizing-homelessness -ranked-choice-voting/.

159. Maura Zurick, "Trump Wants to Make Homelessness Illegal," *Newsweek*, updated April 19, 2023, https://www.newsweek.com/trump-wants-make -homelessness-illegal-1795202.

160. Justine McDaniel, "DeSantis Signs Law Banning Homeless People from Sleeping in Public Places," *Washington Post*, March 21, 2024, https://www. washingtonpost.com/nation/2024/03/21/florida-desantis-homeless-ban-sleeping -public/.

161. Juha Kaakinen and Saija Turunen, "Finnish but Not Yet Finished—Successes and Challenges of Housing First in Finland," *European Journal of Homelessness* 15,

no. 3 (2021), https://www.feantsaresearch.org/public/user/Observatory/2021/EJH _15-3/EJH_15-3_A5_v02.pdf.

CHAPTER NINE

1. This was at the shelter operated by the Community for Creative Non-Violence (CCNV) at Second and D Streets N.W. in Washington, D.C. It was most likely in late 1986 or in 1987, when I was most active with the legal clinic that I and a few other lawyers had started there. I volunteered there in my off-hours from my "day job" in national advocacy.

2. Matthew Chayes, "How 2 families Sparked Nassau's Shelter Mandate," *Newsday*, October 1, 2023 (Janet Koster, then a child, recalling the experience).

3. John Cummings, "Nassau Family's Challenge," *Newsday*, September 25, 1984.

4. Courtney Hagle, "Fox News Zeroes in on a New Target: The Homeless," Media Matters for America, June 4, 2019, https://www.mediamatters.org/fox-news /fox-news-zeroes-new-target-homeless; Bess Levin, "Trump Worried Unsightly Homeless Are Hurting Property Values," *Vanity Fair*, September 17, 2019, https:// www.vanityfair.com/news/2019/09/donald-trump-homeless-property-values.

5. James Powel, "'We Need to Do More': California to Spend $300 Million to Clear Homeless Encampments," *USA Today*, November 28, 2023, https://eu.usatoday .com/story/news/nation/2023/11/28/california-300-million-homeless-encamp-ments/71733895007.

6. Kathleen Ronayne, Michael Casey, and Geoff Mulvihill, "Amid End to COVID Help, Homelessness Surging in Many Cities," AP News, October 6, 2022, https://apnews.com/article/health-california-covid-sacramento-292b0379752d1a2 26a741a70411eb0a9.

7. Pitts v. Black, Pitts v. Black, 208 F. Supp. 696 (SDNY 1994). Eric Pace, "Beneath Grand Central, Home Is a Railway Car," *New York Times*, August 29, 1985, https://www.nytimes.com/1985/08/29/nyregion/beneath-grand-central -home-is-a-railway-car.html.

8. Pitts v. Black, 208 F. Supp. 696 (SDNY 1984).

9. *Committee for the Dignity and Fairness for the Homeless v. Tartaglione* (E.D.PA. September 14, 1984) (unreported order). In 1985, a California state court ruled along similar lines. Collier v. Menzel, 221 Cal. Rptr. 110 (Ct. App. 1985).

10. National Law Center on Homelessness & Poverty (NLCHP), *Photo Identification Barriers Faced by Homeless Persons: The Impact of September 11* (NLCHP, 2004), https://homelesslaw.org/wp-content/uploads/2019/03/Photo-ID-Barriers -Faced-by-Homeless-Persons-2004.pdf.

11. Compl. para. 5, Frank v. Walker, 2:11-cv-01128 (filed December 13, 2011, E.D. Wis.).

12. ACLU, Press Release, ACLU Files Lawsuit Challenging Wisconsin's Unconstitutional Voter ID Law, December 13, 2011, https://www.aclu.org/press-releases/aclu-files-lawsuit-challenging-wisconsins-unconstitutional-voter-id-law.

13. The Conversation, "As Few as 1 in 10 Homeless People Vote in Elections—Here's Why," *U.S. News & World Report*, October 15, 2020, https://www.usnews.com/news/cities/articles/2020-10-15/as-few-as-1-in-10-homeless-people-vote-in-elections-heres-why.

14. Randall Akee, "Voting and Income," EconoFact, February 7, 2019, https://econofact.org/voting-and-income.

15. Courtney Cooperman, *Loss of Place, Loss of Voice: How Homelessness Impedes Political Equality*, Stanford University undergraduate honors thesis, 2020, on file with author, 20. "Eugene" is the pseudonym given by Cooperman.

16. Citizens United v. Federal Election Commission, 558 U.S. 310 (2010); see also Tim Lau, "Citizens United Explained," Brennan Center for Justice, December 12, 2019, https://www.brennancenter.org/our-work/research-reports/citizens-united-explained.

17. Right to Counsel NYC (RTCNYC) and the Community Development Project (CDP), "Profiles of Leaders in the RTC Movement," *Right to Counsel Toolkit* (RTCNYC, 2018), https://www.rtctoolkit.org/chapters/13-profiles-of-leaders-in-the-rtc-movement; New York State Joint Legislative Budget Hearing on Housing, February 14, 2024, Right to Counsel Coalition Testimony on Urgent Need to Fund and Pass Statewide Right to Counsel (S2721) (testimony of Randy Dillard), https://www.nysenate.gov/sites/default/files/admin/structure/media/manage/filefile/a/2024-02/right-to-counsel-coalition-and-community-action-for-safe-apartments-new-settlement-_24.pdf.

18. Lindsey v. Normet, 405 U.S. 56 (1972).

19. NYC Office of Civil Justice (OCJ), *NYC Office of Civil Justice 2016 Annual Report* (OCJ, June 2016), https://www.nyc.gov/assets/hra/downloads/pdf/services/civiljustice/OCJ%202016%20Annual%20Report%20FINAL_08_29_2016.pdf.

20. National Coalition for a Civil Right to Counsel (NCCRC), "The Right to Counsel for Tenants: Enacted Legislation," NCCRC, last modified December 2024. https://civilrighttocounsel.org/uploaded_files/283/RTC_Enacted_Legislation_in_Eviction_Proceedings_FINAL.pdf. The movement is part of a broader effort to secure a right to counsel in civil cases involving critical issues beyond housing, such as child custody, health care, and others. Currently, as interpreted by the US Supreme Court, the Constitution ensures a right to a lawyer only in criminal, not civil, cases.

21. NCCRC, "Tenant Right to Counsel," NCCRC, last modified November 2024, https://civilrighttocounsel.org/uploaded_files/280/Landlord_and_tenant_eviction_rep_stats__NCCRC_.pdf.

22. RTCNYC and CDF, "Profiles of Leaders."

23. Joseph Cepeda, as quoted in Andrew Scherer, "Why a Right: The Right to Counsel and the Ecology of Housing Justice," in *Impact: Collected Essays on Expanding Access to Justice Vol. 2* (Impact Center for Public Interest Law, 2016), 14, https://digitalcommons.nyls.edu/impact_center/17.

24. "Housing Courts Must Change! Campaign," NYCRTC, accessed May 5, 2024, https://www.righttocounselnyc.org/hcmc.

25. See Christopher Essert, "Property and Homelessness," *Philosophy & Public Affairs* 44, no. 4 (Fall 2016).

26. Legal philosopher Christopher Essert offers an incisive description of homelessness as a lack of property, with property defined as legal control over a place. See Essert, "Property and Homelessness"; Christopher Essert, *Property Law in the Society of Equals* (Oxford University Press, 2024); Christopher Essert, emails to the author, December 4 and 8, 2023.

27. There are many variations on these scenarios, including living in a car or RV. While "safe parking lots" are increasing, these offer less than a legal claim to be there: they can be shut down at any time. The same is true of "sanctioned encampments."

28. In a well-known 1991 article, legal and political philosopher Jeremy Waldron noted that "Everything that is done has to be done somewhere. No one is free to perform an action unless there is somewhere he is free to perform it." Waldron argued that homelessness constrains freedom because people who are homeless have no private place where they can consistently be. Jeremy Waldron, "Homelessness and the Issue of Freedom," *UCLA Law Review* 39, no. 2 (1991). More recently, Christopher Essert has argued more broadly that homelessness is the lack of property rights, defined as the ability to exercise control or agency over a space. Essert, "Property and Homelessness."

29. Essert, "Property and Homelessness;" Essert emails; Essert, *Property Law in the Society of Equals*. (Note that as used here, structural subordination is different from the corporate finance term). I am grateful to Christopher Essert for sharing his thoughts with me, along with his full manuscript of *Property Law in the Society of Equals* prior to publication.

30. "We hold these truths to be self-evident, that all men are created equal, that they are endowed by their Creator with certain unalienable Rights, that among these are Life, Liberty and the pursuit of Happiness." "Declaration of Independence: A Transcription," US National Archives and Records Administration, https://www.archives.gov/founding-docs/declaration-transcript.

31. Christopher Essert argues that not solving homelessness undermines the institution of property itself, which is premised on a need to organize relationships among moral equals. Essert, *Property Law in the Society of Equals*. Of course, how property rights are defined matters greatly, and a human rights framework has a critical role here. See also Brandon M. Weiss, "Progressive Property Theory and Housing Justice Campaigns," *UC Irvine Law Review* 10, no. 1 (October 2019).

Progressive property theory, which argues property must center human dignity and flourishing as basic values, could offer a similar perspective.

32. Zia Qureshi, "Rising Inequality: A Major Issue of Our Time," Brookings Institute, May 16, 2023, https://www.brookings.edu/articles/rising-inequality-a -major-issue-of-our-time/; Ann Saphir, "U.S. Income Inequality Grew through Pandemic Years, Fed Survey Shows," Reuters, October 18, 2023, https://www .reuters.com/world/us/us-income-inequality-rose-3-years-through-2022-fed-data -shows-2023-10-18/.

33. Steven Mintz, "Winning the Vote: A History of Voting Rights," The Gilder Lehrman Institute of American History, https://www.gilderlehrman.org/ history-resources/essays/winning-vote-history-voting-rights; "The Founders and the Vote," Library of Congress, https://www.loc.gov/classroom-materials/elections/ right-to-vote/the-founders-and-the-vote/.

34. For a discussion of some of these connections, see "A Way Home America," Aiden Anthony LLC, National Homelessness Law Center (NHLC), and True Colors United, *Slavery as a Cause and Consequence of Homelessness* (Report to the UN Special Rapporteur, 2023), https://homelesslaw.org/wp-content/uploads/2023/04/ UN-Slavery-Homelessness-Report-3-31-2023.pdf.

35. Jeff Stein, Tracy Jan, Josh Dawsey, and Ashley Parker, "Trump Pushing for Major Crackdown on Homeless Camps in California, with Aides Discussing Moving Residents to Government-Backed Facilities," *Washington Post*, September 10, 2019, https://www.washingtonpost.com/business/2019/09/10/trump-pushing -major-crackdown-homeless-camps-california-with-aides-discussing-moving -residents-government-backed-facilities/?arc404=true.

36. Katia Riddle, "Trump's Plan for People Struggling with Mental Illness, Addiction, and Homelessness," NPR, November 12, 2024, https://www.npr .org/2024/11/12/nx-s1-5184507/trumps-plan-for-people-struggling-with-mental -illness-addiction-and-homelessness. Brian Bennett, "Trump Calls for Moving Homeless to 'Tent Cities' in First D.C. Speech Since Leaving Office," *Time*, July 26, 2022, https://time.com/6200821/trump-homeless-tent-cities-2024/. In 2023, with his candidacy officially declared, Trump pledged to "ban urban camping" and arrest violators. Maura Zurick, "Trump Wants to Make Homelessness Illegal," *Newsweek*, updated April 19, 2023, https://www.newsweek.com/trump-wants-make -homelessness-illegal-1795202.

37. Jill Colvin and Bill Barrow, "Trump's Vow to Only Be a Dictator on 'Day One' Follows Growing Worry over His Authoritarian Rhetoric," AP News, updated December 7, 2023, https://apnews.com/article/trump-hannity-dictator -authoritarian-presidential-election-f27e7e9d7c13fabbe3ae7dd7f1235c72.

38. Angela Theisen, "Is Having a Sense of Belonging Important?" Mayo Clinic Health System, December 8, 2021, https://www.mayoclinichealthsystem.org/ hometown-health/speaking-of-health/is-having-a-sense-of-belonging-important.

39. Evan W. Carr, Andrew Reece, Gabriella Rosen Kellerman, and Alexi Robichaux, "The Value of Belonging at Work," *Harvard Business Review*, December 16, 2019, https://hbr.org/2019/12/the-value-of-belonging-at-work.

40. In 2019, Pete Buttigieg, then-mayor of South Bend, Indiana, and presidential candidate, argued that America faced a "crisis of belonging," and proposed a plan for "healing and belonging." Julia Manchester, "Buttigieg Unveils Plan to Strengthen Mental Health Care, Fight Addiction," *The Hill*, August 23, 2019, https://thehill .com/homenews/campaign/458515-buttigieg-unveils-plan-to-strengthen-mental -health-care-fight-addiction/; Kim Samuel, "Politicians Should Talk about Belonging," Medium, September 3, 2019, https://kimsamuelcanada.medium.com /politicians-should-talk-about-belonging-9dbcb0b29709; Pete Buttigieg and David Remnick, "Pete Buttigieg Discusses America's Crisis of Belonging" (interview), *New Yorker*, October 14, 2019, https://www.newyorker.com/video/watch/the-new -yorker-festival-pete-buttigieg.

41. Seligman and Montgomery make the case that belonging is a more powerful concept, and that arguments for universal human rights alone "provide no sense of belonging." While "liberals" promote human rights, the need for belonging, they argue, has instead been appropriated by right-wing populists. But it seems clear that Seligman and Montgomery are defining "human rights" as only civil and political rights, and not including economic, social, and cultural rights, with which they are interdependent. Indeed, the example they cite—"a place where any bloke can come to—no matter what he'd done—and get help"—speaks to those rights. Adam B. Seligman and David W. Montgomery, "The Tragedy of Human Rights: Liberalism and the Loss of Belonging," *Society* 56 (June 2019), 4, https://nsiteam.com/social/ wp-content/uploads/2020/02/2019-Seligman-Montgomery-Society-TragedyOfHu manRights.pdf.

42. "What Are Human Rights?" Council of Europe, https://www.coe.int/en/ web/compass/what-are-human-rights.

43. See, for example, "Poll: OC Residents Want More Housing Support for Homeless" (press release), Othering & Belonging Institute, October 7, 2020, https://belonging.berkeley.edu/poll-oc-residents-want-more-housing -support-homeless; Megan Brenan, "Record-High Worry in U.S. about Hunger, Race Relations," Gallup, March 26, 2021, https://news.gallup.com/poll/341954/ record-high-worry-hunger-race-relations.aspx.

44. Katharina Pistor, *The Code of Capital: How the Law Creates Inequality and Wealth* (Princeton University Press, 2019).

45. Pistor, *Code of Capital*.

46. Alastair Boone, "Housing Activist Dominique Walker Runs for Berkeley Rent Board," *Street Spirit*, October 1, 2020, https://thestreetspirit.org/2020/10/01/ housing-activist-dominique-walker-runs-for-berkeley-rent-board/.

47. Berkeleyside staff, "Election 2020: Who Is Dominique Walker?" *Berkeleyside*, October 4, 2020, https://www.berkeleyside.org/2020/10/04/berkeley-election-2020 -who-is-rent-board-candidate-dominique-walker.

48. "Housing Is a Human Right Slate Sweeps Berkeley Rent Board Election," Alliance of Californians for Community Empowerment (ACCE) Action, November 5, 2020, https://www.acceaction.org/housing_is_a_human_right_slate_sweeps _berkeley_rent_board_election; "Oakland City Councilmember Carroll Fife opens up about struggle with homelessness," KTVU FOX 2, January 8, 2024, https://www .ktvu.com/video/1392654.

49. "City elections in Oakland, California (2020)," Ballotpedia, https://ballotpedia .org/City_elections_in_Oakland,_California_(2020).

50. "What Carroll Stands For," Carroll Fife Oakland City Council District 3, https://www.carrollfife.org/platform.

51. On November 5, 2024, she was recalled. "Sheng Thao," Wikipedia, https:// en.wikipedia.org/wiki/Sheng_Thao.

52. "Cori Bush," Ballotpedia, https://ballotpedia.org/Cori_Bush.

53. "About Cori," US House of Representatives: Cori Bush, https://bush.house .gov/about.

54. Cori Bush, "I Lived in My Car and Now I'm in Congress: We Need to Solve America's Housing Crisis," *Time*, July 30, 2021, https://time.com/6085841/cori -bush-homelessness-crisis/.

55. Unhoused Persons Bill of Rights, H. Res. 634, Introduced July 28, 2023, https://www.congress.gov/bill/118th-congress/house-resolution/634/text?s=1 &r=11.

56. Sunlen Serfaty and Clare Foran, "Freshman Rep. Cori Bush in National Spotlight for Her Activism to Fight Eviction," CNN, updated August 4, 2021, https://www.cnn.com/2021/08/04/politics/cori-bush-eviction-protest/index.html; Glenn Thrush, Michael D. Shear, and Alan Rappeport, "The Biden Administration Issues a New Eviction Moratorium as the Virus Surges," *New York Times*, updated August 7, 2021, https://www.nytimes.com/2021/08/03/us/politics/evictions -housing-moratorium-pelosi-yellen.html?action=click&module=RelatedLinks &pgtype=Article.

57. Carl Romer and Kristen Broady, "In Overturning the Eviction Moratorium, the Supreme Court Continues Its History of Harming Black Households," Brookings Institute, September 14, 2021, https://www.brookings.edu/articles/in -overturning-the-eviction-moratorium-the-supreme-court-continues-its-history-of -harming-black-households/.

58. "Pandemic Eviction Bans Have Spawned a Renters'-Rights Movement, *Economist*, February 16, 2023, https://www.economist.com/united-states/2023/02 /16/pandemic-eviction-bans-have-spawned-a-renters-rights-movement; Natasha Lennard, "Supreme Court Ended Eviction Moratorium, but Pandemic Has Shown Road Map for Fighting Back," *Intercept*, August 27 2021, https://theintercept.com

/2021/08/27/eviction-moratorium-supreme-court-pandemic/; NLIHC, The State of Statewide Tenant Protections (NLICH, 2023), https://nlihc.org/sites/default/files/The-State-of-Statewide-Tenant-Protections.pdf.

59. Lennard, "Supreme Court Ended Eviction Moratorium."

60. Poppy Noor, "'It Was Just Unconscionable': Cori Bush on Her Fight to Extend the Eviction Moratorium" (interview), Guardian, August 8, 2021, https://www.theguardian.com/society/2021/aug/08/cori-bush-interview-eviction-moratorium.

61. Tahiat Mahboob, "Housing Is a Human Right: How Finland Is Eradicating Homelessness," CBC, January 24, 2020, https://www.cbc.ca/radio/sunday/the-sunday-edition-for-january-26-2020-1.5429251/housing-is-a-human-right-how-finland-is-eradicating-homelessness-1.5437402.

62. Florida Republican Kat Kammack, for example, adopted the slogan "from homeless to the House of Representative," but as an avowed "fiscal conservative," has voted to cut funding for housing and other critical social protections. "Promises Made. Promises Kept. Kat's Record of Fighting for You," Kat for Congress, https://katforcongress.com/accomplishments/.

63. Dennis Kucinich and Robert Scheer, "Dennis Kucinich: From Sleeping in a Car as a Kid to 16 Years in Congress" (interview), ScheerPost, June 4, 2021, https://scheerpost.com/2021/06/04/dennis-kucinich-from-sleeping-in-a-car-as-a-kid-to-16-years-in-congress/; Staff writer, "Formerly Homeless Rep. Kucinich on Housing and the Economy," Street Sense Media, December 15, 2003, https://streetsensemedia.org/article/formerly-homeless-rep-kucinich-on-housing-and-the-economy/.

64. Lennard, "Supreme Court Ended Eviction Moratorium."

65. Just a few examples include long-standing advocate Paul Boden, now director of the Western Regional Advocacy Project (WRAP), Karim Walker, homeless outreach worker and organizer at the Safety Net Project of the Urban Justice Center, and Mark Horvath, founder of Invisible People. "Western Regional Advocacy Project," WRAP, https://wraphome.org/; Paul Boden, interview with the author, June 8, 2023; Claudia Irizarry Aponte, "From Shelter to Home to Street: One Man's Homeless Struggle," City, November 21, 2019, https://www.thecity.nyc/2019/11/21/from-shelter-to-home-to-street-one-man-s-homeless-struggle/; Karim Walker, interview with the author, February 22, 2023; "Changing the Story of Homelessness," Invisible People, Invisiblepeople.tv.

66. Some of my former students, including Xyzlo Lee and Luke Cronin, are just a few examples.

67. Joint Center for Housing Studies of Harvard University (JCHS), The State of the Nation's Housing 2023 (JCHS, 2023), https://www.jchs.harvard.edu/sites/default/files/reports/files/Harvard_JCHS_The_State_of_the_Nations_Housing_2023.pdf; JCHS, America's Rental Housing 2024 (JCHS, 2024), https://www.jchs.harvard

.edu/sites/default/files/reports/files/Harvard_JCHS_Americas_Rental_Housing _2024.pdf.

68. Finnish nonprofit leader Juha Kaakinen called affordable social housing and the housing benefit that helps those with low incomes pay for housing the "corner-stones" of the country's successful effort to address homelessness. Juha Kaakinen, interview with the author, October 11, 2023.]

69. "I was hungry and you fed me, thirsty and you gave me a drink; I was a stranger and you received me in your homes, naked and you clothed me; I was sick and you took care of me, I was in prison and you visited me." Matthew 25:35–37 (GNB).

70. NLCHP, *Criminalizing Crisis: The Criminalization of Homelessness in US Cities* (NLCHP, 2011); National Alliance to End Homelessness (NAEH), *Faith-Based Organizations: Fundamental Partners in Ending Homelessness* (NAEH, 2017), https://endhomelessness.org/wp-content/uploads/2017/06/05-04-2017_Faith -Based.pdf; Norm Suchar and John Ashmen, "SNAPS in Focus: Partnerships between CoCs and Faith Based Organizations," HUD, August 13, 2019, https:// www.hudexchange.info/news/snaps-in-focus-partnerships-between-cocs-and-faith -based-organizations/.

71. "The Aims and Means of the Catholic Worker," Catholic Worker Movement, https://catholicworker.org/aims-and-means/.

72. See, for example, Nazila Ghanea, "Religion, Equality and Non-Discrimination," in *Human Rights and Religion: An Introduction*, ed. John Witte Jr. and M. Christian Green (Oxford University Press, 2011), https://www.researchgate .net/publication/233970474_Religion_and_Human_Rights_An_Introduction; Dipti Patel, "The Religious Foundations of Human Rights: A Perspective from the Judeo-Christian Tradition and Hinduism," *Human Rights Law Commentary* 1 (2005), https://www.nottingham.ac.uk/hrlc/documents/publications/hrlcommen-tary2005/religiousfoundationshumanrights.pdf.

73. See, for example, Simone de Beauvoir, *The Ethics of Ambiguity* (Citadel Press, 1949); "Definition of Humanism," American Humanist Association, https:// americanhumanist.org/what-is-humanism/definition-of-humanism/.

74. See, for example, Beauvoir, *The Ethics of Ambiguity*; Hulya Simga, *Beauvoir's Ethics of Ambiguity* and Human Rights, *Philosophia: International Journal of Philosophy* 18, no. 1 (2017), https://ejournals.ph/article.php?id=10687.

75. Fannie Lou Hamer, "Nobody's Free Until Everybody's Free" (speech, Washington, D.C., July 10, 1971), Maegan Parker Brooks and Davis W. Houck, eds., *The Speeches of Fannie Lou Hamer: To Tell It Like It Is* (University Press of Mississippi, 2013).

76. The Declaration of Independence.

77. Charles V. Hamilton, "An Advocate of Black Power Defines It," *New York Times*, April 14, 1968, https://timesmachine.nytimes.com/timesmachine/1968/04 /14/91225005.html?pageNumber=286.

INDEX